THE ALLIED CONVOY SYSTEM 1939-1945

THE ALLIED CONVOY SYSTEM 1939-1945

ITS ORGANIZATION, DEFENCE AND OPERATION

ARNOLD HAGUE

CHATHAM PUBLISHING
LONDON

First published in Canada in 2000 by Vanwell Publishing Limited,
1 Northrup Crescent, P.O. Box 2131, St. Catharines, Ontario L2R 7S2

Vanwell Publishing acknowledges the financial support of the Government of Canada through the Book Publishing Industry Development Program for its publishing activities.

Vanwell Publishing ISBN 1-55125-033-0

First published in Great Britain in 2000 by Chatham Publishing,
61 Frith Street, London W1V 5TA
Chatham Publishing is an imprint of Gerald Duckworth & Co. Ltd.

British Library Cataloguing in Publication Data
A catalogue record for this book is available from the British Library

Chatham Publishing ISBN 1-86176-147-3

Copyright© 2000 by Arnold Hague. All rights reserved. No part of this publication may be reproduced or transmitted in any form or by any means, electronic or mechanical, including photocopying, recording, or any information storage and retrieval system, without either prior permission in writing from the publisher or a license permitting restricted copying. The right of Arnold Hague to be identified as the author of this work has been asserted by him in accordance with the UK Copyrights, Designs and Patents Act 1988.

Design: Linda Moroz-Irvine

Printed and bound in Canada

Canadian Cataloguing in Publication Data

Hague, Arnold
        The allied convoy system, 1939-1945 : its organization, defence and operation

Includes bibliographical references and index.
ISBN 1-55125-033-0

1. Naval convoys – History – 20th century. 2. World War, 1939-1945 – Naval operations.
I. Title.

D770.H338 2000   940.54'5   C00-930141-0

Courtesy Fleet Air Arm Museum (Jeffs collection)

Taken from a collection donated by Lt Cdr Jeffs RNVR, this evocative photograph of a laden convoy in calm conditions is unusual for its clarity. Titled only with the names EMPIRE MACKAY (in the foreground) and EMPIRE MACRAE (distant), it is difficult to identify positively.

There were only two eastbound convoys (the ships are loaded) in which these two ships were together AND the only MAC ships, HX 296 24 June to 2 July 1944 and HX 308 19 to 28 Sept 1944. The plane guard corvette does not, unfortunately, provide a clue even though it is a CASTLE class vessel. Both convoys contained a single such corvette and it is not possible to distinguish the individual pennant number. The corvette was Canadian in both convoys, HMCS ORANGEVILLE in HX 296 and HMCS TILLSONBURG in HX 308. Perhaps a veteran of one of their crews can provide the answer to the puzzle!

ACKNOWLEDGEMENTS

This account of the 1939-1945 convoy system, its origins and methods of working and development over a period of six years, some account of supporting systems and, finally, some relevant statistics, is intended as a reference source for future use. It was written initially at the request of the Naval Historical Branch, Ministry of Defence (Navy), in London as a record to assist in replying to convoy enquiries. It was pointed out that I would not always be available to assist personally in such enquiries, and in 1995 I wrote a short text for office use; it was not intended for publication.

The sudden death of my friend John K Burgess in September 1997 made the point of mortality very clear, and I resolved not only to put my data base in order but also to prepare a proper written reference for NHB. I was also prepared to consider publication but did not feel the subject to be viable.

However, a co-author of John's, Ken Macpherson, who had been pressing me to publish for several years, took it upon himself to interest his Canadian publisher. Vanwell Publishing was interested in the project and I was offered a contract. Having agreed to terms, I am pleased that Vanwell Publishing saw the merit of this book. I hope that the results are both acceptable and appropriate to readers.

I am solely responsible for the content of this work, for opinions expressed (which may or may not have the approval of the publisher) and any errors that it may contain. Where those have occurred despite efforts, I offer my apologies. I must also proffer my thanks to Ken Macpherson, not only for his efforts in obtaining the publisher's interest, but also for granting access to his very extensive photograph collection to illustrate this book.

Other illustrations are reproduced by courtesy of the Fleet Air Arm Museum at RNAS Yeovilton, Somerset, Great Britain, and by the Air Historical and Naval Historical Branches of the Ministry of Defence in London. The provenance of each photograph is indicated by an appropriate title beneath each illustration.

Grateful mention must be made of assistance given by the late John K Burgess of Calgary, Alberta whose co-operation throughout the period 1952 to 1997, and the unstinting sharing of his detailed research in Canadian archives, has added so greatly to my records. John was a close personal friend throughout that time and I miss him very greatly.

Similarly I must thank Don Kindell of Piqua, Ohio. Although our friendship is more recent in origin, his investigations in the USN archive in Washington Navy Yard have added a great deal of information not available in Britain to my records.

In London, not only have I had the greatest encouragement from Michael McAloon, David Ashby and Bob Coppock of the Naval Historical Branch with whom I have worked so closely, but also from their late colleague Alan Francis. Over the years Alan made available to me a great deal of reference material for my research. The support, encouragement and guidance of the Head of the Naval Historical Branch, 1977 to 1999, J D Brown OBE, FRHistS; and his permission to visit his department so freely (even though he no longer employs me!) has been of the greatest help. I value my long association with him and his Branch very much indeed.

The Admiralty Librarian, Miss Jenny Wraight, who was formerly with the National Maritime Museum, Greenwich and the Guildhall Library in the City of London, has also aided my research over a number of years; assistance now ably rendered by her replacement at the Guildhall Library, Declan Barriskill. Both of them have added, and continue to add, to my knowledge.

Finally, to my friend of over fifty years, Michael Crowdy, my thanks for his friendship and assistance. Michael has edited and laid out all my previous publications and, although those tasks for this volume are in the hands of the publisher, he has played a very large part in checking, editing and improvement of this text prior to its despatch to Canada.

A Hague
Esher, Surrey
England
December 1999

GLOSSARY

(A)	The suffix to a naval officer's rank which indicated he was an Air Branch Officer i.e. what was popularly (and is now officially) known as the Fleet Air Arm.
AA	Anti-aircraft.
ACNS	Assistant Chief of Naval Staff. One of several Flag Officers with such a title. Suffixed with the matters for which he was responsible e.g ACNS (Trade).
AFVs	In the context of merchant ship losses, this indicates "armoured fighting vehicles" in the cargo.
ANZAC	Commonly used term to denote Australian and New Zealand troops, often extended to naval and air force units. A 1914 acronym derived from "Australian and New Zealand Army Corps".
Asdic	An acronym used in the RN to define the means of sound detection of submerged submarines. Now known as Sonar.
A/S	Anti-submarine. Applied in various forms eg A/S warfare, A/S ship etc.
Avgas	In the context of merchant ship losses, this indicates a cargo of "aviation gasoline" i.e. aircraft fuel.
BAMS	British Admiralty Merchant Signals. A general broadcast of various signals at a stated time each day, they conveyed general or specific instructions to the recipients.
BdU	Befelshaber der U-boote—Commander of the German Submarine Service, operational, personnel and materiel. An office held from 1935 to 1942 by Captain, later Admiral, Doenitz. BdU became accepted as the acronym for the U-Boat Command as well as a personal title.
B-dienst	The German code breaking organization. Extremely successful from 1939 until a change in British codes in June 1943. Raiding ships carried their own detachment of these experts.
CET	Central European Time, i.e. 2 hours in advance of GMT. CET was kept, for signalling and reporting purposes, by all German warships.
C-in-C	Commander-in-Chief, the supreme Commander in a defined area or of a designated force of a specific Service. The command or force title followed the C-in-C designation e.g. C-in-C Home Fleet.
CHOP	An acronym for "Change of Operational Control," hence "CHOP to," "CHOP line" denoting a position when command changed.
CNO	Chief of Naval Operations, the professional head of the USN.
CTL	This notation occasionally appears in the comments column of losses incurred by a convoy series. It indicates those vessels that were so severely damaged that they were (i) incapable of economic repair, or (ii) repair facilities were too congested to make repair a practical possibility at the time. Usually such ships were broken up (bu), however in some instances the damaged hulls were later repaired in post-war days, when different circumstances existed.
DEMS	Defensively Equipped Merchant Ships. The acronym applied to the ships, the equipment provided, the Service personnel operating it, and the naval shore organisations and staff supporting the entire system.
DF	Direction Finding. Locating the source, world-wide, of a radio transmission and, by plotting the bearings from several receiving stations, obtaining an accurate "fix" on its position. The RN in particular had a world-wide network of such stations with centralised plotting in London and at bases overseas.
EG	Standard British abbreviation for "Escort Group," as in "2EG." Indicates a specific group of ships under the command of a senior officer, who was responsible for the training and administration of the Group as well as its operational control.
EOMP	Eastern Ocean Meeting Point. The position in which escort duty transferred from a UK based group to an Iceland based group.
FDO	Fighter Direction Officer.
FFO	In the context of merchant ship losses this indicates a cargo of "furnace fuel oil" i.e. Admiralty grade bunker fuel.

Gas	In the context of merchant ship cargoes, *(this is not North American usage of the word to mean petrol)*. It refers to ammunition loaded with poison gas! This was shipped overseas from Britain and the USA in large quantities, and stock piled in North Africa, Italy, India and Australia and possibly elsewhere, ready for use if chemical warfare weapons were employed by the Axis powers. In all known cases Allied ammunition was loaded with either mustard gas or phosgene.
General	In the context of merchant ship losses, this indicates a mixed cargo of varied types.
GMT	Greenwich Mean Time. Designated Z time in the RN, i.e. the four-figure time group is suffixed Z. Used for all reports and signals by British warships, and Commonwealth ships pre-1945.
HA	High Angle, i.e. anti-aircraft capable.
HF/DF	High Frequency Direction Finding. An accurate means of detecting VHF transmissions, plotting and homing on their source; developed by the RN in particular. Unknown to the enemy and therefore particularly effective during 1941-45. Often referred to by the nickname "Huff Duff".
HHX	Ships from Halifax NS joining HX convoys originating in New York City. Bore the same number as the parent HX convoy.
HO	Hostilities Only. The abbreviation by which the RN referred to officers and ratings who were entered for service after 1939 "for the duration of hostilities." Such personnel could be either volunteers, or conscripts. The entry of ratings under pre-war term engagements in the period 1939-45 was deliberately limited to reduce over-manning at the end of the war. In the same way, the entry of officer cadets for the RN was also held at pre-war level in the hope of avoiding the "Geddes Axe" position of the 1920s.
HOMP	Halifax Ocean Meeting Point. The position off Halifax NS at which local escorts were exchanged and ships from or for Halifax NS joined or left the convoy.
HON	Ships from Halifax joining an ON convoy for passage southward to Boston, New York City etc. Bore the same number as the ON convoy.
ICOMP	Iceland Ocean Meeting Point. The position at which ships for Iceland left their convoys for that island, or joined a convoy having sailed from Iceland.
MAC	Merchant Aircraft Carrier. A conversion of a bulk grain or oil tanker hull to a flight deck configuration, to operate a small number of A/S aircraft. The vessel remained a merchant ship, with a civilian crew, still able to carry the normal cargo. A small Naval party was embarked to operate and support the aircraft.
MOMP	Mid-Ocean Meeting Point. The position at which the Iceland based escort exchanged duty with a Canadian based escort.
MN	Merchant Navy i.e. British and Commonwealth registered merchant ships and their crews.
MOS	Ministry of Shipping, later amalgamated with the Ministry of Transport to form the Ministry of War Transport.
MOWT	Ministry of War Transport. The Government ministry responsible from 1941 for the control and administration of merchant shipping during the war. Preceded by the Ministry of Shipping.
MSFU	Merchant Ship Fighter Unit. The RAF unit based at Speke, near Liverpool, which supplied the aircraft for CAM ships, provided the maintenance service in the UK and was the holding unit for the embarked RAF personnel.
MT	In the context of merchant ship losses this indicates "motor transport" amongst the cargo.
NCS	Naval Control of Shipping. The Admiralty organization responsible for controlling the movements of merchant shipping. Title applied to the staff e.g. NCS Officer etc.
OR	Operational Research. The investigation of organizations, tactics, weapons and any other matter for the parent Service. Carried out usually by professional, civilian, scientists attached to the RN and RAF specifically for that purpose. Reporting to senior officers of the responsible Service and submitting recommendations and criticisms for improvements, backed by proven facts.
PSTO	Principal Sea Transport Officer. A senior, usually retired, Naval Officer attached to the Sea Transport Organization of the Ministry of Shipping, later the Ministry of War Transport. Responsible for the administration of shipping within a specific port, or group of ports.

RAF	Royal Air Force.
RAS	Replenishment at sea i.e. fuelling and storing.
RCAF	Royal Canadian Air Force.
RNAS	Royal Naval Air Station.
ROP	More properly rendered as RoP, "Report of Proceedings." A written report rendered periodically, usually at the end of a voyage or operation, by the senior officer of a group of ships, or CO of a ship operating alone, to their senior authority recounting the ship's/unit's activities during a stated period.
SD	Sound Detector, the title of specialist rating Asdic operators.
SEA FRONTIER	The title applied to an area of territory, American or foreign, by Presidential Order. It gave total authority to the appropriate Naval Commander over all USN operations in it and within a specified area. Prefixed by the territorial designation e.g. Moroccan Sea Frontier.
SHX	Ships from Sydney CB joining an HX convoy at sea. Bore the same number as the HX convoy.
SOE	Senior Officer of Escort.
STO	Sea Transport Organization, a former Admiralty department transferred to the Board of Trade, later to the MOS, then the MOWT, responsible for the organization of merchant shipping and the fulfilment of the Services' needs for transport of personnel and materiel.
Stores	In the context of merchant ship losses, this indicates a cargo of "government stores" i.e. military supplies.
TAG	Telegraphist Air Gunner. The rating component of a three-man naval aircrew; the rank is self-descriptive.
U-Boat	Unterseeboote, the German title for a submarine. The generic term "U-Boat" was, by Churchill's personal decision, applied to all enemy submarines regardless of nationality.
USN	United States Navy.
VHF	Very High Frequency. Refers to a specific type of radio transmission, both by Morse transmission or voice.
VLR	Very Long Range. A specific conversion of the B 24 Liberator bomber for Coastal Command operations in mid-Atlantic.
V/S	Visual Signal(ing). Communication by flag, semaphore, signal lamp and, after mid-war, by VHF voice transmission. A term also used to describe signal specialist ratings normally found on the bridges of warships in close attendance on the Officer of the Watch and CO.
W App	The common abbreviation of Western Approaches (Command), defined as the North Atlantic excluding areas of national waters, or those reserved by agreement for other control, i.e areas under Canadian or USN control 1941-45.
WACIs	Western Approaches Convoy Instructions, the official Command regulations on all matters pertaining to convoy, its escort and administration.
WATU	Western Approaches Tactical Unit. The central authority at W App HQ in Liverpool responsible for the analysis of enemy attacks; examination of reports and ideas for offence/defence, the promulgation of doctrine to the Command generally and for operational research. This last item additional to the duties of the OR specialists attached to the Command.
WEF	Western Escort Force. RCN escorts based on Halifax and St John's NF for coastal escort in Canadian and US waters. Successor to WLEF.
WHX	Ships from St John's NF joining an HX convoy at sea. The "W" is taken from Wabana, as "S" was already used for the Sydney CB ships.
WLEF	Western Local Escort Force. The original dedicated coastal escort force of the RCN.
WOMP	Western Ocean Meeting Point. The position off St John's NF where the ocean escort joined or left an Atlantic convoy, relieving or being relieved by the RCN escort based on St John's NF.

CONTENTS

Acknowledgements vii

Glossary viii

Chapter 1   **CONTROL OF SHIPPING** 15
                   Definitions: Convoy, Stragglers, Rompers, Nationality
                   Convoys
                   Convoy codewords
                   A brief history of convoy

Chapter 2   **THE INTER-WAR YEARS** 20

Chapter 3   **THE CONVOYS** 23
                   Alterations to the convoy system, and titling
                   Main dangers of attack
                   Convoy formation
                   Convoy command

Chapter 4   **THE TRADE DIVISION** 29
                   The departments and sections of Trade Division
                   Convoy Commodores
                   NCS Officers
                   Overseas control
                   Misuse of shipping

Chapter 5   **VARIATIONS TO THE CONVOY SYSTEM** 35
                   North Atlantic and North Sea 1939-40
                   Variations in 1941
                   Mediterranean convoys 1940-41
                   North Atlantic convoy changes 1942
                   North Atlantic convoy changes 1943
                   Mediterranean convoy changes 1943
                   The first troop convoys
                   The MONSTER convoys
                   The WS convoys
                   Atlantic convoy changes late 1943-45
                   Home waters changes 1944-45
                   Indian Ocean convoys
                   African waters convoys
                   Evasive routing
                   Australian and South-West Pacific convoys
                   Summary

Chapter 6   **THE THREAT** 45
                   The U-Boat and its weapons

Chapter 7   **INTELLIGENCE** 51
                   Enigma and Special Intelligence

Chapter 8	**ESCORTS** 55
	Tactics
	Anti-Submarine weapons
	Escort weapons
	Detection devices
	Sonobuoys
	Magnetic anomaly detection (MAD)
Chapter 9	**WARTIME WEAPON DEVELOPMENT** 65
	Mk X-depth charge
	Ahead-throwing weapons
	Hedgehog
	Squid
	Shark
Chapter 10	**AIRCRAFT A/S TACTICS AND WEAPONS** 73
	Leigh Light
	Retro-bomb
	Acoustic torpedo
	Rocket Projectiles
	Aircraft mounted guns
Chapter 11	**CATAPULT AIRCRAFT MERCHANT SHIPS–CAM SHIPS** 77
	CAM ship design and development
	CAM ship launches
	Helicopter trials afloat
	List of CAM ships
	Fighter Catapult Ships
Chapter 12	**MERCHANT AIRCRAFT CARRIERS––MAC SHIPS** 83
	MAC ship design and development
	Service record
	Descriptive data
Chapter 13	**RESCUE SHIPS** 89
	Description
	List of ships
	Personnel losses
	Rescue trawlers
Chapter 14	**RESCUE TUGS** 93
Chapter 15	**REPLENISHMENT AT SEA** 97
Chapter 16	**DEFENSIVELY EQUIPPED MERCHANT SHIPS (DEMS)** 101
	Admiralty Net Defence
	Mk 29 equipment
	Plastic armour
	Asdic in merchant ships

Chapter 17	CASUALTIES 107
	Personnel
	Ships
	Losses by marine causes
APPENDIX 1	ALPHABETICAL LIST OF CONVOY CODES 109
APPENDIX 2	CONVOY STATISTICS 115
	Oceanic convoys
	UK coastal waters convoys
APPENDIX 3	CONVOY SERIES NOTES AND STATISTICS 123
	HX and HXF convoys
	SC convoys
	SL, SL/MKS and MKS convoys
	OA convoys
	OB convoys
	ON convoys
	ONS convoys
	OS, OS/KMS and KMS convoys
	KMF/MKF convoys
	OG convoys
	HG convoys
	UG convoys
	GU convoys
	CU convoys
	UC convoys
APPENDIX 4	RUSSIAN AND MALTA CONVOYS AND OPERATIONS 187
APPENDIX 5	THE WS CONVOYS 194
APPENDIX 6	SOURCES 197
APPENDIX 7	CONVOY FORM A.1. 200
	INDEX OF SHIP LOSSES 203

Courtesy Fleet Air Arm Museum

A view from a Swordfish, operating from a MAC ship, of a convoy at sea in an unusually tranquil Atlantic.

The original print is, unfortunately, undated so that it is not possible to identify the convoy although it appears to consist of laden ships and is therefore eastbound to the UK from North America.

CHAPTER 1
CONTROL OF SHIPPING

The control of British merchant shipping (and later that of chartered and Allied vessels) during the 1939-45 war, and the word "requisition," are the subject of a considerable degree of misunderstanding. A great many people are convinced that the Admiralty requisitioned, and were responsible for, merchant shipping; very many Army personnel are equally convinced that the troopships in which they proceeded overseas were also run by the Royal Navy. Both impressions are quite incorrect.

The Admiralty became responsible for the control of merchant shipping in late August 1939. This "control" consisted of the authority to decide whether or not a ship was to proceed in convoy and, if not, the courses and speed of its passage to its intended destination. It did NOT extend to deciding the destination, nor the cargo to be carried.

Progressively, between its formation on 13 October 1939 and May 1941, the civilian Ministry of Shipping and its successor, the Ministry of War Transport, received authority to requisition British merchant shipping for national use. Such authority was also extended to Allied and neutral shipping which became, by commercial agreement, chartered to the British Government.

This MOS/MOWT right of requisition carried with it the authority to decide the cargo to be carried and the voyages to be undertaken by merchant ships, the actual management of the ships remaining with their owners or agents.

Requisitioned ships could be specifically allocated for naval use, either as commissioned or non-commissioned auxiliaries. Armed Merchant Cruisers are a prominent example of the former; once so allocated by the Ministry, the ships became the total responsibility of the Admiralty. In the case of such vessels as Rescue Ships or specified tanker tonnage, all were classed as non-commissioned naval auxiliaries. They remained the responsibility of the Sea Transport Organization of the Ministry of Shipping (later War Transport), with their owners responsible for supplying and paying the civilian crews. The arrangement was governed by standard charter agreements between Government and Owner.

The allocation of merchant ships to naval use was, accordingly, quite clearly controlled by a civilian Ministry, which the Admiralty had to convince when requesting tonnage for naval purposes. There was no right of direct acquisition of shipping by the Admiralty for any purpose, except very short-term assumption of control in specific operational areas. For example, naval crews could be placed onboard merchant ships in times of dire necessity if merchant service crews refused duty. A specific example is the Royal Ulsterman when directed to carry ammunition unescorted to Norway on 20 May 1940. A naval crew was provided, and the ship sailed under the White Ensign. Similar arrangements were made on a number of occasions during the siege of Tobruk when local personnel refused to sail in such hazardous circumstances. Such occasions, however, were rare. The

Admiralty responsibility for requisitioned ships was accordingly but a small part of the control of British and Allied merchant shipping.

Troopships, properly titled Personnel Ships, were also directed by the Sea Transport Organization and remained civilian-manned. Their voyages were organized by the STO to provide the requirements of the military authorities for the movement of troops. The Admiralty was responsible for the organization of the convoys, their escort and passage, to comply with the STO needs.

There was a third part of this complex relationship, that provided initially by the Ministry of Transport. That Ministry was responsible for the co-ordination of ship and cargo handling in ports in the UK where, at local level, a complex relationship of port owners, shipping agents, ship owners and railway authorities handled matters pre-war.

The stress of war conditions, with peaks and troughs of arrivals and departures as a result of convoy cycles and the inevitable disruption caused by air raid damage after mid-1940 resulted in major disruption to the system. Port Controllers were appointed with blanket powers to organize their particular ports including the movements of cargo in and out of the port area. While successful, the liaison between the two civilian Ministries of Shipping and Transport was still not as close nor efficient as it could be, so both Ministries were combined in the Ministry of War Transport by Order-in-Council dated 9 May 1941.

Overall responsibility for all aspects of maritime trade and port control in, to, and from Great Britain by a single authority was thus achieved.

Definitions

"Convoy" is quite easily defined, and was understood by the Admiralty as "one or more merchant ships or naval auxiliaries sailing under the protection of one or more warships." The term "convoy" is sometimes used more loosely, for example SLS 64 is usually described as a convoy and is so titled in the numeric run of the SL series. In fact it had no escort whatever when found and attacked by HIPPER and the subsequent losses are properly attributed to "independent passage," not to "losses in convoy".

"Straggler" is another even more emotive word. Its dictionary definition is "a stray, a vagrant" but in the sense of convoy it is more closely defined in official handbooks issued by Trade Division.

Unfortunately the term is very often used, by escort commanders and Commodores alike, for any vessel(s), which became detached from the main body of a convoy. This is not in accord with the Admiralty definition which, from the outbreak of war read, "For the purpose of this article (Article 166 of MERSIGS Vol I) a straggler may be said to be a ship that has definitely become separated from a convoy and is out of sight of her convoy and all escorting vessels".

In 1943 C-in-C W App requested that an even tighter definition be provided for the guidance of Masters generally. On 20 May 1943 accordingly the following revised definition was approved:

(a) A straggler in the sense the term is used in paragraphs b, c and d below is any ship that has definitely become separated through losing touch or inability to keep up and is (i) over five miles from her convoy and unable to rejoin before dark, or (ii) over ten miles from her convoy whether or not she could rejoin before dark. If, however, a vessel which has become separated from her convoy is in the immediate vicinity of an escort vessel which has been detailed to escort her, she is not in these circumstances to be regarded as a straggler.

(b) Should a convoy be reported or attacked by U-boats, a BAMS Message will be made to all stragglers as defined above to proceed direct to the Straggler's Route.

(c) Stragglers, as defined above, should look out for amendments to the Straggler's Route in BAMS Messages.

(d) So long as no BAMS Message is received directing them on to the Straggler's Route, stragglers should continue astern of the convoy until they are quite certain they cannot rejoin within the next 48 hours, and should then draw out to the Straggler's Route.

Vessels which were lost after (by the above definitions) straggling, were dealt with statistically as "independent ships" as were ships which had been detached from a convoy by direct order or in accordance with instructions issued prior to sailing.

"Straggler's Route" is the route laid down in the specific instructions for an individual convoy that required a straggler to pass through certain defined positions, in the same manner as the convoy route. The positions were so sited as to carry the straggler towards its destination, but away from either its former convoy or other convoys in the area. The straggler would, in theory, not become involved with other shipping or, hopefully, with U-boats searching for a convoy. More positively, if shore authorities deemed it necessary to search for a specific straggler, then escorts could be directed to the appropriate area.

"Rompers" was a term applied to vessels that deliberately broke away from the convoy and proceeded on their intended voyage at their best speed. They were, inevitably, ships whose maximum speed exceeded that of the convoy. Romping usually took place during or after an attack on the convoy, when the Master became convinced in his own mind or by pressure from his crew, that the ship would be safer proceeding alone at high speed. As inevitably the speed was less than 15 knots (or the ship would have been routed as an independent), the hope was frequently short-lived and ended in a sinking.

"Nationality". In all cases where the term "British" is used in the context of merchant ships 1939-45, it must be remembered that there was then only a single British Registry. The term therefore includes all vessels of Dominion or Empire ownership. Additionally, for legal reasons (as their Government and Owners were under enemy control), Danish and former French vessels taken over after April 1940 were re-registered for the period of the war as British. The Danish ships retained their Masters and crew in most cases, as did some ex-French vessels. British Masters were not infrequently appointed to ex-French tonnage and all such ships were placed under British management for the period of the war.

Convoys

Convoys were referred to by an alpha code with a numeric suffix, normally sequential. This applied to all convoys where the series was a regularly repetitive cycle or where it was expected that convoy passages would recur, albeit at differing intervals.

A number of convoys, however, were "one-off" and, because they were part of a military operation, bore the operation name. Others, while possessing their own normal coding, were also part of a major operation and have therefore acquired, through common usage, the operation name. Examples are the first convoy to North Russia in 1941; denoted as Operation DERVISH, the convoy was officially referred to as "Convoy Dervish" in orders and dispatches.

The movement of Australian troops home from the Middle East bore the title Operation PAMPHLET; this otherwise unnamed convoy of very large liners has become known as "the Pamphlet Convoy".

More confusing are the major actions to supply Malta, particularly in 1942. While the convoys themselves bore titles, published works and even official papers refer to the convoy by the operation name. Thus convoys GM 1 and MG 1 are referred to as SUBSTANCE, GM 2 and MG 2 as HALBERD, MW 11A and 11B as VIGOROUS and MW 13 as STONEAGE. There are numerous other examples.

Convoy Code Words

A further source of confusion is the use of Convoy Code Words. Obviously, when communicating with aircraft or shore based RAF controllers, where voice radio was the medium, it was unsatisfactory to have to use an alpha/numeric group which was both long-winded and subject to corruption in transmission. All convoys which could expect to receive air support, principally coastal and North Atlantic convoys, were allocated a Convoy Code Word. This was taken from a list drawn up by the RAF and allocated by the NCS organization in strict sequence as convoys were formed. The list was constantly re-used but was of sufficient length to avoid duplication, as the time scale for any one convoy using its Convoy Code Word was usually less than 14 days, frequently only two or three. It follows that a series of convoys with intervals of a number of weeks between each could reuse a code word, and that knowledge of such a word does not and cannot identify a specific convoy. Unfortunately, these words are sometimes used in memoirs, published works and, occasionally, official reports, causing considerable confusion. The classic example is the convoy of CALIFORNIA, DUCHESS OF YORK and PORT FAIRY sailing empty from the UK to Freetown in July 1943 to embark troops from West Africa for India. In official documents the convoy is described as "Special Military Convoy D," while the daily report from the Trade Plot describes it as "CALIFORNIA Convoy" as that ship carried the Commodore. The convoy code word was FAITH, and it is under this erroneous title that descriptions of the attack on it and subsequent sinkings usually appear.

Taken at random from immediately available sailing orders, the Russian outward convoys JW 58 and JW 59 were coded BARBER and BOUQUET respectively. It is of interest that these code words were also used to alert the convoy to imminent air attack and orders were issued that transmission of the words by merchant ships was strictly forbidden, their use being restricted to the escorts and the SOE.

A brief history of convoy, and its origins

The convoy is as old as the exercise of maritime power by sovereign states, its first recorded use in British waters being by Julius Caesar in his initial expedition to Britain over 1900 years ago. In his account, written for political use in Rome, he describes the construction of roomy transports for the legionnaires and their mounted auxiliaries, and the provision of smaller, faster craft as escorts. He also describes, vividly, the assault by infantry against a defended shore, interesting in view of similar ventures in 1942-45.

For England, convoy was an accepted method of trade defence in medieval times when the annual wine/wool trade between England and the King's possessions in Aquitaine attracted enemy attention. Elizabethan adventurers ("licensed pirates" or privateers would be a more accurate description), eagerly sought the Spanish "flotta" which each year conveyed the riches of the New World to Spain. The Dutch wars of Stuart times principally concerned the passage of Dutch trade from and to the Netherlands through the Narrow Seas. The 18th century wars with France frequently involved major actions to try to prevent the passage of convoys either conveying food to France or possible forces to assault British territory.

Convoy imposes restraints upon seamen, a notoriously independent breed, and the edict of the ruler (later government), was insufficient to enforce the system on all. A more effective (if less apparent) force also existed, however: self-interest. A vessel in convoy was less likely to suffer attack and therefore loss; the owner (frequently also the Master) was, in consequence, less likely to lose his investment (and possibly his life), if he conformed to the restrictions of the convoy system.

With the development of marine insurance the economic pressures became greater. Insurance rates for vessels and cargo not in convoy were punitive compared with those for convoyed ships. A Master who broke convoy invalidated whatever insurance the hull and cargo held and was therefore likely to lose his employment or be unable to obtain future insurance if he were an Owner/Master. In the former case he became destitute and liable to the attentions of the Press Gang; in the latter, at best, he found it difficult to obtain freight. In consequence, Owners and Masters accepted convoy, reluctantly but almost universally. Convoys could be large. In 1810, HMS VICTORY'S log recorded that convoys were gathered in the Baltic at Hano and sailed "when they had accumulated to about 500." Indeed, the final convoy of that Baltic season sailed in October 1810 numbering in excess of 1,000 ships.

By the end of the Napoleonic wars in 1815, some five hundred years of accumulated experience made convoy the automatic response to the threat of maritime attack on trade. However, over the succeeding century the vast change in the conduct of trade and (theoretically) of maritime attack caused by the adoption of steam propulsion, provoked much erudite discussion on the merits of the well-tried system.

Although not unanimous, the consensus of long public debate between naval officers, ship owners, traders and marine underwriters was that the correct response to "guerre de course" by a nation opposed to Britain was the blockade of his fleets and the patrolling of the sea routes under threat. In the closing years of the 19th and early years of the 20th centuries, this opinion hardened to the point that discussion of convoy, regarded as "defensive," became anathema to the Royal Navy.

Courtesy Fleet Air Arm Museum (RCAF)

A photograph, taken on 15 Mar 1944, of a MAC ship in convoy HX 283 bound for the UK.

The ship is an oiler, hence the deck park of three folded Swordfish aircraft right aft. She is non-operational in the flying role as she has twenty-two Thunderbolt fighters and a load of crated parts, probably for the USAAF in the UK, lashed down on her flight deck. Note that the Thunderbolts have had their propellers and tailplanes removed for ease of stowage.

Two MAC ships were present in HX 283, AMASTRA and RAPANA, both non-operational in the ferry role. It is not known which of the two is shown here.

In 1914 began the first major maritime war for a century using a new weapon—the submarine—and with a new and vital factor in the equation—starvation. For the first time Britain faced a war in which the populace could not be fed from the resources of the island nation. Successful blockade of British shipping would mean starvation and surrender. Recognising this fact, Germany made two attempts at unrestricted submarine warfare against merchant shipping. In 1915 the campaign was called off in the face of considerable American opposition to its use; in 1917 it was re-introduced as a last resort when Germany faced stalemate in France and increasing shortages at home. The second campaign came very close to achieving a position for negotiation if not, indeed, a German victory.

The Admiralty and many senior Officers of the Royal Navy, trained to the fact that convoy was a defensive measure and therefore unsuitable as a response (and persuaded by misleading statistics on trade that were so inaccurate as to be near fatal to the nation), opposed the introduction of convoy. For once political thought, focused by a rapidly worsening food crisis, was more receptive to change than the professional command and the principle of convoy was reluctantly adopted by the Admiralty after pressure by the civilian government. While not an immediate success, and still opposed by some naval authorities, it turned the tide of German attack and eventually defeated the submarine menace.

It was a lesson relearned by the Royal Navy at grievous cost to the British Merchant Marine, which lost 2,719 ships totalling 6,840,744 grt to submarine action. This figure excluded minelaying activity—principally by submarines—which accounted for a further 510 British ships of 747,085 grt. The Allied losses, of course, increased those figures and neutral (principally Scandinavian) losses were also high. In all, between August 1914 and November 1918, 5,798 ships of 11,311,971 grt were lost, all attributable to direct submarine attack. A further 853 of 1,177,878 grt were lost due to mines, with submarines responsible for the major part of the German mining effort. The lesson was not forgotten in 1939 and convoy was the antidote to submarine attack that was prepared and applied, successfully, during the second war with Germany.

Incredibly, though not strictly pertinent to this work, similar flawed thought regarding the efficiency of convoy came to the fore in post-1950 thinking by some Service and civilian strategists in both Britain and other NATO countries. The protection of SLOC (Sea Lines of Communication: a term much favoured in the 1950s and 60s) by patrolling aircraft and ships, became the favourite theme of theoretical strategists more concerned with saving money in peacetime and advancing theories (and careers) than considering the effects of their proposals on the nation in war. Fortunately, common sense, wartime experience and a study of recent history appear to have defeated this second attempt to endanger the nation's lifeline, not (on this occasion) by an external foe!

CHAPTER 2
THE INTER-WAR YEARS

Predictably, during the 1920s the protection of trade in wartime became a subject of very low priority in Great Britain: the entire convoy organization was dissolved, naval liaison with shipping interests became infrequent, and the politicians assured the Navy that war was a thing of the past—in any case, it would not occur for at least ten years. Indeed, a certain prominent politician, one Winston Churchill, in 1928 made this an automatic annual statement of principle, i.e. each year the government required the Services to accept that war would not occur for ten years hence. It was not until 1936 that the British government made financial provision for re-armament, initially on a limited scale. Shades of 3 September 1939!

Despite such problems, and financial limitations imposed by the very poor state of the British economy, the Admiralty remained aware of its responsibility to the nation and planned ahead as much as it could. By 1932 it was seriously alarmed by the deteriorating position vis-à-vis Japan. In 1933 the election of the Nazi party to government in Germany convinced the Admiralty that a major conflict was, if not inevitable, at least probable. It took politicians and the nation as a whole, believing in the efficacy of the League of Nations, disarmament and with a misplaced faith in human nature, another three years to accept such a likelihood and commence the long overdue strengthening of the Armed Forces.

The Admiralty had great faith in the improvement since 1920 in submarine detection devices, known to the RN as Asdic (now Sonar), and publicly claimed that this had defeated the submarine even though it was untested in other than theoretical investigations. Privately, doubts existed in many minds so that convoy was retained as the principal defence in the event of unrestricted warfare being adopted by an enemy.

As already mentioned, the entire organization required to conduct convoy had been dismantled post-1919 so, in 1935, the Admiralty began to plan its re-creation. The man chosen, Paymaster Rear-Admiral Sir H W Eldon Manisty, KCB, CMG, had served in the 1917-1918 organization and achieved Flag rank prior to his retirement from the Royal Navy. He set to work to lay plans for the new Trade Division and the Naval Control Service (NCS) organization required for the possible introduction of convoy. In so doing, Admiral Manisty had four concurrent tasks:

1. to plan the Trade Division organization in Admiralty and to select and train at least a skeleton staff for immediate service.
2. by the creation and use of committees, to co-operate with ship owners and managers, freight forwarders, marine insurance underwriters and similar professional and civilian organizations and to prepare the arrangements outside the naval service for the control of the nation's shipping—

at that time a very substantial percentage of the entire world tonnage.
3. to prepare, produce and stockpile the necessary minimum equipment (including signal books and written instructions as well as minimal stores and defensive armament) for all merchant ships *and* the necessary shore organization.
4. to devise and prepare the organization overseas *and* make provision for manning it.

The formal planning of the Trade Division in its initial form was well within the Admiral's capability as was his liaison with all the civilian organizations, no one being in much doubt as to the pressing urgency of the task.

The preparation of the material needed for instant distribution posed considerable logistical problems, as did the arrangements for despatch and holding at overseas locations. The most difficult task was, probably, the provision of the manpower required. For even the most minimal convoy requirement foreseen in a limited war involving Germany alone, the numbers were considerable and spanned the world. Admiral Manisty therefore undertook a world tour during which he briefed each overseas C-in-C on the organization for which he would be responsible and advised on its setting up. The Admiral also assisted in finding and selecting suitable retired Officers and Reservists resident overseas to fill the needed appointments and advising them of their specific wartime locations and duties.

The Munich crisis of 1938 acted as a full-scale rehearsal of the new organization, which worked very well indeed. A degree of "fine tuning" was all that was required when the necessity to mobilise came in 1939. The Admiralty assumed control of all British merchant shipping on 26 August by which date the NCS organization was already on a war footing and manning at all but the most distant of its war stations.

Courtesy James Plomer

An excellent view of the Long Range Escort HMS VIDETTE. She was converted from a 1917-built destroyer by the removal of her forward boiler room (hence the absence of a fore funnel) the space being utilised for additional bunkers, stores and accommodation. A gun has been replaced by Hedgehog, while Y gun has been removed to make space for the depth charge parties and spare charges. The after torpedo tubes have made way for a 12pdr HA; modern radars on the bridge (271) and masthead (291) are fitted, as is HF/DF on the slender lattice mainmast.

Interestingly, VIDETTE, SNOWFLAKE and DUNCAN were all units of Gretton's B7 Group which performed in an exemplary fashion in the battle around ONS 5 in May 1943. The photographs of the three ships used in this book were taken by a Canadian officer, then Lt Cdr J Plomer RCNVR, who commanded the corvette HMS SUNFLOWER also of B7 group.

B7, with a considerable reputation, was a very mixed party, HMS SNOWFLAKE's Commanding officer being an Australian, HMS VIDETTE's the only RN officer other than Cdr Gretton. The next senior CO to Gretton, who conducted the latter part of the ONS 5 action after DUNCAN left due to fuel shortage, was a former Merchant Navy officer, Lt Cdr Sherwood RNR in HMS TAY. During the ONS 5 operation, Sherwood controlled both B7 and the supporting ships sent to assist, despite their respective senior officers being a Captain RN in 3rd Escort Group and a Commander RN in 1st Escort Group.

Courtesy Air Historical Branch (Crown Copyright)

Convoy OB 190 seen from an RAF Sunderland flying boat at the end of July 1940. The aircraft is passing across the front of the convoy: the ship in the foreground is the Italian prize EMPIRE ADVOCATE in position 41 (she had been seized in the Clyde only five weeks earlier), the four-master is the DEFENDER (51) and beyond her the Commodore ship NOVA SCOTIA leading column 6. The station keeping of the convoy leaves a lot to be desired!

CHAPTER 3
THE CONVOYS

Convoy was only to be introduced if unrestricted warfare was commenced by an enemy. This proviso was made as it had been accepted that convoy had some detrimental effect on the efficient employment of merchant ships, although the effect was by no means as great as some writers have made out, or the planners feared. It has not been possible to locate the actual signal implementing convoy, which resulted from the sinking of the liner ATHENIA on 3 September 1939. Evidence from notes of Admiralty meetings held on 4 September 1939, however, indicate that while there was a wish that day to implement convoy, adequate escorts were not yet available, as not all Reserve Fleet destroyers had then been deployed. However, convoy in Home waters commenced on the East coast between the Forth and the Thames on 6 September and outward convoys from Liverpool on 8 September. The first convoy (AB 1) had in fact sailed on 2 September, comprising eight tankers from Gibraltar for the Persian Gulf. They had been held at Gibraltar since late August because of possible Italian entry to the anticipated war and were routed via Cape Town, under cruiser escort as far as Freetown, to avoid undue delay to their passage. In the event, Italy delayed its entry to the war until German success appeared to be assured in June 1940.

Initially, convoy was required to cover those routes most threatened by air, surface or submarine action. Accordingly, it was introduced between the Firth of Forth and the Thames, outward from Liverpool (with ships joining from other ports en route). It passed south of Ireland to disperse at sea west of Land's End; from the Downs westward to Liverpool as a coastal convoy with an ocean contingent dispersing west of Land's End; and from a combination of ships from certain OA and OB convoys to Gibraltar.

These series were titled:

- FN Forth North i.e. to the Forth from the Thames
- FS Forth South i.e. to the Thames from the Forth
- OA Outward A (from the Thames via the Channel)
- OB Outward B (from Liverpool and the Bristol Channel)
- OG Outward Gibraltar

The ocean sections of the OA and OB convoys usually, but not always, merged off Land's End to proceed westward and disperse once they were beyond the expected operating area of submarines. The OG convoy, initially a combination of ships from every fifth OA and OB convoy, but later sailed from Liverpool under the OG designation, was escorted throughout its passage.

These series comprised the initial convoy system in UK waters, and outward to overseas ports for what became known as "Trade Convoys," i.e. vessels engaged in the normal commercial traffic. Depending on their final destination, it was usual for ships to detach from the convoy prior to its dispersal, thus ships for West and South Africa might well leave an OB convoy before the main North America-bound body dispersed.

In addition to these convoys there were also "Operational Convoys" consisting of ships on charter for military services. In 1939 such convoys were solely engaged in the transport of the BEF to France and its subsequent support. There were three such series: Cross-Channel steamers used between Southampton and Havre or Cherbourg to move troops, stores convoys between Southampton and other French Channel ports with stores, and a series from Bristol Channel ports to Quiberon Bay for Nantes and St Nazaire carrying principally motor transport. This last series, titled BC for both outward and homeward voyages, was also used in the first half of 1940 to cover coal trade to western France.

Ships from overseas had, of course, to assemble in a suitable port prior to undertaking the passage as a body in order that the Masters could personally receive the relevant instructions before sailing, and be able to make any necessary enquiries directly of the Commodore. Ships from the American East Coast therefore assembled at Halifax, Nova Scotia. Ships from the Mediterranean (and therefore from east of Suez) assembled at Port Said initially, later at Gibraltar. From Africa, the assembly point was at Freetown, and there was a short-lived series from Kingston, Jamaica for the West Indies trade and ships passing through the Panama Canal. Designations were:

HG   Homeward from Gibraltar
HX   Halifax to the UK
KJ   Kingston, Jamaica to UK
SL   Sierra Leone to UK

The HG convoy was escorted throughout its passage, while the remaining three series received a cruiser or armed merchant cruiser escort to the supposed western limit of submarine activity where a destroyer escort (usually from one of the outward convoys) took over. The incoming HX and SL convoys divided off Land's End with ships for Channel ports and London proceeding up Channel. The remaining ships entered the Irish sea via St George's Channel (the southern entrance) and dispersed off Liverpool from which point ships for other ports, e.g. the Clyde, proceeded independently.

All the series mentioned above sailed at set intervals of time (the "convoy cycle"), regardless of the number of ships available at the port of departure. This remained a principle throughout the war. Ships were not to be delayed to "make up numbers"; the only variant would be the cancellation of the convoy if there were no ships ready to sail, or due to stress of weather. Very rarely indeed, enemy action also caused the cancellation or recall of an individual convoy.

Finally, due to the fear that fast German units might repeat 1917 operations by attacking Norwegian-bound shipping, an outward and homeward convoy between the Firth of Forth and Norwegian waters near Bergen commenced in November 1939, continuing until the enemy invasion of Norway in April 1940. Heavily escorted, the convoys are usually thought of as covering the Narvik iron ore trade; in fact, the largest number of ships involved were antiques of Scandinavian and Baltic ownership, small, many under 1,500 grt, dating from the 1880s and 90s, supplying timber and timber products to the UK.

The "convoy cycle" could be adjusted at will. If extended in period it logically increased the number of ships in each convoy and diminished the number of convoys in a set period. This decreased the number of groups of escorts required for a particular convoy series. If the interval was made shorter, convoys became smaller and, in theory, the cargo capacity lost by the use of convoy became less. The trade-off was of course the larger number of escort groups required, and a probable shortening of their lay-over periods in port between convoy sailings. This tendency was always resisted by responsible Flag Officers, as the "lay-over" period was the sole means of resting escort crews, ensuring continuity of training and effecting general repairs to ships. Alterations in convoy cycles were therefore made only after very careful consideration, primarily of the effect on the efficiency of the limited number of available escorts.

Alterations to the convoy system, and titling

Convoy is profligate both in tonnage use due to the inevitable "bunching" of arrivals at destinations, and in the use of escorts. It is accordingly reactionary in its application, i.e. convoy is not usually imposed or maintained in use where there is no threat. The extension of convoy therefore depends upon the perceived danger, and there were many variations and additions to the system throughout the war as circumstances changed. Such alterations are dealt with in subsequent sections; additionally a full alphabetical listing of convoys is given as an Appendix.

In general, convoy codes initially either indicated the port of origin OR purpose of the convoy. Later the most usual form was the use of two letters indicating the ports or area of origin and arrival. As an example: KM being United Kingdom to Mediterranean, the convoys in the reverse direction adopting the reversed initials MK. Occasionally, purely random codes could also be used: JW and RA for Arctic convoys being an example. In fact, the last two codes are the initials of two Staff Officers responsible for routeing convoys at the time of the change.

A third letter was frequently added, usually A, F or S. "A" generally indicated a sub section of the initial convoy, much less commonly a separate convoy. "F" indicated a Fast convoy and "S" a Slow convoy. When used to designate a separate convoy series, e.g. KMS and KMF the distinction was between freighters (the Slow convoy) and personnel ships plus fast freighters in the Fast. The Fast convoy was also usually treated as an Operational convoy as opposed to a Trade convoy, as previously noted.

In some Trade series the F and S suffix was also occasionally used to distinguish between faster and slower convoys within the overall numeric sequence. Here the speed differential was small; a slow convoy was one expected to make seven knots, seven and a half knots from 1941. This was the speed set for the SC convoy series on its inception in 1940. The faster HX convoys were required to steam at nine knots, increased to ten knots from mid-1941.

There are examples of three-letter coding (and one of four) where all the letters indicate ports. Also, during the major amphibious landings and the follow-up period, three-letter codes were common; here the third letter could indicate the type of convoy, e.g. "P" being "Personnel" and "M" being "MT" i.e. vehicles. Direction indications also occur at such times: after Operation Torch (the North African invasion) a series of convoys was styled TE, Torch East, the return convoys to Gibraltar using the reversal code ET.

The RCN maintained very specific records of the HX and SC convoy series, including in almost all instances the average speed of individual convoys. From these records it is possible to state that the average speed of the HX series for 1940 was 8.08 knots; in 1941, 7.56 knots increasing to 8.98 knots when the convoy speed was raised to ten knots. In 1942 the average was 8.95 knots; 1943, 9.15 knots; 1944, 8.81 knots and 1945, 9.24 knots. The drop in HX speeds for 1944 is explicable by the suspension of the SC series and the inclusion of these slower ships in the HX convoys. This resulted from the need to reduce convoys during the mid year to release Escort Groups to protect the Normandy landings.

The equivalent figures for the slower SC series were: 1940, 6.67 knots; 1941, 6.49 knots; 1942, 6.84 knots; 1943, 7.32 knots; 1944, 7.44 knots and 1945, 7.64 knots; i.e. between one and a half and two knots difference. It is noteworthy that the SC convoys of 1944 and 1945 achieved very similar results to the original 1940 and 1941 HX convoy speeds.

Ships that could make 15 knots or more were routed as independents, on the basis that they were capable of evading submarine attack by the use of high, continuous, speed. In general, the maximum surface speed of a submarine was in the range 16-17 knots, and subject to considerable reduction in oceanic sea states.

In November 1940 the minimum speed to qualify as an independent was reduced to 13 knots, considerably increasing the number of independent sailings and the losses amongst them. The decision was taken at Cabinet level, involving the civilian Ministries, and without the benefit of statistics of the number of ships involved in independent passage or the loss ratio. Such statistics were not kept at that time. It also appears that the C-in-C Western Approaches was not consulted, for he raised very strong objections after only two months' experience of the new system. It became clear by May 1941 that the reduction in speed of independents in the North Atlantic had increased the loss ratio of such ships, against that for convoy, by between 250 and 300%.

The 15-knot minimum was re-introduced on 18 June 1941 and led to a rapid reduction in interceptions and loss of independents. In 1943, when fast tanker convoys of some 18 knots speed were instituted by the USN on the Atlantic crossing, other vessels capable of up to 20 knots were included in such convoys wherever possible.

Initially, in the case of the OA, OB and OG convoys, the convoy speed was set at six knots due to the small size and the age of many vessels included. It was felt that this was acceptable in view of the short duration of the escorted passage. By early 1940 the speeds for these convoys, except in isolated cases, had risen to that of the SC series, and every effort was made to increase this wherever possible. At this time neutral ships, which were trading on British behalf, also joined the convoy system. The lower limit for speed in all outward oceanic convoys was eventually set at a nominal 7.5 knots and ships unable to make this had perforce to proceed independently at their own risk. Coastal convoys were of course often slower than this. With the introduction of the ON series, eastbound Atlantic convoys alternated between minimum speeds of 7.5 knots and 9 knots; this arrangement continued until the start of the ONS series in 1943, thereafter all ON convoys had a minimum speed of 9 knots.

In fact, the service speed of many freighters and tankers constructed in the 1920s and 30s was of the order of 10 to 12 knots, tramps some two to three knots less. This simple fact made the organization of convoy series with speed differentials inevitable.

In general the speed of advance, i.e. the average daily rate of progress, of a convoy was approximately one knot less than the nominal speed. This was due to course alterations (zigzagging), weather and the state of ships' hulls and machinery. In the case of westbound vessels, head winds and the large number of vessels in ballast were significant factors.

Main dangers of attack

So far as convoy was concerned in deep waters there were three main dangers: air attacks, surface forces and submarine. In the shallower waters that prevailed in coastal areas there was also the danger of mining. Some convoys faced the possibility of all the dangers simultaneously, the Mediterranean and Arctic being extreme examples. The KJ series was originated purely to counter the possible threat of surface warships deployed prior to hostilities, while the FN and FS series were obliged to cope with air attack and small, fast, surface units plus a high risk of loss or damage from mining. Fortunately, the Atlantic convoys, the most important both in number and content, faced only rare problems from surface vessels, and aircraft were of major concern during late 1940 to mid-1943 only, submarines being by far the principal danger.

Convoy formation

Based on the fact that, faced with submerged attack, the quicker passage is made past the position of the submarine the less the exposure to danger, convoys always adopted a "broad front" formation whenever possible. Obviously this could not be done in confined waters such as a swept channel, off the East Coast of Britain for example, and in those conditions safe navigation became the prime factor governing the formation.

In the extreme, an eight-ship ocean convoy would form in line abreast, designated as eight columns of one ship each. The most usual formation would be between six and nine columns of ships with up to five ships in each column. Early ocean convoys usually comprised approximately 35 ships; indeed, the opinion of many Commodores in the early years was that more than this number could not be properly handled in Atlantic winter conditions.

Ships were allocated their positions prior to sailing, indicated by a number individual to the ship. Columns were numbered from the port hand column (1), consecutively to starboard; ships were numbered within each column from 1 at the head of the column. Thus a ship allocated the number 23 was the third ship of the second column. If the number allocated was a three-figure number, then the first two digits were the column number, e.g. 123 would be the third ship of the 12th column from the port side of the convoy.

For obvious reasons position numbers within a column could not progress beyond 9, and in fact only five in some 3,500 ocean convoys ever had more than 9 ships in any column, then the 10th ship was numbered 9A and the 11th 9B.

Author's collection

Unfortunately untitled, the photograph portrays a Convoy Commodore (right) and the Master of the ship in which he was embarked. Undoubtedly posed by the cameraman, and probably taken while in port, it is nevertheless an excellent illustration of the men who led convoys in the North Atlantic 1939-45. Date of the photograph is uncertain, probably first quarter 1943.

The largest convoy ever to sail, HX 300, between North America and Britain, contained 167 ships in 19 columns of which fourteen contained nine ships and three ten ships. This and several other very large convoys that crossed the North Atlantic in the spring of 1944 were due to the need to withdraw Escort Groups for the Normandy invasion. In consequence the number of convoys at sea at any one time had to be reduced to match the remaining available Escort Groups. Accordingly the slow ONS and SC convoy series were suspended and the ships from them absorbed into the ON and HX codings for some months, resulting in a considerable increase in convoy size. After the successful conclusion of Operation Neptune, the North Atlantic Escort Groups returned to their normal duties, the ONS and SC convoys were reinstated, and convoys reverted to a more normal size.

In column, ships steamed at two-cable (400 yard) intervals until 1943. Increasingly inexperienced Merchant Officers, particularly in American ships, were unwilling to maintain this close interval. As there was no real cure for the problem, column spacing was increased to three- and later four-cable during 1943.

The original distances between columns of three cables by day and five cables by night, was also investigated by OR scientists. They showed that the five-cable spacing of columns presented a lesser, more open, target and the formation was accordingly amended. All convoy sailing plans indicated the masthead height of each ship. The officer on watch was then able to use his sextant to maintain station both in column, and between columns, by taking the relevant angle from a known height. At night, shaded blue stern lights were burned and in fog it was usual to stream a fog buoy (an empty cask or float on an appropriate length of line) to ease station keeping.

As previously stated, convoy size was initially restricted to about 35 ships, regarded by many as the optimum for North Atlantic conditions. However OR proved that there could be a considerable increase in numbers provided the principle of a broad front was kept, without a need to increase the size of the escort to any great degree. This was due to the fact that, in the approved formation, a numerical increase did not cause an equivalent extension of the convoy perimeter requiring defence. Convoy numbers therefore rose to the 60-plus level in up to a dozen columns while maintaining the column length; it was operational necessity in 1944 that drove numbers far beyond that and involved lengthening the columns.

The convoy formation was issued by the NCS to each Master prior to sailing, thereafter the Convoy Commodore was responsible for ordering such alterations as were required or as he thought necessary. For example, a poor stationkeeper would be relegated to the rear of its column to avoid annoyance to ships astern of it. Motor ships, whose diesels made small variations in speed difficult or impossible, were not usually appointed to lead columns. Similar conditions applied to coal burners, where variations in quality of coal, capability of stokers and the periodic need to clean fires, made maintenance of a consistent speed difficult.

All Masters were required, before sailing, to notify the current constant speed capability of their ships; obviously this varied due to loading, time out of drydock etc. Ships were then allocated to a fast or slow convoy accordingly.

Convoy command

In typical British fashion, control of the convoy was twofold. Direct control of the convoy rested with the Convoy Commodore, its protection with the Senior Officer of the Escort (referred to in the RN as SOE). As the escort commander was inevitably junior to the Commodore, it was laid down that the Commodore had no right of intervention with the escort, and that the SOE could, if he became aware of circumstances requiring it, give a mandatory instruction to the Commodore. A good deal of tolerance and understanding between the two officers was therefore essential. In fact, friction was minimal, co-operation normally of a high order and the whole system remarkably effective, with the Commodore dealing solely with the merchant ships of the convoy. The SOE intervened (or detailed another escort) at the specific request of the Commodore to provide any assistance required in controlling the convoy.

The divided command system should be seen in the context of the experience of the two commanders. The Commodores, all elderly men, had practical, personal, experience of the problems of coal fired ships from their younger days. As almost all had started their Commodore's service in the first months of the war they had considerable personal experience of the problems of the Masters whom they led. The escort commanders, much younger officers, lacked that personal knowledge, and the opportunity to obtain it. The system worked in practice, with only rare cases of a personality clash between Commodore and SOE or Commodore and ships' Masters. In such instances, the Admiralty could exercise its prerogative of dispensing with a Commodore's services, or appointing him elsewhere. In the only case known to the writer, the offending Commodore, described as "an intolerant personality who greatly upset the Masters of ships in the convoy," was appointed elsewhere after a short interval. He served the next five years in a single, vital appointment with distinction and great efficiency and, as the Commodore commanding the working-up base at Tobermory in Western Scotland, he was responsible for the training of all newly built or re-commissioned British escort vessels during 1940-45. Indeed not a few RCN and Allied escorts also passed through his hands. He contributed to a very large extent indeed to the efficiency of such escorts and his name became widely known and one to respect and admire. His name? Vice-Admiral Sir Gilbert O Stephenson, also known as "The Terror of Tobermory".

The SOE had sole responsibility for the "safe and timely arrival of the convoy"; i.e. its defence, and could (and did) issue orders, as appropriate, to the Commodore for that purpose. Admiralty instructions to convoys and merchant ships generally (or specifically) were usually contained in BAMS (British Admiralty Mercantile Signals) which were transmitted at specific times on a daily basis using a code held by all merchant ships. In emergency, orders could be passed via the SOE for the attention of the Commodore who would receive them in plain language by line transfer after decoding in the escort.

In the North Atlantic the whole body, convoy and escort, was controlled from the Western Approaches HQ at Liverpool, where C-in-C Western Approaches maintained his command centre. Westbound convoys were controlled to a point known as the Change of Operational Control line (CHOP line) where command was transferred to the Eastern coast of North America, the actual authority varying during the war as is recounted elsewhere. Likewise eastbound convoys came under C-in-C Western Approaches when crossing the same line. In other areas, the appropriate C-in-C exercised control of the convoys within his area, transferring command from or to another C-in-C as appropriate at the Station boundary. In instances where there was an ongoing action condition, the actual transfer could be varied from the CHOP line by signalled agreement.

CHAPTER 4
THE TRADE DIVISION

The Trade Division, as reconstituted in May 1939, consisted of but ten persons: a Captain as Director, five naval Officers and four Admiralty civil servants. By 1942 the number had risen to over 300, all employed within the Admiralty complex.

The functions of the Division were:
1. To control the movements of all merchant ships and convoys.
2. The protection of such ships by the fitting of defensive armament, the provision of trained crews either from Naval or Army resources (DEMS gunners) and the training of MN personnel for the same purpose.
3. Responsibility for the organization and control of the NCS organization and the allocation and distribution of civilian-manned Rescue Tugs.
4. Responsibility for the closest liaison with other Admiralty departments, specifically the Operational Intelligence Centre, MOWT and civilian shipping interests generally.

Trade Division Plot

Initially the Trade Plot was merely a record of the positions of all convoys and merchant ships from the time of their sailing, thereafter updated by dead reckoning plotting. This could be corrected only when the formation or ship made a signal. The routing of convoys was, at that time, the responsibility of Routing Officers elsewhere in Trade Division. The Trade Plot therefore, within its sphere of operations, provided any advice, guidance and recommendation that might be required by other authorities. Specifically, the plotters maintained the closest contact with the Naval Control of Shipping Officers (NCSOs) at UK ports to ensure that incoming ocean ships were allocated to the correct discharging ports and coastal convoy arrangements made where necessary. Similarly, that all the necessary information was available to NCSOs to allocate outward-bound ships to an appropriate convoy sailing.

When the Citadel was nearing completion, as an adjunct to the original Admiralty building in London, the Trade Plot was moved to that more secure area next to but totally independent of the Tracking Room, (the U-boat Plot) maintained by Naval Intelligence. Additionally, the Operational Plot that recorded the movements of all British and Allied warships was amalgamated with the Trade Plot. Eight officers of the Trade Division, in four watches, thus became responsible for the control, routing and plotting of all convoys and independents, and for providing advice, guidance and recommendation for other authorities. The Trade Plot then became the executive authority issuing routing and diversion instructions to Atlantic convoys and independents, after consultation with C-in-C W App.

There was constant contact between the Trade and Submarine Plots, initially on an unofficial basis of liaison between their controllers. This was later made official on the order of Rear-Admiral J H Edelsten, Assistant Chief of Naval Staff (U-boat Warfare and Trade), in early 1943 who laid down that, unless by his specific authority, the advice of the Tracking Room on routing was always to be accepted.

Plotting

Nine officers and sixty-five civilians, who included numerous experienced MN Masters, were responsible for calculating on a daily basis the estimated 0800GMT positions of every convoy and British and Allied merchant ship at sea, these positions being indicated on the previously mentioned Plot.

The section responsible was therefore able to advise authorities, both overseas and at home, of the estimated arrival date of ships requiring discharge, and could also advise warships at sea whether an intercepted vessel could actually be whom she claimed, an important feature when dealing with raiders or blockade runners. Independent ships were also tracked by this means, appropriate advice given as to their due time of arrival, and possible location of loss if gravely overdue.

Administration

The Division was also responsible for the administration of all NCS staff, numbering tens of thousands world-wide, of the Commodores of Convoys and their staffs, and finally for the preparation, stocking and distribution of all publications required by merchant ships. This included records of which individual ships held books and documents.

Convoy Commodores

Convoy Commodores were drawn from a list of volunteers to serve either with Ocean or Coastal convoys. For the former, the choice was made from retired Flag Officers and Captains of the Royal Navy who were appointed as Commodores 2nd Class in the Royal Naval Reserve for the period of their duty. As the war progressed, some senior Officers of the Royal Netherlands and Royal Norwegian Navies were also appointed. In the case of coastal convoys, the list comprised Commanders and Lieutenant-Commanders of the Royal Naval Reserve, i.e. professional seamen, whose age restricted their long-term employment at sea. Almost every Commodore was aged over sixty when he commenced his appointment, some older, and their retired ranks varied from Admiral to Lieutenant-Commander. Shortage of Commodores led to some coastal convoys, and also some ocean convoys, having the Master of one of the merchant ships of the convoy appointed to the task.

Commodores for the North Atlantic routes were drawn from a pool of less than 200 who served almost exclusively in that ocean. Major convoys proceeding east of Gibraltar, such as troop convoys for India via Suez, continued with the UK-based Commodore to Port Said and, occasionally, onward to India. Otherwise, the C-in-C Eastern Fleet had his own small pool of Commodores (or selected Masters) for the Indian Ocean. Russian convoys drew their Commodores from the North Atlantic pool. Convoy systems organized by the Royal Australian and Royal Canadian Navies, principally coastal, were provided with Commodores appointed by those Services.

All Commodores had the right to request reversion to non-active service at any time, while the Admiralty retained the right (and occasionally exercised it) to retire a Commodore from service.

Commodores were assisted in their duties by a Vice-Commodore and, on occasions, by one or more Rear-Commodores. A Vice-Commodore could be either a Commodore RNR from the pool serving as an assistant or the Commodore of another convoy that had joined at sea. This was particularly the case with the SL and MKS convoys, which amalgamated off Gibraltar for the passage to the UK, and of their counterparts, the OS and KMS convoys that sailed as a single unit and divided off Gibraltar. In both cases, one of the Commodores of the individual convoys became the Vice-Commodore of the joint convoy for the period of its existence.

In all other instances the Vice-and Rear-Commodores were Masters of ships in the appropriate convoy. Their duty was to assist the Commodore, and to assume his duties should he be lost during the convoy.

Commodores were accompanied by a staff: a Yeoman of Signals (a Petty Officer of the Communications Branch), three Convoy Signalmen and usually a Telegraphist. The signalmen were young HO ratings, trained as signalmen but without the need for experience in Fleet procedures. They carried considerable responsibility and were, without

The NCS organization at each major port maintained a plot of the adjacent anchorage on which were recorded the anchor berths allocated to ships. This photograph is of the Clyde plot taken in the first four days of Oct 1942, as deduced from the ships shown on the wallboard behind the bearded Captain.

He is Captain H A B Digby-Beste RN, a retired officer of the Royal Indian Navy, who volunteered for duty in 1939. Appointed Temporary Captain RN, he served as Berthing Officer for the Clyde Anchorage from Sept 1940 to the end of 1943. His war service came to an end in late 1945, when he was serving on the staff of C-in-C, British Pacific Fleet in Sydney NSW.

exception, highly efficient visual signallers. It was also usual to provide the Vice-Commodore with two Convoy Signalmen to assist him in his duties.

Commodores and their staffs were based at Liverpool and administered from that port; usually their ship sailed from Liverpool, otherwise they travelled to join the ship at her sailing port. On arrival at their destination in North America, Gibraltar or West Africa they then awaited a convoy returning to the UK.

NCS Officers

A senior Officer, usually of Captain or Commander rank, was appointed at all major British ports, and ports in overseas possessions and the Commonwealth as appropriate, to act for the Trade Division. These officers were retired RN or older Reserve Officers, in the latter case frequently with considerable experience as Merchant Navy (MN) officers. Their duty was the control of all shipping entering their area of authority, monitoring its progress in discharging cargo, effecting repairs, re-supplying and either loading outward cargo or ballast. These matters dealt with by the Port Controller, STO and ships' agents, required close and tactful liaison on the part of the NCSO and his staff.

As a departure date became available for a ship in port, that date and the ship's intended destination as advised by MOWT, was communicated to Trade Division together with the intended convoy from the schedule held by the NCSO.

The NCSO was then required to advise the Master of his sailing date, ensure delivery of all appropriate convoy documentation by hand, ascertain that adequate crew were available, ensure the supply of the requisite quantity of bunkers. Further, he would also obtain the Master's estimate of his vessel's continuous speed applicable to the coming voyage, call the Convoy Conference the day prior to sailing, and arrange the presence of the Master.

The NCSO was also responsible for the preparation of the convoy sailing plan on Form A 1, a copy of which appears as Appendix 7 to this text. Position of ships within the convoy was determined by their destination, armament, value of cargo, number of passengers (if any), whether steam or diesel driven, and speed.

On the departure of the convoy, the NCSO would notify, by signal, the actual as opposed to the intended ships in convoy to both Admiralty and to C-in-C W App. Overseas, advice would be to the area C-in-C who would then notify Trade Division who would circulate the information within Admiralty as required.

The NCSO's task was considerable, and the area of responsibility very variable. For example, the NCSO Clyde was responsible for all merchant shipping within the Clyde, i.e. inside the Cumbrae Gap defences, and all the ports and anchorages of the Clyde Estuary including Glasgow itself. NCSO staffs were therefore of considerable size in large ports, including: Boarding Officers to call personally on ships; boats and crews to handle traffic to ships not alongside; staff to provide a local Plot showing berths allocated to vessels in the port area; a major communications network, etc. A mammoth task as, in a port such as the Clyde or Liverpool, one large ocean convoy a day inward or outward would be quite normal plus the movements within the area of the command. At Southend it was not uncommon for four or even five outward convoys (mostly coastal) to sail each day in the last twelve months of the war.

Older officers, especially with Merchant Navy experience, RNVRs with shipping background and specifically trained RNVR and WRNS officers formed the staffs; the rating establishment had a high proportion of WRNS ratings, including boats' crews.

Overseas control

Overseas the NCS organization functioned in Commonwealth and British colonial ports as in the UK. In Canada and Australia the appropriate Navies, after full mobilisation, gradually took over the NCS duties within their own territories, as staff became available. In neutral ports, an NCS officer was appointed to the local consular staff where necessary; in minor ports the Consul would have to handle such matters himself. In the USA, from 1942, the USN provided a similar NCS organization that made the presence of RN NCS staff in the USA unnecessary. The USN equivalent to a British NCSO was entitled Port Director for the appropriate port.

Communication between the US and British organization was by signal (W/T, cable or Telex) via Trade Division in London.

In some overseas ports in operational areas, e.g. North Africa and India in 1940-42 in particular, overall control rested with the Army and Sea Transport Officers (STO), whose primary duty was to satisfy the requirements of the military authorities. While STOs were, usually, officers drawn from the Retired List of the RN or the Reserves, they were answerable to the Sea Transport Organization of the MOWT. It is noticeable that in such instances, where Trade Division principles were lacking and Ministry control distant, uneconomic use of merchant tonnage occurred. In May 1941, for example, the MOS in London ordered an investigation at Suez. The matter was handled by sending out a senior ship-owner who was attached to MOWT. He discovered that at Suez only one ship was being unloaded every two days and there were, allegedly, 117 ships lying in the roadstead awaiting attention.

The problems arose from the fact that the Ministry representative, an official of over 70 years of age, was based at Alexandria with a minuscule staff and extremely poor communications with Suez. The Sea Transport Officers were elderly, retired RN officers of high rank or younger, more junior officers "whose chief qualification was that no other service was required of them." In the circumstances it is not surprising that chaos reigned in the ships and on the jetties, and that Army demands for items onboard vessels were met though they bore no relation to efficient ship management.

It was stated that there were 117 ships awaiting discharge at Suez when the inspection began, the figure presumably being supplied by one of the two relevant, local authorities. This figure appears high and certainly cannot have been totally made up of ships from the UK. A complete analysis of over 2,500 ships' voyages for 1939-1945 has shown only one vessel, the BLACKHEATH, that lay at Suez for more than 30 days; she was in that area from 23 Feb to 7 April 1941 after her voyage from the UK. This spell included a period when the Canal was blocked to shipping by mines. It is probable that the misinformation arose from the fragmented and inefficient organizations that existed locally. However the decision of the inspecting official to revise local arrangements, and the action taken in London, ensured the creation of a committee along the lines of the Port Directors in the UK, whose chairman was a senior MOWT official. The handling of normal cargoes, including Army stores, was transferred to local, commercially experienced agents and the STO organization was directed to reserve its work for personnel ships and operational vessels. Army profligacy, and a recurring tendency to use loaded ships as floating warehouses, was sharply curbed and a vastly more efficient organization created. This policy was subsequently applied to other overseas areas where similar problems appeared possible or had arisen.

Misuse of shipping

In 1943, the increased losses of the previous fifteen months caused considerable anxiety. The problem was made worse by Allied success in North Africa and Italy, which greatly increased the requirements for ships due to the need to feed and support a very large civilian population. Finally, the necessity to build up supplies for future operations also increased. In consequence, another investigation into the employment of merchant tonnage had to be undertaken.

Incredibly, further examples of Army profligacy came to light; the 8th Army artillery ammunition reserves, for example, held 16 months' expenditure, based on usage during a month which included the heaviest artillery barrage of World War II, that at the Battle of Alamein. Similarly, the reserve of rifles in the Middle East amounted to 14 years' expenditure and of motor transport 4 months' expenditure based on the monthly rate of loss plus usage during 1941, a bad year in North Africa. The remedy applied was to halve the sailings to and within the Indian Ocean theatre, and direct the Army to tailor its operations to conform to that limitation. Given their known reserves, they had more than sufficient supplies to sustain any planned operation or unforeseen Service emergency.

In passing, it must also be mentioned that the tendency of Army authorities to pay little account to the effect of their demands on an overall situation was by no means confined to the UK. The calls on tonnage to support the US Army in the UK (and later Europe) bore little resemblance to actual needs, and this at a time when the British population subsisted on small rations with a national reserve of only eight weeks' consumption.

When considering this matter the differing approach of the UK and USA to the problem of service requirements must be considered. In the UK the MOWT controlled all tonnage and their customers were few: the Ministries of Food, responsible for all food supplies for the UK excluding US personnel; Supply handled all raw materials and war material required for use by industry or use within the UK, again excluding the US forces; Transport for all UK fuel requirements; and the Services, who presented their needs for transport of men and materials overseas for MOWT to satisfy, through the medium of the Sea Transport Office.

The US system was totally different; tonnage was controlled by the War Shipping Administration it is true, but the Navy and Army simply presented to the WSA a statement of their requirements in terms of gross tonnage. These demands had to be met, with no explanation being offered as to how they were arrived at, and the WSA was left to manage with the remaining tonnage at its disposal. The Presidential edict referred to shortly is evidence of the extent of the over estimation by the US Services of their real needs.

After the Normandy landings in June 1944 the situation became even worse, the responsibility of feeding an increasing number of Europeans in a continent devastated by fighting was added to the responsibility with no apparent lessening of the US service requirements. Indeed, with a major withdrawal of US tonnage to the Pacific, it was left to a hard pressed MOWT to balance the need of feeding and supplying the UK, transporting food and fuel to the Continent for the local populations, supplying the British armed forces overseas and, finally, somehow to provide tonnage to create a Fleet Train to support the Royal Navy in the Pacific.

The tendency of Army authorities in particular to use shipping as floating warehouses, to delay unloading entirely or selectively to deal with cargoes rather than emptying a ship, is a common occurrence. It even occurred in 1982 in the Falklands war to a minor degree, when the shore command was highly efficient, amphibious-trained, Royal Marine officers.

The situation became so serious at the end of 1944 that the President of the USA was compelled to intervene, and issued a mandatory instruction to his Joint Chiefs of Staff. Without going into detail, which can be found in Behrens *Merchant Shipping and the Demands of War* in the official British History series, the following extract from the resultant order is of interest.

...It is directed that the following policies be followed by all US commanders of areas under the direction of the US Chiefs of Staff and shall be a guide to US commanders in other areas:

(a) The use of oceangoing ships for storage purposes whether loaded in the US or in the theater, is prohibited.

(b) In arriving at shipping requirements, a realistic appreciation of port and discharge capacity is imperative.

(c) Selective discharge of ships, resulting in partial unloading of a number of vessels, save in the early stages of amphibious operations, will be discontinued.

(d) The misuse of large oceangoing vessels by diversion or delay to discharge or load small tonnages, by partial or selective unloading of cargo; or by inefficient use of ocean tonnage for local small deliveries will be discontinued except in case of emergency which the theater commander cannot meet by other means.

That such a positive directive to Generals Eisenhower and MacArthur, to name but two of the commanders to whom it was addressed, should be necessary underlines the magnitude of the problem that had arisen.

Not only armies were responsible for such actions; similar problems arose with naval authorities though there were some mitigating circumstances. The requirement for deployment of large forces of naval and merchant vessels to ports not equipped to handle such numbers caused major problems in fuel storage. For example, at Freetown, Gibraltar, Scapa Flow and Iceland in particular, demand for bunker fuel far exceeded available shore capacity.

At Scapa Flow the problem was eventually solved by the construction, in hollowed-out hills ashore, of very large oil storage tanks. The resultant spoil was also used to seal the eastern entrances to the Flow and provided the islanders with road communication. However, prior to 1942, the RN was obliged to keep ocean-going tankers idle in the Flow as floating reservoirs of fuel for the Fleet. A similar situation arose at Freetown, where there were minimal shore facilities and a lack of space to build new ones. At Gibraltar the only answer was tunnelling in the rock, and at a number of major escort bases the only answer was the use of a tanker offshore. For example, at Iceland in 1941 the mid-Atlantic escorts used Hvalfjord as a base, while in 1942 and 1943 Seidisfjord became a Home Fleet anchorage for ships covering the Russian convoy routes. There simply was no space ashore for, nor ability to construct, oil terminals and the retention of oceangoing tankers at these bases over a period of three years, was essential.

While it was at times unavoidable, the RN was also not too attentive to relinquishing tonnage when it *was* possible, and there was continual bickering between the Admiralty and MOWT on the subject throughout the war.

CHAPTER 5

VARIATIONS TO THE CONVOY SYSTEM

North Atlantic and North Sea 1939-40

Of the convoys mentioned in an earlier section as commencing the entire system, KJ was short lived and discarded late in 1939. Only two further series were started prior to June 1940, HN and ON; respectively, Homeward from Norway and Outward to Norway. This series escorted the Norwegian trade from and to the limit of Norwegian territorial waters, a NCS officer on the staff of the Consul in Bergen briefing the outgoing Masters and appointing one of their number to lead the convoy out to meet their escort. These series were unique in commencing from a neutral port. The series of course ceased upon the German attack on Norway.

Consequent on the collapse and surrender of France, the situation in the Atlantic changed dramatically. The presence of German forces along the Channel coast, extension of German air power into the western Atlantic and to the whole coast of Britain, and the ability of U-boats to range much further into the Atlantic than hitherto caused a complete re-organization. After June 1940 there had to be considerable extension of the coastal system around Britain, and alterations to the oceanic system.

The OA series from the Downs stopped after a disastrous final passage by OA 178 when the convoy suffered attack by shore batteries, light surface forces and aircraft with considerable loss and damage. The series resumed in July 1940 with sailings from the Firth of Forth north around Scotland, while the OB series was re-routed through the North Channel between Scotland and Ulster, the two convoys (identically numbered) merging northwest of Scotland and proceeding to a dispersal point in the Atlantic. A coastal portion of OA completed the passage to the Clyde so that coastal traffic to and from the east and west coasts had AA and A/S escort.

Channel convoy was introduced to handle coastwise traffic only and was restricted initially to the Downs to Isle of Wight route. From the Isle of Wight, ships sailed as individuals, "coasting" and lying up in ports during the day for protection from air attack. Later, trawler escort was supplied to cover these individual sailings then, finally, a properly organized system from St Helens Roads, Isle of Wight to Milford Haven. The various expedients adopted, rather than the immediate introduction of convoy, were dictated solely by a lack of resources at a critical time.

The necessity of convoy cover for ships from overseas to pass to East coast ports was filled, initially, by a section of the HX and SL convoys which detached from the main body off the west coast of Scotland and passed through the Pentland Firth to Methil (being designated by the suffix A to the convoy title) from where ships proceeded in the FS series southwards as required.

Finally, the heavy losses to slow eastbound independents in the Atlantic required the introduction of a second convoy series and, to avoid overuse of Halifax, it was based in the summer season at Sydney, NS. This port, to avoid signal errors confusing it with

Sydney, New South Wales (Sydney NSW) is always referred to by the Royal Navy as Sydney, Cape Breton (Sydney CB), and the series received the designation SC in consequence. These convoys contained ships previously excluded from convoy due to their speeds being less than 9 knots, and the convoy speed for the series was set at 7 (later seven and a half) knots.

Variations in 1941

The increase in German air activity around western Britain after the surrender of France obliged the convoy systems to be extended with the introduction of Channel convoys terminating at Milford Haven. A further series designated MH covered Milford Haven northwards to Holyhead, the reversal convoy being known as BB, Belfast to Bristol Channel, the southern terminal being, in fact, Milford Haven.

In the North, the eventual cessation of the OA series caused the introduction of the WN convoys from the Clyde to Methil in place of the previously mentioned A section of ocean convoys, with EN in the reverse direction. There was also, for a period in 1941 only, a series known as EC which ran from Southend to the Clyde. This was additional to the northbound FN series and unusual in that there was no corresponding series in the reverse direction.

With these changes there was now a complete system of convoy encircling the British Isles, in both clockwise and anti-clockwise directions. Frequency of sailings of the various series varied according to traffic, but was usually every other day. Numbers in convoys also varied according to traffic from single figures to up to sixty, or even more, ships.

Finally, in 1941, came major changes to the North Atlantic system. The OB convoys had, perforce, been routed further and further north to avoid French based air reconnaissance and attack; also, the escort was extended by basing relief escorts in Iceland. Therefore, use of the series by ships bound for the southern oceans became less desirable, so a series to Freetown was started designated Outward South, OS, in the spring of 1941. Like OB it left Britain via the North Channel but turned southward somewhat short of mid-Atlantic to proceed to Freetown. Also containing ships to be detached for the Caribbean, Panama and beyond Freetown, this series was escorted throughout its passage.

With the restriction of the OB series to North America-bound vessels, and escort about to be extended to Newfoundland, the OB series was replaced by a new series titled Outward North, ON, re-using the 1940 designation originally applied to the Norwegian trade. In this new series, every other convoy was reserved for slower vessels and these convoys are referred to in documents as ON(S). Nevertheless, they bear the consecutive numbering of the ON series and should always be referred to as ON convoys to avoid confusion with a 1943 series that did bear the designation ONS.

Mediterranean convoys 1940-41

Due to the geographical location of Italy, almost all east/west traffic in the Mediterranean ceased in June 1940, and did not resume until after the invasion of North Africa in November 1942. The exceptions of course were the convoys from both east and west to Malta, usually known by their operation names (PEDESTAL, HARPOON etc), rare "through" convoys from Gibraltar to Egypt, and the convoys to and from Tobruk during the siege, these by warships and RN-manned merchant ships. Prior to the overrunning of Greece by German forces in the spring of 1941, the Mediterranean Fleet operated convoys to and from Piraeus and, occasionally, the Dardanelles under the designation Aegean North and Aegean South, AN and AS.

Although technically part of the East Indies Station, mention should also be made of the Red Sea convoys. Until the Italians were defeated in their Eritrean colony and in Abyssinia there was a considerable threat to shipping in the Red Sea, although in fact very few attacks were ever made. A convoy system was operated between Suez and Perim, off Aden, designated BN and BS, Bombay North and Bombay South, these titles being used as the first few convoys in fact originated from Bombay. The convoys are also unusual in that they were locally titled rather than from Trade Division; hence rather than a strict numeric series, or the use of alphabetical suffixes, the local command designated some convoys by halves and quarters. This usage also occurs occasionally in the Indian Ocean convoys later in the war.

North Atlantic convoy changes in 1942

With the German declaration of war on America on 10 December 1941, it had to be expected that submarine warfare would spread much further westward. Such a move was in fact made by BdU and tracked by British Naval Intelligence. Unfortunately, Admiral King, CNO, USN not only chose to ignore the warnings, but also resolutely refused to adopt the proven defence, convoy. It was not until horrific losses off the East Coast of the USA, including a very considerable British tonnage, forced a change of mind that the situation was remedied.

When the Americans reluctantly introduced convoy, they reacted by producing a complex and far ranging system. Based on the need to "feed" ships in and out of the transatlantic convoys, they devised what became known as the "interlocking" convoy system for the East Coast of North America and the Caribbean.

Based on a "day of the week" schedule rather than a cycle of a number of days, a whole series of convoys was created to cover a departure from New York City for ships proceeding to Panama in the west and Trinidad in the south. Thus NG convoys sailed from New York to Guantanamo in Cuba, GN being the northbound versions. From Guantanamo GAT convoys (originally styled WAT and sailing from Key West) sailed to Aruba and Trinidad, the reverse route being TAG. To the westward GZ convoys sailed to the Panama Canal Zone, the reversal being ZG.

As the GN/NG convoys perforce adopted a route somewhat away from the US coast, a further north/south series operated between New York and Key West on the tip of Florida. NK/KN eventually extended westward to serve the US Gulf ports, primarily tanker traffic, with KH/HK between Key West and Galveston Bar i.e. the port of Houston. The Mississippi tanker traffic, terminating at Pilottown in the delta, was catered for by KP/PK. Exchange between the two New York routes was by a Key West to Guantanamo link, KG/GK, while finally, southbound traffic from Trinidad was escorted as far as Bahia in Brazil by TB/BT. The inevitable extension of submarine warfare south as convoy was introduced replaced this last series with TJ/JT from Trinidad to Rio de Janeiro.

Northbound traffic from New York also required convoy, so that the Canadians very quickly introduced the SH/HS series between Halifax NS and Sydney CB, the SQ/QS series between Sydney CB and the St Lawrence Ports, SG/GS for the supply convoys to Greenland from Sydney CB (later from St John's NF). The New York to Halifax traffic was catered for by the US controlled but Canadian escorted BX/XB series between Boston and Halifax. This last series was suspended when, briefly, the Halifax Atlantic terminal was moved south to New York for a period over the winter season of 1942/43. Finally, there was a number of other convoy series to handle Canadian east coast traffic.

The result of these convoy introductions, obviously a progressive operation, was little short of dramatic. As soon as BdU became aware of convoy introduction in a specific area, he ordered the abandonment of those operations and moved the U-boats to where unescorted traffic was still the norm. Hence all operations off the US East Coast ceased, and the U-boats moved to the Caribbean; when convoy was started there, the offensive moved south to the northeast coast of South America. The final move was to the Rio route; when that was also covered by convoy, submarine attacks by large numbers of U-boats ceased entirely and they sought other, easier pickings elsewhere.

The final result of the Interlocking system was in fact to demonstrate conclusively the efficacy of the convoy system in its entirety.

The key to all the US series was the sailing *day* as shown in the accompanying table for the Caribbean. It will be appreciated that, with this knowledge in the hands of the NCSO in ports as remote as Cape Town or Freetown, a ship could be routed via Rio de Janeiro with predicted connections at Trinidad, Guantanamo and New York to sail in a Trans Atlantic convoy, to meet a coastal UK convoy in Loch Ewe, change convoys at Methil and arrive in London for discharge of cargo on a known date. Basically, the convoy system and its promulgated frequency became a vast maritime equivalent of a railway timetable.

Days of departure	Northbound			Southbound		
Sunday	KP			GZ	NG	
Monday	GK	ZG		GAT		
Tuesday	GN	KN	TAG	KG	PK	
Wednesday	No sailings			No sailings		
Thursday	GK	KH		GAT	NG	
Friday	No sailings			HK	KG	NK
Saturday	GN	TAG		No sailings		

North Atlantic convoy changes in 1943

The invasion of North Africa imposed a number of changes, both temporary and permanent, which took effect in October 1942 but which are listed here, as the main effects occurred in 1943.

Firstly, the convoys to and from Gibraltar, OG/HG were suspended, as were the convoys to and from Freetown, SL/OS. This was to clear the path of the invasion convoys and their follow-up reinforcements and, on successful completion of the landings and follow-up, the OS/SL series were reinstated.

The invasion convoys were in four series, two from Britain and two from the USA, one of each pair being troop carrying and one stores. The British pair took the designation KM (United Kingdom to Mediterranean) suffixed F in the case of the troopships and S for the store carriers, hence KMF and KMS. The customary reversal codes applied for the return journey, MKF and MKS. The US convoys adopted UG for (United States to Gibraltar), again suffixed F and S with the reversal code GU, also suffixed F and S.

In the case of all four series the designations were retained after the invasion so that KMF/MKF became the standard series for all troop convoys from the UK to the Mediterranean with an eventual terminal at Port Said, while the KMS/MKS series replaced the old OG/HG series, eventually extending to Port Said. The UGF/GUF series was relatively short, terminating in mid-1943 with a brief revival in early 1944; however, the UGS/GUS continued until the end of the war, albeit using Oran in lieu of Port Said as the eastern terminal from late 1944.

One of the results of the North African invasion was a serious depletion of the oil reserves held in Britain. After a good deal of argument with the Americans (who considered that the British were overly concerned at a reduction of oil stocks to less than two months' consumption), agreement was reached on the institution of special, fast tanker convoys direct from the Caribbean to the UK under the designation CU (Caribbean to United Kingdom) with the return convoys designated UC. This designation became something of a misnomer as, after less than ten fortnightly convoys, the western terminal was shifted from the oil ports of Trinidad and Aruba to New York. The convoys mainly comprised war-built US tankers of relatively high speed (in excess of 15 knots). As a result it became increasingly common for them to include troop transports in that speed range and also fast cargo vessels.

Mediterranean convoy changes in 1943

In the Mediterranean convoy, changes were entirely dictated by military advance. As the Army advanced eastward, eventually into Tunisia, a convoy system had to be created to serve its needs. Similarly, in Libya, the 8th Army needed support in the desert. In the Western Mediterranean the initial sequence was a coastal service from Gibraltar titled TE/ET for Torch East and the usual reversal code. This lasted almost to the end of the Tunisian campaign and then ceased. In the east a service from Alexandria to Tripoli (XT) served the desert troops, again the usual reversal code applied.

By the beginning of 1943 it once again became possible to supply Malta from the east almost without threat, and the Malta West (MW), i.e. Alexandria to Malta, and the reversal ME became a regular rather than an occasional, hard fought series.

When victory came in North Africa, the ability to supply air cover throughout the length of the Mediterranean enabled the reintroduction of regular, through traffic for the first time since June 1940, so that initially a series entitled GTX, Gibraltar/Tripoli/Alexandria and its reversal code XTG, was instituted, superseded by the extension of the KM and UG series and their homeward counterparts to and from Port Said, covering all intermediate ports on the African coast. The supply of Malta, and the forces engaged in Sicily, and later Italy, was then by direct sailings from the UK and USA rather than via the Cape and Eastern Mediterranean.

VARIATIONS TO THE CONVOY SYSTEM

■ Courtesy Air Historical Branch, MoD (Crown Copyright)

An early troop convoy at sea from Canada to the UK. This is convoy TC 6 photographed by a RAF Sunderland flying boat about 28 July 1940. The convoy consisted of seven liners escorted by the battleship REVENGE and cruiser EMERALD. The destroyer escort from the Home Fleet had not yet joined when this picture was taken.

In the background EMPRESS OF AUSTRALIA leads MONARCH OF BERMUDA, the battleship REVENGE leads (probably) ANTONIA while the starboard column is the Polish BATORY leading the Polish SOBIESKI. Out of shot are the liners SAMARIA and DUCHESS OF YORK which are in the port column.

EMPRESS OF AUSTRALIA carried 1,611 personnel; MONARCH OF BERMUDA 1,328; ANTONIA 881; BATORY 1,198; SOBIESKI 1,061; SAMARIA 1,016 and DUCHESS OF YORK 982, all Canadian Army.

In mid-1943 first Sicily and then Southern Italy were occupied bringing the need for maritime supply to those areas, hence the introduction of series that lasted almost until May 1945. They were based loosely on Augusta in Sicily, being fed from the trans-Mediterranean convoys referred to previously, via Malta. Hence the Augusta to Naples series were titled VN for Valetta to Naples with a reversal NV; Augusta to Taranto, Brindisi and Bari was known as AH taken from Augusta to Heel of Italy, with the reversal code HA.

The first troop convoys

Troop convoys, due to the high personnel content and the serious effect that a loss would have upon the conduct of the war, were handled as a naval operation with Trade Division ceding control to the operational side of Admiralty.

Troop convoys were, in the first year of the war, limited to transport of Commonwealth detachments to war stations. The ANZAC troops were conveyed initially to the Middle East, the third such convoy being diverted to Britain in June 1940. The series then reverted to Suez as its destination, all the convoys in a series designated US, the actual derivation of which is not apparent.

Troop convoys from Canada to Britain carried the coding TC, assumed to be Troops from Canada. This series ran in three distinct groups: the transport of the original, regular Canadian Army; the second, the movement of the reserves; the third, the first movement of the wartime volunteers. The reverse designation CT started much later and was used for only a few convoys.

The next, short-lived series in the North Atlantic was NA, again from Canada to the UK and following on from TC; again the derivation is unclear. It also ran partly in conjunction with a US series titled AT, presumably American Troops, which had a reversal TA. This series is dealt with separately.

A final North Atlantic series is again American and ran under the coding UT, possibly derived from United States Troops. It too had a reversal TU for the homeward passage and is possibly unique in that the serial coding was assigned to a specific group of ships rather than a convoy sequence. Hence the employment on another route of the ships from UT 3 caused TU 3 to run AFTER TU 4 and TU 4A!

The Monster convoys

During 1942 the need to transport vast numbers of American servicemen to Britain under the title Operation BOLERO, caused a considerable change in the accepted manner of troop transport across the North Atlantic. Hitherto, personnel ships had moved in strongly escorted convoys on an "as needed" basis; during 1942 there commenced the nearest thing possible to the pre-1939 trans-Atlantic mail service.

Almost the same ships that carried on the luxury Atlantic trade pre-war were used: QUEEN MARY, AQUITANIA, MAURETANIA and the new QUEEN ELIZABETH, the Dutch NIEUW AMSTERDAM, the French ILE DE FRANCE and PASTEUR together with the Royal Mail ANDES, and several other large liners from other sources. The essential requirements were size, to carry large numbers of troops, and a service i.e. constant seagoing speed, of at least 20 knots.

The "convoys" were also unusual in that they were always single ships and were unescorted other than for twenty-four hours at either end of their passage. Off New York or Halifax, the two western terminals, with New York handling a good 80% plus of the traffic, a destroyer escort met the ship at dawn of the last day and brought her into the harbour approaches. In the east, where the terminal in over 90% of passages was the Clyde, the escort consisted of destroyers and an AA cruiser in 1942; later, destroyers only. Similar escort was provided on departure from the terminal ports, also for some twenty-four hours.

There were almost 200 passages in each direction, all under the designations AT, Eastward and TA, Westward. The largest number of troops in a single passage was just over 15,000 in QUEEN ELIZABETH; even the "smaller" liners averaged over 8,000 per eastbound passage. No loss occurred, and there are only three known sightings, and two attacks. In one of these, on 9 Nov 1942, U 704 set up an attack on a large, fast target identified as QUEEN ELIZABETH. Four torpedoes were fired (a detonation of one being heard) but the attack was abortive, probably due to misjudgement of target speed and range.

U 407 also made an attack in the forenoon of 1 Oct 1942 on a "large three-funnelled liner." The abortive attack, in 50.15N 25.32W, was not observed by the QUEEN MARY which was the liner concerned. A third sighting, much later in the war, also of an unknown three-funnelled liner against which no action could be taken, was only identified in the early 1990s. After discussion in MoD (Navy) with one of the submarine crew, who raised an enquiry as to the identity of the target, it was found that ILE DE FRANCE was the only three-funnelled liner in the appropriate area at the time.

There were only two mishaps during the entire series; the more serious was the running down during an eastbound passage by QUEEN MARY of the AA cruiser CURACOA which was cut in half and sank, with very heavy casualties, on 2 October 1942. The second had been earlier in 1942 when the US Army transport WAKEFIELD caught fire during September en route to the UK with troops. It was fortunate that her personnel were taken off without loss and that it was possible to extinguish the fire and tow her back to port for an eighteen-month repair period.

The WS convoys

Other than the ANZAC and Canadian troop movements, there had been little need for the transport of large numbers of personnel until mid-1940, apart from the cross-Channel transport of the BEF in 1939 and the brief incursion to Norway. After the entry of Italy to the war, the reinforcement of the Middle East and India became of prime importance and led to the introduction of the WS series. Generally believed to derive the code letters from "Winston's Special," this series undertook the movement of servicemen from the UK to Suez initially and ran on an approximately monthly schedule.

The first WS convoy was purely troop movement; later convoys also included fast freighters which conveyed the equipment for the troops so that the convoy was, in essence, a complete Divisional organization.

The standard route, although there were of course variations, was from the Clyde to Freetown to refuel and water ship, thence to Cape Town and Durban (the convoy usually splitting between the two ports), and then on to Suez. From 1941, the convoy divided off East Africa with sections going to Suez and Bombay. Two convoys separated a third component at South Africa in late 1941 to take troops to Singapore. Fortunately, the third and last time this occurred the ships had time to divert to India after the fall of Singapore; the second convoy had arrived at Singapore only five days before the collapse and surrender. These three convoys were titled DM when detached from the WS convoy.

The series ceased in mid-1943 when the opening of the Mediterranean to high value ships once again permitted their use of the Suez route. The KMF/MKF series was then extended to Port Said.

Atlantic convoy changes late 1943-45

There was little change in the North Atlantic during 1943-45 except the introduction in 1943 of a "Slow," seven and a half knot outward series to North America from Britain under the title ONS, a series complementary to the ON series and the westbound equivalent of SC.

Both the ONS and SC series were suspended in mid-1944 as the requirements for escorts for the Normandy invasion necessitated stripping the North Atlantic systems. It was during this time that the combination of the HX and SC series produced enormous convoys. Mention has already been made of HX 300 with 167 ships, the largest known convoy of the steam era.

The other principal change took place after August 1944. With the clearance of Northern France after the Normandy invasion, it became possible once again to use the southern route into the Irish Sea (St George's Channel), and the Channel access to Southampton and London. Thus, after August 1944, most incoming convoys entered British waters west of Land's End, dividing there into Channel and Irish Sea portions and proceeding to their destinations accordingly.

Home waters changes 1944-45

Again allowed by the enemy withdrawals in North West Europe, changes occurred in the coastal UK system, not least being the institution of several cross-Channel series to Normandy and, after the clearance of Walcheren at the end of 1944, to Antwerp. In consequence, supplies from America for the armies in Europe could now be sent to French ports or Antwerp, and a convoy system from the Thames to Antwerp and return (TAM/ATM), served the Belgian port. The renewed submarine activities in British coastal waters also caused the revival of two west coast series that had been abandoned with the decline in air attack from 1942 onwards, reviving the former titles BB and MH.

Indian Ocean convoys

Convoy in the Indian Ocean, from 1940 onwards, was a sporadic affair. A dreadful shortage of A/S escorts precluded universal adoption of convoy: traffic was too great and escorts too few to cope, so that only the most vulnerable vessels e.g. loaded troopships, tankers etc received escort. Also apparent with hindsight is the fact that, from 1941 onwards, adequate warning of submarine activity in the Indian Ocean could usually be obtained from signal intelligence. The apparently arbitrary imposition of convoy, and subsequent cancellation, then becomes explicable.

Convoy again proved successful: of 307 mercantile sinkings in the Indian Ocean, only 23 ships were in convoy, and only 14 out of over 1,800 convoys were attacked. These figures include the Aden/Persian Gulf traffic and the Gulf/India traffic.

African waters convoys

This is a massive area, covering the whole African coastline from Tangier via Cape Town to Aden. However, as the submarine threat dictated, convoy was applied out of Freetown (the OS/SL series), southward from Freetown to Nigeria, local convoys from Cape Town and Durban to dispersal in the open ocean, and a series between Cape Town and Durban. The Cape to Aden route was covered, also on an "as required" basis, with a series from the Cape and Durban to Mombasa/Kilindini and onward to Aden. Finally, a series was inaugurated in early 1943 to cover the Gibraltar to Freetown trade during the time when the OS/SL series was suspended.

Evasive routing

From the foregoing it will be apparent that convoy systems were introduced or extended as the threat expanded into new theatres. On occasions convoy extension was not practical, due either to the distances involved, lack of A/S escorts or the small number of ships involved. In these instances evasive routing provided a partial if quite uneconomic solution.

In early 1941 for example, the high level of danger to shipping for Freetown and the Indian Ocean led to ships being sent westward in the OB series to North America. From New York they were then routed south through the US Neutral Zone to Trinidad, then southeastward to Cape Town. In the reverse direction individual ships were routed from Cape Town to Bahia or Pernambuco in Brazil, northward to Trinidad and then to Halifax NS to join the HX convoy series.

In 1942, when the Caribbean and Brazilian coast were brought into the U-boat threat area, even more extreme routing took place. By mid-year the USN had instituted East Coast USA and Caribbean convoy systems as far south as Trinidad and west to Cristobal. Ships from Cape Town were then routed to Punta Arenas in southern Chile, northward to Balboa to join the convoy system at Cristobal. Outward-bound traffic from the USA to the Indian Ocean, in particular arms shipments to Russia via the Persian Gulf, followed the reverse route from Balboa to Cape Town. Such measures greatly extended voyage time and were only resorted to when absolutely necessary.

Australian and South-West Pacific convoys

Convoy in Australian waters was limited initially to major troop movements and the cruiser escort of New Zealand/Canada liner traffic to and from Suva in 1939-41. There were also a small number of convoys from Western Australia to Singapore and the East Indies in the first months of 1942. Otherwise, while there was a NCS organization functioning in Australia from 1939 to handle shipping bound for other areas, the threat was insufficient to make convoy necessary.

On 31 May 1942 the Japanese mounted a submarine attack on Sydney harbour which sank two ships and two more were damaged amongst coastal traffic off south east Australia. While the threat was a minor one in the knowledge that Japanese submarine doctrine was Fleet oriented, and the immense distances involved which restricted the number of submarines available "on task," the political furore was immense. The labour unions for seamen and wharfingers, which carried tremendous power in Australia, forced the implementation of a coastal convoy system covering the area from Melbourne to Darwin via the east coast, which began on 8 June 1942 and operated until signal intelligence persuaded the RAN that the threat no longer existed. In fact the date of cessation of the coastal systems, mid-February 1944, was long after Japanese activity had ceased, the late cancellation being due to political considerations and relations between government and labour unions.

Australian records are understandably somewhat fragmentary after a lapse of fifty years, but it is known that 910 coastal convoys comprising 5,181 ships were sailed. Of these only six convoys were attacked, five of them suffering the loss of six vessels in all with the sixth having two ships damaged.

The RAN also implemented a convoy system from Townsville to New Guinea to supply the Australian Army which was heavily involved in fighting in the island. 254 convoys were operated between December 1942 and March 1944 on this and other forward area routes with a total of 1,148 ships. No losses were incurred in these series.

There were undoubtedly a number of other convoys, not operated on a regular cycle, which must have included major troop movements. Unfortunately there do not appear to be any records of these, a possible answer being that they were organized by the US SW Pacific Command who operated a major transport and freight fleet in the area. It is quite likely therefore that any records which were kept were maintained by the US Army; certainly they do not exist in the RAN archive in Canberra nor have any come to light in the US Navy archive formerly at Washington DC.

Summary

The large number of small series and limitations of space make it impossible to mention here all of the wartime convoys, and reference to the Appendix of convoy code letters will indicate the scale of the operations. To the best of the author's belief, all known convoy series appear in the Appendix.

For the major series, the tables of convoy statistics provide the known number of convoys in each series divided into calendar years, together with the numbers of ships and the losses.

It is impossible to give totally accurate figures for the numbers of ships in all series as statistics were only gradually introduced during the early days of their operation. There has, therefore, been a conscious decision to restrict such figures to the principal North Atlantic convoys and some coastal UK series where definite totals are available. An explanation of the means by which the figures are calculated is given in the Appendix, also the method of computing losses where such figures are quoted.

It is important to keep an open mind on statistics regarding convoys, particularly losses. A participant whose ship was sunk and who survived will have a different viewpoint from the postwar analyst such as the writer; relatives of the dead will also take a different view. The best possible warning is, "anything can be proved by statistics according to the manner of presentation".

One simple example will suffice: there can be no doubt that the Russian-bound convoy PQ 17 was an unmitigated disaster. But, statistically, it could be described as a successful convoy; after all, it lost only three ships out of 39 (including Rescue Ships and Escort Oilers)! The other 21 were lost after the convoy had been dispersed. As such the ships could be, for the purposes of statistical analysis, described as unescorted independents.

If we take the total loss to the PQ 17 ships (24 out of 39 ships sailed), then the loss ratio is just over 60%. But the West Indies to Gibraltar convoy TM 1, lost 7 out of 9 ships, and one Malta convoy lost all four ships. Which convoy had the greatest loss, statistically, and does it really matter?

All that such arithmetical exercises demonstrate is you can prove anything by presenting facts in different ways. The writer has confined himself to quoting figures that are accurate and leaving others to draw whatever conclusions they can from them. There are, undoubtedly, material facts to be deduced from such statistics. Demonstrably, to be within a convoy and therefore escorted was vastly preferable to independent passage, whether as a true independent, a romper or a straggler. It is possible to analyse losses in specific areas and at specific periods, to obtain the balance between mercantile losses and enemy losses in the assault, and to draw lessons therefrom. But care must be taken not to distort statistics (and facts) to fit theories. The author has endeavoured not to.

What is beyond doubt is that some convoys suffered dreadful losses, but many more were fortunate to pass unscathed even at the height of the battle. The system proved its worth as it had on many occasions in the past. Despite appearances, the safer place was in convoy, not "romping" and taking one's chance, or falling out of convoy—"straggling"—without real endeavour to rejoin. Too many ships did, and too many men died in consequence.

■ Courtesy James Plomer

An evocative photograph of HMS SNOWFLAKE escorting a convoy. Although dated 1943, this must be suspect as there is no obvious sign of the Hedgehog mounting that she undoubtedly possessed at that time; a more probable date is the third quarter of 1942.

SNOWFLAKE had a very active existence in the North Atlantic from her completion in Nov 1941 until paying off for refit at the end of 1943. Her actions included the culminating battle around convoy ONS 5 in May 1943, during which she sank U 125 after that boat had been rammed by ORIBI, which finally broke the U-Boat offensive in the North Atlantic.

After her refit and re-commissioning, SNOWFLAKE moved east and served as a convoy escort in the Indian Ocean in the Aden/Bengal/Ceylon Escort Force (ABCEF) until Dec 1945. Then she became the weather ship WEATHER WATCHER, and was finally broken up in Ireland in 1962.

CHAPTER 6
THE THREAT

An appreciation of the forces threatening convoys is essential to the understanding of the entire system, and its extension and variation as a result of changes in the nature of the opposing forces or their operation.

In pre-1939 planning, the problem facing the Admiralty was seen in essentials as being the same as in 1914-18: a German ability to interdict maritime trade based upon naval attack, surface or submarine, with the addition of aerial attack as an option in UK coastal waters only. The sole base for mounting such attacks was Northwest Germany with naval access to the North Sea restricted to the Elbe, Weser and Jade rivers with bases at Emden, Wilhelmshaven and Cuxhaven and via Danish waters through the Kattegat, in both cases giving access to the northern North Sea.

Overseas activities necessitated either the passage of the Straits of Dover and English Channel or passage north of Britain via the Shetland/Iceland or Iceland/Greenland channels. NATO referred to these in later years as the Greenland/Iceland/UK (GIUK) gap. The Admiralty believed, rightly, that the RN could secure the Dover Straits against enemy use even if the events of 1914 recurred and Belgium was occupied as a forward base. Air attack, even if based in Belgium instead of Germany, could really only be effective against East coast traffic.

In any event, British planning was vindicated in September 1939; the German Navy abandoned the Dover Strait passage after several submarine losses, and the oceanic problem became that of defence against surface raiders in the open ocean and submarines in the approaches to the UK.

What the Admiralty cannot be blamed for failing to foresee was the unprecedented success of the German armies in 1940. The occupation of Denmark and Norway in April 1940 eased German access to the North Atlantic but by no means solved their problems as the Royal Navy could still hamper passage via the GIUK gap. The occupation of Belgium and Holland posed greater problems for the East coast traffic, but the disaster for the UK was the German acquisition of the entire French Channel and Atlantic coastlines. The omission of planning against that improbable eventuality can hardly be held against the Admiralty.

Prior to June 1940, the long northern passage for submarines effectively restricted their activities against shipping to the Atlantic east of 12 degrees West, i.e. the Western Approaches. The ability of the U-boats and their crews to greatly extend their range of operations had not, at that time, become apparent even to BdU. There were, in any case, ample targets amongst independent shipping in the focal points off the northern and southern entrances to the Irish Sea and to the Channel. The operating area of U-boats was therefore exposed to surveillance by the RAF, subject to the resources of Coastal Command. Similarly the passage of enemy surface warships could also be monitored by the use of reconnaissance aircraft and submarine patrols between Scotland and southern Norway.

With the use of French Atlantic bases, passage to Atlantic areas became much shorter, extending the effective time on operations, especially for submarines. Practical experience by the excellently trained pre-war U-boat commanders also showed that patrols, much longer in both time and distance, were possible.

Long-range German aircraft could now operate well into the Atlantic west of Ireland, without risk of interference from the RAF when passing over the British Isles. Finally, there was little or no possibility of the RAF obtaining intelligence of enemy movements from the western bases by reconnaissance due to shortage of suitable aircraft.

The immediate effect was to extend westward the area in which escort was required by convoys and, to reduce danger of air attack from French bases, to move the convoy routes northward. This last move, bringing the convoys nearer air cover from Iceland, also lengthened the passage between North America and the UK as the Great Circle routes were abandoned. This in consequence imposed a reduction in cargo delivery to the UK in any given period due to the extended time spent on passage.

The southern approach to British ports, via the English Channel and St George's Channel into the Irish Sea, was also effectively closed so that the port of London was limited in the number of oceangoing ships that could safely be routed via the East coast route. The oil terminal at Southampton suffered similarly, as any tanker traffic had to be routed via Land's End from the West Coast. Air attack on both ports also reduced their capabilities both from direct damage and the threat of loss to shipping in harbour. Henceforth Liverpool and the Clyde, supplemented by Bristol and the Welsh ports, became the major access to the British Isles.

Prior to June 1940 the principal means of attack on shipping were:
1. Surface raider action in distant waters
2. Submarine attack in the Western Approaches
3. Mining of channels and port approaches of the UK
4. Aerial attack on coastal convoys.

After the occupation of the Low Countries and northern and western France in May/June 1940 the likelihood of attack on convoy altered, both in the means employed and the magnitude of each component. In the order in which the means are described in the following text, the list now becomes:
1. Surface raider action in distant waters
2. Mining of channels and port approaches of the UK
3. Aerial attack on convoys, both in the open ocean and UK coastal waters
4. Attack on coastal convoys by fast, light, torpedo craft
5. Submarine attack on an increasing scale and over much extended areas.

The first was dealt with by attempts to bring the raiders concerned to action, successful only in the first phase by the interception of the GRAF SPEE in December 1939 in the River Plate action. Thereafter raider action remained a problem in that two diesel-engine armoured ships ("pocket battleships") and an increasing number of disguised armed merchant ship conversions (usually described as "raiders") with very long endurance, were to operate for a further two years.

Effective as the raiders were (the pocket battleships were singularly unproductive in fact), the total tonnage lost was of minor importance compared with submarine attacks and the problem was largely overcome by 1942.

It must also be remembered that German ability to operate large conventional surface ships in oceanic waters was limited both by their numbers and by design. The two battleships (BISMARCK and TIRPITZ), two battlecruisers (GNEISENAU and SCHARNHORST) and two heavy cruisers (ADMIRAL HIPPER and PRINZ EUGEN) all required frequent refuelling. It was the Royal Navy's ability to intercept and destroy the supply network that limited the effective use of these otherwise formidable ships, aided by a reluctance within the German political and naval hierarchy to hazard them, thereby greatly limiting engagement of major warships. After the loss of BISMARCK, it became standard practice to forbid attack if battleships or aircraft carriers were encountered as part of a convoy escort during a sortie.

The remaining German cruisers available post-June 1940 were quite unsuited to overseas raiding and were never so employed. Indeed, they were a burden on German resources and were used mainly for training purposes, even before the restrictions personally ordered by Hitler after the debacle of the attack on convoy JW 51B at the end of 1942.

Mining of ports and channels was, and remained throughout the war, a cause both of losses and the employment of very large resources of men, materials and effort in preventive minesweeping. It was not, moreover, a threat that could be positively dealt with by the use of convoy. However, convoy did produce a marked reduction in casualties compared with ships on independent passage in mined waters. This was due to the closer control of the ships involved and the ability to route the convoys through swept waters under the supervision of minesweepers.

Likewise, defence against aerial attack on convoy in coastal waters was primarily a RAF responsibility. Naval escort could, and did, reduce the effectiveness of attack but the only real answer to the problem was control of the air, something that only the RAF could impose.

In the Atlantic, so long as there was an air threat to shipping, this could only be met by the use of shipborne aircraft either in the "one off" form of catapult launched fighters or by the use of aircraft carriers. Although CAM ships and, later, escort carriers reduced the number of effective attacks, in the final outcome it was the lessening of effort by the German Air Force caused by more pressing requirements and the occupation of their French bases by ground forces that solved the problem.

Surface attack by light forces on coastal convoys, principally in the English Channel and southern North Sea, remained a hazard from June 1940 until the end. However, while of considerable nuisance value, the use of convoy escort limited the threat, and offensive action by our own similar forces also reduced enemy effectiveness. Set against the volume of traffic in the affected areas, direct assault by light forces was of minor significance. By far the greater threat from them was covert minelaying resulting in losses to mercantile traffic, and the diversion of effort already referred to.

There remains the submarine threat, the principal weapon employed by the enemy against British trade and the only one (other than a successful invasion) which offered the possibility of forcing a dictated peace between the opponents.

Initially the number of submarines available for oceanic employment was small. The number operational in the Atlantic increased slightly during 1941 as the use of French bases shortened passage time to operational areas but new construction barely kept pace with losses. The force available for the Atlantic war was also depleted as boats were diverted to other areas (the Mediterranean and Northern Norway). This was usually for political reasons and the need to withdraw the older U-boats to provide training facilities for new crews. In 1942 the number of U-boats available for operations increased markedly during the year, as the building program became effective, and peaked in the early months of 1943.

At any one time, only 35% of boats would be available for operations from the total strength deployed from the Biscay bases. Refits at the end of each patrol and passage time to and from operational areas accounted for the remainder; this ratio was the aim of BdU, usually achieved.

Both the Admiralty and BdU measured German achievement of sinkings on the basis of numbers and tonnage of vessels available to the Allies sunk, numbers of submarines employed and their losses. As escort efforts improved to affect this equation unfavourably, for whatever reason, the German command looked for new areas where targets were available, attack easier and escort potential less (either in number or efficiency). Thus, when Biscay ports became available, U-boats moved into the area south of Iceland, away from UK based A/S aircraft. The British response was to base ships and aircraft in Iceland, taking over the westbound convoys from UK based escorts and meeting eastbound convoys nearer to their Canadian departure ports. From mid-1941, newly built Canadian vessels and the USN provided escort for the western end of the trans-Atlantic route, the American participation becoming more and more pronounced as the year passed. While these operational changes to escort routine were effective to a degree, the U-boats were simply moved further west to areas where escort was, for a variety of reasons, less effective.

At the end of 1941, the German declaration of war on the USA moved the submarine war right up to the American coast, quite literally, in early 1942 when large numbers of ships were sunk within sight of American coastal cities. Escort throughout the Atlantic passage, desirable since mid-1941, now became essential and also had to be extended southwards along the US coast as the enemy moved to richer hunting grounds. It was not until mid-1942, when the USN finally accepted that convoy was the only answer to the submarine menace, that a US coastal convoy system was implemented.

German attack at once shifted away from the newly escorted area into the Caribbean and southward towards South America, again followed by convoy until the system extended as far south as Rio de Janeiro and north to the St Lawrence River.

In May 1943 a combination of increased escort strength and efficiency, more efficient detection devices unknown to the enemy, the deployment of escort aircraft carriers and long-range, land-based, A/S aircraft greatly reduced the mid-ocean danger area on the Atlantic convoy routes and practically eliminated the submarine threat there. Thereafter, U-boat operations with major success were confined to areas where escort capability had dropped due to long periods of freedom from threat, or where escort numbers were still low. BdU expended ever-increasing effort in locating such areas and arranging passage of U-boats accordingly.

In late 1944 the submarine threat reappeared in UK waters due to new developments in equipment and in the submarines themselves. Firstly, U-boats were now increasingly fitted with the Schnorkel device permitting the use of diesel engines while submerged. This greatly extended their dived range and made detection by surface vessels and aircraft much more difficult.

Their return to coastal UK waters was also forced upon them by their inability to operate in the open ocean, linked with the realisation that detection of a submarine in (relatively) shallow, wreck strewn inshore waters was very difficult.

Secondly, the development by the Germans of very small submersible vehicles had progressed to the point in mid-1944 that quite large operations could be carried out in inshore waters. While not strictly suicide weapons in that there was a theoretical possibility of escape or at least abandonment of the vehicles, personnel losses in these attacks were very high indeed. Nevertheless they continued throughout the remainder of the war and the only defence was extreme vigilance on the part of the escorts.

Finally, the construction of new types of submarines by the Germans, both oceanic and coastal versions, caused great anxiety. Both types were potentially very dangerous and posed major problems of speed, endurance and difficulty of detection for A/S vessels. Fortunately neither type was available in any great number for operational use before the final occupation of the entire German coastline by the Allied armies, the most effective antidote possible to "THE THREAT".

The U-boat and its weapons

The U-boat had been brought to a pre-eminent position by the Imperial German Navy in 1914-18, and its ability to threaten the existence of Great Britain as an enemy had been very convincingly demonstrated. By the Versailles Treaty of 1919 the Allies (and Britain in particular) sought to remove this threat for the foreseeable future.

In fact Germany, in its democratic form 1919-33 and the later totalitarian system, successfully evaded the restrictions by a combination of government guile and deceit and the actions of many individuals both in, or formerly in, Service or Government positions or simply individuals within commerce. Covert organizations existed to maintain design staff, continue research on submarine development etc culminating in the design and construction of submarines for overseas countries (Finland, Spain and Turkey) with the conduct of trials of the completed craft in the hands of German experts. It should not be a surprise therefore to see that U 1 was completed (on 29 June 1935) only five weeks after the repudiation of the Versailles Treaty on 21 May 1935.

While Germany sent to sea almost 1,150 U-boats between that first completion date and the end of hostilities in May 1945, by far the greatest number were of two basic designs and their subsequent variants, Type VII and Type IX. There were also eighteen

U-boats of two distinct specialist designs that had a tremendous influence on mid-war operations, far beyond their minimal numbers.

The Type VII was a relatively small submarine, usually described as the "500 ton" type (in fact varying from 630 to 760 tons!), capable of operations in open waters i.e. the Atlantic. While dimensions etc gradually increased with greater capabilities, its basic armament remained stable, four torpedo tubes forward and one aft, all capable of internal reloading. Designed to operate off the western approaches to Europe, it ultimately ranged far and wide in the Atlantic due to the ingenuity and physical endurance of its crews, and specialist support from auxiliary units. This type is frequently referred to in German naval literature and conversation as "the Atlantic boat." It was fast, handy and with a rapid diving time; a well-handled Type VII could be under water within thirty seconds in an emergency situation. Almost 700 of this type and its variants went to sea operationally.

The Type IX was described as an oceangoing boat and was the standard type for long range work e.g. in the South Atlantic and Indian Ocean, although it was also very active in Atlantic waters. British intelligence reports usually refer to this basic type as the "740 ton" boat. Obviously larger than the Type VII, originally 1,000 tons rising to almost 1,150 in the IXC/40 variant, the armament was again standard with six bow and two stern tubes. Torpedo complement increased in the later variants. Being larger, it was slower in diving, 45 to 60 seconds being usual. Almost 200 of this type became operational.

The two variant designs were Type X and Type XIV. Type XIV, of which only 10 were ever completed, was the most important U-boat type ever built. Known as the "Milch Cow" to the RN, the purpose of its existence was simply to support the smaller U-boats at sea by supplying fuel, lubricating oil, food and, occasionally, torpedoes, to extend their operational service in distant waters. In this form there was no armament except close range AA weapons but 618 tons of diesel fuel, 13 tons of lubricating oil, a variable quantity of fresh and preserved provisions, medical stores etc and a limited number of spare torpedoes could be stowed, and a Medical Officer embarked.

The Type X, designed as a mine layer with stowage for 66 mines in vertical tubes contained within the hull, was also very rapidly converted to the "Milch Cow" role when the value of the Type XIV was realised, especially after the very rapid attrition rate of those valuable vessels soon after their introduction.

Both types, once identified, were specifically targeted by every means possible utilising "Special Intelligence" whenever it became available. Unfortunately, for the German Navy, this was all too frequent and effective.

The principal weapon of the U-boat was, of course, the torpedo. While guns of varying calibre were carried by most oceangoing U-boats, and were used to attack independent shipping early in the war and later in more remote areas, their principal use was as anti-aircraft defence or the finishing off of merchant ships rather than waste a further torpedo, there being only a limited number of those valuable items onboard.

The German Navy torpedo remained a standard weapon throughout the war, varying only in its control mechanism and means of detonation, as improvements were introduced. There were two basic types: a conventional compressed air torpedo, the G7A, very similar to those employed by most other navies, and an electric torpedo using lead/acid accumulators as a power source, the G7E.

The G7A, its presence revealed by the familiar track of bubbles beloved of producers of war films, was a well tried weapon capable of a range of 8,000 metres at a speed of 40 knots, its commonest operating speed. This was the standard pre-war torpedo as, although the G7E design had been completed with specimens built and tested in Sweden as early as 1929, it was only introduced to quantity production shortly before the war. The G7E was initially capable of a speed of 30 knots over a range of only 5,000 metres, though this was improved to 6,500 metres at the same speed by 1944. The G7E was trackless and had the great advantage of taking much less time to build; 1,255 man-hours as opposed to the 1,700 man-hours for the G7A, and that figure was a reduction from the pre-war 3,730 man-hours!

Torpedo production for the German Navy, mostly the G7E, was some 70 per month pre-September 1939 and rose to a peak of 1,700 per month in 1943.

Some 70,000 were probably built, of which 10,000 appear to have been expended operationally, approximately 70% of that total being the G7E type.

German torpedoes were subject to a major defect due to lack of adequate testing, and the deliberate ignoring of defects when these were revealed. Pre-war tests had shown that the torpedo frequently ran deeper than its setting, therefore not striking the target. This fault, also shared by USN torpedoes, was ignored and led to many missed opportunities during 1939 and 1940. When finally properly investigated, the defect was remedied and a number of courts-martial at the highest level of the staff at fault took place.

The means of detonating a torpedo is known as the pistol, the torpedo equivalent of a fuse in a shell. It is contained within the nose of the torpedo and, on contact with an obstruction (hopefully the target), the striker is driven on to a detonator which explodes the warhead. A variant pistol was designed which had two modes of operation, that described above and a magnetic pistol, which detonated the warhead as it passed close beneath a steel hull in a similar manner to the magnetic mine. This German pistol, like the very similar British Duplex pistol, contained both elements; in the magnetic form the torpedo was set to run deep and thus pass below, but close to, the target hull breaking its back with the explosion. Unfortunately, like the British pistol, while theoretically valid it proved unreliable in service and the magnetic element had to be disabled in early 1940 pending further development. Both British and German replacement magnetic pistols became available in 1943.

When the magnetic element was disabled due to its inefficiency, the torpedo had to be used in the contact detonation mode. It was then discovered, through operational experience, that this was also inefficient, operating correctly only when the impact was at right angles to the striker. It followed that an oblique impact, on the slope or curve of a ship's hull below the waterline, could result in a "dud" i.e. no detonation. This matter, discovered in April 1940, also led to courts-martial amongst the torpedo testing staff.

The German torpedo, both G7A and G7E, possessed features not usual in British torpedoes and further refinements came into service during the war. The first difference was that it was possible to set on the torpedo, before firing, a gyro angle that turned the torpedo to a course different from that of the axis of the submarine i.e. the submarine did not itself have to be aimed at the target (or its estimated position after allowance for the running time). This considerably aided the CO in his attack procedure.

A variant was the FAT torpedo, available in both types, which could be set to run for a set distance beyond the target. If it did not hit, and therefore ran that distance, it then reversed its course for a set distance e.g. to within the target area when it then commenced a series of zigzag "legs" until its fuel/batteries were exhausted. The effect was to cross and re-cross the line of advance of the target several times, increasing the possibility of a hit. The system required the U-boat to fire more or less at the beam of the target and was developed due to the increased firing range as U-boats were prevented from closing the convoys by the escorts and were forced to fire salvos at longer ranges.

The final variant, introduced in late 1943, was an anti-escort weapon known to the German Navy as "Zaunkonig," ("Wren" in translation). The British and Canadian name was GNAT, an acronym for German Navy Acoustic Torpedo. A G7E torpedo, it was fitted with acoustic homing designed to receive and attack the cavitation noise of propellers operating at revolution counts equating to speeds in excess of 10 knots i.e. escorts. Great skill was needed in its use, and there were several incidents where the weapon homed onto the firing U-boat, or a consort, with fatal results. It could be avoided by the escort reducing speed below 10 knots, by using a manoeuvre known as "step aside" to avoid detection, by the use of shallow set DCs to countermine the torpedo and, finally, by the use of noise makers towed astern ("Foxer," "Uni-foxer" or "CAT") which decoyed the torpedo to explode in the escorts' wake. The decoys were very simple, consisting of steel pipe in a chain cable harness, which chattered together when towed, the noise confusing the receivers that operated the homing mechanism installed in the torpedo.

CHAPTER 7
INTELLIGENCE

Enigma and Special Intelligence

Most of the requirements of defence are tangible: ships, aircraft, weapons and personnel to handle and support them. One is abstract: Intelligence. Unless a defence can be aware to some degree of enemy intentions, defence must always be a reaction to attack, and therefore initially ineffective. Awareness can come about by detection of the presence of an enemy by some means, by deduction from known facts, by interrogation of enemy personnel, or by foreknowledge of his intentions derived from intercepting signals or documents.

Since wireless communication began it has been necessary to protect, by encoding, vital signals that can of course be read by any radio receiver that is properly tuned to the wavelength used by a particular W/T station. Nations have devoted great effort, and still do, to ensure the security of their own signals and the penetration of those of others, often including those of their friends and allies!

In the 1930s security was obtained by the laborious use of code books by which words and figures were turned into gibberish for transmission, to be decoded by the recipient, a time consuming operation. Electro-mechanical machines were however under development by the major nations to speed the process of encoding and decoding. It was believed that the random nature of the process made it impossible to "break" such coded messages without possession of the appropriate settings to put on a similar machine at the point of receipt. America, Britain, Germany and Japan all had such machines under development, the German machine in particular being viable and commercially available, sold under the name "Enigma".

By 1939, while the RAF had under development a similar machine for British use, it did not meet with naval approval; its frequent emission of sparks and electric flashes as well as code groups caused doubts as to its usefulness within the confines of a warship's signal office. In consequence, the RN still used code books of varying complexity for its communications. The breaking of an opponent's printed code relies principally upon obtaining a sufficiency of coded material, identifying any standard passages and thus relating the coded symbols to plain language. The German Navy operated a service known to them as "B-dienst" whose task was to study RN signal procedure and codes. Due to the increased traffic in code during the tense period 1935-39 (the Abyssinian crisis, Spanish Civil War, Munich crisis) there was considerable RN signal traffic to work on and, by September 1939, B-dienst could readily decode quite large portions of the British naval signal traffic.

Despite changes in the various codes in use, this penetration continued until the end of 1943 in the case of some of the lower level codes, in particular that used in transmissions relating to convoys and for signal traffic to both convoys and authorities overseas.

On the British side this was not so as the use of the German coding machine referred to as "Enigma" meant that no naval traffic could be deciphered. Shortly before September 1939 the Poles had passed to Britain and France specimens of the current German Army version of the machine plus electro-mechanical devices which could attempt to reduce the multiplicity of options the machine produced, and therefore concentrate effort on a much smaller selection of cryptographs. It was these devices, known as "Bombes," that British intelligence experts were to use in an effort to read the Enigma signal traffic; eventually the British cryptanalysts were supplied with "Colossus," the earliest electric computer.

It was not until the recovery in 1941, first of a limited number of documents and machine parts and then of a complete Enigma machine and all its associated settings for a period of weeks, that German naval signal traffic could be read. The final coup, which remained unknown to the enemy throughout the war period and long after, occurred in May 1941.

Decrypted German naval signals were referred to as "Z" intelligence or "Special Intelligence" and classified as "Ultra" for security purposes. Knowledge of the existence of the fact that decryption was being achieved was restricted to a very few senior officers and the staff actually engaged in the interception and processing of signals. The history of the resultant battle of wits is long and complex, and there are many published works claiming (some correctly) to tell the whole story. It is sufficient to say, in broad terms, that until May 1941 it was impossible to break any German naval code. From May 1941 until January 1942 most signals could be read; there was then a blank until the end of 1942 so far as Atlantic submarine traffic was concerned. Thereafter most German naval signal traffic could be read with increasing ease until the end of the war, with certain exceptions never broken due to insufficient material upon which to work. There is an excellent three-volume, four-part, official history by Professor Hinsley devoted entirely to the subject of signal intelligence 1939-45 for those who wish to study the subject. It exposes many of the myths propagated in lesser works since 1970. Reference is also recommended to *Very Special Intelligence* by Patrick Beesley. Beesley was the second-in-command in the Submarine Tracking Room for much of the war period, and his personal account gives a very good insight into the problems of interpreting and acting upon intelligence derived from signal interception, with specific relation to the U-boat war.

It is easy to say that the RN could read German signal traffic from May 1941, but what did that imply? Certainly, due to the manner in which U-boats were then controlled, it meant those positions, courses and intentions were available for all submarines at sea for the rest of that year. But to what effect?

In order to use knowledge of an opponent's intentions it is essential that:
1. The information is received in time to study it and act thereon
2. The means with which to act are available
3. There is sufficient time in which to act effectively i.e. deploy assets, re-route convoys, etc.

Let us take the example of a convoy. For the U-boats to attack the convoy must be located and its position, course and speed signalled to command. BdU would then decide the action to take, bearing in mind the location of other U-boats, and signal accordingly to effect a concentration of several U-boats around the convoy to make a concerted attack.

To obtain the initial contact BdU would form a line of submarines across the probable line of advance of a convoy in order that one boat would make contact and report, then issue the necessary orders previously referred to.

If the order to form the patrol line was intercepted and broken, then the Admiralty could divert the convoy around the line to pass undetected. However, the speed of advance of a convoy was about 8 knots, somewhat less than 10 mph, so that the patrol line of which warning had been received must be sufficiently far ahead of the convoy for effective alteration of course to be made to carry the convoy clear of the line. Even in the best of circumstances the interception of the signal, its decoding, transmission to Admiralty and plotting of the positions must have taken several hours. The subsequent encoding of orders, transmission to the escort, decoding and initiation of action also took time so that it might well be impossible to act in sufficient time to prevent an interception of the convoy, despite foreknowledge.

If the intercept gave a specific position of a submarine or supply vessel in the future e.g. a supply rendezvous, was there time before that position was reached to deploy aircraft or ships to effect an interception? Were those assets available and if so within reach of the intercept position? If not, the knowledge gained was of academic interest only.

Much of the information gained by decryption, certainly in 1941 and 1942, failed the test of viability under one or all of these headings. Only from 1943 onwards was the decryption process so speedy and the improvement in material assets so great as to permit effective use of the information by the Allies.

It is interesting to note that B-dienst had similar problems. At the crisis point in the U-boat campaign in the North Atlantic in May 1943 it is recorded that, in the first twenty days, 177 Allied signals pertaining to convoys were decoded. However, only 10 of these signals were of operational use to BdU owing to the delay in decryption, or inability to deploy U-boats.

Finally, in mid-1944 there came a further lapse in information available to the Allies due to a change in German procedure. With submarines deployed close inshore, BdU exercised less control as the individual boats perforce awaited targets presenting themselves rather than hunting for them. In consequence submarines were allocated a specific area in which to operate prior to their departure; other than an order to change area, to return or to demand a report BdU exercised no further control. Signal traffic to U-boats therefore greatly decreased, transmissions by U-boats were almost non-existent, and decrypts and information very much scarcer.

Intelligence gained from signals certainly played a large part in the Atlantic war but was only one of a number of factors. In 1941 successful diversion of some convoys can certainly be credited to that source. The destruction in 1941 of the German supply ship network in the North Atlantic was entirely due to signal intelligence and was a major factor in reducing the danger to convoys in that theatre. Similar successes elsewhere also came from decoded signals and greatly reduced the German ability to operate effectively, for example, in the Indian Ocean.

In 1943 and 1944, the principal benefit of signal intelligence was the ability it provided to divert the Support Groups at sea in the Atlantic to convoys known to have been located, and therefore provide targets for those groups, usually with considerable success; an instance of both the availability of assets and time to react effectively.

In the Indian Ocean and off the Canadian East Coast, signal intelligence was frequently used from 1943 to 1945 to decide whether or not to use convoy at all. If signals indicated the departure of submarines from the area, convoy was suspended until such time as the next arrival was identified, when convoy could be selectively introduced in the appropriate areas.

Finally, the steady accumulation of information and knowledge in the Admiralty, in Ottawa and in Washington from "special intelligence" and aerial reconnaissance enabled accurate estimates of existing disposition and number of submarines, and accurate forecast of future strength. These forecasts, proven by post-war research to be extremely accurate, were of inestimable value to those responsible for the anti-U-boat war in the Admiralty.

Courtesy James Plomer

HMS DUNCAN had served on the China Station pre-1939, and was, in common with all the "D"s, in a poor state of hull repair at the outbreak of war. By the time she became a North Atlantic escort in 1943 after further service in the Indian Ocean, her general condition and stability was very suspect. She served as SOE of B7 Group from Mar to Nov 1943, commanded by Commander (later Vice-Admiral) P Gretton. She then had a long refit and completed her war service principally in UK waters.

In this view she displays the "B VII" funnel insignia of the Group and is re-armed for escort work. She has retained B gun with a Hedgehog in A position, and has a 3-inch HA in lieu of the forward torpedo tubes. The after set has also been removed as has Y gun. Note that she still uses the old Mk II depth charge thrower, the shaft of carriers can be seen at the after end of the after superstructure. Six single 20mm Oerlikon are mounted, two each forward of the searchlight, between the funnels and in the bridge wings. HF/DF is at the head of the lattice mast aft, 291 radar at the foremasthead and the 271 radar "lantern" at the after end of the bridge.

CHAPTER 8
ESCORTS

As previously mentioned, there was a tendency, both in the Royal Navy and elsewhere, to regard convoy as a defensive measure. On the outbreak of war "hunting groups" based on an aircraft carrier with accompanying destroyers were formed to search for and destroy submarines. This measure, while foreshadowing the Support Group, ignored the fact that convoy escort was in fact an offensive operation. The large carriers, all that were available in 1939, were a scarce asset and it was merely by good luck that only one of the two so employed was lost. A convoy acted as a honeypot to attract the wasps; sooner or later a submarine or submarines would present themselves as a target with, provided the escort was efficient and large enough, almost inevitably fatal results to the submarine. This was the ideal scenario, difficult to achieve in 1939-1941 with inadequate escort forces available.

Early convoy escorts were too few to operate efficiently, tactics too crude to be really effective, weapons and sensors inefficient and understanding of enemy tactics rudimentary. The composition and operation of the hunting groups was also flawed and the sole result was the loss of one large aircraft carrier, COURAGEOUS and a near fatal encounter by another, the modern ARK ROYAL. Similar operations in 1943 and subsequently utilised the smaller escort carriers; together with effective A/S escorts they were highly effective. An added bonus was that the loss of a small carrier from a much larger pool of ships existing, would not have been the disastrous blow that the sinking of COURAGEOUS was. It must be remembered that, in 1939, that ship represented 25% of the effective carrier force available to the RN, ARGUS, EAGLE and HERMES being too old, slow or small to be truly effective World War II carriers.

British orders produced for the conduct of convoy laid down quite clearly that the paramount duty of the escort was "THE SAFE AND TIMELY ARRIVAL OF THE CONVOY." These orders, in the 1939-1941 period, prevented a positive and extended reaction to submarine attacks, reflected in the low number of successes during that time. However, this was inevitable with the restricted number of ships available for escort duty.

The initial organization of the A/S war in the Atlantic was based on the existing C-in-C Plymouth, whose "dormant appointment" for many years had specified his appointment as C-in-C W App at the start of hostilities. He and his staff therefore had pre-prepared plans and a paper organization for the task, which remained based in the Plymouth HQ as the principal maritime traffic for Britain entered coastal waters via the gap between Ushant and Ireland.

In the very early days of mobilisation, escorts allocated to the new Command were whatever was available rather than selected ships. Thus the Local Flotillas of the three Naval Home Commands (the Nore, Portsmouth and Plymouth), which comprised a selection of elderly destroyers and certain brand new ships, formed the core of the force. As time allowed, the most modern ships were withdrawn, additional older destroyers came forward from Reserve and the larger requisitioned trawlers were completed for A/S work. Such ships were based at focal points so that the whole of W App Command decentralised to Flag Officers at the major commercial ports of Liverpool and the Clyde. East coast traffic was excluded from W App Command, and its escort force, based on the Nore and Rosyth, remained independent of the Atlantic system throughout the war.

Initially, escorts were loosely organized by type and area, hence the use of such terms as "Clyde Special Escort Force" (the RCN destroyers), "Liverpool Sloop Division" and "Liverpool Escort Division." These organizations were, basically, purely administrative and actual convoy escorts were formed from those ships which were available so that there was neither common doctrine, training nor experience in operating together.

A major improvement in the preparation of new or re-commissioned ships was the formation of the working-up base at Tobermory. Initially planned to be established at Lorient for joint Anglo-French use under the command of a retired Flag Officer (Vice-Admiral Sir G O Stephenson) serving as a Commodore, this idea was overtaken by the surrender of France. Finally established at Tobermory in July 1940, this organization became responsible for the initial training and work-up of all Atlantic A/S escorts based in the UK. The Commodore became universally known as the "Terror of Tobermory" and was undoubtedly responsible for the high standard of individual efficiency of every escort sent into active service in 1940-45.

The shift of maritime traffic from the southern approaches to the northern, around Northern Ireland, occurred in August 1940, forced by the enemy occupation of France. It rapidly became clear to the C-in-C W App that it was not possible to exercise his command from Plymouth, and that the affairs of Plymouth Command had to take second place to the main task. Accordingly, the duties of the two Cs-in-C were separated, a new C-in-C Plymouth appointed, and conversion of part of Derby House in Liverpool as the new W App Command HQ was commenced, the new organization becoming operational early in 1941.

By the end of 1940, numbered Groups began to be formed containing a variety of types (destroyers of several classes, corvettes, a few sloops and A/S trawlers) and attempts were made to make up convoy escorts from one Group but not necessarily all its ships. While an improvement, there was still a lack of co-operation and shared knowledge between Groups and therefore relative inefficiency of escorts, however good their individual, initial training.

During 1941 and early 1942 the escort situation gradually improved. Groups became smaller and were operated more as a single unit and tactical training within groups improved. The breakthrough came with the establishment of the Western Approaches Tactical Unit (WATU) ashore at Liverpool where proper tactical training of Commanding Officers could be undertaken as Groups rested, and convoy actions could be properly analysed and the results promulgated. Most importantly, tactics devised by the experienced Group commanders could be formalised and passed to all Groups in the form of specific printed instructions available to all.

Previously each SOE had devised his own tactics, and some were remarkably similar, being based on common experience and training. These tactics were however each known by the code name devised by the originator, causing confusion within mixed escorts.

Control of forces in the North Atlantic was, due to the distance involved, divided between the east and west. From a specified (and variable) boundary in mid-Atlantic, control to the westward was vested in a Canadian based command. As trans-Atlantic escort was impracticable until mid-1941 no great problems arose from this division. Western command was initially vested in Flag Officer 3rd Battle Squadron at Halifax, NS, a Royal Navy officer commanding the battleships and armed merchant cruisers that provided the ocean escorts to the HX convoy system. The RCN local command handled the provision of coastal escorts from their own resources, also based in Halifax.

From mid-1941, as the submarine war moved inexorably westward, the USN entered the scene with increasing involvement in the escort of British convoys within the US imposed "Neutrality Zone," basically the Western Atlantic. The arrangements for this escort included the operation of US forces from their newly acquired base at Argentia in the colony of Newfoundland, RCN ships from a base at St John's NF, the elimination of the 3rd Battle Squadron organization at Halifax, and the subordination of the RCN operations to an American Flag Officer.

One result of this unusual command organization was the increasing use of USN terminology, RN and RCN escort groups bearing the normal titling such as 2 EG, being referred to in signal traffic as TU (Task Unit) XX.XX.X, a numeric acronym designating a specific group of vessels. Later in 1941, with a further reorganization, purely North Atlantic Groups became designated as A, B or C (American, British or Canadian) followed by a number. This practice continued until 1945, albeit with the abolition of the A groups when the USN withdrew from the North Atlantic scene in mid-1943, but it applied solely to convoy escort groups in that area. The normal numeration system e.g. 2 EG, continued for those groups employed in the support role, on the Freetown/UK route and, from 1943, in the Mediterranean. Confusingly, some convoy escort groups with B or C designations were also employed for varying periods in 1943 and 1944 in the support role, B7 being a specific example.

A common policy based on the best ideas of a group of experienced escort commanders, and greatly improved training ashore when resting between convoys, improved efficiency. With a regular pattern of sea duty based on the convoy cycle and guaranteed rest and repair periods for escorts (albeit brief), the efficiency of individual ships and of the composite Groups improved dramatically.

By mid-1942 the position regarding both numbers of escorts available and their individual and collective efficiency had so improved that C-in-C W App could begin to form specified Groups, not to escort convoys but to reinforce those under threat. Such a presence would enable these "Support Groups" to remain over a contact and hunt it to destruction, while the convoy escort continued with its appointed task. Unfortunately, there were only limited numbers of ships available for such duty and they, plus a number of the existing Escort Groups, had to be withdrawn from the North Atlantic to provide cover for the North African invasion of November 1942. There was therefore a major shortfall of escorts in the six months October 1942 to March 1943, exacerbated by the appalling weather of that winter which dramatically decreased the effi-

■ Courtesy Fleet Air Arm Museum

The concept of a support group and an associated escort carrier was explored in Western Approaches Command in Sept 1942. However the experiment had to be abandoned to provide both resources to Operation Torch, and could not be revived until the RAF and USAAF had established suitable airfields and fighters in North Africa. One of the two escort carriers employed, HMS AVENGER, was lost after Torch, and only BITER remained to re-enter the North Atlantic with the formation of 5th Escort Group on 23 Mar 1943. This consisted of BITER as SOE with, at first, two escorting destroyers, increased later as more were borrowed from the Home Fleet.

BITER, illustrated here, scored the first two sinkings of U-boats in the North Atlantic by escort carriers in conjunction with surface vessels, U 203 on 25 Apr and U 89 on 12 May. The third success, by the newly available ARCHER which sank U 752 on 23 May, and the advent of an increased VLR Liberator force, so positively closed the "air gap" in the North Atlantic that the area was no longer viable for U-boat operations.

The principal asset of the escort carrier was the antiquated Swordfish, hardly comparable with the Liberator. However it possessed the inestimable advantage of being with or close to a convoy, unlike the Liberator which faced a protracted long-distance flight to reach its escort goal. In late 1943 and subsequently, this close aerial escort role was assumed by the mercantile manned MAC ships with trans-Atlantic convoys when escort carriers were diverted to convoys requiring fighter protection in addition to A/S escort, or to other duties.

ciency of escorts and imposed additional dockyard "down time".

Following the intense attacks and large losses of March 1943 C-in-C W App insisted upon the return of his escorts and the provision of extra vessels drawn from the Home Fleet. This drastic action together with a refusal (after dispute at the highest level), to upset the Escort Group routine by shortening the convoy cycle, resulted in a dramatic change in fortune in the A/S war in the North Atlantic in May 1943.

While the reaction to the March losses included the provision of additional VLR Liberator aircraft, it was the operation of experienced destroyer Groups from the Home Fleet which had trained and operated together with the North Russian convoys, specialist W App Groups commanded by highly experienced officers such as Gretton, Tait and Walker, and the provision of escort carriers to operate with them that made such a dramatic change in the fortunes of North Atlantic convoy possible. By mid-year also, the increased Naval Aviation and RAF presence in mid-ocean had removed the benefit of the "black pit," as the Germans referred to the air gap, for U-boats who were forced to turn to other and less dangerous areas for operations. The setback was one from which the German submarine service never completely recovered.

With the introduction of MAC ships, the need to deploy escort carriers in the North Atlantic declined and that scarce asset could be deployed where the need was greater, the Gibraltar and North Russian routes, where fighter as well as anti-submarine aircraft were required.

The deployment of Escort Groups in the support role continued, and indeed was greatly enhanced as more ships became available, and proved the deciding factor in the attack on submarines. With the assistance of signal intelligence derived from the breaking of German codes, support groups were deployed to convoys about to become at risk. A U-boat sighted by an aircraft, even if not sunk, was forced to dive. An escort might then attack and sink the contact but, if not, it could be handed over to the Support Group who were able to remain over the contact until exhaustion of air and battery power or cumulative damage forced the boat to surface, or to be destroyed by relentless hunting.

By the end of 1943, the plenitude of escorts available in the North Atlantic meant that every convoy even remotely threatened by submarine attack received immediate cover from one or more additional Escort Groups. Indeed, experienced Groups were also lent outside the Atlantic, particularly to the Home Fleet for North Russian escort when the threat in that area changed from airborne to submarine attack.

In May 1944, circumstances forced a major change in North Atlantic tactics, as it became necessary to remove a large number of the most efficient Groups in order to ensure the safety of Operation Neptune. The task of W App Cmd and Coastal Command was to prevent any access by U-boats into the Channel for possible attack on the invasion convoys. This was largely achieved by swamping the passage area from the U-boat bases to the Channel with escorts and aircraft in such numbers that submarine passage became all but impossible.

The price paid was to decrease the number of convoys at sea in the North Atlantic to conform to the number of Escort Groups remaining. This was achieved by stopping the two Slow series ONS and SC for the middle months of 1944, incorporating their ships into the ON and HX series and extending the interval between convoys. During this period these two series added the letter F (Fast), M (Medium) and S (Slow) to their existing titles while retaining the sequence of numbers. The other, and most obvious effect, was a considerable increase in numbers of ships in individual convoys, rising from the average of 60 to in excess of 100; the largest convoy of the war being HX 300 with 167 ships.

Once the US Army had cleared the French Atlantic coast and occupied or isolated the submarine base ports, the Western Approaches escort groups returned to the North Atlantic and convoys reverted to normality in both size, title and frequency.

Tactics

The tactics of escort varied widely between the Atlantic and other areas of operations. With very limited exceptions, the problem in the Atlantic was of submarine attack only and the variation in tactics was dictated initially by the number of escorts available and later by the current philosophy devised by WATU.

In other areas of operations, the threat was quite different and caused a varied outlook and approach. In the Mediterranean, from 1940 to mid-1943, surface and air attack posed a much greater problem than submarines and both escort tactics and composition of the escort reflected this. In the South Atlantic and Indian Ocean, very limited escort resources until as late as mid-1944 and the sporadic nature of submarine operations in those areas, meant that escort tactics even as late as 1944 much resembled the North Atlantic in 1941.

British A/S doctrine pre-1939 was influenced by British submarine tactics, which presupposed operating close to an enemy coast in defined patrol areas, so that submarines operated as individual units. Furthermore, in such circumstances, a dived patrol during the day in the allocated area, withdrawing to more open waters to charge batteries during the dark hours, was the usual pattern of operations.

In the RN, which had to protect convoys approaching the British coast, it was considered that similar tactics could be expected from the enemy. In the period to August 1940 this view was basically valid in that German submarines had to operate in relatively restricted waters subject to air patrol. However, from August 1940 their ability to operate in the open waters of the Atlantic with minimal or no aircraft intervention caused a fundamental change in the manner of attack, an alteration to tactics already devised by BdU and trained for since 1935.

Once the true Battle of the Atlantic commenced, with the extension of submarine attack into the distant ocean, escorts had to contend with submarines operating on the surface at night. German doctrine was to attack in that manner, with the boat rigged for diving but not in a semi-submerged state. Only the small conning tower offered a target (little larger than a motor boat) for visual discovery; furthermore the boat was undetectable by Asdic, as that sensor operated only against a submerged target.

A submarine was difficult to handle except in a relatively calm sea, somewhat unusual in mid-Atlantic, so attacks were usually carried out with wind and sea astern. If possible, the attack was also made with the convoy silhouetted against the moon. Finally, the shore-based BdU controlled the preparations for attacks until permission was given for individual boats to attack.

In consequence, German tactics were for a patrol line of submarines to lie across the anticipated path of convoys. When a sighting was made the boat concerned reported the convoy and shadowed it, on the surface, from astern making periodic reports. BdU planned and oversaw the concentration of submarines in the area and, when a sufficient force had been assembled, released boats to make their individual attacks. Commanders of U-boats, when released, made their own plans and attacked in their individual styles subject to the general training they had all received. Each CO prefaced his attack with a very brief signal so that BdU and (more importantly) his colleagues were aware of the situation and his own presence.

The convoy found itself faced with a series of individual attacks at very close intervals likely to continue throughout the dark hours. As a submarine's surface speed was almost double that of most convoys and aircraft escort was rarely available, except in relatively close proximity to the British Isles until 1943, the convoy was followed on the surface during the subsequent day. The convoy could expect further attacks that night, a process repeated either until torpedoes were exhausted or air cover prevented surfaced shadowing during daylight.

With few and inadequately equipped escorts, i.e. until mid to late 1941, little could be done except to react to events. Experienced SOEs learned to dispose escorts ahead during the day to drive under any submarines lying in wait, at dusk to have a search astern by the fastest escort to deter overtaking boats, and to have the escort watch the dark, windward side of the convoy was as much as could be done.

Once effective radar came into general service after June 1941 and escort numbers increased, one of the screening dispositions laid down by in WACIs (W App Convoy Instructions) could be adopted, the number of escorts available dictating the choice. These orders provided for two, three or four ships ahead of the convoy, distanced from one another by their joint effective radar range, to provide a "fence" against submarines ahead of the convoy during daylight hours. Amended positions could be ordered

Courtesy K Macpherson (National Archives of Canada)

Titled by NAC as taken 25 Sept 1944, this shows HMS HIGHLANDER. Other than HAVANT all built in Britain for the Brazilian Navy, she and her sisters were taken over in 1939 and completed in 1940. All were employed as Senior Officer's ships in North Atlantic Escort Groups. HIGHLANDER, when photographed, was SOE of B4 Group en route to join convoy HX 310 at WOMP on 26 Sept 1944.

Badly damaged by pack ice 14 Apr 1945 she had to be towed to Bay Bulls for slipping and repair which took until Sept 1945. She was sold post-war and broken up at Rosyth in Aug 1947.

during the dark hours if imminent contact with U-boats was expected. An escort on either flank of the convoy plus one astern (the stern escort, usually the fastest), was responsible for sweeping astern at dusk and dawn to "put down" any shadowing submarine. If a shadower were suspected, and the tactics mentioned were successful, then the convoy had a good chance of making an evasive turn during the day and shaking off the shadower.

At night, if an attack was intercepted or a ship was torpedoed, starshell and lighting rockets (Snowflake) were employed to illuminate the surface, expose the submarine and attack. Once submerged, not only was the submarine slower than the convoy and thus losing ground, but it was also subject to Asdic search and detection. The instinct of a less experienced U-boat officer on being approached by an escort at night was to dive to seek safety. In fact (up until late 1941) he was worse off if he did dive: escape on the surface was a far better option in pre-radar days. Experienced U-boat COs were wont to forbid their junior officers to dive in those circumstances, and there are recorded cases where the order was disobeyed in the heat of a sudden, close encounter leading to the loss of the boat.

Once a U-boat was forced under and detected, search by two escorts able to co-ordinate attacks was desirable. However, such luxury could be inhibited by the number of escorts available, whether or not further submarine attacks were being made or expected, the fuel and ammunition states of escorts etc. At all times the mandatory protection of the convoy rather than a hunt to exhaustion of a single submarine had to be uppermost in mind.

With the introduction of a second Group in the support role, and of more numerous escorts, longer and more co-ordinated attacks on contacts could be carried out. May to the end of 1943 was the main time for these; thereafter the enforced movement of submarines away from the Atlantic routes due to major losses reduced the targets available around convoys.

Once U-boats were forced away from the main convoy routes and became accustomed to using the Schnorkel to avoid air detection, coastal activity again became a viable proposition and U-boats returned to inshore waters around the UK. This posed a problem as the shallower water permitted submarines to lie stopped on the bottom. The multiple wrecks, shoals of fish and underwater obstructions generally in coastal waters produced a plethora of "non sub" contacts and made hunting very difficult. In many cases escorts reverted to "reaction" techniques at this time, "swamping" the vicinity of an attack on a merchant ship and awaiting the inevitable, eventual, movement of the bottomed U-boat.

Anti-Submarine weapons

Any consideration of the weapons used by escorts must commence with a brief overview of the escorts themselves. It is a widely held belief that destroyers were the natural anti-submarine vessel. This is not so, as use of the destroyer's high speed nullifies the advantage of its detection equipment, sound detectors of whatever type becoming useless at speeds much in excess of 15 knots due to propeller and general water noise interference.

However, destroyers remained the principal source of escorts, if only due to their availability. Accepted practice, also enshrined in international treaties, was that the effective life of a destroyer hull was twenty years, and that it became of declining value as a Fleet unit after ten years. In consequence, there were readily available to the RN for escort duties the numerous destroyers of the S and V & W classes and their variants. As the war progressed and new construction destroyers entered service from 1940 onwards, some ships of the A to I classes were also withdrawn from Fleet duties and joined Western Approaches Command, as did many of the fifty ex-US vessels acquired in September 1940 in exchange for bases.

Initially such ships were unchanged but, as the war progressed and tactics and weapons improved, alterations were made varying from the reduction of gun armament and increased depth charge stowage to major rebuilding. This last comprised the reduction of boiler numbers to increase bunker capacity, with greater range of action in consequence. The space available in the former boiler room, above the fuel bunkers, also provided extra accommodation for the increased crews called for by new weapons, etc, and for larger store rooms to cope with the increased sea time arising from the extended range of action.

The second ship type to be employed in the escort role was the sloop, with construction continuing throughout the war using the final pre-war design almost unchanged.

The need for smaller escorts, intended for the expected inshore role, was met by the requisition and conversion of the larger and more modern deep-sea trawlers and the design and construction of the first corvettes, loosely based on a commercial whale-catcher design. While both types were very seaworthy, neither was ever intended for oceanic escort work and the designs were too small to operate as such without greatly degrading the crews' effectiveness due to fatigue and very poor living conditions. The initial corvette type was widely constructed in Britain and Canada and referred to as the FLOWER class. There were numerous alterations and improvements, both to existing ships and new construction, although lack of facilities greatly delayed alterations in the Canadian corvette force. Later the FLOWER type was succeeded by the refined CASTLE class, which proved a greatly superior vessel to the original FLOWER design, indeed to subsequent variants, and continued in construction until the end of the war.

As time permitted a new ship design, the frigate, was evolved to overcome the problems inherent in the small corvette. The supplementary design was specifically intended for the North Atlantic with an optimum length (300 feet) to suit the sea conditions found in that ocean. Bigger, therefore somewhat faster, better armed and with superior habitability, the frigate formed the mainstay of the escort force from 1942 onwards. Similar frigates were also constructed in Canada in large numbers to supplement the British building program.

The new frigates, named after rivers in Great Britain, became known as the RIVER class. The Canadian vessels were named after Canadian towns and were usually referred to in the RCN simply as "frigates." The basic RIVER design was followed by the even more successful LOCH class later in the war, complete with new A/S weapons. A variant, based on the RIVER design, was also constructed in America using American shipbuilding practice and basic equipment, some vessels being lent to the RN and referred to as COLONY class frigates.

Facilities in Britain and Canada being insufficient to build the numbers of ships planned, Britain placed orders in America in early 1941 for additional vessels, orders that were later funded under the Lend-Lease agreement. The design was specified by the Admiralty in the most general terms: dimensions, speed, armament and complement being the basic parameters, and it was accepted that the detailed design would be American and make use of American equipment.

The type was designated, using USN terminology, BDE—British Destroyer Escort—and the target was production of 50 ships initially and 300 eventually. While the design went into service, it did not do so until after America entered the war at the end of 1941, whereupon the design became known as "DE"—Destroyer Escort—and production was diverted to the USN. 78 ships were supplied to the RN under Lend-Lease, the number exceeding the original order, but not the first fifty hulls completed. The ships were referred to by the RN as "frigates" and, while of two differing propulsion types, all received names of naval officers and were known as the CAPTAIN class.

Also received under Lend-Lease in May 1941 were ten US Coast Guard cutters, vessels analogous to the RN sloop, although with many greatly differing characteristics. Initially deployed in the North Atlantic, the West African route and then the Indian Ocean became their usual operational area due to their considerable range. They were almost always referred to in the RN by the title of "cutter".

Within coastal waters, particularly the Canadian coast, the Mediterranean and the Indian Ocean, considerable use was also made of minesweepers as anti-submarine escorts. All classes were used: the pre-war HALCYON class serving in North Russian waters, the Atlantic and the Mediterranean particularly. The small BANGOR class vessels, both British and Canadian, were widely used as coastal escorts on both Atlantic seaboards and in the Mediterranean, as were the larger ALGERINE type. In the Indian Ocean and Mediterranean, the BANGORs and the Australian BATHURST class, manned by the RAN and the RIN, served in the escort role with considerable success, even to engaging large surface raiders on one occasion with excellent results.

Escort weapons

As far as convoy escorts were concerned, their available weapons in 1939 were little different from those employed in 1918. Ships were reliant upon the depth charge set, by a hydrostatic pressure fuse, to explode at the estimated depth of a target. Positioning of the charge(s) was a matter for judgement by the attacking CO.

An ahead-throwing weapon, regarded as essential by the A/S School, had been under development in 1934 but was abandoned due to restriction of funds by the Treasury.

Air attack relied upon a RAF-developed A/S bomb, a weapon renowned for its theoretical efficiency and practical uselessness. It presented more danger to the aircraft dropping it than it did to the intended target, several aircraft being lost due to the explosion of their own bomb or the bomb ricocheting from the surface and actually striking the aircraft, causing its destruction. This happened to two Skua aircraft from ARK ROYAL who attacked U 30 on 14 September 1939. Both aircraft had to ditch, their aircrew suffering the ignominy of rescue by their intended victim who surfaced and took them on board as prisoners of war.

Detection of a target was, for an aircraft, a matter of visual sighting; for a surface ship, possibly visual detection followed by acquisition by Asdic, or initial detection by that means. It is important to note that Asdic would not (and will not even in 1999) detect a surfaced target and therefore in darkness a surfaced submarine remained safe. Also, most important, contact is lost by Asdic on approaching a submerged target as the sound transmission eventually overshoots the contact and fails to record an echo. The acquisition and destruction of submarine targets was therefore an uncertain art in 1939 and so continued until 1941. In some sea areas with major thermal layers, such as Arctic waters and the St Lawrence estuary, the difficulty in locating a submerged target beneath such a layer persisted until the end of the war and beyond. The problem is in fact still present, aggravated by the much deeper diving abilities of modern submarines.

By 1941 the RAF had admitted the defects of the A/S bomb (which the RN had pointed out prior to the outbreak of war) and replaced it with the standard naval depth charge modified with simple fins and a shaped nose to assist accurate entry into the water. However, the level of successful attacks remained low and it was only when analysis of attacks by civilian OR scientists proved that the depth settings were hopelessly deep and a new fuse giving shallower settings was devised, that matters improved.

It required further evidence from cameras to convince the RAF that the gallantry of the aircrews' low level attacks was not equalled by their skill or their observations. Despite aircrew statements, camera records revealed fundamental aiming errors resulting in missed targets, and a new bomb sight had to be designed and training changed before aircrew were able to reap the reward of their considerable efforts.

From September 1939 to June 1941 Coastal Command aircraft made 215 attacks on proven submarine contacts. Only five achieved any success with one submarine sunk and four damaged. Using the adapted naval depth charge with a 50-foot depth set fuse, 127 attacks between June and December 1941 produced two sinkings and thirteen seriously damaged submarines. The first six months of 1942, with an even shallower 33-foot setting available, saw four sunk and nineteen damaged submarines for only 79 attacks. Further major improvements were later achieved with the final, 25-foot setting, improved tactics and training and bombsights, to enable Coastal Command to make its major contribution to the defeat of the U-boat attack.

Detection devices

The naval problem of surface detection and then accurate attack was partially solved in 1941 by the introduction of type 271 centimetric radar, followed by successive marks of the type with increased efficiency. With pulses recorded on the now familiar circular scan, a surfaced U-boat could rarely escape detection at night or in foul weather when within operating range. Improved Asdic, and experience in its use, also increased the detection and proper interpretation of submerged contacts. However, the problem of evasion by the enemy in the "lost contact" period of an attack remained.

Another device, widely used by the RN with great success, was the detection of High Frequency wireless transmissions using sophisticated semi-automated equipment known as HF/DF, usually referred to in conversation as "Huff Duff." VHF radio was widely used by the German Navy to communicate between the shore-based headquarters referred to elsewhere in this text and submarines at sea. The effective detection of such signals except by large land based stations were throughout the war regarded by the Germans as impossible, a view upheld after repeated investigation on several occasions. However, viable seaborne detection devices had been developed in the late 1930s by British and French scientists working independently. The French scientists, together with their apparatus, succeeded in leaving France in late 1940 for America where further development introduced the system to the USN. In Britain, work also continued and an operational system went to sea in 1941, well in advance of the USN. The details were delivered to the USN to assist their program, operational sets were fitted to some US warships at British bases, and experienced British officers embarked to instruct USN crews. The RCN of course used the system extensively in its own escorts.

The system was capable of detecting a transmission of extremely short duration and recording its bearing on a scan similar to that of a radar set, the bearing being accurate to within a degree. A skilled operator could also positively identify whether the signal was "ground wave" i.e. within 25 miles, or the longer-range transmissions, which were bounced off the ionosphere. It was therefore possible for an escort to run down the bearing of a ground wave (with a good estimate of the distance to cover derived from the strength of the signal) and to surprise a surfaced submarine. With the greatly increased range compared with the 271 radar, HF/DF made more impact on the detection capability of escorts than radar itself.

All escort groups in the North Atlantic from mid-1941 included at least one HF/DF equipped ship, while the Rescue Ships by then in use were also so fitted, enabling cross bearings to be provided to the SOE. HF/DF was also fitted in Coastal Command aircraft, with similar success. The value of the system was increased by the failure of the German Navy to realise the existence of HF/DF, it being always assumed that references to the system, and the detailed observation by agents of the distinctive Adcock aerials, referred to a radar system, something for which the German Navy had a healthy respect. In consequence, until the abandonment of group tactics by submarines and the adoption of fully submerged operations in coastal waters late in the war, German use of VHF radio remained unrestricted and identifiable to the Allies.

Sonobuoys

The Sonobuoy is an airborne method to detect submerged targets, previously immune to searching aircraft, and still in use after great refinement over fifty years. It involves dropping small, battery-powered buoys into the sea in a set pattern in the area of a suspected target. The buoys can be employed in two modes, passive or active; in the former sound transmissions from a submarine (engine noise, cavitation of propellers etc) are detected and passed to the parent aircraft. In the active mode, Asdic signals are transmitted in the usual way and the aircraft receives any responses, again via the sonobuoy. In both cases, plotting of bearings and depths of contacts transmitted from the pattern of buoys provide a "fix" on the suspected target. The passive role has the advantage that the U-boat has no warning of the search, and it would usually be employed when the aircraft sighted a periscope or Schnorkel, there being a reasonable chance then that the U-boat would be unaware of the presence of the aircraft. Attack, by any of the variety of airborne weapons, would accordingly come as a surprise thus limiting the U-boat's ability to take evasive action.

Magnetic Anomaly Detection (MAD)

Another method of detection, also of a submerged target, resulted from scientific investigation into magnetic anomaly i.e. the variation in the earth's magnetic field caused by the passage through the water of a metal hull. The problems are enormous given the minute signal and the inherent difficulty of operation; however it was developed as a viable system in mid-1943 and still remains a potent means of detection in the 21st century.

Courtesy Jack Tice

USS NIBLACK, typical of the USN fleet destroyers which escorted Atlantic convoys from late 1941 onwards. As the photograph is undated, other than "a North Atlantic convoy in 1942," no identification can be made. The tankers in the background appear to be in ballast, so that it is one of a possible six ON convoys escorted by NIBLACK.

CHAPTER 9
WARTIME WEAPON DEVELOPMENT

An escort attacking a submarine usually tracked its target at the optimum Asdic speed (8 to 10 knots). When contact was lost, i.e. at about 300 yards from the target, the escort increased speed as much as possible to close the gap and placed depth charges in the estimated position of the target, the escort making due allowance for the target's depth and the sinking rate of the charges. It was this sudden increase in speed that warned the target of an impending attack and permitted a final effort to avoid destruction by a combination of rapid change of course and depth. It must be remembered that the theoretical lethal radius of a depth charge in 1939 was 30 feet, in practice found to be an over-estimate!

Depth charges were either rolled over the stern from racks in which they were stowed, or fired from throwers sited on the beam aft in the escort. Initially a carrier (the arbour) was inserted in the barrel of the thrower with the charge rested on a tray attached to the end of the arbour, carrier and charge being projected; this was the Mk II thrower. A later type of thrower, the Mk IV, in which the arbour and tray were integral to and retained with the thrower, was soon developed and placed in service resulting in greater stowage space for charges and reduced loading effort and time. The Mk II thrower remained in use in many British and almost all Canadian ships completed before 1942. A recently seen photograph of HOTSPUR, taken in June 1943 after her refit for escort work, clearly shows her as still mounting the Mk II thrower. The reason for such an anomaly is not known.

Charges were at first used in patterns of five, three dropped by gravity in line from the racks and one projected from each thrower to produce a diamond shaped pattern. The fitting of two throwers on each beam, and the introduction of a "heavy" charge (iron weights strapped to the side of the charge) resulting in a more rapid sinking rate, meant that by varying the selection of light and heavy charges with different depth settings, ten charges in two superimposed patterns bracketing the submarine could be produced. A special thrower, the Mk V was developed for the "heavy" charge.

The next variant was to increase the throwers to four per side, further vary the mix of charge weight and depth settings, to produce a fourteen-charge pattern at three different depths. This unfortunately was a complete failure, it being found that the explosion of the earliest charges countermined the whole pattern; the idea was therefore abandoned and ships reverted to a four-thrower fit and the use of the ten-charge pattern.

Mk X Depth Charge

A problem that frequently faced escorts was that German submarines were designed for far greater depths than their British counterparts, a fact not apparent until the examination of the captured U 570. British depth charges could be fused down to 300 feet, whereas a U-boat could happily lie in stopped trim at depths of 600 feet, impervious to attack. Once this fact was accepted, new fuses were

◇ THE ALLIED CONVOY SYSTEM 1939-1945

■ Courtesy Vosper-Thornycroft Ltd

Shown here is the later Mk V depth charge thrower. It differed from the Mk IV only in the capacity of the chamber in which the cordite charge was placed. In the Mk V a larger charge was used to project heavy, i.e. weighted, charges, further than the Mk IV.

It will be seen that the carrier and tray are integral to the thrower. When fired the stalk of the carrier was forced up the barrel and sharply arrested at the end of its travel; the charge, released automatically from its retaining strop, continued its parabolic flight. In firing, the stalk had compressed a recoil spring integral to the thrower; two men were able to re-set the tray in the loading position by hauling down on the edge of the tray by hand. Depth charge patterns were, then, limited only by the number of charges carried (or supplied at sea), not by the stock of carriers. The thrower in the background is the 1917 pattern Mk II which also appears in the photograph of HMCS MORDEN's A/S equipment.

introduced with appropriate depth settings, but it was still difficult to attack a boat at that depth, and the time span for the target to react and evade had lengthened.

Meanwhile, in order to increase the destructive power of a DC attack, an ultra-heavy charge had been developed: the Mk X. It is of interest that something of this nature had been proposed pre-1939 with the suggestion of linking three standard DCs together and laying them as a single unit. The Mk X as introduced was a 21-inch diameter cylinder carrying 2,000 lb of explosive detonated by the usual hydrostatic fuse. Due to its weight and size it was designed to be carried in, and fired from, the torpedo tube mounting of a destroyer. The charge had small buoyancy chambers at either end that controlled its sinking, in an approximately horizontal position in slow descent, with the fuse operable at depths up to 200 feet. The slow descent permitted the movement of the escort to a safe distance from the explosion. The

WARTIME WEAPON DEVELOPMENT

Courtesy Ed O'Connor

An interesting view of the starboard waist of HMCS MORDEN in 1942. The two starboard depth charge throwers can be seen in the background, in the foreground the stowage of both DCs and carriers. When loaded, the shaft of the carrier, seen uppermost in the stowage, was inserted into the barrel of the mortar. The DC was then placed in the semi-circular tray at the end of the shaft. A cordite charge was loaded into the chamber of the thrower; when ignited it projected carrier and charge away from the beam of the firing ship. The DC separated from the carrier in flight; it follows that carriers and charges had to be carried in equal quantity. Ships fitted with the old Mk II thrower can be readily identified by the array of carriers to be seen on the upper deck as shown here.

effect of a single Mk X charge was rated as equal to that of a complete 10 charge pattern of standard DCs. Use of the charge was intended not so much to sink a submarine as to cause such alarm and equipment damage as to force it nearer the surface and betray its exact position by its movement.

When it was realised, from inspection of U 570, just how deep the standard U-boat could dive and survive, new fuses were devised for standard DCs permitting detonation as deep as 600 feet, at 50 foot intervals. At the same time the Mk X was modified as the Mk X* by removing the buoyancy chamber from one end thus causing a vertical descent at a more rapid rate, and with the provision of a fuse capable of settings to 900 feet. At that depth it was calculated that even a slow moving escort would escape damage.

Three or four such charges were carried in escort destroyers still fitted with tubes, either one Mk X and two Mk X* in triple tube ships or two of each in quadruple tube ships. In the CAPTAIN class frigates, certain ships carried two Mk X* charges in racks which delivered the charge over the transom from a position between the normal DC racks.

A final variant, Mk X**, with a fuse capable of being set to 1,200 feet was developed by late 1944, but did not enter operational service.

Ahead-Throwing Weapons
Hedgehog

The real answer to the inevitable loss of Asdic contact during an attack was, of course, the ahead-throwing weapon idea of the 1930s, which would project charges ahead of the ship while still in Asdic contact,

67

without the warning of a sudden increase in speed. Several such weapons were devised and tested, that selected being known as Hedgehog. This consisted of a spigot mortar, i.e. a bomb with a propellant contained in a hollow stem ending in stabilising vanes, the whole placed on a spike or spigot. The propellant was electrically detonated to launch the bomb.

Twenty-four such spikes in six horizontal rows of four formed the weapon mounting, and these were fired in sequence of row at brief intervals to minimise recoil effect. The twenty-four bombs of each firing were projected to land in an ovoid formation 300 yards ahead of the ship. The intention was that the pattern of bombs should land on and bracket the hull of the U-boat. The bombs were contact fused and only detonated on striking the target, so that there was no warning to the submarine of an unsuccessful attack.

Theoretically an excellent weapon, it remained almost ineffective from its introduction in January 1942 until late in 1943. The problems were multiple,

Courtesy K Macpherson, National Archives of Canada

The Hedgehog mounting of HMCS MOOSE JAW in 1944. The safety caps are in position on the projectiles, covering the arming vanes and the fuses. The weather cover is in the raised position to the rear of the mounting.

WARTIME WEAPON DEVELOPMENT

Courtesy K Macpherson

In 1943 the Admiralty had on order in Britain a new, large class of corvette armed with a new A/S weapon, the Squid. The RN had a manpower shortage and the RCN was asked to assist in manning some of the new ships. Unlike the situation in 1940 when some early FLOWERS, built in Canada for the RN, were RCN-manned and later in the war when the RCN also manned some RIVER class frigates; the CASTLE class ships involved were transferred outright to Canadian ownership. No financial transaction took place; the RN received ALGERINE minesweepers building in Canada for the RCN in an exchange deal. The RCN ships, already allocated British names and pennant numbers, were re-named and received pennants in the RCN sequence. Seen here, just after commissioning, is HMCS BOWMANVILLE formerly HMS NUNNEY CASTLE K 446.

Note the single Squid in B position, a naval style bridge and lattice mast which carries the new 277 radar and HF/DF aerials. The squared transom quarterdeck is almost empty. So certain was the RN of the effectiveness of the new Squid, ordered from the drawing board, that only two depth charge throwers, two rails and 15 depth charges were provided. BOWMANVILLE was sold in 1947 by the RCN, for commercial service, to Chinese owners. She was reportedly seized by the Communist forces after the collapse of the Chiang Kai-shek government and taken back into naval service; apparently to serve until the early 1980s.

including inefficient fitting of the mounting, poor training of crews, poor maintenance (many ships did not receive any advice or manuals) and incorrect use by Commanding Officers, usually too high an attack speed. When these matters were overcome, and attack speeds reduced in late 1943, the success rate increased dramatically and the weapon finally achieved acceptance in the escort community. It is interesting to note that the acceptance of the correct, slow approach took place at the same time as the introduction of a German acoustic torpedo specifically designed to attack escorts. It so happens that the correct Hedgehog attack speed coincided with the ideal speed to avoid detection by the new torpedo.

The Hedgehog suffered from inherent shortcomings; a miss did not produce the morale enhancing (or depressing if you were the target) BANG, its explosive charge was light (32 lb) and it still relied upon standard Asdic and therefore approximate estimation of depth and consequent sinking time for the bombs. A further weapon with an associated depth-finding Asdic was therefore a pressing requirement.

The question of depth-finding, as opposed to range and bearing, Asdic had been under consideration for some time and was finally solved by, in effect, fitting two sets, one at right angles to the other. The scan of the additional set was in the vertical not the horizontal plane and of a narrow horizontal angle, locked in con-

◊ THE ALLIED CONVOY SYSTEM 1939-1945

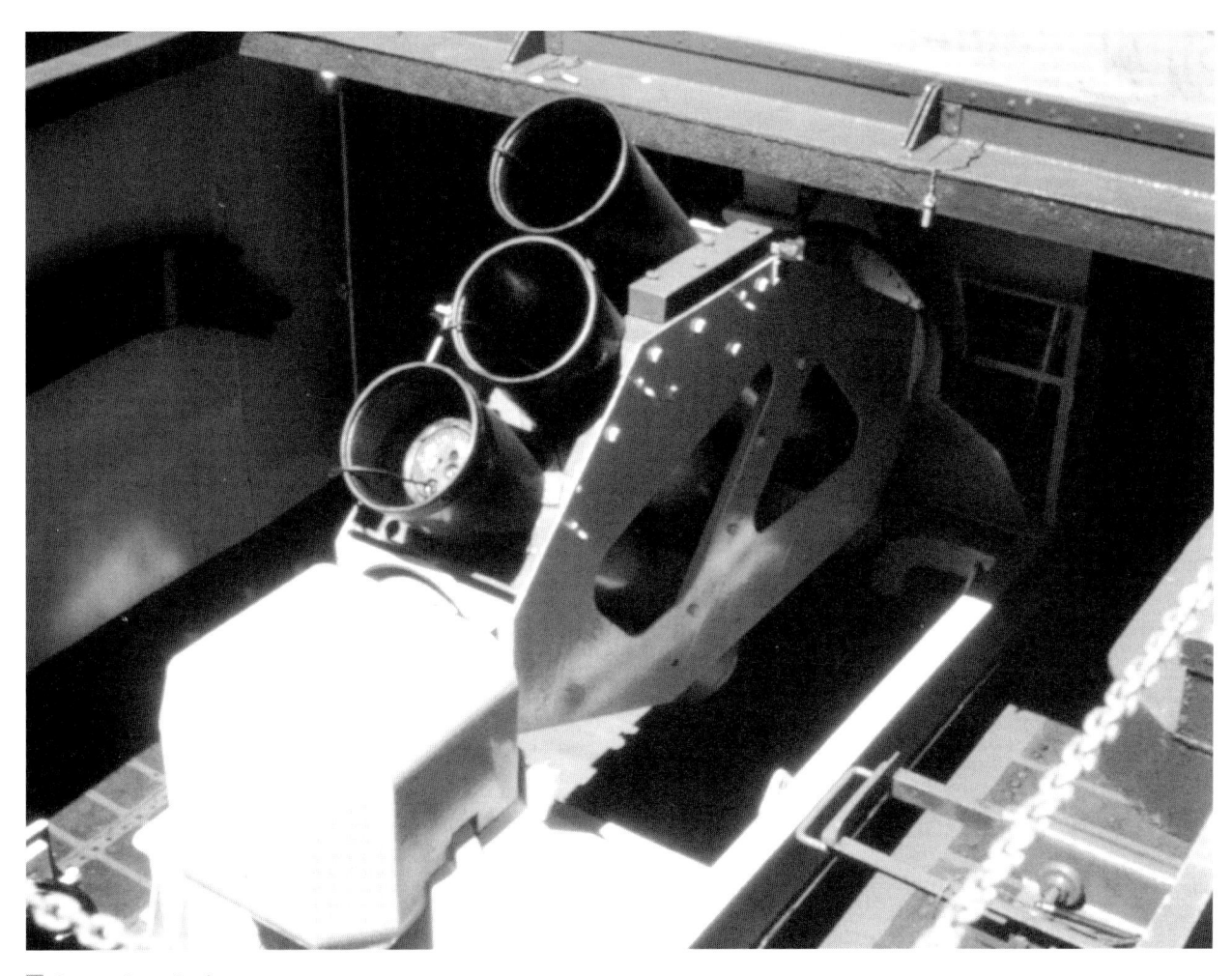

Courtesy Roger Steed

A Squid mounting shown on a postwar Royal Canadian Navy frigate.

cert with the main transmission. The location of a contact by the normal transmission therefore also produced a contact showing the position in the vertical; simple control mechanics in the searching vessels produced a bearing, range and depth solution.

Squid

The weapon to operate with the new Asdic commenced development in February 1942 and the design was in fact extrapolated from data gathered during the development of a rival to the Hedgehog that had been abandoned at trial stage. The new weapon, Squid, consisted of a three-barrelled mortar in which the bomb was inserted in the mortar tube via the muzzle when the mounting was laid in a horizontal position on its side. The mortar mounting contained three barrels permanently elevated at 45 degrees, with the centre barrel slightly offset. The pattern of bombs therefore landed in a triangle so that the lethal area of each bomb overlapped the other two. In ships carrying two Squid (the LOCH class frigates), the offset barrels were handed in the two mountings so that a six charge firing produced a hexagonal pattern.

Depth settings from the Asdic were automatically fed into the bombs while in the mortar tubes, and the mountings fired automatically when the range of the target coincided with the range of the mounting. The bombs were exploded by a hydrostatic fuse that had been automatically set with the Asdic reported depth of the target at the moment of firing.

Squid went to sea trials in Oct 1943, the first operational system sailed in Dec 1943, and Squid achieved its first sinking in Aug 1944. The ships in which it was fitted (CASTLE class corvettes with a single Squid and LOCH class frigates with two) were designed specifically for the weapon when it was itself still on the drawing board.

One RCN Commanding Officer commented that he only ever fired his Squid twice, once in training and the second time when he sank the submarine!

A persistent problem for escorts throughout the war was the problem of dealing with a surfaced submarine. The tough pressure hull with its continuously curved surface was impervious to many of the guns mounted in escorts. Even a 4.7-inch firing semi-armour piercing ammunition could have the shell deflected if the angle of impact was too oblique. Ramming, the most effective method, caused serious damage to an escort, leading possibly to damage to propellers and shafts and subsequent loss of the escort in some cases. At best a "controlled ramming," where a damaged and inert submarine was contacted by the escort's stem and gradually pushed over to roll the submarine under, could be resorted to. This was far from a guaranteed method as CROCUS found off Freetown when so dealing with U 333, which succeeded in returning to France albeit heavily damaged.

Shark

The problem led to the development of Shark. In effect, this was a non-self-propelled version of the RAF 3-inch rocket projectile. Manufactured in various calibres from 4.7-inch downward, it consisted of a 25lb AP warhead as in its aircraft relative, and a solid shaft carrying steadying vanes at the after end. The projectile was loaded into the breech of a gun of the appropriate calibre, and fired by a cordite propellant charge. Aimed to strike the water at a slight angle some 20 yards short of the target, Shark behaved in the same way as the aircraft rocket: it commenced to rise after an initial dive to strike the target on or slightly below the waterline. If a hit was achieved, velocity was sufficient to guarantee penetration. Brought into service in escorts during late 1943 it was used in action on several occasions to ensure the destruction of submarines forced to the surface by other means.

■ Courtesy Air Historical Branch (Crown Copyright)

Liberator bombers of 120 Squadron RAF at their base in N Ireland. In May 1943 this was the only operational squadron with these VLR aircraft for the North Atlantic and eight of the total of seventeen of them are seen here. The fuselage numbers of the two aircraft nearest the camera set the date of the photograph at between Feb and Sept 1943. The first two aircraft have ASV II radar, the third ASV III. ASV III centimetric radar, the aerial equivalent of the naval 271 radar, was not authorised for use in Coastal Command until Feb 1943. By the combination of radars, aircraft numbers and the new Control Tower building in the background, the Air Historical Branch date the photograph in the last days of April 1943.

CHAPTER 10

AIRCRAFT A/S TACTICS AND WEAPONS

A/S aircraft eventually received airborne radar enabling detection to be made at night in poor visibility or through cloud. The efficacy of attack after such a detection relied entirely on the skill and determination of the pilot, as the approach had to remain undetected by the target as long as possible. The attack had to be made at low level and pressed home despite all counter fire from the target. Ideally, depth charges would be placed in a diagonal line to straddle the target while the conning tower was still visible above the surface thus ensuring that all charges were within the lethal radius of the target. The conning tower was used as the aiming mark with the intention of the line of charges centring upon it.

As the diving time of an efficient U-boat was less than 45 seconds (30 seconds was normal for Type VII U-boats), RN and RAF pilots had to react very sharply indeed to achieve success. With the progress of the war, additional means of detection and attack were devised for aircraft use.

A/S aircraft of Coastal Command operated in two distinct roles. The purely offensive role which centred on the interdiction of U-boats crossing, in particular, the Bay of Biscay to and from their operational areas, and the convoy escort role. Quite definitely the second was also an offensive action so far as the Command was concerned, but the simple act of forcing a U-boat to dive when in the vicinity of a convoy was almost as important as an actual attack. Forcing a U-boat to dive, due to its slow speed, could very easily cause it to lose contact with the convoy. It was therefore a significant part of a VLR aircraft's operational role, even after expending its load of depth charges or other ordnance, to remain in the vicinity of the convoy as long as possible as its sheer presence was an effective deterrent against potential attack by a U-boat.

The Leigh Light

Night attack, despite detection by radar, was not easy even under the best of circumstances until the invention by a RAF Officer (Wing Commander Leigh) of the Leigh Light. This consisted of a naval searchlight mounted within or beneath the aircraft and powered by accumulators installed in the plane. The aircraft, having detected a target at night by radar, manoeuvred to approach at low level and exposed the light when less than two miles from the target, and illuminated it. The pilot, hitherto flying by instruments, could then acquire the target visually and carry out his attack in the normal manner. Such an attack required the most careful flying (it was not unknown for aircraft to fly into the darkened surface of the sea) and most accurate instructions to the pilot from the radar operator during the approach.

Additional weapons were also developed for use by aircraft, some still in use, others used only in 1943-45.

Retro-bomb

This weapon was specifically developed for use with MAD, which has a fundamental drawback when attacking with conventional bombs or depth charges. MAD records the exact position of a submerged target only when the investigating unit is vertically above it; it follows that any object dropped from the aircraft at that moment will strike ahead of the target due to the forward velocity imparted by the bomber.

The retro-bomb consisted of a small bomb fitted with a rocket in the nose that ignited on leaving the bomb bay. The approach speed of the aircraft was adjusted so that the reverse thrust of the rocket equalled the forward motion of the plane, the bomb therefore fell vertically onto the target area.

With a small size (35lb) and the inevitable possibility of slight error in use, the bombs were employed in patterns of eight with three patterns (the total bomb load) being dropped during the attack. Design of the bomb racks, speed of aircraft approach and timing of release resulted in a theoretical impact zone of three overlapping 100-foot diameter patterns covering a length of approximately 200 feet.

The weapon was deployed only in Catalina flying boats (PBY in US usage, Canso to the RCAF) of the USN. The first recorded success was against U 761 on 24 Feb 1944 in conjunction with depth charges and gunfire from surface ships and another aircraft.

Acoustic torpedo

The second weapon was developed for use specifically with the sonobouy system but was equally effective with MAD or, indeed, visual sightings. This was the earliest operational form of acoustic A/S torpedo, pre-dating the German Navy version. It was developed in the US at the request of the USN, the program commencing in December 1941. Design work was completed in October 1942 with the first production model being delivered in March 1943, an amazing performance for a totally new concept. The weapon was slow—only 12 knots—had an approximate range of 4,000 yards and endurance of 10 minutes, and could be avoided by deep diving. Due to very careful restrictions on the method and area of use, its existence remained unknown by the enemy until post-war; it therefore proved a very effective means of destruction.

The restrictions demanded that the torpedo be dropped only after a U-boat had shut down and commenced diving; visual sighting was therefore impossible. The U-boat was also at its most vulnerable when diving. Recovery of a torpedo by the enemy was avoided by its use being restricted to the open Atlantic so that the possibility of an accidental beaching and discovery by the Germans did not exist.

It entered service in May 1943, the first consignment of the weapon reaching the RAF in Northern Ireland on 27 April 1943. Its first operational victory was the sinking of U 456 on 12 May by Liberator B of 86 Sqdn RAF. Just fewer than 350 weapons were expended 1943-1945: 102 of which were rated as successful, 68 U-Boats being sunk and 33 damaged. The slow speed of the weapon would have minimised its effectiveness against the 1945 Type XXI and XXIII U-boats. The concept, vastly improved, is still the main aircraft A/S weapon in use today.

The weapon was particularly effective against a diving U-boat due to the German method of operation. In the act of diving, to ensure rapid submergence, the German practice was not only to vent ballast tanks but also to drive the boat under by using maximum engine power. This produced high cavitation noise, which was the principal factor in the homing ability of the torpedo; very rapid submergence was also likely to generate other mechanical noise above the usual operating level.

When designed it was code-named "Fido," later changed to "Proctor," referred to officially as the "Mk 24 mine" and nicknamed "Wandering Annie" by the USN aircrews. In a number of contemporary reports by aircraft it is also referred to as the "600lb D/C".

Rocket projectiles

Both the foregoing weapons were devised for relatively large, modern aircraft; something smaller and simpler was needed for carrier borne aircraft or small aircraft operating inshore. In late 1941 the RAF had demonstrated a small (3.5-inch calibre) rocket projectile for use by Hurricane fighters against tanks, specifically for the Western Desert. The weapon consisted of a 25lb AP head attached to a four-foot long steel tube containing cordite propellant, the tube being fitted with stabilising fins. This rocket was adopted and used most effectively by the RAF.

In October 1942 trials were carried out with naval Swordfish Mk II aircraft; these proved that the weapon was perfectly practical for use against submarine, indeed all, maritime targets. The only alterations required to the aircraft, other than the actual rails and firing equipment, was the provision of aluminium covered panels on the lower mainplane adjacent to the launching rails instead of the normal fabric.

The effectiveness of the attack depended entirely on the skill of the pilot who had to adjust the height and angle of his approach and range of firing to achieve the desired result. Providing he flew in and released his rockets at a flight angle of 20 degrees from the horizontal at a range of 400 yards, then the projectiles achieved their maximum velocity as they entered the water. On so doing, they dived and then turned upwards again to emerge from the water some 20 yards from entry point. Aircraft attacking usually fired rockets in pairs, one from each wing to lessen the yawing effect on the aircraft's course, using several firings to cross the target, opening fire at approximately 400 yards. Four rockets were carried on each lower mainplane and, if fired in pairs, the line of fire crossed the target.

The aim was to penetrate the hull of the submarine with at least one pair of rockets, thus rendering it unfit to dive. In that state, the submarine either sank as a result of the attack, or was helpless in the face of other aircraft or surface ships summoned by the attacker and was either then sunk or forced to scuttle. The weapon entered service in May 1943 and was immediately successful, causing U 752 to scuttle on 23 May after an attack by Swordfish G of 819 Sqdn Royal Navy, operating from the escort carrier ARCHER. The attack was the classic textbook operation with a fighter, Martlet B of 892 Sqdn, providing strafing fire to reduce the U-boat's AA defence, aiding the attack by the slower Swordfish.

The pilot fired too soon, the first pair of rockets being released at 800 yards and falling short. The second pair, fired at 400 yards, was also short but close. The third pair, fired at 300 yards as the U-boat dived, fell almost alongside the target, dived, and one struck and penetrated the pressure hull. The final pair, fired at close range, struck the hull right aft without entering the water as the U-boat's stern was still above the surface. Flooding, the U-boat surfaced and, after attempting a further dive, had to scuttle after being attacked by further fighter aircraft who killed the CO and another man on the conning tower.

Aircraft-mounted guns

Even the 20mm cannon mounted in World War II aircraft were quite ineffective against the main hull of a submarine, although capable of causing heavy casualties to exposed personnel and superficial damage to casing, conning tower etc. Larger calibre weapons were not viable for the relatively small carrier-borne aircraft of that era, but the RAF did develop a variant of the Army 6pdr automatic gun for use in Mosquito aircraft. These planes were employed in the Biscay submarine transit area at first and, using armour piercing shell, demonstrated the effectiveness of the gun against surfaced targets providing the attack could be pressed home at low level and close range. The first success of this form of attack was the sinking of U 976 on 25 Mar 1944 by a Mosquito of 248 Sqdn. Further successes followed, particularly in the Kattegat in the closing days of the war.

Courtesy K Macpherson (National Archives of Canada)

A magnificent photograph of EMPIRE DARWIN in the CAM ship role, taken on 27 Sept 1941 while in convoy SC 27. It shows very clearly the positioning of the rocket-powered catapult on the port side of the foc's'le. The ship was obliged to moor starboard side to in order to work No 1 hatch. Note, on the starboard side abeam the foremast, the handling davit for the paravane which is stowed on deck abeam No 1 hatch. The haul-down chains for this gear can be seen leading down from the starboard bulwarks of the foc's'le head. Unusually, the ship sports a most surreal camouflage which compensates somewhat for her otherwise stark and utilitarian appearance. The light fore topmast, unusual in war-built freighters, is probably for her radar and VHF aerials.

CHAPTER 11

CATAPULT AIRCRAFT MERCHANT SHIPS—CAM ships

CAM ships design and development

After the occupation of the French Atlantic Coast in June 1940, air attack by enemy aircraft against convoys in areas outside RAF fighter cover became a serious menace. The FW 200 aircraft, with a considerable radius of action, operating both as a reconnaissance aircraft to locate and signal the presence of convoys, and an efficient bomber to attack convoys and individual ships, caused an unacceptable measure of damage as the war loss records bear witness.

Protection of the convoys at that time was limited to a few auxiliary anti-aircraft ships armed with twin 4-inch HA and any escorts with a particular convoy that might possess HA weapons; effectively, only the pre-war sloops. The problem was made worse by the lack of an efficient HA control system in the RN, a deficiency only made good long after the threat under discussion had evaporated, and even then from American resources.

The effective answer to the problem was, of course, fighter aircraft but no aircraft carriers were available; the pre-1939 Staff Requirement for a "trade defence carrier" having been stillborn in the face of Treasury parsimony.

The RN proposed an answer in the Fighter Catapult Ship (FCS) which consisted of the ageing catapult test ship PEGASUS and several conversions of Ocean Boarding Vessels and an auxiliary anti-aircraft ship, all being fitted with a naval catapult and a Fulmar aircraft. While potentially effective, there were major difficulties such as the large number of trained RN personnel involved for a relatively small return, and the problems inherent in a warship proceeding to areas where entry to a neutral harbour might be involved.

The RAF took the initiative in proposing the fitting of a catapult to mercantile freighters to carry a single fighter, a proposal tabled in late 1940, but opposed as no such catapult existed. It was considered that such a fitting would be detrimental to the cargo capacity of the ship, presumably by preventing the use of No 1 hatch and hold. Eventually, the proposal and consequent dispute came to the attention of the Prime Minister, who ruled that a catapult should be designed and produced and that 250 ships were to be fitted, 200 of them RAF responsibility and 50 RN.

It is noteworthy that, with two Services and Royal Aircraft Establishment, Farnborough involved, very rapid and satisfactory progress was made by March 1941. By that time a simple, rocket driven catapult had been designed and tested. The number of ships proposed had been reduced to a more practical 50, and the RAF had agreed to provide the aircraft, pilot and maintenance crew while the RN provided the radar, Fighter Direction Officer and radar operator.

The final arrangements, other than for the freighter MICHAEL E which was exclusively a RN commitment, were that the squadrons of 9 Group, RAF "adopted" two or three CAM ships each and provided the pilots and VHF equipment for them. The personnel and equipment were formally taken over by the Merchant Ship Fighter Unit based at RAF Speke near Liverpool, the RN appointed a Sub Lieutenant FDO (trained by the RAF) and appropriate ratings direct to each merchantman.

Two hundred aircraft, Hurricane Mk 1, were to be provided to Speke for use with a further one hundred held at RCAF Dartmouth, NS as replacements. The immediate initial allocation to Speke in April 1941 was sixty aircraft. The pilots, trained at Farnborough and Gosport, were appointed for two round voyages only, despite the RN requesting permanent allocation. The RAF reasonably contended that, as the pilot would not be flying *at all* unless called to action or when flying off to return to Speke, his flying skills would deteriorate in the probable 18 or 19 weeks involved in two transAtlantic round voyages, and that permanent allocation of individuals was therefore totally unacceptable.

The RAF pilot was in command of the joint party with the RN FDO as his deputy. Catapult maintenance rested initially with the ship's Engineer Officer, later the RN FDO, while the MN Wireless Officer handled the actual operation of the catapult. All the Service party was signed on Ship's Articles in the same manner as DEMS ratings.

The catapult, a simple girder structure with a fitted trolley onto which the aircraft was loaded and the rockets attached, was installed on the fo'c'sle offset to port. Number 1 hatch could therefore be worked providing the ship berthed starboard side to, and deck cargo could be stowed on number 2 hold and further aft. The aircraft, brought by road from Speke, was loaded at Liverpool and disembarked at Halifax, also by crane and road, for servicing at Dartmouth NS or replacement as circumstances dictated. On return to the UK, the aircraft was catapulted and flown to Speke for maintenance.

Operation was vested in the Master of the CAM ship, who was responsible for the decision to launch, the FDO thereafter controlling the aircraft. After, hopefully, successfully attacking an enemy or driving it off, the pilot could either attempt to reach a shore airfield if within his remaining fuel range or he homed onto the convoy and made a parachute escape close to an escort to be picked up.

In any event, only thirty-five CAM ships were completed, the first RAF sponsored CAM ship aircraft launch being on 31 May 1941 by the newly built EMPIRE RAINBOW in the Clyde. The RN sponsored MICHAEL E carried out an earlier trial off Belfast and she was the first CAM ship to sail, in convoy OB 327, on 28 May 1941. Unfortunately, U 108 sank her on 2 June, after dispersal of the convoy. Thankfully her 47 survivors included both of the aircrew, the FDO and all nine RAF aircraftmen. One of the aircrew, Sub Lieutenant M A Birrell, had fought with the RAF in 79 Squadron in the Battle of Britain when a Midshipman.

Initially the ships were confined to the North American convoys but in September 1941 were also included in the Gibraltar series with a small maintenance party at Gibraltar's North Front airstrip; ships proceeding to Freetown were also added to the list later. Aircraft were not embarked in the Atlantic ships in January and February 1942 as experience showed that the winter weather rendered them unfit for flying and incapable of maintenance. They recommenced duty on 6 March 1942. In April 1942 North Russian convoys were added to the list requiring protection. The Russian servicing terminal was set up at Archangel, where a small RAF party was based until the end of September 1942. The base was then closed due to the imminent icing up of the port, and the party withdrawn. Subsequently air cover for Russian convoys was provided by escort carriers, commencing with PQ 18.

In August 1942 it was deemed unnecessary to continue CAM ship protection in the North Atlantic except for convoys in the Gibraltar and Freetown series, the FW 200 attacks then being confined to the Biscay area and west of the Iberian peninsula. At the same time the new escort carriers were about to enter service in the North Atlantic carrying both fighter and A/S aircraft.

By then 26 CAM ships were still in service and the number was reduced to 16 with eight of the ten redundant ships having their catapults removed. The Canadian servicing base was shut down and its aircraft handed over to the RCAF (who had always provided the servicing personnel) for their use.

In March 1943 the RAF became impatient at the absence of trained pilots and pressed for complete abolition of CAM ships, maintaining that the detachments, MSFU and the Gibraltar unit were equivalent to two full fighter squadrons lost. The Admiralty agreed and it was decided to close the operations of the Unit on 15 July 1943. However, two ships, EMPIRE DARWIN and EMPIRE TIDE were still at sea, returning to the UK in convoy SL 133. They made the final operational launches on 27 July when both aircraft broke up an attack by seven FW 200s destroying one and damaging a second.

Judged simply on the basis of actual launches and victories the operations of the CAM ships were not impressive. 170 round voyages by a total of 35 CAM ships, 8 operational launches resulting in seven "kills" and the loss of one pilot, F/O J B Kendall RAF from EMPIRE MORN in convoy QP 12 when his parachute failed to deploy properly on bailing out.

However it must be remembered that the CAM ship was a one-off defence; once launched there could be no recovery or second chance so the decision was rightly delayed as long as possible to maximise the effect. Finally, the presence of the CAM ship was in itself a protection by causing enemy aircraft to stay clear of the convoy. Whilst not deterring shadowing and reporting, it certainly prevented a number of bomb attacks, attacks which had, until the advent of the CAM ship, been unpleasantly successful.

CAM ships operated normally at the head of the port column of the convoy where the restricted view ahead from the bridge posed the least problems for the Master. On launch also, the aircraft was immediately clear of "friendly fire," as gunners in merchant ships were understandably liable to shoot at anything airborne in the circumstances of the time regardless of appearance, markings or number of engines!

Two ships, CAPE CLEAR and CITY OF JOHANNESBURG were fitted with dummy catapults and aircraft as a deception, for a limited period only, about the end of 1941.

Helicopter trials afloat

It is worthy of note that DAGHESTAN, still equipped with her VHF equipment and radar, was used after the end of her CAM ship service for experiments with operating helicopters as A/S aircraft. A timber landing pad was erected aft, protected by removable timber windbreaks, and a very early model helicopter embarked and operated during an eastward passage. The small machine was incapable of carrying a weapons load and the trials were simply to test the ability of the aircraft to operate under extreme conditions. The trials, conducted during the passage of convoy HX 274 from 6 to 21 Jan 1944, were adjudged a success and both the RN and USN decided upon the future use of helicopters as an A/S weapon system as and when suitable airframes had been developed.

CAM ship launches

Date	CAM ship	Pilot	Score
1.11.41	EMPIRE FOAM	P/O G W Varley RAFVR	-
25.5.42	EMPIRE MORN	F/O J B Kendall RAF	1 kill, 1 damaged
25.5.42	EMPIRE LAWRENCE	F/O A J Hay RAF	2 kills
14.6.42	EMPIRE MOON	P/O A V Sanders RAF	1 damaged
18.9.42	EMPIRE MORN	F/O A H Burr RAF	2 kills
1.11.42	EMPIRE HEATH	F/O N Taylor DFM RAF	1 kill
28.7.43	EMPIRE TIDE	F/O P J R Flynn RAF	1 kill
28.7.43	EMPIRE DARWIN	F/O J A Stewart RAF	1 damaged

List of Catapult Aircraft Merchant Ships

DAGHESTAN	
DALTON HALL	
EASTERN CITY	
EMPIRE BURTON	sunk by U 74 on 20.9.41 in SC 44
EMPIRE CLIVE	
EMPIRE DARWIN	
EMPIRE DAY	
EMPIRE DELL	sunk by U 124 on 12.4.42 in ON 92
EMPIRE EVE	
EMPIRE FAITH	
EMPIRE FOAM	
EMPIRE FLAME	
EMPIRE FRANKLIN	
EMPIRE GALE	
EMPIRE HEATH	
EMPIRE HUDSON	sunk by U 82 on 10.9.41 in SC 42
EMPIRE LAWRENCE	sunk by aircraft on 27.5.42 in PQ 16
EMPIRE MOON	
EMPIRE MORN	
EMPIRE OCEAN	aground 4.8.42, refloated and sank 5.8.42
EMPIRE RAINBOW	
EMPIRE RAY	
EMPIRE ROWAN	
EMPIRE SHACKLETON	sunk by U 406, U 123 & U 435 on 29.12.42 in ON 154
EMPIRE SPRAY	
EMPIRE SPRING	sunk by U 576 on 14.2.42 after dispersal from ON 63
EMPIRE STANLEY	
EMPIRE SUN	sunk by U 751 on 7.2.42 while on independent passage
EMPIRE TIDE	
EMPIRE WAVE	sunk by U 562 on 2.10.41 in ON 19
HELENCREST	
KAFIRISTAN	
MICHAEL E	sunk by U 108 on 2.6.41 after dispersal of OB 327
NOVELIST	
PRIMROSE HILL	sunk by UD 5 on 29.10.42 after dispersal of ON 139

Note: Some of the ships listed above were lost after their service as CAM ships had been discontinued; the loss data quoted is of ships serving as CAM ships at the time of loss.

Courtesy Fleet Air Arm Museum

The Fighter Catapult Ship HMS SPRINGBANK. She had been converted into an Auxiliary Anti-Aircraft Ship when taken over by the Royal Navy and refitted with a naval type bridge structure carrying a High Angle Director. Fore and aft appropriate superstructure was erected and four twin 4-inch High Angle mountings were installed, two forward and two aft. This gave the ship, and similar conversions, an anti-aircraft armament which equalled that of a cruiser.

When the need arose to provide ship-borne fighter aircraft to protect convoys from the FW 200 aircraft operating from western France, several of these AA ships were adapted by fitting a catapult and providing them with a naval two-seat Fulmar fighter. This aircraft can be seen abaft the funnel on its catapult, trained to starboard ready for launch.

Fighter Catapult Ships (FCS)

These ships, commissioned into the Royal Navy, were fitted with a catapult and embarked Fulmar aircraft to operate in a similar fashion to the CAM ships. They were, of course, manned by naval officers and ratings. Catapults were cordite operated in PEGASUS and SPRINGBANK and rocket operated in ARIGUANI and MAPLIN, the type fitted in PATIA is not recorded.

HMS PEGASUS	Converted from a catapult trials ship. Reverted to catapult training duties 26 July 1941
HMS SPRINGBANK	Converted from an auxiliary anti-aircraft ship, sunk by U 201, 27 Sept 1941 in convoy HG 73
HMS MAPLIN	Converted from an Ocean Boarding Vessel. Ship paid off and reverted to trade 30 June 1942
HMS ARIGUANI	Converted from an Ocean Boarding Vessel, torpedoed by U 83, 26 Oct 1941 in convoy HG 75, towed to Gibraltar, laid up and reverted to trade 27 Dec 1941. Later towed to UK
HMS PATIA	Converted from an Ocean Boarding Vessel, sunk by air attack 27 Apr 1941 on post-conversion trials

1. PEGASUS operated in support of nine convoys between 3 Dec 1940 and 26 July 1941 making three operational launches. All launches used Fulmar aircraft.
In the first, on 11 Jan 1941 with convoy SL 49; the enemy evaded action.
The second launch on 7 June 1941 was with convoy HG 63; the enemy was driven off and the fighter landed at Belfast.
The final launch on 7 July 1941 was with convoy OG 67; no interception took place. The fighter endeavoured to return to Northern Ireland, crashing into a hillside in bad visibility, with the loss of the pilot, Sub Lieutenant (A) T R V Parke RNVR and his TAG, Ldg Telegraphist B F Miller.

2. SPRINGBANK operated Fulmar aircraft between 10 May 1941 (convoy HX 126) and her loss in convoy HG 73 on 27 Sept 1941.
Her first launch was with HX 129 on 10 June 1941; the enemy evaded action and the Fulmar returned to Belfast.
The second launch was on 18 Sept 1941 with HG 73; the enemy was attacked but escaped. On arrival of the aircraft at Gibraltar it was found that all but one of the Fulmar's guns had jammed due to faulty ammunition. U 201 torpedoed the ship on 27 Sept 1941.

3. MAPLIN embarked one, after 23 Feb 1942 increased to three, Hurricanes. She operated with nine convoys between June 1941 and June 1942, making three operational launches.
The first launch was with convoy OB 346 on 18 July 1941; the convoy's gunfire shot down the enemy as the Hurricane commenced its attack.
The second launch with convoy SL 81 on 3 Aug 1941 resulted in a FW 200 being shot down. The pilot (Lt (A) R W H Everett RNVR) bailed out and was rescued. Lt Everett was later awarded the DSO.
The final launch was with convoy HG 72 on 14 Sept 1941 when the fighter carried out repeated attacks over a period of an hour. Although damaged, the FW 200 eventually escaped; the fighter pilot (S-Lt (A) C W Walker RNVR) bailed out and was rescued.

4. ARIGUANI initially operated a single Fulmar from May 1941, reinforced with a Hurricane in August. She served with eleven convoys before being torpedoed by U 83 on 26 Oct 1941. Towed to Gibraltar, she was eventually stripped and returned to mercantile service.
She made two launches, the first of a Fulmar on 27 Aug 1941 when with convoy OS 4 when interception was evaded. The Fulmar returned to Ireland, landing briefly in Eire and finally arrived at Eglinton.
The second launch, also of a Fulmar, was on 4 Oct 1941 with convoy OG 75. The enemy was attacked and damaged before escaping in cloud. The Fulmar pilot bailed out and was recovered by an escort.

5. PATIA was lost on post-conversion trials prior to embarking her aircraft.

CHAPTER 12

MERCHANT AIRCRAFT CARRIERS–MAC ships

The escalation of submarine warfare apparent in early 1942, and anticipated to increase in the succeeding 12/18 months, led to considerations of providing additional air cover in the large areas of the Atlantic beyond the range of existing shore-based aircraft. The problem had been foreseen during the 1930s, and a "trade defence carrier" figured in the Naval Staff needs of that period; lack of finance prevented its development however. A substitute was devised in 1941 with the conversion of the prize HANOVER as the first escort carrier and she proved, during her short career, the viability of the type. American resources undertook the construction, initially by conversion of existing hulls and later by the use of a standard mercantile design converted on the ways, of considerable numbers of escort carriers (CVE in US parlance), several being employed in A/S warfare in the North Atlantic by both the RN and the USN.

MAC ship design and development

The potential rate of construction of such ships in the UK and the provision of both naval aviation and general service personnel was a cause of acute anxiety on the British side. An alternative that would not involve the loss of cargo carrying capacity nor cause large naval personnel involvement was sought. In early 1942 therefore the Admiralty produced a Staff Requirement detailing the minimum needs for a flight deck, ancillary below deck stowage for hangar, stores, fuel etc, all to be carried on a standard war construction hull.

The provision of an overall flight deck precluded the use of any vessel requiring loading via conventional hatchways; the choice of hull was therefore restricted to tankers and bulk grain carriers that both loaded and discharged by flexible pipework. The initial order was for two ships, adapted from bulk grain carriers under construction, and the detailed design work was entrusted to the mercantile builders, Burntisland Shipbuilding Co Ltd, who were to submit plans using the broad outline of the Staff Requirement.

Inevitably some compromise had to be made as the initial outline design proved too optimistic. Nevertheless the builders were able to submit, by May 1942, plans for a vessel with a flight deck of approximately 420 feet by 62 feet, a small hangar to accommodate four aircraft, a single lift and four arrester wires. The standard diesel machinery of the original design was upgraded to produce 3,300BHP rather than 2,500BHP to give a margin of speed for operation and manoeuvre.

The plans having been approved by the Admiralty, the initial order for two ships was increased to six in October 1942 with two builders, Denny and Lithgows, being added to the leading yard, each building two ships. The first ship was ordered from Burntisland in June 1942, keel laid in August and launched in December; delivery of the completed ship was made in April 1943 and the first operational voyage in May. Such speed was only obtained by a combination of forceful management

◇ THE ALLIED CONVOY SYSTEM 1939-1945

Courtesy Fleet Air Arm Museum (RCAF)

An excellent view of the tanker MAC ship EMPIRE MACCOLL, which illustrates the visual differences between the two types.

Reading from aft, where two Swordfish are folded and the third ranged for launch, note the windbreak palisades on either side to protect the deck park of aircraft. Further forward the island is distinctive, a two-level structure with an open bridge above the upper level; the mast is stepped abaft the upper level onto the lower level. The upper level is the chartroom, the lower the aircrew ready room etc.

Forward of the bridge can be seen the A frames which, when erected hydraulically, spread the barrier required during flying operations in a ship relying on deck-parked aircraft. This photograph was taken 30 Apr 1944 when EMPIRE MACCOLL was operating with convoy HX 289 en route to the UK.

by the builders in refusing to brook changes in design after the acceptance of their plans and the Admiralty making a considerable effort to refrain from interference.

Attention was then turned to tanker hulls to be altered in the same way; here problems arose. Complaints that the carriage of aviation fuel would increase the hazard to the ships were dismissed early in consideration, the hazards of tanker cargoes were little more than that arising from grain dust explosions and any additional risk was minimal. The most important difference was the difficulty of installing a hangar, which would have required major redesign and delay. As this was not acceptable, the longer flight deck (460 feet) of the tanker allowed the use of the after end as a permanent deck park.

The basic design changes having been agreed in October 1942, four hulls under construction were taken up for conversion as were nine ships already at sea, with a further thirteen ships planned but not actually converted or built. Hulls on the ways required an additional three months' work to complete to the carrier form; conversions of ships already at sea took six months with much of the structural steel being prefabricated away from the building yard.

The aircraft used was the standard Swordfish Mk II biplane, with four aircraft embarked in the grain carrier conversions and three in the deck stowage tankers. The Air Staff Officer, aircrew and maintenance personnel were, of course, drawn from the Air Branch of the Royal Navy; a naval Medical Officer was also carried. A small number of general service ratings were drafted as flight deck party and three signalmen would handle the increased V/S and voice communication anticipated. Aircraft were part of an administrative Squadron, 836, and were embarked as detached Flights, designated A to S for a total of 63 aircrews embarked.

Other than the naval party, the ships were manned by Merchant Navy personnel (two were in fact Dutch owned and manned), the naval party signing Ship's

◇ 84

Articles, coming under the disciplinary control of the Master and being accommodated and fed by the ship's owners. The naval party embarked at the port of departure in the UK, Clyde in the case of tankers, Liverpool for grain ships. Aircraft were flown on from their parent station, RNAS Maydown in Northern Ireland after sailing. The turnaround of the ships, generally at Halifax, was brief as they were all bulk loaded. Aircraft were flown ashore to RCAF Dartmouth NS where spares and replacement aircraft were available, flown on again for the return passage. On return to the UK aircraft flew ashore for maintenance. Unserviceable aircraft were landed by dockside crane after berthing and removed by road; replacement aircraft were supplied in Canada as required.

The aircraft carried out patrols as required by the SOE, subject only to weather conditions. Inability to operate due to weather problems was minimal, visibility or lack of wind speed over the deck being the two most frequent causes. Unserviceability of aircraft due to accidents on deck was unfortunately quite common. This reflected the very cramped flight deck area available to the pilots. The general servicing record of the Flights reflects great credit on aircrew operating in open, unheated cockpits and with the maintenance being carried out on open decks in two thirds of the ships. Twelve contacts resulting in attacks were made on targets resulting in possible damage to two U-boats.

While this may seem a small number of attacks it must be remembered that, during the operational service of MAC ships (late 1943-45), U-boat activity against the North America/UK traffic was at a minimum. The MAC ship operations also had the effect of reducing the need for VLR aircraft of Coastal Command to operate in mid-Atlantic, enabling more profitable use to be made of a most valuable asset still, even at that time, in none too plentiful supply.

One major disaster occurred on 8 July 1944 when a positive sighting was made and attacked (after a check with the controlling MAC ship that no friendly submarines were in the area) by aircraft from the two MAC ships in convoy ON 243. Rocket projectiles sank the submarine and a number of survivors were seen in the water. Only one remained alive when an escort arrived on the scene at which stage it was discovered that the submarine was the French LA PERLE on passage from the USA after refit. The subsequent Board of Enquiry ascertained that the MAC ships had not been advised, due to an error in the senior escort vessel, of the submarine's presence and the consequent attack restrictions.

Two of the tanker MAC ships were Dutch owned and were the first carriers under the Netherlands flag. Both operated aircraft flown by Dutch aircrew, later followed by the formation of the Dutch Air Branch and the acquisition of a British escort carrier eventually replaced by a light fleet carrier also from Britain.

Service record

The last MAC ship to serve as such was EMPIRE MACKAY, which arrived in the UK to convert to normal tanker configuration on 28 June 1945, 836 Squadron, itself having been disbanded on 21 May. During the early months of 1944, some MAC ships did not operate their Flights eastbound, being used instead as transports with their flight decks crammed with replacement aircraft for discharge in the UK, eleven passages being made in this role. A deckload would typically be twenty twin-engined medium bombers and some crated stores. The embarked Swordfish were stowed aft of a barrier built out of the crated stores, and enclosed by their windbreak palisades if a tanker; grain ships struck their aircraft down into the hangar.

During 1943 there were 27 MAC ship passages in the North Atlantic, 216 in 1944 and 80 in 1945 for a total of days at sea of 378; 2,938; and 1,131 respectively. Total sorties flown were 282; 2,603; and 1,292 during which 114 aircraft were either lost or irreparably damaged while operating from the extremely cramped flight decks; however, only eight aircrew (six officers and two leading airmen) were lost in these operations.

While the number of lost aircraft may appear high, it must be appreciated that with an extremely cramped flight deck and no hangar in two-thirds of the ships, a flight deck accident frequently required the ditching of the aircraft to enable another aircraft to be landed on. The rule of thumb was that the flight deck must be operable within thirty minutes of the initial accident; three other lives could well depend on that.

■ Courtesy Fleet Air Arm Museum (RCAF)

EMPIRE MACRAE in convoy HX 289 on 30 Apr 1944. This ship is built as a bulk grain carrier, and differs markedly from her half-sisters which were oil tankers.

Reading from aft, where a single Swordfish is ranged for take-off, note the absence of windbreak palisades. As the four aircraft carried could be struck down into the hangar, there was no need for a deck park, hence no barrier was fitted.

The island superstructure, sited further forward than in the tanker variant, is a simple single-level structure containing the chartroom, with an open bridge on the top. The pole mast is stepped against the after end of the island, and continues down to flight deck level.

■ Courtesy Robert Eakins

An extremely interesting photograph of the MAC ship MACOMA. She was Netherlands owned and manned, and her Swordfish aircraft were flown by Royal Netherlands Navy aircrew. Available information suggests that this photograph was taken during convoy SC 168 or SC 175, as MACOMA is acting as escort oiler. These were the only two convoys in which she so operated.

The fuelling hose can be seen led over the round down of the flight deck aft of the deck park. This of course means that the hose passes over the arrester wires and, on its way from a forward oiling point, obstructs the already narrow flight deck. Despite this, there are records of take-off in this dangerous situation when operational necessity called for an unexpected sortie.

Another unusual point is that oiler MAC ships operated flights of three Swordfish, however clearly four such aircraft are embarked in this photograph. The usual restriction of numbers was due to flight deck space; all aircraft had to remain on deck in the absence of a hangar.

Reference is made in Chapter 15, "Replenishment at Sea," to the supply operations to escorts by MAC ships during their operational service..

Descriptive data

Grain ship hulls

Name	Builder	In service
EMPIRE MACALPINE	Burntisland	Apr 1943
EMPIRE MACANDREW	Denny	July 1943
EMPIRE MACCALLUM	Lithgows	Dec 1943
EMPIRE MACDERMOTT	Denny	May 1944
EMPIRE MACRAE	Lithgows	Sept 1943
EMPIRE MACKENDRICK	Burntisland	Dec 1943

Oil tanker hulls

Name	Builder	In service
EMPIRE MACCABE	Swan Hunter	Dec 1943
EMPIRE MACCOLL	Cammell Laird	Nov 1943
EMPIRE MACKAY	Harland & Wolff, Govan	Oct 1943
EMPIRE MACMAHON	Swan Hunter	Dec 1943

Oil tanker conversions

Name	Owner	In service
ACAVUS	Anglo-Saxon Petroleum Co Ltd	Oct 1943
ADULA	Anglo-Saxon Petroleum Co Ltd	Feb 1944
ALEXIA	Anglo-Saxon Petroleum Co Ltd	Dec 1943
AMASTRA	Anglo-Saxon Petroleum Co Ltd	Sept 1943
ANCYLUS	Anglo-Saxon Petroleum Co Ltd	Oct 1943
GADILA	N V Petroleum Maatschappij	Mar 1944
MACOMA	N V Petroleum Maatschappij	May 1944
MIRALDA	Anglo-Saxon Petroleum Co Ltd	Jan 1944
RAPANA	Anglo-Saxon Petroleum Co Ltd	July 1943

MAC ship particulars

Detail	Grain ships	Tankers
Tonnage	8,000 grt approx.	11,000 grt approx.
Speed	12.5 knots	11.5 knots
Flight deck length	410 to 420 feet	460 feet
Flight deck width	62 feet	62 feet
Flight deck freeboard	28 to 30 feet	30 to 32 feet
Aircraft	4 Swordfish	3 Swordfish
Aircraft stowage	Hangar and lift	Deck park
Flight deck arrangements	4 wires	4 wires, crash barrier
Gun armament	1 4in LA	1 4in LA
	2 40mm Bofors	2 40mm Bofors
	4 20mm Oerlikon	6 20mm Oerlikon
Cargo capacity as MAC ships	80% of designed	90% of designed

■ Courtesy Fleet Air Arm Museum

An undated photograph of a Mark II Swordfish of B Flight, 836 Squadron airborne, probably over the Irish Sea. The aircraft is armed with the standard Rocket Projectile, four under each lower mainplane. Note the light-coloured aluminum-panelled area of the lower mainplanes, to protect that part from the flame of the propellant on discharge.

The photograph is posed, not operational, as only the Pilot is present. On an operational flight the Observer would have been in the cockpit abaft the Pilot and the Telegraphist Air Gunner in the rear cockpit, though there were occasions when he was omitted from the flight crew on operational flights.

Note, in addition to the B2 number, indicating aircraft 2 of B Flight 836 Squadron, the airframe number (LS 276) and the MERCHANT NAVY title under and forward of the tailplane, replacing the more usual ROYAL NAVY. 836 Squadron aircraft routinely carried this titling. The aircraft is painted in the matte white common to all MAC ship and RAF Coastal Command aircraft operating in the anti-submarine role.

CHAPTER 13
RESCUE SHIPS

The original convoy orders, printed on the sailing plan, laid down that the rear ship of each column should act as rescue ship in the event of sinking of one of the ships ahead of her. Although the rescue of survivors is an automatic reaction of any seaman, the task imposed considerable danger to the rescuer. Also the freeboard of a freighter or tanker in ballast, and the unwieldy nature of merchant ships' boats, made recovery of men in the water very difficult.

As soon as this problem became apparent with the increased sinkings of ships after-mid 1940, the Admiralty sought to requisition certain small vessels for the specific duty of Rescue Ships. These were principally small freighters with passenger accommodation, and a good deal of work was required to fit them for their new role. In view of the physical and morale advantage of dedicated Rescue vessels, it is surprising that the MOWT actively opposed the allo-

Courtesy K Macpherson (NMM photo N 34332)

Rescue Ship FASTNET with an eastbound convoy with supplies for Britain. FASTNET entered service after the withdrawal of U-boats from the North Atlantic in mid-1943, and her duties mostly involved her in providing medical aid to ships of the convoys which she accompanied.

cation of additional vessels after the initial conversions. Although the allocation was finally agreed, when a further need for more ships arose later in the war, five CASTLE class corvettes on the ways but surplus to escort needs were converted to the rescue role. These ships survived postwar as small troopships in Army service in the Mediterranean.

Description

Two-berth cabins were built in the 'tween-deck spaces for officer survivors, while messdecks with bunk or hammock accommodation for up to 150 men were also provided. Galley and food storage areas were enlarged as needed, additional sanitary arrangements made and a properly fitted sick bay and operating theatre provided with accommodation for a naval doctor and sick bay staff. Boats more suitable for open sea work were provided in lieu of the standard lifeboats, as were recovery aids such as scrambling nets and the like.

The completed vessels were allocated to convoys as a specific Rescue Ships and usually stationed at the rear of the centre column of the convoy. The Master was under the control of the Commodore, while responding to the requests of the Senior Officer of the Escort and reporting submarine bearings, etc direct to him.

An additional benefit of the Rescue Ships was that almost all were eventually fitted with High Frequency Direction Finding equipment, and three Radio Officers specially trained in its use were embarked additional to the normal complement. They were therefore able to take bearings on enemy radio transmissions and pass these to the SOE to provide a cross bearing in conjunction with his set. This facility added materially to the defence of the convoy and was of great value to the Escort Commander.

A feature of the Rescue Ships was the consistent service of many of their crews. Masters were meticulous in their recruitment of crews, with very positive views on seamanship. One Master recruited his deck complement solely from Hebridean seamen, renowned for their seamanship and boat-handling ability.

There was continuous development of recovery and transfer tactics, and of specialised equipment, developed through experience by the crews themselves. The shore organization, Clyde based, provided by the PSTO ensured that such improvements were monitored, approved and the knowledge at once passed to other Rescue Ships.

The PSTO, Clyde, appointed a specific Rescue Ship Officer in June 1941 whose sole responsibility thereafter was the fitting out and general care of all Rescue Ships. Later a further officer was appointed as Inspecting Officer charged with the care of the Rescue Ships when in port in Glasgow. As the incumbents remained in office throughout the remainder of the war, continuity and very close personal involvement was ensured, a fact undoubtedly adding greatly to the effectiveness of the organization.

Surprisingly, given their exposure to attack during their work, relatively few of the Rescue Ships were lost. They were greatly admired both by their colleagues in the convoy and by the crews of escort vessels, and escorts went to considerable lengths whenever possible to give cover to "their" Rescue Ship.

From their introduction to the North Atlantic convoy routes in late 1940 (the system was later extended to cover other major routes including North Russia) 4,194 survivors were picked up; 2,296 Britons, 951 Americans, 369 Norwegians, 141 Greeks, 104 Russians, 81 Panamanians, 75 Dutch, 56 French, 40 Latvians, 34 Swedes, 21 Yugoslavs, 20 Filipino, 2 Czechs and 4 German U-boat survivors from a total of 119 ships. These figures include 32 aircrew picked up as a result of crashes, principally from MAC ships of the convoy. Seven hundred and ninety-seven voyages in convoy were recorded over a distance of some two and a quarter million miles. The attribution of nationality is that given by the Rescue Service. It is probable that this was decided by the nationality of the Register upon which the ship appeared. Thus "Panamanian" is quite likely to consist largely of American seamen. British DEMS ratings serving in Dutch or Norwegian ships might well also be listed under those nationalities.

The foregoing is only the briefest survey of a little known group of important ships. *Convoy Rescue Ships 1940-45* by this author, published November 1998 by World Ship Society, ISBN 0 905617 88 6, contains more detailed research.

List of Rescue Ships

In the list below, the ship's name is followed by her gross registered tonnage/year of build. The date on which the ship became operational appears next, followed by the number of convoys in which she took part and the total of numbers rescued. Finally, a note shows the ships lost with relevant data.

Name	GRT/Year	Operational	Convoys	Rescued	Notes
ABOYNE	1,020/37	11/06/43	26	20	
ACCRINGTON	1,678/10	26/07/42	36	141	
BEACHY	1,600/36	?/01/41	5	-	Sunk 11/1/41 by aircraft
BURY	1,686/11	27/12/41	48	237	
COPELAND	1,526/23	29/01/41	71	433	
DEWSBURY	1,686/10	29/09/41	43	5	
DUNDEE	1,541/34	08/08/43	24	11	
EDDYSTONE	1,500/27	06/11/43	24	64	
EMPIRE COMFORT	1,333/45	25/02/45	8	-	
EMPIRE LIFEGUARD	1,333/44	07/03/45	6	-	
EMPIRE PEACEMAKER	1,333/45	10/02/45	8	3	
EMPIRE REST	1,327/44	12/11/44	11	-	
EMPIRE SHELTER	1,336/45	16/04/45	6	-	
FASTNET	1,415/28	07/10/43	25	35	
GOODWIN	1,569/17	28/04/43	25	133	
GOTHLAND	1,286/32	05/02/42	41	149	
HONTESTROOM	1,875/21	11/01/41	11	69	Withdrawn from service 5/41
MELROSE ABBEY	1,908/29	11/02/42	46	85	
PERTH	2,258/15	05/05/41	60	455	
PINTO	1,346/28	05/12/42	10	2	Sunk 8/9/44 by U 482
RATHLIN	1,599/36	02/10/41	47	634	
ST CLAIR	1,636/37	01/07/44	14	-	
ST SUNNIVA	1,368/31	07/12/42	1	-	Foundered 23/1/43, probably due to icing up
STOCKPORT	1,683/11	22/10/41	16	413	Sunk 23/2/43 by U 604
SYRIAN PRINCE	1,989/36	18/11/43	19	-	
TJALDUR	1,130/16	26/10/41	3	-	Withdrawn as unsuitable 12/41
TOWARD	1,571/23	24/10/41	45	337	Sunk 7/2/43 by U 402
WALMER CASTLE	906/36	12/09/41	1	81	Sunk 29/1/41 by aircraft
ZAAFARAN	1,567/21	23/03/41	26	220	Sunk 5/7/42 by aircraft
ZAMALEK	1,565/21	26/02/41	68	665	

Note: The Master of ZAMALEK claimed a total of 665 rescues, although shore records only list 611; the former figure has been used.

Personnel losses

Two hundred and nine crew of the Rescue Ships were lost in the sinkings recorded above plus 22 known survivors onboard at the time. Distribution is as follows:

PINTO	16 crew
ST SUNNIVA	64 (total) crew
STOCKPORT	63 (total) crew, plus any survivors on board at the time
TOWARD	54 crew & 2 medical cases
WALMER CASTLE	11 crew & 20 survivors
ZAAFARAN	1 crew lost

Rescue Trawlers

An unusual position arose in 1943 regarding the Rescue Service. Two Rescue Ships had been lost early in the year, the number of trans-Atlantic convoys was increasing and the individual convoys were also much larger. Obviously, C-in-C Western Approaches became concerned about the ability of the Rescue Ships to cope, and requested replacements and a further increase in numbers. This was opposed by MOWT on the very valid grounds that the number of suitable vessels was now exceedingly limited, and they were required for trade purposes. This situation arose just prior to the defeat and withdrawal of U-boats from the North Atlantic in May 1943.

The RN accepted the decision and decided to convert five corvettes then building to civilian-manned Rescue Ships. These incomplete hulls, and others, had become surplus to needs after the defeat of U-boats in the North Atlantic in May. Unfortunately, the transformation of mass-produced escorts to individually finished, specialised mercantile hulls involved extended building times, and these replacements would not be available for some twelve months. The increase in escort strength and change in the strategic situation had however also made the highly experienced A/S trawlers of Western Approaches Command less essential to the escort force strength. In consequence a number of these veterans were refitted for service as Rescue Trawlers.

The conversion, in fact a modest refit, involved a slight reduction in A/S armament (as much to clear deck space as anything) and the provision of basic rescue equipment. The size of the ships precluded any provision of sickbay or operating facilities and only the most minimal accommodation for survivors. This is amply illustrated by the experience of NORTHERN SPRAY when with convoy ONS 5. When detached to St John's NF the 150 foot vessel carried 134 survivors additional to her own complement; her consort NORTHERN GEM had been detached earlier with a total of 78 survivors.

The ships remained naval-manned (principally by their original Patrol Service crews) and were attached to convoys as an addition to an existing Rescue Ship. When no Rescue Ship was available, two Rescue Trawlers were usually attached to a single convoy.

Where survivors were recovered, and the vastly smaller losses from mid-1943 onwards made this an infrequent occurrence, the trawler either transferred the survivors to the Rescue Ship at the earliest opportunity or detached to the nearest port to land them.

The trawlers were capable of reverting to escort work, indeed a number did so and took part in convoy escort in the Channel in the post D-Day operations.

CHAPTER 14
RESCUE TUGS

Salvage firms have for many years maintained ocean-going tugs at strategic locations on either side of the Atlantic for the specific purpose of assisting ships suffering mishap. Dutch deep sea tugs in particular were specialists in this field, and with long-distance tows, pre-1939. During the war the recovery of damaged vessels and their crews was to become of prime importance. Accordingly when war broke out in Sept 1939 the Admiralty set up a similar organization to that of the 1917-19 period, using commercial tugs and their crews on charter to the Government.

The financial cost of these chartered vessels however proved too high for their limited capacity and use. In September 1939 the Admiralty also arranged at the same time that tug owners at the principal British ports would pool resources and keep one tug permanently available at each, at no public charge. Costs would be recovered, and profit made, from the usual fees and salvage awards for work completed.

The largest of these tugs, the NEPTUNIA, was unfortunately lost on 13 Sept 1939 when torpedoed by U 29. Thereafter, tug crews became reluctant to proceed to sea in their unarmed vessels. Accordingly, a proposal to set up an armed Rescue Tug service was approved on 12 Oct 1939 whereby suitable tugs were made available from the very limited naval supply, and from requisitioned commercial tugs of oceangoing capability. These ships were to be manned by qualified civilian crews under a variant of the T124 Agreement. This Rescue Tug Service replaced both previous arrangements and proved far more satisfactory to all parties.

The T124T Agreement offered tug officers and crews employment for the duration of the war, as naval personnel subject to the Naval Discipline Act, serving in ships wearing the White or Blue Ensign. Naval commissions were granted to officers appropriate to their qualifications, and suitable ratings to the crew. The Agreement included payment on the basis of the national agreement on mercantile pay i.e. somewhat in excess of naval rates so far as ratings were concerned, plus a monthly bonus of £10.

As the Agreement ran for the term of the war, ratings' pay was effectively doubled in the majority of cases. This led to a good deal of ill-feeling when RN ratings found themselves serving in a vessel at half the daily rate of pay of their fellow crew members. This especially applied to those recruited directly for the Rescue Tug service but as Hostilities Only ratings. As a result a postwar review by the Commander in Charge Rescue Tugs recommended that, in any future revival of the Service, all personnel should be entered as Hostilities Only on basic Service rates of pay.

All Navigating and Engineer tug officers were given temporary commissions if professionally qualified; otherwise, they received temporary acting appointments. It was found by experience that Warrant Engineers and Engine Room Artificers would be eminently suitable as Engineer Officers for the tugs, as was indeed the case with most RN escort vessels.

A detailed examination of all available British registered tugs was carried out and by Jan 1940 twelve vessels were in service. Their Navigating Officers and seamen were almost exclusively experienced tug personnel, or were drawn from professional small ship seamen such as Scottish trawlermen.

In June 1940, the conquest of Holland by Germany and the surrender of France made available (by consent or seizure) some additional deep-sea tonnage and the tug figure rose to 19. The Dutch tugs in particular were of the greatest value in view of the vast experience that became available from their owners and crews.

The Admiralty also commenced a large tug construction program covering a range of sizes and equipment, and the 1941 Lend-Lease legislation in the USA also offered the opportunity to increase the fleet. Accordingly the figures of vessels available rose steadily throughout the rest of the war, as shown below:

Date	Rescue Tugs available
1.41	33
6.41	31
1.42	33
6.42	37
1.43	51
6.43	61
1.44	77
6.44	83

Rising to a peak figure of 85 ships in April 1945.

The training of Officers recruited for, or appointed to, tugs was at first carried out solely "on the job," by the experienced tugmasters available. Subsequently harbour training was conducted, also by the existing tugmasters, at the Campbeltown base and short Divisional Courses at the Naval Barracks, Portsmouth was arranged for new entrants.

The ranks of the seamen ratings were supplemented by recruitment from the fishing fleet and Merchant Navy generally, and in 1941 by the recruitment and training of young men specifically for the Rescue Tug fleet but as Hostilities Only ratings of the RN. This last category were men recruited and trained at the Campbeltown base, their training being tailored to suit the specific requirements of tugs. They replaced ratings drafted from General Service who could then be returned to RN service.

The Rescue Tug fleet was controlled by a Commander in Charge Rescue Tugs (CCRT) based at HMS NIMROD at Campbeltown who was responsible for the actual deployment of ships and personnel, discipline, training and organization. Spare crews were held initially at Campbeltown and later at HMS BADGER, the Harwich base. Subsequently pools of spare personnel were established at Gibraltar, St John's NF, Algiers, Malta and Colombo.

Rescue Tugs were initially based at suitable ports as near as possible to the Atlantic battlefield: Londonderry, Oban, Loch Ewe, etc. As the submarine war spread westward ships were based in Iceland and the main non-UK base, St John's NF. Tugs were also placed at Gibraltar and, after January 1943, Algiers and Malta. The few tugs based at Alexandria from June 1940 were controlled directly by the Commander-in-Chief Mediterranean Fleet. Finally, a number of vessels became available for service in the Indian Ocean and were based on Colombo under the control of the Eastern Fleet.

Initially Rescue Tugs were to respond to casualties, being sailed under the orders of the C-in-C Western Approaches. As more tugs became available the Allied Flag Officer in Newfoundland acquired some ships, HMS TENACITY being based at St John's NF for a long period. This base also had the use of several very efficient Canadian civilian operated ships.

As strength further increased the practice started of having a Rescue Tug accompany a convoy so that reaction to a casualty could be much more prompt. Such tugs were usually accompanied by a Rescue Trawler (ex A/S trawler) which could be detached with the tug and tow if required.

Rescue Tugs were also called upon to perform long-distance tows not necessarily connected with salvage. Thus a number of crews found themselves committed to the transit of floating docks, generally involving a tow of long duration probably at a speed of advance of some 3 knots. While not rescue work, it was nevertheless essential to the maritime war.

British and Empire Warships of the Second World War by Lenton, lists all Rescue Tug tonnage available in 1939 and built subsequently for the RN, plus a list of requisitioned units. It is clear from two Confidential Admiralty Fleet Orders on the subject that not all of this tonnage was regarded by the Admiralty as "Rescue Tugs" capable of such service. Furthermore, a number of the vessels listed in the CAFO were EMPIRE tugs that do not appear in Lenton's lists.

It is also apparent that the term "Rescue Tug" was frequently applied, both officially and in general terminology, to all naval-manned tugs even when employed purely on passage towing duty as opposed to assisting action and marine casualties. Indeed, there are occasions where the term has been applied at the highest level to a tug that was on passage in a convoy for overseas duty and assisted another vessel in the convoy after it had been damaged. Similarly the T 124T Agreement also seems to have been used to man all White Ensign tugs regardless of their official, operational designation.

It must be stressed, in this necessarily brief statement of the Rescue Tug organization, that however badly damaged a ship might be, if the hull (or portion thereof) could be brought into harbour then some part of the cargo might be saved. A repair, including if need be the construction of a new hull section, could return the ship to service, or major equipment be salved for use in new construction. This applied particularly to tanker tonnage; the construction of such ships made them difficult to sink (especially when in ballast). A salvaged hull could yield cargo, a repairable ship, save on the production of new engines and complex pumping systems or, at worst, become a static fuel hulk at a remote base.

For example, the tanker OHIO brought into Malta (admittedly by naval vessels, not tugs), so badly damaged that she sank after entry nevertheless yielded over 90% of her cargo for use in the island. The tanker DENBYDALE had her engines removed and incorporated in the tanker DERWENTDALE, while the tanker ATHELVISCOUNT, towed 750 miles in 10 days with her entire aft end and engine room destroyed, was rebuilt and traded for a further 15 years.

Such instances were numerous and the majority owed their success to the Rescue Tug service and crews, of whom little has been written and in consequence little remains known even to those who study the maritime war 1939-45.

During the war years, excluding all fishing vessels and all ships of under 500grt, 750 British, 140 American and 245 other Allied and neutral merchant vessels suffered major damage worldwide but were brought into port for repair. Some of this total of 1,135 ships required salvage activity after having been sunk in shallow water or beached. Almost all of the ships concerned involved the services of ocean-going tugs at some point in the recovery and transit to repair ports.

Courtesy K Macpherson

Far from a good photograph, but indicative of the difficulties and dangers of fuelling at sea in poor conditions. BEACONSTREET, a highly experienced escort oiler, is here seen re-fuelling by the astern method.

CHAPTER 15

REPLENISHMENT AT SEA

Today it is normal practice for the majority of fuel used by HM Ships to be transferred at sea and the term RAS (Replenishment At Sea) is used officially and is widely known.

Prior to 1939, however, the practice was hardly known in the RN. This was due to the fact that warships carried out strictly defined voyages and exercises and obtained their requirements of fuel and stores at one of the multiplicity of naval bases and depots available world-wide to the Royal Navy in those days. The problem of fuelling warships in wartime on distant stations, where fuelling in a neutral country was restricted to visits once every 90 days, was accepted. The problem was to be overcome by the provision of naval or naval controlled tankers who would transfer fuel to warships by berthing the recipient alongside in sheltered areas outside territorial waters, such methods and locations having been used since 1914. Where such opportunity was not available, then the accepted method was for the supplying vessel to pass a tow to the recipient who, while maintaining steerage way, would keep tension on the towline and receive the fuel via a delivery hose stopped in bights onto the tow.

The provision of buoyant hose, dispensing with the tow, was considered in the 1930s but finance for the development of the necessary equipment was not available. Indeed, the first buoyant hose in use in the RN was German, recovered from a captured supply ship in 1941. The first practical experience of properly equipped abeam refuelling was obtained in 1945 from US tankers in the Pacific and from the captured German tanker NORDMARK, renamed BULAWAYO, in the immediate postwar years.

An alternative method was for the ships supplying fuel to suspend the delivery hose from the jib of a crane with the hose supported in a sling, the outboard end being taken in by the receiving ship which steamed abeam. This method was used where large warships (capital ships and cruisers) equipped with aircraft cranes supplied smaller escorts. A sophisticated version is now, of course, the standard method of fuel supply at sea. However, mercantile tankers, even now at the end of the 20th century, are not usually fitted with cargo derricks and winches nor was it practicable to provide such sophisticated equipment during the war. There was therefore no alternative in 1941 when trans-Atlantic convoy with continuous escort became a necessity, than the occasional beam refuelling where derricks were available, or the improvisation based on the astern supply method mentioned.

The RFA tankers, whose crews had some experience of the crude 1930s system, were far too few, small and slow for the requirements so that a considerable program of adaptation of commercial tankers had to be undertaken. This consisted of supplying tankers with adequate towing gear, flexible hose and adapted piping or hose arrangements onboard to deliver fuel to a point right aft in the tanker, this not being a normal discharging position.

Providing the weather was suitable, not always the case in the North Atlantic, and that the crew of the tanker ensured that the tank from which fuel was to be

◼ Courtesy K Macpherson

Another astern fuelling, the ships unknown. The better weather conditions show more clearly the lead of the fuel hose and tow over the starboard quarter, and the roller fitted to protect the hose.

◼ Courtesy James Plomer

BEACONSTREET fuelling HMS HEATHER at sea by the abeam method. The crudity of the rig can clearly be seen, a simple hose suspended at only one point and subject to considerable stress in other than flat calm conditions. Fortunately these prevail in this case, but it illustrates why the method was little used in preference to the astern position.

drawn was adequately pre-heated to ensure a free flow of the bunker oil, then it was possible for the recipient escort to obtain fuel at a reasonable rate and adequate to "top up" during the passage of a convoy.

In the case of UK-bound convoys, the fuel was drawn from the normal cargo of tankers freighting furnace fuel oil (FFO as naval oil fuel was described), the tankers being designated as "escort oilers" in the convoy orders. For outward bound convoys, between 500 and 1,000 tons of FFO would be specifically embarked (or retained) by the tanker for the purpose of fuelling escorts. It is noteworthy that such tankers frequently remained with their colleague Escort Group, berthing at Londonderry or the Clyde. It is apparent indeed from the ships' movements that some tankers, after supplying the eastbound escort, discharged most of their cargo at Londonderry either to other escorts or the oiler lying off Moville. They only needed to call briefly at the oil terminal in the Clyde either to discharge the balance of the cargo less the 500 tons needed for the westbound crossing or, if complete discharge had occurred at Londonderry, to top up with the necessary amount to carry out their duty.

As the astern method was normally used, it became the practice for escort oilers to be stationed in the central columns of the convoy, with an empty berth astern of them, i.e. they would be second ship in the column with the next astern occupying the fourth position. An alternative was to station two tankers in the second position of two columns of three, with the central column consisting of the leading ship only. There was therefore adequate space for the recipient escort to steam up the empty column and for the tanker to move outward from its usual berth into the clear area for the fuelling operation.

Given the passage time of even the slowest convoys and the more basic rations issued in the period 1939-45, the supply of fresh provisions at sea was not considered necessary, as it is today. However, escorts routinely heavily used one item of stores and without it they were severely handicapped in their duties. There are many instances where escorts expended all their depth charges and were impotent in the face of further submarine attack.

To overcome this deficiency it became the practice for escorts to carry an excess of firing pistols, the hydrostatic fuses which initiate a depth charge's explosion, and for ships in the convoy to embark deck stores of unfused depth charges. Two methods of supply were used: a messenger line was passed to an escort steaming alongside, the charges suspended from a cargo derrick that was then swung out towards the escort to haul in the load; or, by lashing the depth charges to a float, hoisting them out and streaming them astern to be recovered by the escort. The former system was preferred by all parties.

Cargo ships routinely carried between 24 and 48 charges in racks arranged on either beam in its after well decks; tankers could carry 60 charges, occasionally more. Other than token supplies to test the organization on board ships, transfer was only made if escorts had expended a major proportion of their stowage. The ability to replenish did remove any inhibition that escort commanders might have felt in attacking even dubious contacts, or in prosecuting those regarded as positive, and the co-operation of merchant ships (many of them foreign flag vessels), and their crews was greatly appreciated.

It is worthy of note, in the present era of "one-stop" extremely expensive RFA replenishment vessels, that in 1943 it was quite usual for a tanker MAC ship to operate three A/S aircraft from a crude flight deck with no hangar facilities, to refuel escorts *and* to carry spare depth charges. All this was incidental to the delivery of a commercial cargo of liquid fuel. Indeed the reports of the Air Staff Officer of several MAC ships make it clear that it was not unknown for aircraft to be flown off during a refuelling operation when the necessity arose.

In the case of the OS and SL convoys to and from Freetown, certain tankers were allocated for the specific duty of replenishing the escorts. The tankers loaded in the UK, sailed in the southbound convoy and refuelled all the escorts at the appropriate point of the passage. On completion, the tanker transferred to a northbound SL convoy and repeated the process for that escort before detaching to Gibraltar where it topped up its tanks from supplies at that base. The pattern was then repeated, joining a southbound convoy to replenish the escort, then switching to a northbound convoy and return to the UK. In some cases, the tanker appears to have been based on Gibraltar for a considerable period on this duty.

Courtesy Robert Eakins

HMCS SMITHS FALLS, one of the later-construction RCN corvettes. She displays all the benefits of her late building (completed end Nov 1944): her late pattern 4-inch gun is mounted on a bandstand to assist in preventing washing-down in heavy seas, with rocket rails on each side of its shield for the Snowflake rocket illuminant. The Hedgehog mounting can be seen abaft and to starboard of the gun. The marked sheer to the hull and the foc's'le carried well aft is in contrast to the early-construction ships of both the RN and RCN.

CHAPTER 16
DEFENSIVELY EQUIPPED MERCHANT SHIPS

Traditionally, merchant ships may arm themselves and permit their non-combatant crews to use arms for the purpose of defending the ship against attack by either combatants or criminals without endangering their non-combatant status. This right is established in modern international law.

The Admiralty had laid aside, in depots in Britain and its dependent territories overseas, such surplus weapons and equipment as had survived the post-1918 disarmament process. The object was to be able to equip all vessels of the British Merchant Navy with adequate defensive means, specified as:

1. At least one low angle gun of 3, 4 or 6 inch calibre (dependent on the size of the vessel) mounted aft as a defence against surface attack.
2. A high angle weapon for defence against air attack, usually a 12pdr on a HA mounting.
3. One or more rifle calibre machine guns for defence against low level air attack.

The initial supply of weapons being very limited, many small ships in coastal waters received only machine guns, and then frequently on a loan basis, the guns being withdrawn when the ship moved to a less dangerous area.

As supply improved, the 20mm Oerlikon began to be allocated to merchant ships in lieu of lesser calibre weapons; some larger vessels also received the 40mm Bofors.

Strictly defensive items supplied were kite balloons and kites, designed to be flown as a barrage to deter low flying aircraft; "wiping" and "de-gaussing," (the former a temporary and the latter a permanent) defence against magnetic mines, and Admiralty Net Defence fitted to certain vessels as a partial protection against torpedoes. Paravane gear as a defence against moored contact mines was also fitted to many merchant ships.

Scientific measures included the fitting of Asdic to a limited number of ships, and High Frequency Direction Finding to detect and give warning of enemy wireless transmissions in the vicinity, and therefore of the possibility of attack.

There were also several devices provided in the early days whose principal purpose was the maintenance of morale; however, danger from the devices was more likely to the user than the intended recipient. These included the Holman Projector, with which a primed hand grenade would be ejected by steam pressure from a metal tube aimed at an aircraft, PAC (Parachute and Cable), a rocket-propelled device that ejected a small parachute with a dependent wire into the track of an approaching aircraft and "Pigtrough" which, both trainable and with variable elevation, launched a series of small rockets at a target. All this equipment, plus the work to the ships to fit it and the ratings to operate it, came under the generic term of DEMS, an acronym familiar to all merchant seamen of 1939-45.

The guns' crews were mainly naval, drawn from pensioners and young HO ratings entered for the period of the war and trained in the appropriate equipment. Their small number onboard was usually commanded by a NCO (Petty Officer, Sergeant Royal Marines or a Leading Seaman); only the larger ships would embark a junior naval officer. Both before the war, and as a continuing program, the RN undertook the training of large numbers of Merchant Navy officers and men who, in wartime, supplemented the DEMS gunners allocated to their ship.

The numbers of men involved was very large and eventually overwhelmed the RN system; even additional conscripts could not be handled by the training schools. The Army was therefore requested to assist in overcoming the shortage and did so, not by training naval gunners nor by transferring trained gunners to the Navy, but by raising the Maritime Regiment of Artillery to serve at sea alongside RN personnel. This compromise, unlikely though it may seem, worked very well and mixed DEMS crews of Navy, Army and Merchant Navy personnel were quite usual.

DEMS crews, always referred to as "gunners" by the Merchant Navy, were allocated as needed to ships from pools of men held available at the major ports. Their records and pay accounts were held centrally by their Service and were almost invariably devoid of any details as to where the men actually were.

On allocation to a ship, DEMS personnel were required to sign Ship's Articles in the same way as a merchant seaman, thereby becoming subject to the Master for discipline, and the responsibility of the ship owner for accommodation, food and advances of pay. The cost of food, and any advance of pay, was recouped from the Services in due course plus any adjustment for breakages, disciplinary offences etc. It will therefore be seen that the *only* satisfactory record of DEMS service rests in the Articles. While the Registrar of Seamen at Cardiff holds these, a prerequisite of access is that the name of the ship and dates of service are known. As this is usually the first information an inquirer wants, effective search is impossible as neither the Royal Navy nor the Army can supply such information other than in the most exceptional cases. While no doubt recorded at the time by the DEMS Officer at the appropriate base, these records do not seem to have survived the post-May 1945 euphoria, incredible though this may seem nowadays.

It is known that records were kept by the RCN for their DEMS ratings. In 1995 William A Cowling, a Canadian, published privately an account of his father's naval service as a DEMS gunner titled *1,413 Days In the Wake of a Canadian DEMS Gunner*, available under ISBN 0-9699212-0-9. The frontispiece is a copy of Cowling's service drafts, including merchant ships and dates. I have no doubt that a very similar document would have been kept by the RN. Regrettably, the likelihood of it having passed to the rating on demobilisation is slight; it is rare that any documents handed over to a man, such as his Service Certificate, have survived the fifty plus years since demobilisation.

DEMS personnel and their mercantile counterparts are little known and frequently ignored participants in the maritime war. Their contribution, both material and in morale, to the defence of the Merchant Navy is very great indeed and should never be overlooked by anyone studying the wartime service of the Allied merchant fleets.

Total personnel involved in DEMS work was large, peaking in 1944 when the approximate figures were 600 officers and 38,000 men of whom 24,000 were naval and 14,000 military. Additionally, over 150,000 merchant navy personnel received gunnery training during the war period.

DEMS casualties to the end of the European war were 2,731 naval killed and missing and 1,222 military killed and missing; 168 naval and 74 army personnel became prisoners of war. Merchant Navy casualties are, of course, included with the general MN figures; DEMS trained MN personnel were not separately identified in statistics.

Admiralty Net Defence

These notes are but a resumé of a great deal of research carried out by the late Lawrence Norbury-Williams, who had served at sea 1939-45 in some ships fitted with the system. His interest and depth of research was such that, given the materials, there is no doubt that he could have produced a working set of nets and onboard equipment. An abridged form of his research was printed in *Warship 1989*, published by Conway Maritime Press Ltd under ISBN 0-85177-530-6, which should be referred to for greater detail.

DEFENSIVELY EQUIPPED MERCHANT SHIPS

Courtesy K Macpherson (Hill Wilson Collection)
An unusual view of a new-construction freighter, either a FORT or a PARK built in Canada, testing the Admiralty Net Defence with which she is fitted. Note that the ship has yet to fit any armament, indicating that she is probably still in her builders' hands. The steel A frame forward is for the bow defence gear i.e. a paravane.

The introduction of the "locomotive torpedo" (the original title of what is now referred to simply as a torpedo), also initiated an ongoing search for preventive measures against such attack and protection against its results. An early expedient was the production of steel wire netting which, supported by a series of booms along each side of a major warship, provided a curtain covering some 90% of the ship's length when in the rigged position. Such protection could only be used when steaming very slowly and preferably when stationary. The objective of the net was to prevent penetration by the torpedo and impact with the hull of the ship.

The system, fitted to almost all large warships in the period 1880 to 1910, received little operational use, only the Russo-Japanese war providing an opportunity for true operational experience. Larger and faster torpedoes, and the general fitting of net cutters to the weapons, rendered the nets ineffective and all navies abandoned the system during the 1914-18 war.

The losses sustained in the 1915 unrestricted submarine campaign, and again in 1917-18, revived interest in net defence but this time for use by ships under way. The principle was not to prevent the torpedo passing through the net, but to entangle the missile during its passage, usually by its tail with the vulnerable vertical and horizontal rudders and propellers.

The use of lighter wire for the construction of the mesh negated the effect of net cutters, and the reduced weight of the net made its use at sea a viable proposition. With initial trials proposed by the Torpedo School based in HMS ACTAEON, the system became known as "Actaeon Net Defence." Successful trials were carried out in late 1917 and early 1918, but the Armistice removed the need for further development of the scheme.

In 1935, as part of the preparations for DEMS equipment, interest was revived in the system and some further experiments were carried out. In 1939 production and fitting of equipment to merchant

103

ships was considered but abandoned owing to the problems of operating the gear in oceanic conditions, although some trials were carried out by the AMC HMS QUEEN OF BERMUDA.

The losses of 1941 reopened interest, and improvements and simplification in design produced a system capable of use at sea under way, which was widely adopted. The nets were suspended from long booms on either beam which could be swung out and locked in position at right angles to the centre line of the ship. The nets, rolled up and stowed along the booms, were then unrolled and their head drawn along a stay connecting the head of the booms. Similarly, they could be brailed up and the booms stowed inboard while under way; a reduction of speed was required during both operations. The effect of streamed nets was to reduce the ships' speed by 17%; with the faster trade convoys steaming at 9.5 knots and most war built tonnage (to which the nets were fitted) capable of 11 to 12 knots, this was acceptable.

The amended system, known as "Admiralty Net Defence" (AND), was widely fitted to wartime construction and proved very effective. The coverage of the nets varied between 50 and 80% of the ship's length, dependent on the number and siting of the booms, so that the bow and stern inevitably remained at risk. However, the lethal area (and of course the main target), received considerable protection. There was also a considerable improvement in morale and confidence amongst crews in ships so fitted.

The US Maritime Commission used an almost identical system equally successfully, referred to as "Torpedo Net Defence."

Mk 29 EQUIPMENT

The principle of AND being the arresting of the passage of the torpedo, thereby preventing impact on the hull and explosion, it is not surprising that the USN conducted trials to achieve the same results by less cumbersome means.

The result was complex equipment theoretically effective but, in practical terms, somewhat of a nightmare. It consisted of two buoyant lines which, when streamed from booms forward, were towed parallel to the ships' hulls in a similar fashion to the AND. The lines each contained a series of explosive charges to be fired electrically from a console in the wheelhouse, the resultant explosion deflecting the torpedo from its course, or countermining its warhead prior to impact.

The problem of the equipment lay in the necessity of accurate judgement by the observing Officer as to which charge to fire and when. Obviously, darkness and weather conditions impeded vision and prevented accurate or indeed, any observation. That the majority of German naval torpedoes were electric and therefore left no track seems to have been ignored. Furthermore, the fact that a torpedo running at 40 knots at 20 feet depth is some 100 yards ahead of the apparent wake (if any), added to the problems of assessment of the time to fire.

Despite these drawbacks, effectively limiting its use to defence against aerial torpedoes (which did leave a wake and were usually launched in daylight hours), and a tendency on the part of the equipment to detonate spontaneously, usually while being streamed or recovered, a few successes were recorded.

Plastic armour

In the early days of the war, with merchant ships lacking effective AA armament, low-level attacks by aircraft became common and all too easily could render a ship helpless by wrecking the bridge and killing key personnel. Also the Master's quarters and W/T office were usually adjacent to or beneath the bridge and the entire structure was, at best, of light steel construction or even timber, affording no protection against bomb splinters or machine gun attack.

The obvious counter of plating vital, exposed positions in armour was not possible for several reasons: lack of armour plate, far greater priority for its use by the Services and possible stability problems and most important of all, the effect on the magnetic compass which was a standard item in almost all merchant ships.

The widely used alternative that was developed became known as "plastic armour" and was used to panel the exterior of bridge structures, exposed gun positions, W/T offices and the like. The material was composed of a mixture of bitumen and granite chippings, almost identical to road surfacing material, formed into sheets or panels. Its resistance to penetration lay in its ability to absorb energy on impact (by the bitumen), and the retarding and deflecting effect of the granite chips.

Merchant Navy crews were initially inclined to regard the material with the gravest reservations, if not open derision, and its proponents and those fitting it were able to overcome that outlook only by practical demonstration. This consisted of several rounds of .303 rifle fire at a target placed on a light steel plate resulting in penetration of both plate and target. The fact that armour-piercing rounds were used was not mentioned.

The second demonstration, against a paper target applied to the "armour" by means of drawing pins stuck into the bitumen, also involved firing five rounds of .303 ammunition at close range, this time standard ammunition. Critics were generally silenced when the expended bullets of the second demonstration were dug out with a penknife and passed around for examination!

The "armour" was an extraordinarily effective and economic means of protection, easily produced and fitted and providing both physical and morale protection to crews.

Asdic in merchant ships

Asdic was the acronym used by the Royal Navy, prior to 1943, to indicate the means of locating a submerged submarine; the system is now known by the US term Sonar.

Basically, Asdic consisted of a means of transmitting ultrasonic sound, the reception of reflected echoes and the provision of a highly trained operator with excellent hearing to interpret the results. The last requirement was essential to efficient operation.

Having a very sensitive receiver, Asdic could also be used in the "passive" mode simply as a hydrophone and provide accurate information on the bearing and course of engine-driven objects. By this means, warning of torpedoes running (and whether or not the weapon was aimed at the receiving ship), was possible.

It is now common to use the sophisticated sonar of the 1990s in the "passive" mode, i.e. listening to sounds other than the sonar transmitter and its return signal. The method was little used in 1939-45 except as a defensive measure.

Certain war-built merchant ships, usually in the over-15-knot cargo liner category, were fitted with a simple form of Asdic purely for this purpose. As no provision appears to have been made for RN ratings of the SD specialisation to be embarked, it must be assumed that ships' officers, possibly Radio Officers, operated the equipment.

Unfortunately, no statistics have been found indicating the success of this measure. It would only have been effective when the ship was steaming independently, i.e. without other distracting noises. Attack in such instances after 1943, at which time the first Asdic fitted merchant ships appeared, was less common than previously, possibly leading to the absence of comment on the efficiency of the equipment.

Courtesy K Macpherson

HMS VANQUISHER after her conversion to Long Range Escort. The date of the photograph is indeterminate. The LRE conversion has taken place as she has lost the fore funnel, A and Y guns, and that re-building took place at Portsmouth Dockyard from Sept 1942 to the end of Apr 1943. However she has still not received 20mm Oerlikon nor Hedgehog in A position. The photograph cannot therefore have been taken in Halifax in 1942 as originally captioned. It was possibly taken while, during her refit in Feb 1943, she carried out trials of the Asdic Type 147Q; fitting Hedgehog later. At this stage she is also still fitted with the old Mk II throwers.

CHAPTER 17
CASUALTIES

Personnel

There are problems in assessing merchant seaman casualties during the conflict, arising from the fact that some deaths occurred of British seamen serving in foreign vessels or those requisitioned by the Royal Navy. However, the total fatal casualties notified to the Registrar General from 3 September 1939 to 31 August 1945 were 29,180 plus 814 men lost in fishing vessels. These figures include foreign seamen serving in British ships and British seamen serving in foreign ships chartered to or requisitioned by H M Government.

The 2,176 British ships, excluding fishing vessels, lost in the war and the annual totals of ships, total crews and casualties for those ships are shown below. The figures used are those kept by Trade Division of Admiralty and differ from the Registrar General's statistics. Foreign seamen possibly account for the discrepancy in total deaths in British ships.

Year	Ships lost by S/M attack	Ships lost by all causes	Total of crew and DEMS in ships lost by S/M attack	Total of crew & DEMS in ships lost by all causes	Deaths caused by S/M attack	Total deaths
1939	50	95	2,361	3,857	260	495
1940	225	512	11,285	22,923	3,375	5,622
1941	288	569	14,426	25,345	5,632	7,838
1942	452	590	28,259	36,200	8,413	9,736
1943	203	266	13,104	17,412	3,826	4,606
1944	67	101	4,440	5,916	1,163	1,510
1945	26	43	1,322	1,983	189	322
Total	1,311	2,176	75,197	113,636	22,858	30,129

Ships

Ship casualties are also ambiguous as some statistics use as a basis "ships of all tonnages" while others record only those exceeding 100 gross registered tons. Listed below in the first table, by calendar year, are the numbers of merchant ships, British, Allied and neutral lost by varying types of enemy action and in the second table, also by calendar year, those losses occurring due to marine causes.

The second category might be assumed to cover the normal hazards of maritime trade, but it must be borne in mind that collision in particular was a hazard increased by the close proximity of ships in convoy. This was compounded by the fact that ships steamed "darkened ship," i.e. no lights of any nature visible including steaming lights, and that the risk of foundering was higher due to the unusual cargoes carried and stowage not normal to trade e.g. large deck cargoes. Casualties were increased partly by the almost complete absence of navigational lights (lighthouse, light vessels and most buoys) and also by ships being obliged to sail in conditions where, in peacetime, a prudent seaman would have delayed his passage.

Year	By S/M	By mine	By surface attack	By aircraft	Other causes	Total
1939	103	83	15	10	4	215
1940	440	201	96	177	78	992
1941	429	108	102	323	167	1,129
1942	1,155	48	85	143	139	1,570
1943	462	37	10	76	10	595
1944	132	25	13	19	8	197
1945	54	19	5	5	5	88
Total	2,775	521	326	753	411	4,786

NOTES

1. "Surface ships" in the above table covers, in fact, three disparate types. Initially the losses were caused by the operation of conventional, large units in oceanic cruises, particularly the so-called "pocket battleships," later 8" gun cruisers and the battlecruisers GNEISENAU and SCHARNHORST. These ships were later supplemented and eventually replaced by disguised mercantile conversions normally referred to as "raiders" in British terminology; in fact, Armed Merchant Cruisers with the offensive features concealed and in some cases of considerable complexity. The final part of the equation was the *Schnellboote,* referred to by British sources (including official ones) as "E-boats." They were, in RN terminology, motor torpedo boats and were of extremely effective design, operated by highly skilled crews and used both for torpedo attack and as covert minelayers.

2. "Other causes" covers a variety of headings and a detailed analysis would undoubtedly allocate many of them to one of the other categories, particularly submarines. However, in a number of cases the cause of loss can only be guessed at, hence the category. Also included in this subtotal are ships seized in occupied ports, loss incidental to destruction of another vessel e.g. explosion of an ammunition ship and other unusual causes.

Losses by marine causes of ships over 100 grt

Year	Foundered	Overdue presumed lost	Fire & explosion	Collision	Wrecked	Total
1939	11	11	10	14	62	108
1940	47	43	30	74	162	356
1941	61	17	48	59	112	297
1942	42	9	48	59	132	290
1943	62	5	26	42	102	237
1944	55	8	40	44	99	246
1945	29	2	24	20	33	108
Total	307	95	226	312	702	1,642

The heading of "overdue (and) presumed lost" can also be misleading in that detailed investigation will reveal that submarines sank some of these ships or, possibly, surface raiders. The subsequent loss of an enemy submarine prior to an attack report, and the ambiguity of certain Japanese records, renders this section difficult to analyse. The loss of a ship due to war causes rather than marine causes is difficult to attribute properly in the absence of enemy records and survivors.

APPENDIX 1

ALPHABETICAL LIST OF CONVOY CODES

AB	Two "one off" convoys of early date (one from August 1939!).
AB	Commenced in Sept 1942, Aden to Bombay.
ABF	The Fast, i.e. troopship, successor to AB, Aden to Bombay.
AC	A 1941 series, Alexandria to Cyrenaica i.e. Tobruk.
AG	Alexandria to Greece, a 1941 series.
AH	Aruba to Halifax, a brief tanker series in 1942.
AH	Augusta to Heel of Italy, post Sept 1943.
AJ	Aden to Colombo. "J" probably refers to Jaffna.
AK	Aden to Kilindini, commenced in 1942.
AKD	Aden to Kilindini and Durban.
AM	Chittagong to Madras.
AN	Aegean Northward, i.e. Alexandria to Piraeus 1940 & 1941.
AN	A Pacific series, Admiralty Islands to New Guinea.
AP	The early troop convoys UK to Egypt in mid 1940.
ARG	Boston to Argentia—USN convoys.
ARM	A local Mediterranean code, little used.
AS	Aegean Southward, i.e. Piraeus to Alexandria 1940 & 1941.
AS	America to Suez, convoys New York to Suez via Freetown in 1942.
AT	Alexandria to Tobruk commencing late 1941.
AT	USA to UK troopship series 1942-45.
ATM	Antwerp to Thames, a late 1944 & 1945 series.
AW	Aruba to Curacao (Willemstad) local tanker traffic.
BA	Bombay to Aden, reversal of AB.
BAF	Bombay to Aden Fast, troopships, reverse of ABF.
BB	Belfast to Bristol Channel 1940 to 1943.
BB	Clyde to Bristol Channel 1945.
BC	Beira to Durban, probably coded as Beira-Cape.
BC	Bristol Channel to Biscay, outward & return carried same number.
BD	White Sea to Dikson Sept 1943 onward, new numbers each year.
BEC	The retitled EBC series—qv.
BF	Bahia, Brazil to Freetown, a US series from 1943.
BG	A Pacific series, Milne Bay to New Guinea.
BG	A Pacific series, Brisbane to Gladstone.
BHX	Bermuda to rendezvous with the same number HX convoy.
BK	A little used Bombay to Karachi series in 1943.
BK	White Sea to Kola Inlet Sept 1943 onward, new numbers each year.
"Blue"	The early Port Said to Gibraltar convoys of 1939.
BM	Bombay to Singapore to Jan 42 then Bombay/Colombo traffic.
BN	Bombay Northward, (Bombay to Suez, then Aden to Suez), 1940-41.
BN	A later, Pacific, series, New Britain to New Guinea.
BP	Bombay to Persian Gulf.
BRN	Bahia, Brazil, Recife Northward.
BS	Suez to Aden late 1940 and early 1941.
BS	A brief Canadian series Corner Brook to Sydney CB.
BS	French convoys Brest to Casablanca 1939-40.
BT	Bahia, Brazil to Trinidad commenced Jan 1943.
BT	Sydney NSW to USA troop convoys 1943-44.
BT	Brisbane to Townsville.
BTC	Bristol Channel to Thames 1944-45.
BV	A Pacific series, Brisbane to Townsville.
BW	Sydney CB to St John's NF commenced 1942.
BX	Boston to Halifax.
BZ	Proposed Bombay-Kilindini-Aden series, not used.
C	Colombo to dispersal, 1942 series.
CA	Capetown southward to dispersal.
CB	Durban to Beira.
CD	Capetown to Durban.
CE	Channel Eastward i.e. St Helens Roads to Southend.
CF	Capetown to W Africa and UK, a little used series.
CF	Colombo to Fremantle, occasional use only.
CG	Casablanca to Gibraltar.

CH	Chittagong to Calcutta.
CJ	Calcutta to Colombo.
CK	Havana (Cuba) to Key West.
CK	Charleston SC to UK, rarely used 1944 series.
CL	St John's NF to Sydney CB.
CM	Capetown Military, Capetown-Kilindini-Aden.
CN	Capetown Northward to dispersal.
CNF	Special designation for Sicily invasion.
CO	Newcastle, NSW to Melbourne & Adelaide in 1942.
COC	Late 1944 early 1945 Plymouth to Brittany series.
CP	Curacao to Panama, 1942 series.
CRD	Casablanca to Dakar.
CT	UK to Canada troopship series in 1941.
CT	Corsica-Sardinia-Bizerta series in 1944.
CU	Curacao-UK tanker series, New York to UK after CU 9.
CV	Cyrenaica to Valetta, rarely used, 1944.
CW	Cristobal to Key West.
CW	Channel Westward i.e. Southend to St Helens Roads.
CX	Colombo to Addu Atoll, both outward and return passages.
CZ	Curacao to Cristobal (Canal Zone).
D	Dakar to Casablanca.
DB	Dikson to White Sea from 1942, new numeration for each year.
DBF	Dakar-Bathurst-Freetown, 1943 series.
DC	Durban to Capetown.
DF	Clyde to Faroes, military ferry service.
DG	Thursday Island to Merauke, New Guinea.
DK	Durban to Kilindini.
DKA	Durban-Kilindini-Aden.
DLM	Durban to Lourenco Marques.
DM	Durban to Malaya, 1941-42, three convoys only.
DN	Durban Northwards to dispersal.
DR	Dakar to Gibraltar, 1944 series.
DRC	Dakar to Casablanca.
DS	Clyde to Reykjavik, military ferry service.
DSF	Dakar to Freetown.
DSL	Dakar to Freetown & Lagos.
DSP	Dakar to Freetown & Pointe Noire.
DST	Dakar to Freetown & Takoradi.
DT	Darwin to Thursday Island.
DWI	Dutch West Indies to UK, proposed in 1943, not used.
E	Trinidad to dispersal southward.
EBC	Bristol Channel coastal convoy to France June to Oct 1944.
EBM	Bristol Channel MT convoy to France June 1944.
EC	Southend to Oban via Firth of Forth, 1941.
ECM	Falmouth to France June/early July 1944.
ECP	Portland & Solent Personnel convoys to Seine Bay June to Oct 1944.
EMM	Two convoys Belfast to France June/July 1944.
EMP	Two personnel convoys Belfast to France July 1944.
EN	Methil to Oban via Loch Ewe. Two series, interrupted by EC.
EPM	Portland to France via Solent MT convoys July to Sept 1944.
EPP	Portland to France via Solent personnel convoys July to Sept 1944.
ET	North Africa to Gibraltar, Nov 1942 to early 1943.
ETC	Thames to France coaster convoys June to Oct 1944.
ETM	Thames to France MT convoys June to Oct 1944.
EWC	Spithead to Normandy beaches, coaster convoys June 1944
EWL	Isle of Wight to France convoys, mainly landing ships & craft June 1944.
EWM	Isle of Wight to France MT convoys Sept and Oct 1944.
EWP	Isle of Wight to France personnel convoys.
EXP	June to Oct 1944 invasion series.
FB	Freetown to Bahia, Brazil.
FBC	Seine Bay to Bristol Channel coaster convoys June to Oct 1944.
FD	Faroes to Clyde, military ferry.
FC	France to W of England convoy series June/July 1944.
FCP	France to W of England personnel convoys June/July 1944.
FFT	Freetown to Trinidad 1942 to 1943.
FG	Fremantle to Adelaide, 1942 onward.
FH	Saint John NB to Halifax, late 1942 onward.
FJ	Florianopolis to Rio de Janeiro.
FM	Milne Bay to Port Moresby.
FN	Forth North, Thames to Firth of Forth 1939 to 1945.

FP	Troop convoys to Norway Apr/May 1940.	HG	Homeward from Gibraltar 1939-42.
FPM	France to Portland MT convoys, invasion series.	HGF	Homeward from Gibraltar Fast.
FPP	France to Portland personnel convoys July/Aug 1944.	HHX	Halifax ships joining HX convoys which originated at New York.
FS	Forth South, Firth of Forth to Thames 1939 to 1945.	HJ	Halifax to St John's, NF.
		HK	Galveston (Houston) to Key West.
FSD	Freetown to Dakar, small craft 1944.	HM	Holyhead to Milford Haven.
FTC	France to Thames coaster convoys 1944.	HN	Homeward from Norway i.e. Bergen to Methil 1939-40.
FTM	France to Thames MT convoys 1944.		
FWC	France to Isle of Wight coaster convoys June 1944.	HON	Ships joining, from Halifax NS, a NYC-bound ON convoy.
FWL	France to Isle of Wight landing craft convoys 1944.	HP	Heel of Italy to Piraeus.
		HS	Halifax to Sydney CB.
FWM	France to Isle of Wight MT convoys June/July 1944.	HT	Halifax to Trinidad preceded HA.
		HX	Halifax to UK, later New York City to UK.
FWP	France to Isle of Wight personnel convoys June/Sept 1944.	HXA	English Channel section of HX 1939-40 & 1944-45.
FXP	France to UK invasion series June to Oct 1944.	HXF	Halifax to UK, Fast 1939-40 only.
		IG	Philippines to New Guinea.
G	Guantanamo to San Juan PR.	IXF	Italy (Taranto & Naples) to Alexandria & Pt Said.
GAT	Guantanamo-Aruba-Trinidad.		
GB	New Guinea to Milne Bay.	JA	Colombo to Aden.
GC	Gibraltar to Casablanca.	JC	Colombo to Calcutta.
GD	Merauke to Thursday Island.	JF	Rio de Janeiro to Florianopolis.
GF	Adelaide to Fremantle.	JG	Kingston, Jamaica to Guantanamo.
GI	New Guinea to Philippines.	JH	St John's NF to Halifax NS.
GJ	Guantanamo to Kingston, Jamaica.	JM	India to Madagascar via Mombasa 1943 only.
GK	Guantanamo to Key West.	JMG	Assault convoy for Malaya Sept 1945.
GM	Gibraltar to Malta.	JN	St John's, NF to Labrador.
GM	Galveston to Mississippi.	JR	Rio de Janeiro to Recife.
GN	Guantanamo to New York City.	JS	Colombo to Singapore Nov 41 to Feb 42.
GP	Guantanamo to Panama.	JT	Rio de Janeiro to Trinidad, 1943-45.
GP	Sydney NSW to Townsville and Brisbane.	JW	UK to North Russia. Replaced PQ.
"Green"	Gibraltar to Port Said, late 1939.	K	Casablanca to Brest, sometimes suffixed F or S.
GREYBACK	Dieppe-Newhaven ferry service.		
GS	Greenland to Sydney CB or St John's NF.	KA	Kilindini to Aden.
GS	Humber (Grimsby) to Southend 1940.	KB	Kola Inlet to White Sea, fresh numeration annually.
GT	Gladstone to Townsville.		
GTX	Gibraltar-Tripoli-Alexandria 1943 only.	KM	Karachi to Bombay.
GUF	Oran or Naples to USA Fast.	KD	Kilindini to Durban.
GUS	Port Said to USA Slow.	KG	Key West to Guantanamo.
GZ	Guantanamo to Canal Zone 1942 onward.	KH	Key West to Galveston (Houston).
HA	Halifax to Curacao 1942 only.	KJ	Kingston, Jamaica to UK, 1940, also KJF.
HA	Heel of Italy to Augusta 1943 onwards.	KM	Kilindini to Diego Suarez (Madagascar).
HB	Troop convoys Australia to India 1945.	KMF	UK to Mediterranean Fast Nov 1942 onward.
HC	Calcutta to Chittagong.	KMS	UK to Mediterranean Slow Nov 1942 onward.
HF	Halifax to Saint John, NB.		

KN	Key West to New York City.
KP	Key West to Pilottown, Mississippi.
KP	Karachi to Persian Gulf.
KP	Kola Inlet to Petsamo 1944-45, fresh numbers annually.
KR	Kilindini to Ceylon.
KR	Calcutta and Arakan ports to Rangoon 1945.
KS	Key West South, i.e. New York to Key West.
KS	Variation on the French K series.
KW	Key West to Havana.
KX	UK to Gibraltar Oct 42 onward.
LC	Sydney CB to St John's NF.
LE	Levant East i.e. Port Said to Haifa.
LGE	Lagos Eastbound, local West African traffic.
LGW	Lagos Westbound, local West African traffic.
LM	Lagos to Matadi.
LMD	Lourenco Marques to Durban.
LN	St Lawrence to Labrador.
LQ	Barrier Reef to Brisbane.
LS	Lagos to Freetown.
LSD	Lagos to Dakar via Freetown.
LTS	Lagos-Takoradi-Freetown.
LU	Humber to Elbe, May 1945.
LW	Levant West i.e. Haifa to Port Said.
MA	Mombasa to Aden.
MA	Madras to Chittagong 1943.
MB	Colombo to Bombay.
MB	Port Moresby to Fall River.
MC	Aden-Mombasa-Durban-Capetown.
MD	Madagascar to Durban, one convoy only.
ME	Malta East, i.e. Malta to Alexandria & Port Said.
MF	Port Moresby to Milne Bay & Fall River.
MG	Malta to Gibraltar.
MG	Mississippi to Galveston.
MH	Milford Haven to Holyhead.
MK	Madagascar to Kilindini.
MKF	Mediterranean to UK Fast Nov 1942 onward.
MKS	Mediterranean to UK Slow Nov 1942 onward.
MN	Mauritius to Seychelles.
MO	Marseilles to North Africa.
MR	Madras to Rangoon.
MS	Melbourne to Singapore Nov 41 to Feb 42.
MS	Marseilles to Naples 1944 to1945.
MT	Methil to Tyne 1940 & 1941.
MT	Port Moresby to Townsville 1942.
MTC	Seine Bay to Southend, replacing FTC.
MTM	Seine Bay to Southend, replacing FTM.
MV	Milne Bay to Townsville.
MW	Malta Westward, Alexandria to Malta.
NA	Canada to UK troop convoys.
NA	Langemak Bay, New Guinea to Admiralty Islands.
NAP	A southbound series, mainly from Dover to France Dec 44.
NB	New Guinea to New Britain.
NC	Walvis Bay to Capetown 1943.
NCF	Fast Sicily invasion convoys 1943.
NCS	Slow Sicily invasion convoys 1943.
NE	New Zealand to Panama.
NG	New York City to Guantanamo.
NJ	Newfoundland coast to St John's NF.
NK	New York City to Key West.
NL	Labrador to St Lawrence.
NLY	Lingayen/Hollandia/Leyte convoys.
NP	Norwegian troop convoys Apr-May 1940.
NP	Turkey to Port Said.
NR	Norway to Methil, 1945.
NS	New Caledonia to Sydney NSW.
NSF	North African ports to Naples, troop convoys.
NT	New Guinea to Townsville.
NV	Naples to Augusta.
NYC	New York City to UK via Bermuda & E Coast USA ports.
OA	Thames to Liverpool, with an Atlantic element 1939 to July 1940. After July 1940, Methil to Liverpool northwards, to disperse in North Atlantic, sometimes after juncture with OB of same number.
OB	Liverpool outward, usually joined by the OA of same number.
OC	Melbourne to Newcastle, NSW.
OG	Outward to Gibraltar from UK.
OM	Oran to Marseilles, 1944 series.
ON	Outward to Norway, Methil to Bergen, in 1939-40.
ON	Outward North. Liverpool etc to North America 1941 onwards.
ON(F)	Alternate convoys of the ON sequence (see above).
ON(S)	Alternate convoys of the ON sequence (see above).
ONS	Outward North Slow, Liverpool etc to North America 1943 onwards.
OS	Outward Southbound, Liverpool etc to Freetown 1941 onwards.

Code	Description
OSS	Southward extension of OS from Freetown.
OT	Outward Trinidad. Two series, one local Caribbean, one to North Africa.
OW	Outward Westward, Australia/India, numbers re-used.
PA	Persian Gulf to Aden.
PB	Persian Gulf to Bombay.
PG	Brisbane to Sydney NSW.
PG	Panama to Guantanamo, 1942 series.
PGE	Pointe Noire southward, local traffic.
PH	Piraeus to Heel of Italy.
PK	Pilottown, Mississippi to Key West.
PN	Port Said Northbound to Turkey.
PQ	Iceland to North Russia, 1941 and 1942.
PQ	Townsville to Port Moresby 1942.
PR	Piraeus to Rabbit Island (Dardanelles), 1945.
PAD	Pointe Noire-Freetown-Dakar.
PT	Paramaribo to Trinidad.
PT	Pearl Harbor to Tarawa.
PTS	Pointe Noire-Takoradi-Freetown.
PV	Melbourne to Townsville.
PW	Portsmouth-Wales.
QL	Brisbane to Townsville.
QP	North Russia to Iceland 1941-42.
QS	Quebec to Sydney CB.
RA	North Russia to Iceland, later UK 1942-45. Replaced QP.
RB	A single convoy of small passenger liners USA to UK 1942.
"Red"	Early Gibraltar to Far East convoy.
RJ	Recife to Rio de Janeiro.
RK	Rangoon to Arakan and Calcutta, 1945.
RK	Colombo to Kilindini, 1944.
RM	Rangoon-Madras-Colombo, 1945.
RN	Methil to Norway, May 1945.
RP	Dardanelles (Rabbit Island) to Piraeus, 1945.
RS	Gibraltar to Freetown 1943.
RT	Capetown to Freetown, 1941.
RT	Recife to Trinidad, 1943.
RU	Reykjavik to Loch Ewe, later Belfast. 1941-45.
SB	Sydney CB to Corner Brook from 1942.
SBF) SBM)	Assault convoys for Sicily invasion.
SC	Sydney CB later Halifax or New York to UK. Commenced 1941.
SD	Iceland to Clyde, military ferry service.
SD	Seychelles to Diego Suarez, 1944.
SG	Southend to Humber (Grimsby) 1940.
SG	Sydney CB later St John's NF to Greenland, 1942 onwards.
SH	Sydney CB to Halifax.
SHX	Sydney CB component joining HX convoys.
SILVERTIP	Newhaven-Dieppe ferry service.
SJ	San Juan PR to Guantanamo.
SJ	Singapore to Colombo, Nov 41 to Feb 42.
SJ	Santos to Rio de Janeiro.
SL	Freetown to UK.
SLF	Freetown to UK Fast.
SLS	Freetown to UK Slow.
SM	Batavia to Fremantle, Dec 41 to Feb 42.
SM	Naples to Marseilles, 1944.
SN	Sydney NSW to New Caledonia.
SNF	South from Naples, Fast troopships Naples to North Africa.
SQ	Sydney CB to Quebec.
SR	Sandheads (Calcutta) to Rangoon 1941-42.
SR	Freetown to Gibraltar 1943-44.
ST	Freetown to Takoradi.
ST	Sydney NSW to Townsville 1943.
STC	Freetown-Takoradi-Capetown.
STL	Freetown-Takoradi-Lagos.
STP	Freetown-Takoradi-Pointe Noire.
STW	Freetown-Takoradi-Walvis Bay.
SU	Suez to Australia 1940-41.
SV	Sydney NSW to Townsville.
SW	Suez to Mombasa or Durban, 1940-41.
T	Hollandia to Manila.
TA	UK to USA, large troopships.
TA	Tobruk to Alexandria.
TAC	Thames to Ostend 1945.
TACA	Thames to Antwerp, later retitled TAM.
TAG	Trinidad-Aruba-Guantanamo 1942 onwards.
TAM	Thames to Antwerp Military, retitled from TAC qv.
TAP	Thames to France 1945.
TAW	Trinidad-Curacao-Key West 1942.
TB	Trinidad to Bahia, Brazil.
TBC	Thames to Bristol Channel, 1944-45.
TC	Troops from Canada, troop convoys to UK 1939-41.
TC	Tunisia to Corsica, 1943-44.

Code	Description
TCU	Occasional CU convoys containing troopships.
TD	Thursday Island to Darwin.
TD	New Zealand to Northern Australia.
TE	Trinidad Eastward to dispersal.
TE	Torch Eastward, Gibraltar to North Africa 1943.
TF	Trinidad to Freetown.
TG	Trinidad to Guantanamo.
TGE	Takoradi, Lagos Eastward to dispersal.
TH	Trinidad to Halifax 1942.
TJ	Trinidad to Rio de Janeiro.
TJF) TJM) TJS)	Assault convoys for Sicilian invasion.
TLDM	Takoradi-Lagos-Duala-Matadi. The longest purely alpha code.
TM	Norwegian troop convoys Apr-May 1940 only.
TM	Trinidad to Mediterranean 1942.
TMC	The retitled ETC series–qv.
TMM	The retitled ETM series–qv.
TN	Townsville to New Guinea.
TO	North Africa to Caribbean.
TO	Trinidad to Curacao.
TP	Troop convoy from Norway to UK May 1940.
TP	Trinidad to Paramaribo.
TP	Tarawa to Pearl Harbor.
TR	Trinidad to Recife.
TRINIDAD	Trinidad to dispersal southeast.
TS	Takoradi to Freetown.
TS	Townsville to Sydney NSW & Brisbane.
TSD	Takoradi-Freetown-Dakar.
TSF) TSM) TSS)	Assault convoys for Naples landings.
TU	UK to USA military convoys, reversal of UT.
TV	Tripoli (Libya) to Valetta.
TX	Tripoli (Libya) to Alexandria.
UA	UK to Azores, three convoys to occupy the islands in 1943.
UC	UK to New York, reversal of CU. Occasionally a T suffix.
UGF	USA to Gibraltar, later Naples, started Nov 1942.
UGL	USA to Gibraltar, landing craft convoys.
UGS	USA to Gibraltar, later Port Said Nov 42-May 45.
UL	Elbe to Humber post May 1945.
UR	Loch Ewe (later Belfast) to Reykjavik (Iceland),
US	Australia to Suez. US 3 diverted to UK via Cape.
UT	USA to UK troop convoys 1943-44.
VB	Townsville to Brisbane.
VC	Valetta to Cyrenaica 1943-44.
VK	Sydney NSW to Wellington.
VN	Augusta to Naples, also used for Malta to Naples, late 1944 Naples to Leghorn
VS	Townsville to Sydney NSW.
VT	Valetta to Tripoli, Libya.
WA	Curacao to Aruba.
WAP	Oct to Dec 1944 invasion series.
WAT	Key West-Curacao-Trinidad.
WDC	Sept to Dec 1944 invasion series.
WEC	Isle of Wight to France Dec 1944 to May 1945.
WEL	Isle of Wight to France, landing craft 1944-45.
WEP	Isle of Wight to Cherbourg series, Dec 1944.
WFM	Oct and Nov 1944 invasion series.
WMP	Isle of Wight to Arromanches Nov & Dec 1944.
WN	Clyde, Oban & Loch Ewe to Firth of Forth.
WNC	Isle of Wight to Havre Dec 1944 to May 1945.
WNL	Isle of Wight to France Apr to May 1945.
WO	India to Australia troop convoys.
WP	Wales-Portsmouth i.e. Milford Haven to Solent.
WS	Wabana to Sydney CB.
WS	UK to Suez and Bombay, troop convoys 1940-43.
WTS	Walvis Bay-Takoradi-Freetown.
WVP	Isle of Wight to France Dec 1944 to May 1945.
WX	Western Desert ports to Alexandria.
XB	Halifax to Boston.
XIF	Alexandria & Port Said-Italy (Taranto & Naples).
XK	Gibraltar to UK.
XT	Alexandria to Tripoli (Libya).
XTG	Alexandria-Tripoli-Gibraltar 1943 only.
XW	Alexandria to Western Desert ports.
ZC	Cristobal to Curacao.
ZG	Cristobal to Guantanamo.
ZT	New Zealand to Sydney NSW.

APPENDIX 2

CONVOY STATISTICS

The tables that follow set out the number of convoys in each calendar year for each series, or group of series, detailed in the individual headings. Each year contains those convoys that completed their voyages on or before 31 December.

Numbers of ships quoted are the total that completed the voyage, or would have done so except for loss, i.e. numbers do NOT include ships which sailed but returned to the port of origin or another port in the same area. They are the statistics used by Trade Division.

Straggler losses are an obvious term (but see the previous detailed definition of "straggler"), and the Admiralty regarded such losses as effectively independent ships. Losses "out of convoys" are of ships which had been detached (for whatever reason) and were subsequently lost, ships lost after the dispersal of the convoy, or lost in the absence of an escort. However, in the Convoy Data Tables in Appendix 3 for the HX and SL series two convoys, HX 77 and SL 64S, are shown with major losses. These do so as, in the author's opinion, they are significant and should be so recorded.

Wherever possible ships lost due to marine causes WHILST IN THE CONVOY, and which can be attributed to the circumstances of the convoy rather than true accident, have been included in the "Convoy losses" section.

Students of Operation Torch will note that the losses of US vessels involved in the initial convoys are omitted. The action leading to these losses took place when the ships were lying in a relatively open anchorage after the arrival of the convoys, and has been omitted deliberately.

The initial group of tables is of the North Atlantic convoys and reference to Appendix A will indicate those series that might, statistically, be linked, for example HX, SC and CU for North America to UK.

Where convoys entered the Mediterranean, e.g. the UG and KM series and their reversals, figures quoted are for the ATLANTIC PASSAGE ONLY. Because of the numerous ports of arrival and departure and consequent joiners and leavers in the Mediterranean, meaningful figures for that sea cannot be provided.

The second group of tables is for the United Kingdom coastal convoy system. Here the convoys have been paired so that, for example, the north and southbound East Coast convoy tables follow one another. Also, convoys in the same area appear close to their fellows, thus the EC and MT series that also operated on part of the East Coast, follow the FS/FN series.

Great care should be taken in interpreting the tables, especially in the coastal series. It has not, for example, been possible to isolate the ship and loss figures for the coastal voyages of the OA series that, prior to July 1940, would be grouped with the Channel convoys and after July 1940, with the Methil to Oban series.

Similarly, the BB figures are obviously, from the years listed, two separate series with 1940-43 being subject only to air attack and 1945 to submarine. A further complication in this series, for all years, is that the western UK component of the outward OB (after Aug 1940) and ON convoys proceeded on the same route as BB, HM and MH under the designation OBM and ONM. Separate figures for number of convoys, ships and losses are unclear.

Finally, the Channel figures for late 1944 and 1945 are also greatly distorted by the fact that the Thames component of KMS, ON and OS outward and HX, MKS and SL inwards operated in this area under their appropriate designations, but without separate statistics existing. Frequently also, the three sections proceeded as a single unit for the greater part of the Channel passage.

In passing it must also be mentioned that there are no statistics available to indicate the number of independent passages to and from the UK in the North Atlantic prior to mid 1941, and only sparse figures thereafter. There is also no record of independent sailings outside the North Atlantic. In consequence, it is difficult to arrive at any coherent picture of this facet of the maritime war other than the actual losses.

In this respect it is interesting to note that BdU kept careful records of the number of ships sunk by U-boats in each month, for clearly defined areas, and similarly of U-boat losses. While not totally correct, due to late arrival of information for example, it gave a very clear indication when a satisfactory ratio of sinkings of merchant ships versus U-boats lost was deteriorating. It was at that point that BdU ordered a move of his operational strength to waters thought to be more profitable.

THE ALLIED CONVOY SYSTEM 1939-1945

Postwar the naval historian D Waters used precisely the same method to demonstrate the success of convoy. He had more accurate figures as a result of postwar research and possession of German records, and he used them in a slightly different way. Waters was able to produce statistics, both numerical and graphical, to illustrate the "exchange rate" of merchant losses versus submarine losses in attacks on convoys, and for attacks on independent ships. Clear indications, on a monthly basis, were then available on the progress of the mercantile war.

The figures are illuminating when taken in the context of merchant ships lost in convoy set against losses inflicted by escorts (sea and air) on the attackers. In Feb 1943 34 ships were lost in North Atlantic convoy at a cost of 12 U-boats, a ratio of 1:3. In March, a month of savage attacks on two convoys, the figures rose to 72 ships lost for 6 U-boats, 1:12. In April the ratio dropped again to 1:3 while in May it had altered dramatically: 14 ships lost in convoy at a cost of 25 U-boats, 2:1. No service could withstand such losses for so little return, and the U-boats quit the North Atlantic.

It should be clearly understood in this context that only U-boats sunk in action against convoys are included. The toll taken of U-boats by ships and aircraft operating away from convoys in the Bay of Biscay, for example, is not taken into account. Independently routed merchant ship losses are also excluded.

Oceanic convoys
HX Convoys

Year	Convoys	Total ships	Convoy losses	Straggler losses	Losses out of convoy	Total
1939	22	431	1	-	2	3
1940	91	3,424	48	22	24	94
1941	70	3,050	21	18	7	46
1942	54	1,811	8	6	3	17
1943	53	2,958	27	14	-	41
1944	55	4,085	2	-	-	2
1945	32	1,985	3	-	-	3
TOTAL	377	17,744	110	60	36	206

SC Convoys

Year	Convoys	Total ships	Convoy losses	Straggler losses	Losses out of convoy	Total
1940	16	508	29	13	4	46
1941	44	1,740	46	18	6	70
1942	52	1,903	40	10	2	52
1943	37	1,661	26	12	-	38
1944	14	601	2	1	-	3
1945	14	393	2	-	-	2
TOTAL	177	6,806	145	54	12	211

SL and MKS Convoys

Year	Convoys	Total ships	Convoy losses	Straggler losses	Losses out of convoy	Total
1939	21	302	1	1	-	2
1940	69	1,502	7	14	1	22
1941	45	1,150	34	11	15	60
1942	38	1,216	18	6	-	24
1943	33	1,409	13	1	-	14
1944	39	1,555	2	-	-	2
1945	31	733	-	-	-	-
TOTAL	276	7,867	75	33	16	124

HG and XK Convoys

Year	Convoys	Total ships	Convoy losses	Straggler losses	Losses out of convoy	Total
1939	14	473	-	-	3	3
1940	61	1,718	4	5	2	11
1941	28	570	25	5	1	31
1942	14	233	5	-	-	5
1943	9	163	-	1	-	1
1944	8	60	-	-	-	-
1945	3	12	-	-	-	-
TOTAL	137	3,229	34	11	6	51

OA Convoys

Year	Convoys	Total ships	Convoy losses	Straggler losses	Losses out of convoy	Total
1939	60	1,067	-	-	1	1
1940	166	3,782	16	5	13	34
TOTAL	226	4,849	16	5	14	35

OB Convoys

Year	Convoys	Total ships	Convoy losses	Straggler losses	Losses out of convoy	Total
1939	60	1,012	2	3	2	7
1940	201	5,273	21	19	44	84
1941	84	3,038	30	8	84	122
TOTAL	345	9,323	53	30	130	213

OG & KX Convoys

Year	Convoys	Total ships	Convoy losses	Straggler losses	Losses out of convoy	Total
1939	11	437	-	-	-	-
1940	58	2,197	6	3	-	9
1941	30	1,004	21	34	-	55
1942	12	256		11	1	12
1943	8	269	-	-	-	-
1944	5	24	-	-	-	-
1945	1	6	-	-	-	-
TOTAL	125	4,193	27	48	1	76

OS & KMS Convoys

Year	Convoys	Total ships	Convoy losses	Straggler losses	Losses out of convoy	Total
1941	14	505	8	2	1	11
1942	34	1,379	8	1	18	27
1943	29	1,545	28	1	-	29
1944	39	1,351	4	-	-	4
1945	31	599	3	1	-	4
TOTAL	147	5,379	51	5	19	75

ON Convoys

Year	Convoys	Total ships	Convoy losses	Straggler losses	Losses out of convoy	Total
1941	49	1,994	1	7	2	10
1942	106	3,523	44	25	35	104
1943	61	3,012	33	9	1	43
1944	57	4,023	2	2	-	4
1944	34	2,312	1	-	-	1
TOTAL	307	14,864	81	43	38	162

ONS Convoys

Year	Convoys	Total ships	Convoy losses	Straggler losses	Losses out of convoy	Total
1943	24	898	16	3	-	19
1944	13	488	-	-	-	-
1945	14	387	-	-	-	-
TOTAL	51	1,773	16	3	-	19

UC Convoys

Year	Convoys	Total ships	Convoy losses	Straggler losses	Losses out of convoy	Total
1943	8	162	-	-	-	-
1944	54	1,399	2	1	-	3
1945	41	808	-	-	-	-
TOTAL	103	2,369	2	1	-	3

CU Convoys

Year	Convoys	Total ships	Convoy losses	Straggler losses	Losses out of convoy	Total
1943	9	159	-	-	-	-
1944	43	1,364	3	-	-	3
1945	22	732	-	-	-	-
TOTAL	74	2,255	3	-	-	3

RU Convoys

Year	Convoys	Total ships	Convoy losses	Straggler losses	Losses out of convoy	Total
1941	1	6	-	-	-	-
1942	53	382	-	-	-	-
1943	49	327	1	-	-	1
1944	47	229	-	-	-	-
1945	16	64	1	1	-	2
TOTAL	166	1,008	2	1	-	3

UR Convoys

Year	Convoys	Total ships	Convoy losses	Straggler losses	Losses out of convoy	Total
1941	3	21	-	-	-	-
1942	52	425	-	-	1	1
1943	50	301	-	1	1	2
1944	46	212	1	2	-	3
1945	16	74	2	-	-	2
TOTAL	167	1,033	3	3	2	8

KMF Convoys

Year	Convoys	Total ships	Convoy losses	Straggler losses	Losses out of convoy	Total
1942	5	112	1	-	-	1
1943	19	216	-	-	-	-
1944	15	191	-	-	-	-
1945	9	109	-	-	-	-
TOTAL	48	628	1	-	-	1

MKF Convoys

Year	Convoys	Total ships	Convoy losses	Straggler losses	Losses out of convoy	Total
1942	7	79	2	-	-	2
1943	19	206	-	-	-	-
1944	16	163	-	-	-	-
1945	9	115	-	-	-	-
TOTAL	51	563	2	-	-	2

UGS Convoys

Year	Convoys	Total ships	Convoy losses	Straggler losses	Losses out of convoy	Total
1942	2	85	-	-	-	-
1943	27	1,603	3	5	-	8
1944	39	2,747	-	-	-	-
1945	32	1,443	-	-	-	-
TOTAL	100	5,878	3	5	-	8

GUS Convoys

Year	Convoys	Total ships	Convoy losses	Straggler losses	Losses out of convoy	Total
1942	-	-	-	-	-	-
1943	28	1,231	-	-	-	-
1944	38	2,352	-	-	-	-
1945	31	1,383	-	-	-	-
TOTAL	97	4,966	-	-	-	-

UGF Convoys

Year	Convoys	Total ships	Convoy losses	Straggler losses	Losses out of convoy	Total
1942	3	59	-	-	-	-
1943	9	177	-	-	-	-
1944	10	120	-	-	-	-
1945	4	15	-	-	-	-
TOTAL	26	371	-	-	-	-

GUF Convoys

Year	Convoys	Total ships	Convoy losses	Straggler losses	Losses out of convoy	Total
1942	3	58	-	-	-	-
1943	7	130	-	-	-	-
1944	9	124	-	-	-	-
1945	24	342	-	-	-	-
TOTAL	43	654	-	-	-	-

UK Coastal waters convoys

FS Convoys

Year	Convoys	Total ships	Convoy losses	Straggler losses	Losses out of convoy	Total
1939	55	1,069	4	-	-	4
1940	299	9,361	29	1	1	31
1941	301	11,082	34	4	3	41
1942	307	10,488	22	1	1	24
1943	321	10,043	1	-	-	1
1944	362	9,592	1	-	-	1
1945	195	2,882	6	-	-	6
TOTAL	1,840	54,517	97	6	5	108

FN Convoys

Year	Convoys	Total ships	Convoy losses	Straggler losses	Losses out of convoy	Total
1939	52	1,155	3	-	-	3
1940	314	10,008	17	2	3	22
1941	204	7,251	38	2	7	47
1942	306	11,064	16	-	-	16
1943	315	9,459	6	-	-	6
1944	360	8,764	-	-	-	-
1945	193	2,574	1	-	-	1
TOTAL	1,744	50,275	81	4	10	95

EC Convoys

Year	Convoys	Total ships	Convoy losses	Straggler losses	Losses out of convoy	Total
1941	90	6,080	10	2	2	14
TOTAL	90	6,080	10	2	2	14

MT Convoys

Year	Convoys	Total ships	Convoy losses	Straggler losses	Losses out of convoy	Total
1940	171	2,334	-	-	-	-
TOTAL	171	2,334	-	-	-	-

SG Convoys

Year	Convoys	Total ships	Convoy losses	Straggler losses	Losses out of convoy	Total
1940	29	293	-	-	-	-
TOTAL	29	293	-	-	-	-

WN Convoys

Year	Convoys	Total ships	Convoy losses	Straggler losses	Losses out of convoy	Total
1940	60	1,285	6	-	-	6
1941	163	3,875	2	2	-	4
1942	151	2,970	1	-	-	1
1943	174	2,212	-	-	-	-
1944	147	1,916	-	-	-	-
1945	26	169	-	-	-	-
TOTAL	721	12,427	9	2	-	11

EN Convoys

Year	Convoys	Total ships	Convoy losses	Straggler losses	Losses out of convoy	Total
1940	46	849	2	1	-	3
1941	71	1,565	1	-	1	2
1942	151	3,579	-	-	-	-
1943	158	2,370	-	-	-	-
1944	142	1,815	-	-	-	-
1945	29	239	2	-	-	2
TOTAL	597	10,417	5	1	1	7

BB Convoys

Year	Convoys	Total ships	Convoy losses	Straggler losses	Losses out of convoy	Total
1941	114	1,530	-	-	1	1
1942	132	1,755	-	-	-	-
1943	69	625	-	-	-	-
1944	-	-	-	-	-	-
1945	115	743	-	-	-	-
TOTAL	430	4,653	-	-	1	1

MH Convoys

Year	Convoys	Total ships	Convoy losses	Straggler losses	Losses out of convoy	Total
1941	57	220	-	-	-	-
1942	68	366	-	-	-	-
1943	-	-	-	-	-	-
1944	-	-	-	-	-	-
1945	115	1,064	-	-	1	1
TOTAL	240	1,650	-	-	1	1

HM Convoys

Year	Convoys	Total ships	Convoy losses	Straggler losses	Losses out of convoy	Total
1941	1	5	-	-	-	-
1942	90	392	-	-	-	-
1943	33	94	-	-	-	-
TOTAL	124	491	-	-	-	-

CE Convoys

Year	Convoys	Total ships	Convoy losses	Straggler losses	Losses out of convoy	Total
1940	14	198	-	-	-	-
1941	42	632	1	-	-	1
1942	77	1,272	-	-	-	-
1943	90	1,582	-	-	-	-
1944	38	766	-	-	-	-
TOTAL	261	4,450	1	-	-	1

CW Convoys

Year	Convoys	Total ships	Convoy losses	Straggler losses	Losses out of convoy	Total
1940	19	352	13	3	3	19
1941	42	644	4	1	-	5
1942	82	1,287	1	-	-	1
1943	89	1,626	3	-	-	3
1944	38	738	2	-	-	2
TOTAL	270	4,647	23	4	3	30

WP Convoys

Year	Convoys	Total ships	Convoy losses	Straggler losses	Losses out of convoy	Total
1941	88	1,425	1	-	-	1
1942	179	3,070	7	-	1	8
1943	193	2,605	1	-	-	1
1944	88	1,146	3	-	-	3
TOTAL	548	8,246	12	-	1	13

PW Convoys

Year	Convoys	Total ships	Convoy losses	Straggler losses	Losses out of convoy	Total
1941	88	1,408	-	-	-	-
1942	178	3,067	5	-	1	6
1943	179	2,801	1	-	-	1
1944	74	1,024	-	-	-	-
TOTAL	519	8,300	6	-	1	7

BTC Convoys

Year	Convoys	Total ships	Convoy losses	Straggler losses	Losses out of convoy	Total
1944	19	435	1	-	-	1
1945	146	2,559	7	-	-	7
TOTAL	165	2,994	8	-	-	8

TBC Convoys

Year	Convoys	Total ships	Convoy losses	Straggler losses	Losses out of convoy	Total
1944	18	429	1	-	-	1
1945	144	3,179	4	-	-	4
TOTAL	162	3,608	5	-	-	5

APPENDIX 3

CONVOY SERIES NOTES AND STATISTICS

These notes on convoy series expand the details in the main text to deal with the individual series. The data has, of necessity, to be brief but provides date of sailing and arrival at terminal ports. "TDS" indicates "Trade Division Statistics" and is the number of merchant ships by Trade Division definition in each convoy, i.e. it excludes warships and auxiliaries attached for passage; also Rescue Ships and Tugs.

The cargo and personnel losses in the loss section are derived from Lloyd's of London sources.

The information shown in the CONVOY SERIES is directly comparable with the appropriate sections that appear under CONVOY STATISTICS earlier in the book. The losses shown numerically against specific convoys relate ONLY to those earlier figures.

The list of names etc that appear under the heading "Losses incurred in…excluding stragglers" does NOT relate to the totals included in either of the sections referred to in the previous paragraph.

The reason for the difference is that losses by marine causes have been included as have losses classified by the Admiralty as "Ex convoy." In other words, losses incurred when either no escort had been provided, the escort had not joined or had already detached at the time of the attack, or the ship(s) concerned were not with the convoy due to specific orders. This last category includes, for example, Rescue Ships (whether of the Rescue Service or simply vessels nominated by the Convoy Commodore) which detached in the course of their duty.

In the case of convoys of the KM, MK, UG and GU series (both the Fast and Slow variants) the statistics shown in the CONVOY STATISTICS and CONVOY DATA lists relate only to the Atlantic portion of their passage. As has been explained earlier, the large variation in convoy numbers in the course of a Mediterranean passage, make it impossible to produce meaningful figures. It is, however, appreciated that readers will expect Mediterranean losses for those series to be listed; they have therefore been shown in a subsection with the specific warning that they cannot be related to the Atlantic passage figures for the appropriate convoy designation.

In the context of the loss dates of casualties it should be noted that, on occasions, sections of a convoy may have sailed one day prior to the main body, or arrived one or two days after it. For example, ships departing Milford Haven to join a convoy sailing from Liverpool or ships bound for Milford Haven detaching from a convoy arriving at Liverpool. This apparent anomaly exists ONLY where the "FEEDER" convoy bore the same designation as the main body e.g. OBM (OB ex Milford Haven) to join the main body of the relevant OB convoy.

Note: All dates in the tables in this Appendix are given in the standard British format of day,day/month,month/year,year. The anniversary of the Canadian declaration of war against Germany is shown therefore as 10/09/39, i.e. 10 September 1939, possibly a style strange to some North American readers.

In the convoy data tables which follow, in the interest of brevity, the column headed "GRT" records tonnage followed by a two digit number which is the last two digits of the year of build, and an abbreviated nationality which should be obvious e.g. Br = British, Du = Dutch etc. As this book covers the period 1939-1945 it follows that all abbreviated digits in excess of 45 are prefixed 18 i.e. 98 = 1898 year of build. Digits 00 to 45 are prefixed 19, i.e. 45 = 1945.

HX convoy series 1939-1945

The HX series was, with the exception of the East Coast UK coastal convoys, the longest continuous convoy series of the war. HX 1 sailed from Halifax NS on 16 Sept 1939, HX 358 sailed on 23 May 1945. The convoys perpetuated the designation of a similar series, also from Halifax to the UK, in the 1917-18 period.

With the HX convoy speed set initially at 9 knots, there was a number of ships in Canadian waters, or routed there from the Panama Canal and the Caribbean, whose speed was sufficiently high to require special convoys. Their speed was insufficient to justify inclusion in the independent category so Fast convoys designated HXF were run to accommodate them. These HXF convoys sailed a few days prior to or after the appropriate HX convoy and bore the same numeric designation; thus, HXF 1 sailed 19 Sept 1939. As there were insufficient fast ships to require regular convoys, the HXF series is incomplete. Only 1, 2 and 6 to 20 inclusive actually sailed.

Uniquely, HX 3 sailed in two parts, a Slow section sailing 24 hours ahead of the main convoy and amalgamating when overtaken by the main body.

For some time it was the practice for a "feeder" convoy to sail from Bermuda and join the HX convoy at sea. The Bermuda convoy, BHX, bore the same number as the HX convoy it was to meet. The BHX numeration accordingly spans 41 to 137 inclusive. One convoy, BHX 104, did not meet its HX counterpart and proceeded direct to the UK as a separate entity.

There were therefore a total of 377 convoys between North America and the UK in the HX series, 359 under HX, 1 under BHX and 17 under HXF designations. Of these, 38, just 10%, suffered loss by direct attack on the formed body. Of the total of 110 merchant ships so sunk, 96 were from submarine attack and 14 from other causes, 5 of these, from HX 84, by raider. In this context it is of interest that the TDS figure is incorrect in showing 6 ships lost. There was a sixth ship, MOPAN, which was an independent upon whom SCHEER stumbled shortly before attacking the convoy. The necessity of silencing MOPAN so as not to alarm HX 84 led to a delay of approximately an hour in the attack on the convoy itself, undoubtedly thereby saving HX 84 even greater loss than it actually suffered.

Sixty stragglers were sunk and 36 ships were lost due to attack prior to the arrival of A/S escort or after detachment from the convoy for one reason or another including its scattering following attack. In the case of the fifteen ships lost prior to the arrival of the A/S escort, these have been included in the chronological list of convoy losses. There were also several losses due to marine causes, which can safely be ascribed to war conditions, and these have likewise been included in the loss list for the series that appears following the listing of convoys.

Initially the HX series provided the only means of escorted, eastbound passage to the UK. The RCN provided A/S escort for twenty-four hours out of Halifax from its meagre resources and the ocean passage was covered by units of the 3rd Battle Squadron. This was a Halifax based RN shore command whose ships were at first cruisers specifically allocated for escort, which were gradually replaced by Armed Merchant Cruisers and old battleships of the "R" class, all based at Halifax. The force was also supplemented as needed by British and French submarines. Ocean escort was provided from Halifax to the edge of the U-boat danger zone, approximately 12W.

A/S escort for Atlantic convoys was provided by UK based vessels as the focus of U-boat operations lay to the west of the British Isles. It therefore followed that eastbound convoys usually obtained their escort from westbound convoys, after they had passed out of the danger zone. Until the late summer of 1940 this was usually in the zone 12 to 15W.

After the collapse of France and the occupation of the Biscay bases, convoys were routed further north and, gradually, escort was extended westward; eventually escorts left the westbound convoys to refuel in Iceland. In consequence the HX convoys then received their A/S escort in more northerly and westerly positions.

In May 1941 a number of escorts were based in Iceland to extend A/S cover. It then became normal practice for westbound convoys to exchange their UK based escort at Eastern Ocean Meeting Point (EOMP) for an Iceland based group who took the convoy west to Mid Ocean Meeting Point (MOMP). It was then at MOMP that HX convoys received their first A/S escort, with another exchange at EOMP. Shortly after this change the regular ocean escort by 3rd Battle Squadron ceased, and that command was abolished.

The BdU response was, of course, to extend U-boat activity even further west. In consequence the RCN, by then receiving increased numbers of corvettes from Canadian yards, undertook escort from the vicinity of Newfoundland to MOMP, the new, western meeting point being known as Western Ocean Meeting Point (WOMP). A further change was that following an agreement between Britain, Canada and the USA, the USN also started escorting the convoys between WOMP and MOMP, a passage area that lay within the US Neutrality Zone. In consequence, the RCN vessels came under the control of an USN Flag Officer, as did the convoys themselves.

In December 1941, with the German declaration of war on the USN, the trans-Atlantic convoy system was completed with local RCN escort between Halifax NS and WOMP. When re-fuelling at sea became practical, MOMP was discontinued and the escort from WOMP to the UK for a convoy was provided by a single Escort Group. Ultimately, the increasing number of merchant ships commencing their ocean voyages from New York City caused the western terminal of the HX series to move to that port from Halifax.

When the HX western terminal became New York City, changes were required in the escort routine and the final re-organization was for a RCN local escort to handle the NYC/HOMP (Halifax Ocean Meeting Point) passage, relieved by another RCN escort from HOMP to WOMP.

The numeric series remained constant with no variations until HX 229. Due to extreme congestion in New York harbour, this convoy was sailed as two distinct bodies, HX 229 and HX 229A, and proceeded throughout their passage as separate convoys. From April 1944, to accommodate slower ships, the HX convoys sailed with differing speed parameters. This was necessary due to the suspension of the SC series as escorts were withdrawn from the Atlantic to protect the Normandy invasion. SC convoys were re-instituted in October 1944. In consequence, from HX 287 to HX 310, the convoys were suffixed F, M or S according to their speed of advance. After HX 311 this practice ceased and all HX convoys thereafter reverted to a standard speed.

The move of the western terminal to NYC also altered the composition of the HX convoys. For a period of some months the newly instituted Boston/Halifax system was stopped, and ships for passage northward to Canada generally were included in the HX convoy. At HOMP the replacement RCN escort brought out ships from Halifax to join the convoy for the UK; the NYC/Halifax escort escorted in the Canadian-bound vessels to Halifax. The few merchant ships joining from Sydney CB and St John's NF were provided with a small, local, escort.

Also included in HX convoys from mid-1941 were ships for Iceland. The garrison of the island had changed in June 1941 with the relief of the Canadian

Author's collection

On her way to the Atlantic Charter meeting between Winston Churchill and President Roosevelt in Argentia Bay, Newfoundland; HMS PRINCE OF WALES passes through the lines of convoy HX 143.

garrison by US troops, who were supplied from the USA; civilian traffic to Iceland also now needed escort. Initially such ships were escorted from the HX convoys to Iceland by the returning Iceland based escort. When "through escort," WOMP to UK, was introduced, a detachment of USCG cutters was based in Iceland to handle traffic to and from Iceland from the trans-Atlantic convoys. The rendezvous for such transfers became known as Iceland Ocean Meeting Point (ICOMP), and remained a feature of both east and westbound convoys until late in 1943. Then, due to the trans-Atlantic routes moving further south, Iceland-bound ships were routed to Loch Ewe in Northwest Scotland to join a convoy series from there to Iceland.

HX convoy data

CONVOY	DEP. PORT	DEP. DATE	ARRIVAL PORT	ARR. DATE	TDS	MV SUNK	MV DMGD
HX 1	HALIFAX	16/09/39	LIVERPOOL	30/09/39	15		
HX 2	HALIFAX	23/09/39	LIVERPOOL	10/10/39	15		
HX 3	HALIFAX	30/09/39	LIVERPOOL	14/10/39	20		
HX 3S	HALIFAX	29/09/39	RV with HX	14/10/39	4		
HX 4	HALIFAX	08/10/39	LIVERPOOL	22/10/39	10		
HX 5	HALIFAX	17/10/39	LIVERPOOL	29/10/39	16	1	
HX 6	HALIFAX	25/10/39	LIVERPOOL	10/11/39	52		
HX 7	HALIFAX	02/11/39	LIVERPOOL	16/11/39	29		
HX 8	HALIFAX	10/11/39	LIVERPOOL	25/11/39	34		
HX 9	HALIFAX	18/11/39	LIVERPOOL	02/12/39	30		
HX 10	HALIFAX	26/11/39	LIVERPOOL	10/12/39	33		
HX 11	HALIFAX	04/12/39	LIVERPOOL	18/12/39	45		
HX 12	HALIFAX	12/12/39	LIVERPOOL	27/12/39	35		
HX 13	HALIFAX	20/12/39	LIVERPOOL	04/01/40	27		
HX 14	HALIFAX	29/12/39	LIVERPOOL	12/01/40	40	1	
HX 15	HALIFAX	06/01/40	LIVERPOOL	19/01/40	24		
HX 16	HALIFAX	14/01/40	LIVERPOOL	28/01/40	25		
HX 17	HALIFAX	22/01/40	LIVERPOOL	07/02/40	49		
HX 18	HALIFAX	31/01/40	LIVERPOOL	16/02/40	43		
HX 19	HALIFAX	07/02/40	LIVERPOOL	22/02/40	45		
HX 20	HALIFAX	16/02/40	LIVERPOOL	04/03/40	55		1
HX 21	HALIFAX	18/02/40	LIVERPOOL	04/03/40	16		
HX 22	HALIFAX	22/02/40	LIVERPOOL	09/03/40	35	1	
HX 23	HALIFAX	26/02/40	LIVERPOOL	12/03/40	26		
HX 24	HALIFAX	02/03/40	LIVERPOOL	17/03/40	40		
HX 25	HALIFAX	05/03/40	LIVERPOOL	20/03/40	25		
HX 26	HALIFAX	09/03/40	LIVERPOOL	26/03/40	39		
HX 27	HALIFAX	13/03/40	LIVERPOOL	28/03/40	28		
HX 28	HALIFAX	18/03/40	LIVERPOOL	02/04/40	61		
HX 29	HALIFAX	21/03/40	LIVERPOOL	04/04/40	29		
HX 30	HALIFAX	25/03/40	LIVERPOOL	09/04/40	38		
HX 31	HALIFAX	29/03/40	LIVERPOOL	13/04/40	30		
HX 32	HALIFAX	02/04/40	LIVERPOOL	17/04/40	31		
HX 33	HALIFAX	06/04/40	LIVERPOOL	20/04/40	34		
HX 34	HALIFAX	10/04/40	LIVERPOOL	26/04/40	28		2
HX 35	HALIFAX	14/04/40	LIVERPOOL	29/04/40	36		
HX 36	HALIFAX	18/04/40	LIVERPOOL	03/05/40	22		
HX 37	HALIFAX	22/04/40	LIVERPOOL	07/05/40	32		
HX 38	HALIFAX	26/04/40	LIVERPOOL	12/05/40	41		
HX 39	HALIFAX	30/04/40	LIVERPOOL	15/05/40	44		
HX 40	HALIFAX	04/05/40	LIVERPOOL	19/05/40	28		
HX 41	HALIFAX	08/05/40	LIVERPOOL	23/05/40	44		
HX 42	HALIFAX	12/05/40	LIVERPOOL	28/05/40	47		
HX 43	HALIFAX	16/05/40	LIVERPOOL	31/05/40	43		
HX 44	HALIFAX	20/05/40	LIVERPOOL	03/06/40	33		
HX 45	HALIFAX	24/05/40	LIVERPOOL	08/06/40	63		
HX 46	HALIFAX	28/05/40	LIVERPOOL	12/06/40	46		
HX 47	HALIFAX	02/06/40	LIVERPOOL	17/06/40	57	2	
HX 48	HALIFAX	05/06/40	LIVERPOOL	20/06/40	38		
HX 49	HALIFAX	09/06/40	LIVERPOOL	24/06/40	50	1	
HX 50	HALIFAX	13/06/40	LIVERPOOL	30/06/40	49		
HX 51	HALIFAX	17/06/40	LIVERPOOL	02/07/40	35		
HX 52	HALIFAX	21/06/40	LIVERPOOL	06/07/40	29		
HX 53	HALIFAX	25/06/40	LIVERPOOL	10/07/40	44	1	
HX 54	HALIFAX	29/06/40	LIVERPOOL	14/07/40	43		
HX 55	HALIFAX	03/07/40	LIVERPOOL	18/07/40	40	2	1
HX 56	HALIFAX	07/07/40	LIVERPOOL	22/07/40	48		
HX 57	HALIFAX	11/07/40	LIVERPOOL	26/07/40	51		
HX 58	HALIFAX	15/07/40	LIVERPOOL	31/07/40	65		
HX 59	HALIFAX	19/07/40	LIVERPOOL	03/08/40	54		
HX 60	HALIFAX	23/07/40	LIVERPOOL	07/08/40	60	3	
HX 61	HALIFAX	27/07/40	LIVERPOOL	11/08/40	45		
HX 62	HALIFAX	31/07/40	LIVERPOOL	15/08/40	76		
HX 63	HALIFAX	04/08/40	LIVERPOOL	19/08/40	53		
HX 64	HALIFAX	08/08/40	LIVERPOOL	23/08/40	62		
HX 65	HALIFAX	12/08/40	LIVERPOOL	27/08/40	51	5	1
HX 66	HALIFAX	16/08/40	LIVERPOOL	31/08/40	51	4	
HX 67	HALIFAX	20/08/40	LIVERPOOL	04/09/40	37		
HX 68	HALIFAX	24/08/40	LIVERPOOL	08/09/40	47		
HX 69	HALIFAX	28/08/40	LIVERPOOL	12/09/40	47		
HX 70	HALIFAX	01/09/40	LIVERPOOL	16/09/40	42		2
HX 71	HALIFAX	05/09/40	LIVERPOOL	20/09/40	34	1	
HX 72	HALIFAX	09/09/40	DISPERSED	21/09/40	47	6	3
HX 73	HALIFAX	13/09/40	LIVERPOOL	28/09/40	43	1	1
HX 74	HALIFAX	17/09/40	LIVERPOOL	02/10/40	33		1
HX 75	HALIFAX	21/09/40	LIVERPOOL	07/10/40	56		
HX 76	HALIFAX	26/09/40	LIVERPOOL	10/10/40	38		
HX 77	HALIFAX	30/09/40	LIVERPOOL	15/10/40	39	6	

APPENDIX 3

CONVOY	DEP. PORT	DEP. DATE	ARRIVAL PORT	ARR. DATE	TDS	MV SUNK	MV DMGD
HX 78	HALIFAX	04/10/40	LIVERPOOL	18/10/40	32		
HX 79	HALIFAX	08/10/40	LIVERPOOL	23/10/40	49	10	
HX 80	HALIFAX	12/10/40	LIVERPOOL	27/10/40	33		
HX 81	HALIFAX	16/10/40	LIVERPOOL	02/11/40	39		
HX 82	HALIFAX	20/10/40	LIVERPOOL	06/11/40	39		
HX 83	HALIFAX	24/10/40	LIVERPOOL	07/11/40	36	1	
HX 84	HALIFAX	28/10/40	DISPERSED	05/11/40	38	6	
HX 85	HALIFAX	01/11/40	SYDNEY CB	09/11/40	28		
HX 85/1	SYDNEY CB	11/11/40	LIVERPOOL	25/11/40	28		
HX 86	HALIFAX	10/11/40	LIVERPOOL	26/11/40	37		
HX 87	HALIFAX	14/11/40	LIVERPOOL	29/11/40	31		1
HX 88	HALIFAX	14/11/40	LIVERPOOL	30/11/40	51		
HX 89	HALIFAX	17/11/40	LIVERPOOL	01/12/40	30		
HX 90	HALIFAX	21/11/40	LIVERPOOL	05/12/40	35	3	2
HX 91	HALIFAX	25/11/40	LIVERPOOL	11/12/40	29		
HX 92	HALIFAX	29/11/40	LIVERPOOL	12/12/40	24		
HX 93	HALIFAX	03/12/40	LIVERPOOL	18/12/40	29		
HX 94	HALIFAX	06/12/40	LIVERPOOL	22/12/40	17		
HX 95	HALIFAX	10/12/40	LIVERPOOL	27/12/40	24		
HX 96	HALIFAX	14/12/40	LIVERPOOL	30/12/40	30		1
HX 97	HALIFAX	18/12/40	LIVERPOOL	03/01/41	24		
HX 98	HALIFAX	22/12/40	SYDNEY CB	29/12/40	23		
HX 98/1	SYDNEY CB	02/01/41	LIVERPOOL	17/01/41	22		
HX 99	HALIFAX	26/12/40	LIVERPOOL	11/01/41	22		
HX 100	HALIFAX	01/01/41	LIVERPOOL	18/01/41	35		
HX 101	HALIFAX	06/01/41	LIVERPOOL	22/01/41	25		1
HX 102	HALIFAX	11/01/41	LIVERPOOL	29/01/41	30		
HX 103	HALIFAX	15/01/41	LIVERPOOL	01/02/41	11		
HX 104	HALIFAX	21/01/41	LIVERPOOL	08/02/41	21		
HX 105	HALIFAX	25/01/41	LIVERPOOL	09/02/41	35		
HX 106	HALIFAX	30/01/41	LIVERPOOL	18/02/41	41		
HX 107	HALIFAX	03/02/41	LIVERPOOL	28/02/41	21		1
HX 108	HALIFAX	09/02/41	LIVERPOOL	27/02/41	47		1
HX 109	HALIFAX	13/02/41	LIVERPOOL	04/03/41	36	1	1
HX 110	HALIFAX	19/02/41	LIVERPOOL	11/03/41	41		
HX 111	HALIFAX	23/02/41	LIVERPOOL	12/03/41	23		
HX 112	HALIFAX	01/03/41	LIVERPOOL	20/03/41	41	5	2
HX 113	HALIFAX	05/03/41	LIVERPOOL	21/03/41	27		
HX 114	HALIFAX	11/03/41	LIVERPOOL	30/03/41	40	2	3
HX 115	HALIFAX	17/03/41	LIVERPOOL	03/04/41	30		2
HX 116	HALIFAX	21/03/41	LIVERPOOL	09/04/41	28		
HX 117	HALIFAX	27/03/41	LIVERPOOL	15/04/41	43		1
HX 118	HALIFAX	31/03/41	LIVERPOOL	18/04/41	33		
HX 119A	HALIFAX	06/04/41	LIVERPOOL	22/04/41	34		
HX 119B	HALIFAX	06/04/41	LIVERPOOL	22/04/41	19		
HX 120	HALIFAX	10/04/41	LIVERPOOL	29/04/41	37		
HX 121	HALIFAX	16/04/41	LIVERPOOL	03/05/41	47	4	
HX 122	HALIFAX	20/04/41	LIVERPOOL	08/05/41	27		
HX 123	HALIFAX	25/04/41	LIVERPOOL	13/05/41	34		
HX 124	HALIFAX	30/04/41	LIVERPOOL	20/05/41	36		
HX 125A	HALIFAX	06/05/41	LIVERPOOL	22/05/41	40		

CONVOY	DEP. PORT	DEP. DATE	ARRIVAL PORT	ARR. DATE	TDS	MV SUNK	MV DMGD
HX 125B	HALIFAX	06/05/41	LIVERPOOL	22/05/41	27		
HX 126	HALIFAX	10/05/41	LIVERPOOL	28/05/41	29	4	
HX 127	HALIFAX	16/05/41	LIVERPOOL	02/06/41	56		
HX 128	HALIFAX	20/05/41	LIVERPOOL	06/06/41	43		
HX 129	HALIFAX	27/05/41	LIVERPOOL	12/06/41	57		
HX 130	HALIFAX	01/06/41	LIVERPOOL	20/06/41	46		
HX 131	HALIFAX	06/06/41	LIVERPOOL	23/06/41	42		
HX 132	HALIFAX	10/06/41	LIVERPOOL	28/06/41	34		
HX 133	HALIFAX	16/06/41	LIVERPOOL	03/07/41	51	5	2
HX 134	HALIFAX	20/06/41	LIVERPOOL	09/07/41	48		
HX 135	HALIFAX	26/06/41	LIVERPOOL	12/07/41	52		
HX 136	HALIFAX	30/06/41	LIVERPOOL	18/07/41	46		
HX 137	HALIFAX	06/07/41	LIVERPOOL	22/07/41	53		
HX 138	HALIFAX	11/07/41	LIVERPOOL	27/07/41	47		
HX 139	HALIFAX	16/07/41	LIVERPOOL	31/07/41	60		
HX 140	HALIFAX	22/07/41	LIVERPOOL	06/08/41	70		
HX 141	HALIFAX	27/07/41	LIVERPOOL	11/08/41	60		
HX 142	HALIFAX	01/08/41	LIVERPOOL	18/08/41	65		
HX 143	HALIFAX	05/08/41	LIVERPOOL	20/08/41	73		
HX 144	HALIFAX	10/08/41	LIVERPOOL	30/08/41	60		
HX 145	HALIFAX	16/08/41	LIVERPOOL	31/08/41	83		
HX 146	HALIFAX	21/08/41	LIVERPOOL	06/09/41	62		
HX 147	HALIFAX	29/08/41	LIVERPOOL	12/09/41	64		
HX 148	HALIFAX	04/09/41	LIVERPOOL	17/09/41	48		
HX 149	HALIFAX	10/09/41	LIVERPOOL	25/09/41	57		
HX 150	HALIFAX	16/09/41	LIVERPOOL	30/09/41	44		
HX 151	HALIFAX	22/09/41	LIVERPOOL	07/10/41	46		
HX 152	HALIFAX	28/09/41	LIVERPOOL	14/10/41	58		1
HX 153	HALIFAX	05/10/41	LIVERPOOL	19/10/41	56		
HX 154	HALIFAX	10/10/41	LIVERPOOL	23/10/41	51		
HX 155	HALIFAX	16/10/41	LIVERPOOL	31/10/41	52		
HX 156	HALIFAX	22/10/41	LIVERPOOL	05/11/41	43		
HX 157	HALIFAX	28/10/41	LIVERPOOL	13/11/41	41		
HX 158	HALIFAX	03/11/41	LIVERPOOL	18/11/41	40		
HX 159	HALIFAX	08/11/41	LIVERPOOL	23/11/41	32		
HX 160	HALIFAX	15/11/41	LIVERPOOL	30/11/41	62		
HX 161	HALIFAX	21/11/41	LIVERPOOL	06/12/41	42		1
HX 162	HALIFAX	27/11/41	LIVERPOOL	11/12/41	31		
HX 163	HALIFAX	03/12/41	LIVERPOOL	19/12/41	43		
HX 164	HALIFAX	08/12/41	LIVERPOOL	23/12/41	43		
HX 165	HALIFAX	15/12/41	LIVERPOOL	30/12/41	48		
HX 166	HALIFAX	21/12/41	LIVERPOOL	05/01/42	33		
HX 167	HALIFAX	27/12/41	LIVERPOOL	11/01/42	41		
HX 168	HALIFAX	02/01/42	DISPERSED	13/01/42	36		
HX 169	HALIFAX	08/01/42	LIVERPOOL	23/01/42	36		
HX 170	HALIFAX	13/01/42	LIVERPOOL	28/01/42	29		
HX 171	HALIFAX	20/01/42	LIVERPOOL	01/02/42	42		
HX 172	HALIFAX	26/01/42	LIVERPOOL	07/02/42	53		
HX 173	HALIFAX	01/02/42	LIVERPOOL	14/02/42	30		1
HX 174	HALIFAX	07/02/42	LIVERPOOL	21/02/42	27		
HX 175	HALIFAX	13/02/42	LIVERPOOL	25/02/42	27		

THE ALLIED CONVOY SYSTEM 1939-1945

CONVOY	DEP. PORT	DEP. DATE	ARRIVAL PORT	ARR. DATE	TDS	MV SUNK	MV DMGD
HX 176	HALIFAX	19/02/42	LIVERPOOL	06/03/42	24		
HX 177	HALIFAX	25/02/42	LIVERPOOL	09/03/42	24		
HX 178	HALIFAX	03/03/42	LIVERPOOL	17/03/42	22		
HX 179	HALIFAX	09/03/42	LIVERPOOL	22/03/42	21		
HX 180	HALIFAX	15/03/42	LIVERPOOL	27/03/42	35		
HX 181	HALIFAX	21/03/42	LIVERPOOL	02/04/42	25		
HX 182	HALIFAX	27/03/42	LIVERPOOL	09/04/42	34		
HX 183	HALIFAX	02/04/42	LIVERPOOL	15/04/42	23		
HX 184	HALIFAX	08/04/42	LIVERPOOL	20/04/42	30		
HX 185	HALIFAX	14/04/42	LIVERPOOL	27/04/42	33		
HX 186	HALIFAX	20/04/42	LIVERPOOL	02/05/42	21		
HX 187	HALIFAX	26/04/42	LIVERPOOL	08/05/42	24		
HX 188	HALIFAX	03/05/42	LIVERPOOL	15/05/42	28		
HX 189	HALIFAX	10/05/42	LIVERPOOL	20/05/42	20		
HX 190	HALIFAX	17/05/42	LIVERPOOL	28/05/42	18		
HX 191	HALIFAX	24/05/42	LIVERPOOL	06/06/42	24		
HX 192	HALIFAX	31/05/42	LIVERPOOL	11/06/42	27		
HX 193	HALIFAX	07/06/42	LIVERPOOL	19/06/42	31		
HX 194	HALIFAX	14/06/42	LIVERPOOL	26/06/42	32		
HX 195	HALIFAX	21/06/42	LIVERPOOL	02/07/42	30		
HX 196	HALIFAX	29/06/42	LIVERPOOL	10/07/42	42		
HX 197	HALIFAX	06/07/42	LIVERPOOL	17/07/42	24		
HX 198	HALIFAX	12/07/42	LIVERPOOL	23/07/42	29		
HX 199	HALIFAX	19/07/42	LIVERPOOL	30/07/42	29		
HX 200	HALIFAX	27/07/42	LIVERPOOL	07/08/42	34		
HX 201	HALIFAX	02/08/42	LIVERPOOL	14/08/42	30		
HX 202	HALIFAX	09/08/42	LIVERPOOL	21/08/42	43		
HX 203	HALIFAX	16/08/42	LIVERPOOL	28/08/42	37		
HX 204	HALIFAX	23/08/42	LIVERPOOL	04/09/42	45		
HX 205	HALIFAX	30/08/42	LIVERPOOL	11/09/42	56		
HX 206	HALIFAX	06/09/42	LIVERPOOL	18/09/42	45		
HX 207	HALIFAX	13/09/42	LIVERPOOL	25/09/42	36		
HX 208	NYC	17/09/42	LIVERPOOL	02/10/42	59		
HX 209	NYC	24/09/42	LIVERPOOL	09/10/42	35	1	1
HX 210	NYC	01/10/42	LIVERPOOL	16/10/42	36		
HX 211	NYC	08/10/42	LIVERPOOL	24/10/42	29		
HX 212	NYC	18/10/42	LIVERPOOL	02/11/42	43	5	
HX 213	NYC	26/10/42	LIVERPOOL	10/11/42	42		
HX 214	NYC	03/11/42	LIVERPOOL	18/11/42	27		
HX 215	NYC	11/11/42	LIVERPOOL	25/11/42	42		
HX 216	NYC	19/11/42	LIVERPOOL	06/12/42	42		
HX 217	NYC	27/11/42	LIVERPOOL	14/12/42	26	2	
HX 218	NYC	05/12/42	LIVERPOOL	21/12/42	55		
HX 219	NYC	13/12/42	LIVERPOOL	29/12/42	45		
HX 220	NYC	21/12/42	LIVERPOOL	09/01/43	33		
HX 221	NYC	29/12/42	LIVERPOOL	14/01/43	36		
HX 222	NYC	06/01/43	LIVERPOOL	22/01/43	34	1	
HX 223	NYC	14/01/43	LIVERPOOL	02/02/43	48		
HX 224	NYC	22/01/43	LIVERPOOL	05/02/43	57	2	
HX 225	NYC	30/01/43	LIVERPOOL	13/02/43	38		
HX 226	NYC	08/02/43	LIVERPOOL	24/02/43	43		
HX 227	NYC	18/02/43	LIVERPOOL	06/03/43	66		
HX 228	NYC	28/02/43	LIVERPOOL	15/03/43	60	4	
HX 229	NYC	08/03/43	LIVERPOOL	23/03/43	38	12	
HX 229A	NYC	09/03/43	LIVERPOOL	26/03/43	34		
HX 230	NYC	18/03/43	LIVERPOOL	02/04/43	41		
HX 231	NYC	25/03/43	LIVERPOOL	10/04/43	62	3	
HX 232	NYC	01/04/43	LIVERPOOL	16/04/43	47	3	
HX 233	NYC	06/04/43	LIVERPOOL	21/04/43	54	1	
HX 234	NYC	12/04/43	LIVERPOOL	29/04/43	43	1	1
HX 235	NYC	18/04/43	LIVERPOOL	05/05/43	36		
HX 236	NYC	24/04/43	LIVERPOOL	09/05/43	46		
HX 237	NYC	01/05/43	LIVERPOOL	17/05/43	46		
HX 238	NYC	07/05/43	LIVERPOOL	22/05/43	45		
HX 239	NYC	13/05/43	LIVERPOOL	28/05/43	42		
HX 240	NYC	19/05/43	LIVERPOOL	04/06/43	56		
HX 241	NYC	25/05/43	LIVERPOOL	10/06/43	43		
HX 242	NYC	31/05/43	LIVERPOOL	15/06/43	61		
HX 243	NYC	07/06/43	LIVERPOOL	21/06/43	76		
HX 244	NYC	15/06/43	LIVERPOOL	30/06/43	86		
HX 245	NYC	23/06/43	LIVERPOOL	07/07/43	84		
HX 246	NYC	30/06/43	LIVERPOOL	14/07/43	63		
HX 247	NYC	08/07/43	LIVERPOOL	22/07/43	71		
HX 248	NYC	15/07/43	LIVERPOOL	29/07/43	89		
HX 249	NYC	23/07/43	LIVERPOOL	06/08/43	62		
HX 250	NYC	30/07/43	LIVERPOOL	12/08/43	75		
HX 251	NYC	07/08/43	LIVERPOOL	23/08/43	87		
HX 252	NYC	14/08/43	LIVERPOOL	28/08/43	52		
HX 253	NYC	20/08/43	LIVERPOOL	04/09/43	50		
HX 254	NYC	27/08/43	LIVERPOOL	12/09/43	81		1
HX 255	NYC	02/09/43	LIVERPOOL	16/09/43	52		
HX 256	NYC	09/09/43	LIVERPOOL	21/09/43	59		
HX 257	NYC	16/09/43	LIVERPOOL	30/09/43	75		
HX 258	NYC	22/09/43	LIVERPOOL	06/10/43	59		
HX 259	NYC	28/09/43	LIVERPOOL	13/10/43	41		
HX 260	NYC	05/10/43	LIVERPOOL	20/10/43	61		
HX 261	NYC	11/10/43	LIVERPOOL	26/10/43	65		
HX 262	NYC	18/10/43	LIVERPOOL	02/11/43	59		
HX 263	NYC	24/10/43	LIVERPOOL	08/11/43	47		
HX 264	NYC	31/10/43	LIVERPOOL	17/11/43	65		
HX 265	NYC	06/11/43	LIVERPOOL	21/11/43	51		
HX 266	NYC	13/11/43	LIVERPOOL	27/11/43	76		
HX 267	NYC	19/11/43	LIVERPOOL	03/12/43	61		
HX 268	NYC	26/11/43	LIVERPOOL	11/12/43	45		
HX 269	NYC	02/12/43	LIVERPOOL	16/12/43	43		
HX 270	NYC	10/12/43	LIVERPOOL	26/12/43	61		
HX 271	NYC	15/12/43	LIVERPOOL	29/12/43	53		
HX 272	NYC	22/12/43	LIVERPOOL	06/01/44	73		
HX 273	NYC	29/12/43	LIVERPOOL	14/01/44	45		
HX 274	NYC	06/01/44	LIVERPOOL	21/01/44	38		
HX 275	NYC	13/01/44	LIVERPOOL	28/01/44	62		
HX 276	NYC	22/01/44	LIVERPOOL	07/02/44	73		

CONVOY	DEP. PORT	DEP. DATE	ARRIVAL PORT	ARR. DATE	TDS	MV SUNK	MV DMGD
HX 277	NYC	28/01/44	LIVERPOOL	13/02/44	69		
HX 278	NYC	05/02/44	LIVERPOOL	20/02/44	51		
HX 279	NYC	13/02/44	LIVERPOOL	29/02/44	59		
HX 280	NYC	20/02/44	LIVERPOOL	09/03/44	63		
HX 281	NYC	27/02/44	LIVERPOOL	15/03/44	37		
HX 282	NYC	06/03/44	LIVERPOOL	22/03/44	96		
HX 283	NYC	13/03/44	LIVERPOOL	29/03/44	62		
HX 284	NYC	21/03/44	LIVERPOOL	06/04/44	80		
HX 285	NYC	28/03/44	LIVERPOOL	12/04/44	54		
HX 286	NYC	05/04/44	LIVERPOOL	20/04/44	87		
HX 287	NYC	12/04/44	LIVERPOOL	26/04/44	71		
HX 288	NYC	18/04/44	LIVERPOOL	04/05/44	89		
HX 289	NYC	27/04/44	LIVERPOOL	13/05/44	130		
HX 290	NYC	05/05/44	LIVERPOOL	19/05/44	93		
HX 291	NYC	10/05/44	LIVERPOOL	27/05/44	99		
HX 292	NYC	19/05/44	LIVERPOOL	02/06/44	128		
HX 293	NYC	27/05/44	LIVERPOOL	09/06/44	97		
HX 294	NYC	02/06/44	LIVERPOOL	19/06/44	113		
HX 295	NYC	10/06/44	LIVERPOOL	24/06/44	80		
HX 296	NYC	19/06/44	LIVERPOOL	03/07/44	91		
HX 297	NYC	24/06/44	LIVERPOOL	11/07/44	116		
HX 298	NYC	03/07/44	LIVERPOOL	18/07/44	115		
HX 299	NYC	11/07/44	LIVERPOOL	24/07/44	85		
HX 300	NYC	17/07/44	LIVERPOOL	03/08/44	166		
HX 301	NYC	25/07/44	LIVERPOOL	08/08/44	130		
HX 302	NYC	04/08/44	LIVERPOOL	17/08/44	96		
HX 303	NYC	11/08/44	LIVERPOOL	27/08/44	104		
HX 304	NYC	17/08/44	LIVERPOOL	01/09/44	89		
HX 305	NYC	25/08/44	LIVERPOOL	10/09/44	98	2	
HX 306	NYC	31/08/44	LIVERPOOL	17/09/44	120		
HX 307	NYC	06/09/44	LIVERPOOL	20/09/44	73		
HX 308	NYC	13/09/44	LIVERPOOL	28/09/44	59		
HX 309	NYC	16/09/44	LIVERPOOL	03/10/44	74		
HX 310	NYC	21/09/44	LIVERPOOL	05/10/44	56		
HX 311	NYC	28/09/44	LIVERPOOL	14/10/44	60		
HX 312	NYC	05/10/44	LIVERPOOL	21/10/44	76		
HX 313	NYC	10/10/44	LIVERPOOL	24/10/44	43		
HX 314	NYC	15/10/44	LIVERPOOL	29/10/44	63		
HX 315	NYC	20/10/44	LIVERPOOL	03/11/44	42		
HX 316	NYC	25/10/44	LIVERPOOL	10/11/44	39		
HX 317	NYC	30/10/44	LIVERPOOL	13/11/44	44		
HX 318	NYC	04/11/44	LIVERPOOL	19/11/44	36		
HX 319	NYC	09/11/44	LIVERPOOL	25/11/44	46		
HX 320	NYC	14/11/44	LIVERPOOL	30/11/44	39		
HX 321	NYC	19/11/44	LIVERPOOL	05/12/44	36		
HX 322	NYC	24/11/44	LIVERPOOL	08/12/44	38		
HX 323	NYC	29/11/44	LIVERPOOL	13/12/44	40		
HX 324	NYC	04/12/44	LIVERPOOL	21/12/44	55		
HX 325	NYC	09/12/44	LIVERPOOL	23/12/44	59		
HX 326	NYC	14/12/44	LIVERPOOL	27/12/44	48		
HX 327	NYC	19/12/44	LIVERPOOL	02/01/45	44		
HX 328	NYC	24/12/44	LIVERPOOL	08/01/45	51		
HX 329	NYC	29/12/44	LIVERPOOL	12/01/45	36		
HX 330	NYC	03/01/45	LIVERPOOL	17/01/45	45		
HX 331	NYC	08/01/45	LIVERPOOL	22/01/45	62		
HX 332	NYC	13/01/45	LIVERPOOL	28/01/45	47	1	1
HX 333	NYC	18/01/45	LIVERPOOL	01/02/45	52		
HX 334	NYC	23/01/45	LIVERPOOL	06/02/45	74		
HX 335	NYC	28/01/45	LIVERPOOL	10/02/45	53		
HX 336	NYC	02/02/45	LIVERPOOL	14/02/45	47		
HX 337	NYC	07/02/45	LIVERPOOL	21/02/45	68		
HX 338	NYC	12/02/45	LIVERPOOL	27/02/45	70		
HX 339	NYC	18/02/45	LIVERPOOL	03/03/45	79		
HX 340	NYC	23/02/45	LIVERPOOL	10/03/45	53		
HX 341	NYC	28/02/45	LIVERPOOL	15/03/45	72		
HX 342	NYC	04/03/45	LIVERPOOL	19/03/45	71		
HX 343	NYC	09/03/45	LIVERPOOL	24/03/45	66		
HX 344	NYC	14/03/45	LIVERPOOL	28/03/45	71		
HX 345	NYC	19/03/45	LIVERPOOL	02/04/45	74		
HX 346	NYC	24/03/45	LIVERPOOL	07/04/45	61		1
HX 347	NYC	29/03/45	LIVERPOOL	14/04/45	62		
HX 348	NYC	03/04/45	LIVERPOOL	20/04/45	80	2	
HX 349	NYC	08/04/45	LIVERPOOL	23/04/45	56		
HX 350	NYC	13/04/45	LIVERPOOL	28/04/45	87		
HX 351	NYC	18/04/45	LIVERPOOL	03/05/45	57		
HX 352	NYC	23/04/45	LIVERPOOL	08/05/45	75		
HX 353	NYC	29/04/45	LIVERPOOL	15/05/45	64		
HX 354	NYC	03/05/45	LIVERPOOL	18/05/45	65		
HX 355	NYC	09/05/45	LIVERPOOL	25/05/45	57		
HX 356	NYC	13/05/45	LIVERPOOL	26/05/45	47		
HX 357	NYC	19/05/45	LIVERPOOL	03/06/45	83		
HX 358	NYC	23/05/45	LIVERPOOL	06/06/45	56		

HXF convoy data

CONVOY	DEP. PORT	DEP. DATE	ARRIVAL PORT	ARR. DATE	TDS	MV SUNK	MV DMGD
HXF 1	HALIFAX	29/09/39	LIVERPOOL	29/9/39	8		
HXF 2	HALIFAX	25/09/39	LIVERPOOL	04/10/39	1		
HXF 6	HALIFAX	24/10/39	LIVERPOOL	02/11/39	6		
HXF 7	HALIFAX	31/10/39	LIVERPOOL	12/11/39	13		
HXF 8	HALIFAX	08/11/39	DOVER	21/11/39	12		
HXF 9	HALIFAX	17/11/39	LIVERPOOL	29/11/39	13		
HXF 10	HALIFAX	25/11/39	DOVER	09/12/39	10		
HXF 11	HALIFAX	02/12/39	LIVERPOOL	15/12/39	14		
HXF 12	HALIFAX	10/12/39	LIVERPOOL	24/12/39	9		
HXF 13	HALIFAX	19/12/39	LIVERPOOL	30/12/39	11		
HXF 14	HALIFAX	27/12/39	LIVERPOOL	08/01/40	20		
HXF 15	HALIFAX	04/01/40	LIVERPOOL	15/01/40	12		
HXF 16	HALIFAX	12/01/40	DOVER	24/01/40	13		
HXF 17	HALIFAX	20/01/40	DOVER	01/02/40	12		
HXF 18	HALIFAX	28/01/40	LIVERPOOL	08/02/40	8		
HXF 19	HALIFAX	04/02/40	LIVERPOOL	17/02/40	8		
HXF 20	HALIFAX	12/02/40	LIVERPOOL	25/02/40	9		

◇ THE ALLIED CONVOY SYSTEM 1939-1945

■ Author's collection

When SCHEER attacked convoy HX 84 sinking HMS JERVIS BAY and five merchant ships, several others were damaged. One, the tanker SAN DEMETRIO, was loaded with petrol and caught fire, her Master and crew not unnaturally abandoned ship. The following day, 7 Nov 1940, a junior officer in charge of one boat sighted smoke and steered towards hopeful rescue and safety. He was somewhat startled to find himself approaching his own ship, afloat and with only residual smoke rising from the gutted midships section. He and his fellow survivors boarded the ship and found the fires had burned out although petrol was freely leaking onto the tank deck.

As the midships structure, containing all controls, navigational aids and officers accommodation was totally gutted, he had his lifeboat hoisted in, rigged emergency steering aft and ordered her diesels re-started. Steering with his lifeboat compass in a vaguely easterly direction he succeeded, after six days, in reaching the west coast of Ireland. Here he anchored, went ashore and succeeded, with local assistance, in finding a telephone and contacting Liverpool. There the somewhat startled naval authorities ordered a tug and escorts to proceed at once to his aid. No doubt provided with some signals assistance and charts from the escort, the MN officer declined a tow and, under escort, brought his ship into the Clyde.

She is seen here arriving to be berthed by tugs; note the burnt out island superstructure amidships and the "S.O.S" message painted on the face of the bridge, the only means of communication onboard! Incredibly, 11,000 tons of her petrol cargo of 11,200 tons was landed intact.

Losses incurred in HX and HXF convoys, excluding stragglers

Convoy	Ship's Name	GRT	Date of loss	Cause of loss	Comments
HX 5	MALABAR	7,976 38 Br	27/10/39	U 34	Tobacco, lumber, general. 5 dead
HX 14	EL OSO	7,267 21 Br	11/01/40	MINED	9,238 tons crude oil, 511 tons petrol.
HX 20	CASTLEMOOR	6,574 22 Br	25/02/40	FOUNDERED	9,400 ton steel ingots. 42 dead
HX 22	COUNSELLOR	5,068 26 Br	08/03/40	MINED	General cargo. No dead
HX 26	ROSSINGTON COURT	6,922 28 Br	13/03/40	COLLISION	Wheat & lumber. No dead Collision with ATHELVIKING
HX 47	ERIK BOYE	2,238 24 Br	15/06/40	U 38	3,568 tons wheat. No dead
HX 47	ITALIA	9,973 39 Nor	14/06/40	U 38	13,000 tons petrol, 19 dead

Convoy	Ship's Name	GRT	Date of loss	Cause of loss	Comments
HX 49	SAN FERNANDO	13,056 19 Br	22/06/40	U 47	13,500 tons crude oil, 4,200 tons FFO. No dead
HX 53	HUMBER ARM	5,758 25 Br	08/07/40	U 99	1,000 tons steel, 5,450 tons paper. No dead
HX 55	MANIPUR	8,652 20 Br	17/07/40	U 57	General including metals. 14 dead
HX 55	SCOTTISH MINSTREL	6,998 22 Br	17/07/40	U 61	9,200 tons FFO. 9 dead
HX 60	GERALDINE MARY	7,244 24 Br	04/08/40	U 52	6,112 tons newsprint. 3 dead
HX 60	GOGOVALE	4,586 27 Br	04/08/40	U 52	6,386 tons flour. 3 dead
HX 60	KING ALFRED	5,272 19 Br	04/08/40	U 52	6,750 tons pitprops. 5 dead

APPENDIX 3

Convoy	Ship's Name	GRT			Date of loss	Cause of loss	Comments
HX 65	ATHELCREST	6,825	40	Br	25/08/40	U 48	Diesel oil. 30 dead
HX 65	CAPE YORK	5,027	26	Br	26/08/40	AIRCRAFT	3,500 tons grain, 4,180 tons lumber. No dead
HX 65	FIRCREST	5,394	07	Br	25/08/40	U 124	7,900 tons iron ore. All crew (40) dead
HX 65	HARPALYCE	5,169	40	Br	25/08/40	U 124	Approx 8,000 tons steel. No dead
HX 65	REMUERA	11,445	11	Br	26/08/40	AIRCRAFT	4,801 tons frig, 1,646 tons general. No dead
HX 66	CHELSEA	4,804	25	Br	30/08/40	U 32	7,600 tons maize. 24 dead
HX 66	KYNO	3,946	24	Br	28/08/40	U 28	4,499 tons general. 5 dead
HX 66	MILL HILL	4,318	30	Br	30/08/40	U 32	6,750 tons pigiron & steel. 34 dead
HX 66	NORNE	3,971	30	Nor	30/08/40	U 32	Scrap metal. Dead unknown
HX 71	TREGENNA	5,242	19	Br	17/09/40	U 65	8,000 tons steel. 33 dead
HX 72	BLAIRANGUS	4,409	30	Br	21/09/40	U 48	1,825 fathoms pitprops. 7 dead
HX 72	CANONESA	8,286	20	Br	21/09/40	U 100	7,265 tons frig & general. 1 dead
HX 72	DALCAIRN	4,608	27	Br	21/09/40	U 100	8,000 tons wheat. No dead
HX 72	ELMBANK	5,156	25	Br	21/09/40	U 99 & U 47	Timber & metals. 1 dead
HX 72	INVERSHANNON	9,154	38	Br	21/09/40	U 99	13,241 tons FFO. 16 dead
HX 72	TORINIA	10,364	39	Br	21/09/40	U 100	13,815 tons FFO. 5 dead
HX 73	DALVEEN	5,193	27	Br	28/09/40	AIRCRAFT	7,398 tons wheat. 11 dead
HX 77	BRANDANGER	4,624	26	Nor	11/10/40	U 48	8,000 tons lumber & metals. 6 dead
HX 77	DAVANGER	7,102	22	Nor	11/10/40	U 48	10,000 tons fuel oil. 17 dead
HX 77	PACIFIC RANGER	6,865	29	Br	12/10/40	U 59	8,235 tons lumber & metals. No dead
HX 77	PORT GISBORNE	10,144	27	Br	11/10/40	U 48	Frig & general cargo. 26 dead
HX 77	ST MALO	5,779	17	Br	12/10/40	U 101	7,274 tons general. 28 dead
HX 77	STANGRANT	5,804	12	Br	13/10/40	U 37	7,715 tons steel and scrap. 9 dead
HX 79	BILDERDIJK	6,856	22	Du	19/10/40	U 47	8,640 tons grain & general. No dead
HX 79	CAPRELLA	8,230	31	Br	20/10/40	U 100	11,300 tons fuel oil. 1 dead
HX 79	LA ESTANCIA	5,185	40	Br	20/10/40	U 47	8,333 tons sugar. 1 dead
HX 79	MATHERAN	7,653	19	Br	19/10/40	U 38	3,000 tons iron, 1,200 tons zinc etc. 9 dead
HX 79	RUPERRA	4,548	25	Br	19/10/40	U 46	Steel, scrap, aircraft. 30 dead
HX 79	SHIRAK	6,023	26	Br	19/10/40	U 47 & U 48	7,771 tons petrol. No dead
HX 79	SITALA	6,218	37	Br	20/10/40	U 100	8,444 tons crude oil. 1 dead
HX 79	UGANDA	4,966	27	Br	19/10/40	U 38	2,006 tons steel, 6,200 tons wood. No dead
HX 79	WANDBY	4,947	40	Br	20/10/40	U 47	8,900 tons lead, zinc & wood. No dead
HX 79	WHITFORD POINT	5,026	28	Br	20/10/40	U 47	7.840 tons steel. 37 dead
HX 83	SCOTTISH MAIDEN	6,993	21	Br	05/11/40	U 99	3,000 tons dieso, 6,500 tons FFO. 16 dead
HX 84	BEAVERFORD	10,042	28	Br	05/11/40	SCHEER	8,425 tons food & general. 77 dead
HX 84	FRESNO CITY	4,955	29	Br	05/11/40	SCHEER	8,129 tons maize. 1 dead
HX 84	KENBANE HEAD	5,225	19	Br	05/11/40	SCHEER	General cargo. 23 dead
HX 84	MAIDAN	7,908	25	Br	05/11/40	SCHEER	General & MT. 91 dead
HX 84	TREWELLARD	5,201	36	Br	05/11/40	SCHEER	7,800 tons steel, 12 a/c. 16 dead
HX 90	APPALACHEE	8,826	30	Br	01/12/40	U 101	11,076 tons avgas & oil. 7 dead
HX 90	CONCH	8,376	31	Br	02/12/40	U 47 & U 95	11,214 tons FFO. No dead
HX 90	GOODLEIGH	5,448	38	Br	02/12/40	U 52	1,000 tons spelter, 8,400 tons wood. 1 dead
HX 90	KAVAK	2,782	29	Br	02/12/40	U 101	1,745 tons bauxite, 1,650 tons pitch. 25 dead
HX 90	LADY GLANELY	5,497	38	Br	02/12/40	U 101	2,000 tons wheat, 6,125 tons wood. 33 dead
HX 90	STIRLINGSHIRE	6,022	28	Br	02/12/40	U 94	7,600 tons sugar, lead & frig. No dead
HX 90	TASSO	1,586	38	Br	02/12/40	U 52	1,300 tons greenheart logs. 5 dead
HX 90	W HENDRIK	4,360	25	Br	03/12/40	AIRCRAFT	1,500 tons steel, 5,000 tons timber. 5 dead
HX 90	WILHELMINA	6,725	09	Br	02/12/40	U 94	6,365 tons general. 5 dead
HX 91	DIONYSSIOS STATHATOS	5,168	19	Gk	12/12/40	FOUNDERED	Wheat. No survivors
HX 92	MACEDONIER	5,227	21	Bel	12/12/40	U 96	6,800 tons phosphates. 15 dead
HX 92	ROTORUA	10,890	11	Br	11/12/40	U 96	10,803 tons frig & general. 21 dead
HX 92	TOWA	5,419	30	Du	11/12/40	U 96	7,778 tons grain, 48 MT. 18 dead
HX 93	ANTHEA	5,186	24	Br	08/12/40	COLLISION	Grain, MT. No dead Collision with MAASDAM.
HX 97	CITY OF BEDFORD	6,402	24	Br	30/12/40	COLLISION	General. 48 dead Collision wtih BODNANT.
HX 100	SOEMBA	6,718	23	Du	07/01/41	FOUNDERED	Steel & scrap. 34 dead
HX 109	CADILLAC	12,062	17	Br	01/03/41	U 552	17,000 tons avgas. 35 dead
HX 112	BEDUIN	8,136	36	Nor	16/03/41	U 99	11,000 tons petrol. 4 dead
HX 112	FERM	6,593	33	Nor	16/03/41	U 99	8,935 tons fuel oil. No dead
HX 112	J B WHITE	7,375	19	Br	17/03/41	U 99	2,500 tons steel, 4,500 tons paper. 2 dead
HX 112	KORSHAMN	6,673	20	Sw	17/03/41	U 99	7,979 tons general. 26 dead
HX 112	VENETIA	5,728	27	Br	16/03/41	U 99	7,052 tons maize. No dead
HX 114	HIDLEFJORD	7,639	28	Nor	01/04/41	AIRCRAFT	10,600 tons petrol. 29 dead
HX 114	SAN CONRADO	7,982	36	Br	01/04/41	AIRCRAFT	10,700 tons petrol. No dead
HX 115	HYLTON	5,197	37	Br	29/03/41	U 48	6,900 tons lumber, 1,500 tons wheat. No dead
HX 115	GERMANIC	5,352	36	Br	29/03/41	U 48	7,982 tons wheat. 5 dead
HX 115	LIMBOURG	2,936	38	Bel	29/03/41	U 48	3,450 tons phosphate. 2 survivors
HX 121	CALEDONIA	9,892	36	Nor	28/04/41	U 96	13,745 tons dieso & fuel oil. 12 dead
HX 121	CAPULET	8,190	32	Br	28/04/41	U 512 & U 201	11,200 tons FFO. 9 dead
HX 121	OILFIELD	8,516	38	Br	28/04/41	U 96	11,700 tons benzine. 47 dead
HX 121	PORT HARDY	8,897	23	Br	28/04/41	U 96	4,000 tons meat, 3,000 tons foodstuffs. 1 dead

131

◇ THE ALLIED CONVOY SYSTEM 1939-1945

Convoy	Ship's Name	GRT			Date of loss	Cause of loss	Comments
HX 126	BARNBY	4,813	40	Br	22/05/41	U 111	7,250 tons flour. 2 dead
HX 126	BRITISH SECURITY	8,470	37	Br	20/05/41	U 556	11,200 tons benzine & paraffin. 53 dead
HX 126	COCKAPONSET	5,995	19	Br	20/05/41	U 556	6,250 tons steel, TNT & general. No dead
HX 126	DARLINGTON COURT	4,974	36	Br	20/05/41	U 556	8,116 tons wheat, a/c. 25 dead
HX 126	ELUSA	6,235	36	Du	21/05/41	U 93	8,000 tons dieso. 3 dead
HX 126	HARPAGUS	5,173	40	Br	20/05/41	U 109	8,250 tons grain. 32 dead
HX 126	JOHN P PEDERSEN	6,128	30	Nor	20/05/41	U 94	9,100 tons army fuel oil. 22 dead
HX 126	NORMAN MONARCH	4,718	37	Br	20/05/41	U 94	8,300 tons wheat. 26 dead
HX 126	ROTHERMERE	5,356	38	Br	20/05/41	U 98	1,998 tons steel, 4,750 tons paper. 22 dead
HX 133	BROCKLEY HILL	5,297	19	Br	24/06/41	U 651	7,000 tons grain. No dead
HX 133	GRAYBURN	6,342	38	Br	29/06/41	U 651	10,300 tons steel & scrap. 35 dead
HX 133	MAASDAM	8,812	21	Du	26/06/41	U 564	9,120 tons general. 32 pass. 2 dead
HX 133	MALAYA II	8,651	21	Br	26/06/41	U 564	6,250 tons metal, wheat & TNT. 39 dead
HX 133	SOLOY	4,402	29	Nor	24/06/41	U 203	7,880 tons wheat. No dead
HX 148	SOCONY	4,404	36	Br	09/09/41	COLLISION	Lub oil. 2 dead. Collision with TONGARIRO
HX 150	NIGARISTAN	5,993	12	Br	24/09/41	FIRE	7,000 tons general. No dead
HX 173	DVINOLES	3,946	31	Russ	04/02/42	COLLISION	Collision with EVITA
HX 174	ANDERSON	1,694	25	Nor	10/02/42	WRECKED	Cargo unknown. 8 dead
HX 194	KAAPAREN	3,386	30	Sw	14/06/42	COLLISION	Collision with TUNGSHA
HX 209	ROBERT H COLLEY	11,651	38	Amer	04/10/42	U 254	154,000 barrels FFO. 33 survivors
HX 212	BARRWHIN	4,998	29	Br	29/10/42	U 436	8,200 tons grain & stores. 24 dead
HX 212	GURNEY E NEWLIN	8,225	42	Amer	27/10/42	U 436 & U 606	12,000 tons petrol & paraffin. 60 dead
HX 212	KOSMOS II	16,966	31	Nor	28/10/42	U 606 & U 624	21,000 tons crude oil. 40 dead
HX 212	PAN-NEW YORK	7,701	38	Amer	29/10/42	U 624	12,500 tons "clean oil". 42 dead
HX 212	SOURABAYA	10,107	15	Br	27/10/42	U 436	7,800 tons fuel oil. 77 dead
HX 217	CHARLES L D	5,273	33	Br	09/12/42	U 553	6,517 tons general. 36 dead
HX 217	EMPIRE SPENSER	8,194	42	Br	08/12/42	U 524	10,000 tons benzine. 1 dead
HX 222	VESTFOLD	14,547	31	Pan	17/01/43	U 268	17,386 tons oil. 3 LCTs, 19 dead
HX 223	KOLLBJORG	8,259	37	Nor	24/01/43	FOUNDERED	Unknown quantity of oil. 12 dead
HX 223	NORTIND	8,221	41	Nor	26/01/43	U 358	11,000 tons oil. No survivors
HX 224	INVERILEN	9,456	38	Br	03/02/43	U 456	13,000 tons clean oil. 31 dead
HX 224	JEREMIAH VAN RENSSELAER	7,177	42	Amer	02/02/43	U 456	9,000 tons general. 46 dead

Convoy	Ship's Name	GRT			Date of loss	Cause of loss	Comments
HX 228	ANDREA F LUCKENBACH	6,565	19	Amer	10/03/43	U 221	General & explosives. 21 dead
HX 228	BRANT COUNTY	5,001	15	Nor	11/03/43	U 757	5,330 tons general, 670 tons TNT. 6 dead
HX 228	TUCURINCA	5,412	26	Br	10/03/43	U 221	4,000 tons general. 1 dead
HX 228	WILLIAM C GORGAS	7,197	43	Amer	11/03/43	U 444 & U 757	Gen, expl, deck cargo. Only 12 survivors
HX 229	CANADIAN STAR	8,293	39	Br	18/03/43	U 221	7,806 tons frig cargo. 29 dead
HX 229	CORACERO	7,252	23	Br	17/03/43	U 384	5,758 tons frig cargo. 5 dead
HX 229	ELIN K	5,214	37	Nor	16/03/43	U 603	7,000 tons wheat & frig. No dead
HX 229	HARRY LUCKENBACH	6,366	19	Amer	17/03/43	U 91	General. All crew (80) dead
HX 229	IRENEE DU PONT	6,125	41	Amer	17/03/43	U 600 & U 91	3,200 tons oil, 5,800 tons general. 24 dead
HX 229	JAMES OGLETHORPE	7,176	42	Amer	17/03/43	U 758 & U 91	8,000 tons general. 44 dead
HX 229	NARIVA	8,714	20	Br	17/03/43	U 600 & U 91	5,600 tons frig cargo. No dead
HX 229	SOUTHERN PRINCESS	12,156	15	Br	17/03/43	U 600	10,053 tons oil fuel, 463 tons general. 4 dead
HX 229	TERKOELI	5,158	23	Du	17/03/43	U 632	Zinc, wheat, mail. 36 dead
HX 229	WALTER Q GRESHAM	7,191	43	Amer	18/03/43	U 221	9,000 tons foodstuffs. 27 dead
HX 229	WILLIAM EUSTIS	7,196	43	Amer	17/03/43	U 435 & U 91	7,400 tons foodstuffs. No dead
HX 229	ZAANLAND	6,813	21	Du	17/03/43	U 758	Frig cargo, wheat & zinc. No dead
HX 229A	SVEND FOYN	14,795	31	Br	19/03/43	FOUNDERED	Oil. 187 dead
HX 231	BRITISH ARDOUR	7,124	28	Br	05/04/43	U 706	10,000 tons fuel oil. No dead
HX 231	SHILLONG	5,529	39	Br	04/04/43	U 635	8,000 tons zinc, 3,000 tons general. 65 dead
HX 231	WAROONGA	9,365	14	Br	06/04/43	U 630	6,000 tons food, 1,500 tons lead. 19 dead
HX 232	FRESNO CITY II	7,261	42	Br	12/04/43	U 563 & U 706	3,000 tons ore, 5,965 tons general. No dead
HX 232	PACIFIC GROVE	7,117	28	Br	12/04/43	U 563	7,184 tons gen, 1,500 tons dieso. 11 dead
HX 232	ULYSSES	2,666	18	Du	12/04/43	U 563	3,372 tons general. No dead
HX 233	FORT RAMPART	7,134	43	Br	17/04/43	U 628 & U 226	1,400 tons metal, 7,300 tons lumber. 6 dead
HX 234	AMERIKA	10,218	30	Br	22/04/43	U 306	8,844 tons general. 86 dead incl 37 passengers
HX 235	EL ALMIRANTE	5,248	17	Pan	22/04/43	COLLISION	Collision ELIAS BOUDINOT. 12 dead
HX 245	EMPIRE IBEX	7,028	18	Br	02/07/43	COLLISION	General cargo. No dead. Coll. with EMPIRE MACCALPINE
HX 252	J H SENIOR	11,065	31	Pan	19/08/43	COLLISION[1]	Avgas
HX 252	J PINCKNEY HENDERSON	7,176	43	Amer	19/08/43	COLLISION[1]	General
HX 252	SANTOS	4,639	28	Nor	19/08/43	COLLISION	General. 2 dead

◇ 132

Convoy	Ship's Name	GRT			Date of loss	Cause of loss	Comments
HX 270	FREDERICK BARTHOLDI	7,201	43	Amer	25/12/43	WRECKED	General. Salved, bu on Clyde
HX 276	EMPIRE MANOR	7,017	43	Br	28/01/44	COLLISION	Cargo incl bullion. No dead. Collision with EDWARD KAVANNAGH
HX 300	ELISABETH DAL	4,258	10	Br	03/08/44	COLLISION	Grain. Collision in Mersey. CTL. Coll. with JACKSONVILLE
HX 305	EMPIRE HERITAGE	15,702	30	Br	08/09/44	U 482	16,000 tons FFO, 1,900 tons deck. 113 dead
HX 305	PINTO	1,346	28	Br	08/09/44	U 482	Rescue ship. 21 dead
HX 326	JAMAICA PLANTER	4,098	36	Br	27/12/44	COLLISION	Refrigerated cargo. No dead. Collision with WELLESLEY
HX 332	SOLOR	8,262	38	Nor	27/01/45	U 825	Oil, gliders. 4 dead
HX 348	CYRUS H MCCORMICK	7,181	42	Amer	18/04/45	U 1107	6,364 tons construction gear. 6 dead
HX 348	EMPIRE GOLD	8,028	41	Br	18/04/45	U 1107	10,500 tons white spirit. 43 dead
HXF 7	MATRA	8,003	26	Br	13/11/39	MINED	5,750 tons general. 16 dead
HXF 11	CHANCELLOR	4,607	16	Br	02/12/39	COLLISION	General. Collision with ATHELCHIEF and OROPESA

1. The collision was between both these ships and the resultant fire from JH SENIOR'S cargo destroyed both. There were only 9 survivors from the combined crews.

SC convoy series 1940-1945

This was the second eastbound trans-Atlantic series, introduced in Aug 1940, to convoy the slower, older vessels. Prior to this, the 9-knot minimum speed of the HX series had excluded such ships that were obliged to proceed unescorted, with dire results. The SC series, with an initial minimum speed of seven and a half knots, at least reduced their exposure from the hazards facing slow, independent ships.

To avoid undue congestion at Halifax, the series at first used Sydney, Cape Breton as its western terminal; hence the RN, to avoid confusion in signals with SYDNEY NSW, always used the convoy code SC. SYDNEY CB. The possibility of the "W" being omitted (or added) in a corrupted signal caused the usage of "CB" rather than the usual "NS" for Nova Scotia.

SC 1 sailed 15 Aug 1940 and, with SC 15 sailing 8 Dec 1940, the service then transferred to Halifax NS for the winter season. Whilst Sydney CB does not completely ice up, navigation does become more difficult in the winter season.

Sailings from Sydney CB re-commenced with SC 33 on 1 Jun 1941, continuing until the next winter and terminating with SC 64. The winter sailings from Halifax were SC 65 to 84, then returning to Sydney CB for a brief period. SC 85 to 94 sailed from Sydney CB but SC 95 reverted to Halifax NS for its sailing on 4 Aug 1942. The HX series was about to move its terminal from Halifax to NYC, thus freeing Halifax as an assembly port for the SC convoys.

With SC 102 sailing 19 Sept 1942, the SC series also moved further south to NYC where it remained until SC 125 sailing on 31 Mar 1943, once again from Halifax NS. The series remained Halifax based thereafter until the last convoy, SC 177, which sailed 26 May 1945.

Except for the seasonal changes of the sailing port, the operation of this series and the arrangements for escorts was broadly similar to that already described in the preceding notes on the HX convoys.

The series was continuous, except for a pause in mid-1944. Convoy SC 157 sailed 17 Apr 1944 and the series resumed with SC 158 sailing on 4 Oct 1944. This pause was to permit the withdrawal of a number of Escort Groups to cover the Normandy invasion routes. The vessels displaced from the SC series were absorbed into the SLOW convoys of the HX series run during that period. (See comment in the notes on HX convoys)

Of all the SC convoys only three failed to complete their passages as formed bodies. SC 52 suffered a heavy attack by submarines soon after sailing and was ordered to return to Sydney CB after circumnavigating Newfoundland. SC 62 and SC 63 both met appalling weather in mid-January 1942, were hove to and scattered, and accordingly ships were ordered to complete their individual passages as independents.

Of the 177 convoys containing a total of 6,806 ships, 29 were attacked and suffered loss. 145 ships were lost in attacks on convoys, 143 sunk by U-boats and 2 by aircraft. Two ships, BLAIRMORE of SC 1 and TOWARD of SC 118, were also sunk by U-boats while detached on rescue duty. 18 merchant ships were lost from marine causes, and are included in the listings as these can reasonably be described as losses incurred due to the exigencies of war. Finally one ship, ALMA DAWSON of SC 11, sank when she blundered into a British minefield.

Comparison with the HX convoys, for similar periods, show that the 1940 convoys were broadly comparable, HX convoys lost 24 ships to SC convoys' 29 ships. In 1941 and 1942 there were horrifying differences, HX convoys lost 21

THE ALLIED CONVOY SYSTEM 1939-1945

and 8 respectively, SC convoys 46 and 40. 1943, 1944 and 1945 showed almost equal losses to both series.

The dreadful bias against the slower SC convoys is partially attributable to reduced ability to divert the slower convoys from known danger and, to a degree, to the fact that slower, older and smaller ships are a good deal more susceptible to loss during a concerted attack. The fact that almost double the number of SC convoys was located and attacked as opposed to those of HX has the greatest bearing on the matter however.

The figures indicate why merchant seamen hated being included in a SC convoy as opposed to an HX. It must however be appreciated that this division was due entirely to the rated speed of the individual ship, and that the alternative was a reversion to the unescorted days pre-August 1940. This was not an alternative that any authority or individual was prepared to enforce.

SC convoy data

CONVOY	DEP. PORT	DEP. DATE	ARRIVAL PORT	ARR. DATE	TDS	MV SUNK	MV DMGD
SC 1	SYDNEY CB	15/08/40	LIVERPOOL	29/08/40	40		
SC 2	SYDNEY CB	25/08/40	LIVERPOOL	10/09/40	53	2	
SC 3	SYDNEY CB	02/09/40	LIVERPOOL	18/09/40	47	2	
SC 4	SYDNEY CB	10/09/40	LIVERPOOL	26/09/40	30		
SC 5	SYDNEY CB	19/09/40	LIVERPOOL	04/10/40	43		
SC 6	SYDNEY CB	27/09/40	LIVERPOOL	12/10/40	38	3	
SC 7	SYDNEY CB	05/10/40	LIVERPOOL	21/10/40	34	15	
SC 8	SYDNEY CB	15/10/40	LIVERPOOL	31/10/40	40		
SC 9	SYDNEY CB	24/10/40	LIVERPOOL	09/11/40	29		
SC 10	SYDNEY CB	29/10/40	LIVERPOOL	13/11/40	14		
SC 11	SYDNEY CB	09/11/40	LIVERPOOL	26/11/40	34	7	
SC 12	SYDNEY CB	13/11/40	LIVERPOOL	29/11/40	17		
SC 13	SYDNEY CB	22/11/40	LIVERPOOL	07/12/40	32		
SC 14	SYDNEY CB	30/11/40	LIVERPOOL	17/12/40	21		
SC 15	SYDNEY CB	08/12/40	LIVERPOOL	23/12/40	21		
SC 16	HALIFAX	15/12/40	LIVERPOOL	31/12/40	15		
SC 17	HALIFAX	23/12/40	LIVERPOOL	08/01/41	19		
SC 18	HALIFAX	02/01/41	LIVERPOOL	19/01/41	27		
SC 19	HALIFAX	12/01/41	LIVERPOOL	02/02/41	27	3	
SC 20	HALIFAX	22/01/41	LIVERPOOL	08/02/41	38		
SC 21	HALIFAX	31/01/41	LIVERPOOL	18/02/41	38		
SC 22	HALIFAX	08/02/41	LIVERPOOL	28/02/41	32	1	1
SC 23	HALIFAX	18/02/41	LOCH EWE	09/03/41	34	1	
SC 24	HALIFAX	28/02/41	LIVERPOOL	19/03/41	26		
SC 25	HALIFAX	10/03/41	LIVERPOOL	29/03/41	32		
SC 26	HALIFAX	20/03/41	LIVERPOOL	08/04/41	23	6	2
SC 27	HALIFAX	30/03/41	LIVERPOOL	18/04/41	29		
SC 28	HALIFAX	09/04/41	LIVERPOOL	28/04/41	31		
SC 29	HALIFAX	19/04/41	LIVERPOOL	08/05/41	42		
SC 30	HALIFAX	29/04/41	LIVERPOOL	20/05/41	28		
SC 31	HALIFAX	09/05/41	LIVERPOOL	30/05/41	32		
SC 32	HALIFAX	19/05/41	LIVERPOOL	07/06/41	28		
SC 33	SYDNEY CB	01/06/41	LIVERPOOL	21/06/41	43		
SC 34	SYDNEY CB	10/06/41	CLYDE	29/06/41	34		
SC 35	SYDNEY CB	21/06/41	CLYDE	09/07/41	34		
SC 36	SYDNEY CB	01/07/41	LIVERPOOL	19/07/41	40		
SC 37	SYDNEY CB	12/07/41	CLYDE	28/07/41	41		
SC 38	SYDNEY CB	22/07/41	LIVERPOOL	08/08/41	22		
SC 39	SYDNEY CB	01/08/41	LIVERPOOL	19/08/41	29		
SC 40	SYDNEY CB	10/08/41	LIVERPOOL	29/08/41	46		
SC 41	SYDNEY CB	24/08/41	LIVERPOOL	11/09/41	64		
SC 42	SYDNEY CB	30/08/41	LIVERPOOL	15/09/41	65	15	
SC 43	SYDNEY CB	05/09/41	LIVERPOOL	20/09/41	55		
SC 44	SYDNEY CB	11/09/41	LIVERPOOL	30/09/41	54	4	
SC 45	SYDNEY CB	18/09/41	LIVERPOOL	04/10/41	58		
SC 46	SYDNEY CB	24/09/41	LIVERPOOL	10/10/41	53		
SC 47	SYDNEY CB	29/09/41	LIVERPOOL	20/10/41	63		
SC 48	SYDNEY CB	05/10/41	LIVERPOOL	22/10/41	52	9	
SC 49	SYDNEY CB	11/10/41	LIVERPOOL	27/10/41	31		
SC 50	SYDNEY CB	17/10/41	LIVERPOOL	04/11/41	41		
SC 51	SYDNEY CB	23/10/41	LIVERPOOL	09/11/41	38		
SC 52	SYDNEY CB	29/10/41	SYDNEY CB	05/11/41	34	4	
SC 53	SYDNEY CB	04/11/41	LIVERPOOL	24/11/41	52		
SC 54	SYDNEY CB	10/11/41	LIVERPOOL	26/11/41	70		
SC 55	SYDNEY CB	16/11/41	LIVERPOOL	05/12/41	46		
SC 56	SYDNEY CB	22/11/41	LIVERPOOL	10/12/41	45		
SC 57	SYDNEY CB	28/11/41	LIVERPOOL	15/12/41	33	3	
SC 58	SYDNEY CB	04/12/41	LIVERPOOL	21/12/41	50		
SC 59	SYDNEY CB	10/12/41	LIVERPOOL	27/12/41	39		
SC 60	SYDNEY CB	16/12/41	LIVERPOOL	31/12/41	22		
SC 61	SYDNEY CB	21/12/41	LIVERPOOL	07/01/42	16		
SC 62	SYDNEY CB	27/12/41	DISPERSED IN 56.49 N 09.12W	12/01/42	28		
SC 63	SYDNEY CB	03/01/42	DISPERSED	13/01/42	27		
SC 64	SYDNEY CB	09/01/42	LIVERPOOL	23/01/42	29		
SC 65	HALIFAX	17/01/42	LIVERPOOL	04/02/42	36		
SC 66	HALIFAX	23/01/42	LIVERPOOL	09/02/42	29		
SC 67	HALIFAX	30/01/42	LIVERPOOL	15/02/42	22	1	
SC 68	HALIFAX	04/02/42	LIVERPOOL	20/02/42	20		
SC 69	HALIFAX	10/02/42	LIVERPOOL	27/02/42	25		
SC 70	HALIFAX	15/02/42	LIVERPOOL	07/03/42	31		
SC 71	HALIFAX	22/02/42	LIVERPOOL	10/03/42	23		
SC 72	HALIFAX	28/02/42	LIVERPOOL	17/03/42	19		
SC 73	HALIFAX	06/03/42	LIVERPOOL	24/03/42	24		
SC 74	HALIFAX	12/03/42	LIVERPOOL	28/03/42	34		
SC 75	HALIFAX	18/03/42	LIVERPOOL	03/04/42	27		
SC 76	HALIFAX	24/03/42	LIVERPOOL	11/04/42	25		
SC 77	HALIFAX	30/03/42	LIVERPOOL	16/04/42	51		

… APPENDIX 3

CONVOY	DEP. PORT	DEP. DATE	ARRIVAL PORT	ARR. DATE	TDS	MV SUNK	MV DMGD	CONVOY	DEP. PORT	DEP. DATE	ARRIVAL PORT	ARR. DATE	TDS	MV SUNK	MV DMGD
SC 78	HALIFAX	05/04/42	LIVERPOOL	22/04/42	12			SC 128	HALIFAX	25/04/43	LIVERPOOL	13/05/43	31		
SC 79	HALIFAX	11/04/42	LIVERPOOL	27/04/42	53			SC 129	HALIFAX	02/05/43	LIVERPOOL	21/05/43	24	2	
SC 80	HALIFAX	17/04/42	LIVERPOOL	03/05/42	29			SC 130	HALIFAX	11/05/43	LIVERPOOL	26/05/43	37		
SC 81	HALIFAX	23/04/42	LIVERPOOL	09/05/42	68			SC 131	HALIFAX	18/05/43	LIVERPOOL	31/05/43	31		
SC 82	HALIFAX	30/04/42	LIVERPOOL	16/05/42	31			SC 132	HALIFAX	26/05/43	LIVERPOOL	11/06/43	44		
SC 83	HALIFAX	07/05/42	LIVERPOOL	23/05/42	62			SC 133	HALIFAX	05/06/43	LIVERPOOL	19/06/43	49		
SC 84	HALIFAX	14/05/42	LIVERPOOL	29/05/42	45			SC 134	HALIFAX	16/06/43	LIVERPOOL	01/07/43	74		
SC 85	SYDNEY CB	29/05/42	LIVERPOOL	12/06/42	60			SC 135	HALIFAX	27/06/43	LIVERPOOL	11/07/43	73		
SC 86	SYDNEY CB	05/06/42	LIVERPOOL	20/06/42	35			SC 136	HALIFAX	08/07/43	LIVERPOOL	23/07/43	47		
SC 87	SYDNEY CB	12/06/42	LIVERPOOL	27/06/42	41			SC 137	HALIFAX	19/07/43	LIVERPOOL	03/08/43	41		
SC 88	SYDNEY CB	19/06/42	LIVERPOOL	04/07/42	33			SC 138	HALIFAX	30/07/43	LIVERPOOL	12/08/43	50		
SC 89	SYDNEY CB	26/06/42	LIVERPOOL	11/07/42	51			SC 139	HALIFAX	09/08/43	LIVERPOOL	24/08/43	56		
SC 90	SYDNEY CB	03/07/42	LIVERPOOL	16/07/42	32			SC 140	HALIFAX	21/08/43	LIVERPOOL	05/09/43	73		
SC 91	SYDNEY CB	10/07/42	LIVERPOOL	24/07/42	39			SC 141	HALIFAX	03/09/43	LIVERPOOL	17/09/43	75		
SC 92	SYDNEY CB	17/07/42	LIVERPOOL	31/07/42	43			SC 142	HALIFAX	15/09/43	LIVERPOOL	29/09/43	51		
SC 93	SYDNEY CB	24/07/42	LIVERPOOL	07/08/42	41			SC 143	HALIFAX	28/09/43	LIVERPOOL	12/10/43	39	1	
SC 94	SYDNEY CB	31/07/42	LIVERPOOL	13/08/42	30	10		SC 144	HALIFAX	11/10/43	LIVERPOOL	27/10/43	38		
SC 95	HALIFAX	04/08/42	LIVERPOOL	19/08/42	41	1		SC 145	HALIFAX	24/10/43	LIVERPOOL	07/11/43	31		
SC 96	HALIFAX	11/08/42	LIVERPOOL	27/08/42	27			SC 146	HALIFAX	06/11/43	LIVERPOOL	22/11/43	32		
SC 97	HALIFAX	22/08/42	LIVERPOOL	07/09/42	59	2		SC 147	HALIFAX	19/11/43	LIVERPOOL	04/12/43	50		
SC 98	HALIFAX	29/08/42	LIVERPOOL	13/09/42	69			SC 148	HALIFAX	02/12/43	LIVERPOOL	16/12/43	41		
SC 99	HALIFAX	05/09/42	LIVERPOOL	20/09/42	59			SC 149	HALIFAX	15/12/43	LIVERPOOL	30/12/43	33		
SC 100	HALIFAX	12/09/42	LIVERPOOL	28/09/42	20	3		SC 150	HALIFAX	30/12/43	LIVERPOOL	14/01/44	19		
SC 101	HALIFAX	19/09/42	LIVERPOOL	05/10/42	26			SC 151	HALIFAX	14/01/44	LIVERPOOL	31/01/44	33		
SC 102	NYC	19/09/42	LIVERPOOL	06/10/42	34			SC 152	HALIFAX	29/01/44	LIVERPOOL	15/02/44	29		
SC 103	NYC	26/09/42	LIVERPOOL	14/10/42	48			SC 153	HALIFAX	13/02/44	LIVERPOOL	02/03/44	18		
SC 104	NYC	03/10/42	LIVERPOOL	21/10/42	47	7		SC 154	HALIFAX	28/02/44	LIVERPOOL	15/03/44	30		
SC 105	NYC	11/10/42	LIVERPOOL	31/10/42	50			SC 155	HALIFAX	14/03/44	LIVERPOOL	29/03/44	46		
SC 106	NYC	16/10/42	LIVERPOOL	05/11/42	24			SC 156	HALIFAX	29/03/44	LIVERPOOL	13/04/44	40	2	
SC 107	NYC	24/10/42	LIVERPOOL	10/11/42	41	15		SC 157	HALIFAX	17/04/44	LIVERPOOL	01/05/44	48		
SC 108	NYC	01/11/42	LIVERPOOL	19/11/42	37			SC 158	HALIFAX	04/10/44	LIVERPOOL	18/10/44	72		
SC 109	NYC	09/11/42	LIVERPOOL	30/11/42	45	1	1	SC 159	HALIFAX	18/10/44	LIVERPOOL	02/11/44	63		
SC 110	NYC	17/11/42	LIVERPOOL	06/12/42	33			SC 160	HALIFAX	02/11/44	LIVERPOOL	17/11/44	47		
SC 111	NYC	25/11/42	LIVERPOOL	17/12/42	20			SC 161	HALIFAX	17/11/44	LIVERPOOL	04/12/44	49		
SC 112	NYC	04/12/42	LIVERPOOL	25/12/42	52			SC 162	HALIFAX	02/12/44	LIVERPOOL	17/12/44	59		
SC 113	NYC	12/12/42	LIVERPOOL	02/01/43	54			SC 163	HALIFAX	17/12/44	LIVERPOOL	31/12/44	48		
SC 114	NYC	19/12/42	LIVERPOOL	07/01/43	31			SC 164	HALIFAX	01/01/45	LIVERPOOL	18/01/45	42		
SC 115	NYC	27/12/42	LIVERPOOL	15/01/43	18			SC 165	HALIFAX	16/01/45	LIVERPOOL	31/01/45	32		
SC 116	NYC	04/01/43	LIVERPOOL	29/01/43	48			SC 166	HALIFAX	31/01/45	LIVERPOOL	13/02/45	26		
SC 117	NYC	12/01/43	LIVERPOOL	03/02/43	21			SC 167	HALIFAX	16/02/45	LIVERPOOL	02/03/45	38	2	
SC 118	NYC	24/01/43	LIVERPOOL	12/02/43	61	8		SC 168	HALIFAX	25/02/45	LIVERPOOL	13/03/45	19		
SC 119	NYC	03/02/43	LIVERPOOL	22/02/43	39			SC 169	HALIFAX	07/03/45	LIVERPOOL	21/03/45	20		
SC 120	NYC	13/02/43	LIVERPOOL	05/03/43	56			SC 170	HALIFAX	17/03/45	LIVERPOOL	31/03/45	27		
SC 121	NYC	23/02/43	LIVERPOOL	14/03/43	57	7	1	SC 171	HALIFAX	27/03/45	LIVERPOOL	10/04/45	22		
SC 122	NYC	05/03/43	LIVERPOOL	24/03/43	51	8		SC 172	HALIFAX	06/04/45	LIVERPOOL	22/04/45	30		
SC 123	NYC	14/03/43	LIVERPOOL	03/04/43	45			SC 173	HALIFAX	18/04/45	LIVERPOOL	04/05/45	17		
SC 124	NYC	20/03/43	LIVERPOOL	09/04/43	33			SC 174	HALIFAX	28/04/45	LIVERPOOL	14/05/45	33		
SC 125	HALIFAX	31/03/43	LIVERPOOL	15/04/43	34			SC 175	HALIFAX	07/05/45	LIVERPOOL	21/05/45	29		
SC 126	HALIFAX	08/04/43	LIVERPOOL	23/04/43	38			SC 176	HALIFAX	16/05/45	LIVERPOOL	29/05/45	26		
SC 127	HALIFAX	16/04/43	LIVERPOOL	03/05/43	55			SC 177	HALIFAX	26/05/45	LIVERPOOL	08/06/45	32		

THE ALLIED CONVOY SYSTEM 1939-1945

Losses incurred in SC convoys, excluding stragglers

Convoy	Ship's Name	GRT		Date of loss	Cause of loss	Comments
SC 1	BLAIRMORE	4,141 28	Br	24/08/40	U 37	Pitprops. 4 dead
SC 2	MARDINIAN	2,434 19	Br	09/09/40	U 28	3,500 tons pitch. 6 dead
SC 2	POSSIDON	3,840 09	Gk	08/09/40	U 47	5,410 tons sulphur, phosphate. 17 dead
SC 3	ALEXANDROS	4,343 06	Gk	15/09/40	U 48	4,500 tons timber & paper. 5 dead
SC 3	EMPIRE VOLUNTEER	5,319 21	Br	15/09/40	U 48	7,700 tons iron ore. 6 dead
SC 6	DELPHIN	3,816 06	Gk	09/10/40	U 103	Maize, wheat. No dead
SC 6	GRAIGWEN	3,697 26	Br	10/10/40	U 103 (9.10) & U 123	6,160 tons maize. 7 dead
SC 6	ZANNES GOUNARIS	4,407 07	Gk	09/10/40	U 103	Phosphate rock. 1 dead
SC 7	ASSYRIAN	2,962 14	Br	19/10/40	U 101	3,700 tons general. 17 dead
SC 7	BEATUS	4,885 25	Br	18/10/40	U 46	1,926 tons steel, 5,874 tons wood. No dead
SC 7	BOEKELO	2,118 30	Du	19/10/40	U 100 & U 123	Timber. No dead
SC 7	CONVALLARIA	1,996 21	Sw	18/10/40	U 46	Pulpwood. No dead
SC 7	CREEKIRK	3,917 12	Br	18/10/40	U 101	5,900 tons iron ore. 36 dead
SC 7	EMPIRE BRIGADE	5,154 12	Br	19/10/40	U 99	750 tons copper, 980 tons steel. 6 dead
SC 7	EMPIRE MINIVER	6,055 18	Br	18/10/40	U 99	10,700 tons iron & steel. 3 dead
SC 7	GUNBORG	1,572 30	Sw	18/10/40	U 46	Pulpwood. No dead
SC 7	LANGUEDOC	9,512 37	Br	17/10/40	U 48	13,700 tons fuel oil. No dead
SC 7	NIRITOS	3,854 07	Gk	18/10/40	U 99	5,426 tons sulphur. 1 dead
SC 7	SCORESBY	3,843 23	Br	17/10/40	U 48	Pitprops. No dead
SC 7	SEDGEPOOL	5,556 18	Br	19/10/40	U 123	8,720 tons wheat, 3 dead
SC 7	SNEFJELD	1,643 01	Nor	19/10/40	U 99	Lumber. No dead
SC 7	SOESTERBERG	1,904 27	Du	19/10/40	U 101	Pitprops. 6 dead
SC 7	THALIA(Gk)	5,875 17	Gk	19/10/40	U 99	Steel, lead & spelter. 22 dead
SC 11	ALMA DAWSON	3,985 17	Br	24/11/40	MINED	British mined area. No dead
SC 11	BRADFYNE	4,740 28	Br	23/11/40	U 100	7,900 tons grain. 39 dead
SC 11	BRUSE	2,205 33	Nor	23/11/40	U 100	Lumber. 16 dead
SC 11	BUSSUM	3,636 17	Du	23/11/40	U 100	5,200 tons grain. 29 survivors
SC 11	JUSTITIA	4,562 35	Br	22/11/40	U 100	5,161 tons wood, 2,248 tons steel. 13 dead
SC 11	LEISE MAERSK	3,136 21	Br	23/11/40	U 100	4,500 tons grain & gen. 17 dead
SC 11	SALONICA	2,694 12	Nor	23/11/40	U 100	Pitprops. 9 dead
SC 13	EUGENIA CAMBANIS	3,470 98	Gk	28/11/40	FOUNDERED	Grain. No dead
SC 13	KOLCHIS	2,219 09	Gk	23/11/40	FOUNDERED	Grain. 23 dead
SC 13	LISIEUX	2,594 19	Br	27/11/40	FOUNDERED	Plywood, spelter, lead. No dead
SC 19	AIKATERINI	4,929 13	Gk	29/01/41	U 93	7,844 tons grain. No dead
SC 19	KING ROBERT	5,886 20	Br	29/01/41	U 93	7,942 tons grain. No dead
SC 19	W B WALKER	10,468 35	Br	29/01/41	U 93	13,338 tons petrol & avgas. 4 dead
SC 21	MIDDLETON	4,297 35	Br	18/02/41	COLLISION	Steel & MT. No dead
SC 22	KERVEGAN	2,018 22	Br	09/02/41	FOUNDERED	Pulpwood. No survivors
SC 22	ROTULA	7,981 35	Du	01/03/41	AIRCRAFT	10,699 tons avgas. 16 dead
SC 23	EMPIRE FROST	7,005 40	Br	13/03/41	AIRCRAFT	9,150 tons wheat. 6 dead
SC 26	ALDERPOOL	4,313 30	Br	03/04/41	U 46	7,200 tons wheat,. No dead
SC 26	BRITISH RELIANCE	7,000 28	Br	02/04/41	U 46	9,967 tons gas oil. No dead
SC 26	HELLE	2,467 18	Nor	04/04/41	U 98	350 tons steel, 2,600 tons pulp, No dead
SC 26	INDIER	5,409 18	Bel	03/04/41	U 73	6,300 tons steel & gen. 42 dead
SC 26	LEONIDAS Z CAMBANIS	4,274 17	Gk	03/04/41	U 73	6,500 tons wheat. 2 dead
SC 26	WESTPOOL	5,724 18	Br	03/04/41	U 74	7,144 tons scrap iron. 35 dead
SC 42	BARON PENTLAND	3,410 27	Br	10/09/41	U 652 & U372	1,512 standards lumber. 2 dead
SC 42	BERURY	4,924 19	Br	11/09/41	U 207	2,100 tons general. 1 dead
SC 42	BULYSSES	7,519 27	Br	10/09/41	U 82	9,300 tons gas oil. 4 dead
SC 42	EMPIRE CROSSBILL	5,463 19	Br	11/09/41	U 82	6,686 tons steel. 49 dead
SC 42	EMPIRE HUDSON	7,456 41	Br	10/09/41	U 82	9,562 tons wheat. 4 dead
SC 42	GARM	1,231 12	Sw	11/09/41	U 432	502 standards lumber. 6 dead
SC 42	GYPSUM QUEEN	3,915 27	Br	11/09/41	U 82	5,500 tons sulphur. 10 dead
SC 42	JEDMOOR	4,392 28	Br	16/09/41	U 98	7,400 tons iron ore, 31 dead
SC 42	MUNERIC	5,229 19	Br	09/09/41	U 432	7,000 tons iron ore. 63 dead
SC 42	SALLY MAERSK	3,252 23	Br	10/09/41	U 81	4,527 tons wheat. No dead
SC 42	SCANIA	1,980 01	Sw	11/09/41	U 82 & U 202	Lumber. No dead
SC 42	STARGARD	1,113 15	Nor	10/09/41	U 432	1,600 lumber. 2 dead
SC 42	STONEPOOL	4,815 28	Br	11/09/41	U 207	7,000 tons grain, 528 tons oats, MT. 42 dead
SC 42	THISTLEGLEN	4,748 29	Br	10/09/41	U 85	5,200 tons steel, 2,400 tons pigiron. 3 dead
SC 42	WINTERSWIJK	3,205 14	Du	10/09/41	U 432	4,278 tons phosphates. 20 dead
SC 44	BARBRO	6,325 34	Nor	20/09/41	U 552	9,000 tons petrol. No dead
SC 44	EMPIRE BURTON	6,966 41	Br	20/09/41	U 74	9,106 tons wheat. 3 dead
SC 44	PINK STAR	4,150 26	Pan	20/09/41	U 552	General. 11 dead
SC 44	T J WILLIAMS	8,212 21	Br	20/09/41	U 552	10,036 tons petrol. 17 dead
SC 46	EMPIRE KUDU	6,622 19	Br	26/09/41	WRECKED	Scrap steel. 1 dead
SC 46	EMPIRE MALLARD	4,957 18	Br	26/09/41	COLLISION	Steel. No dead. Collision with EMPIRE MOON
SC 46	SOUTH WALES	5,619 29	Br	26/09/41	COLLISION	Grain. No dead
SC 48	BARFONN	9,739 31	Nor	16/10/41	U 432	13,300 tons gas oil. 14 dead
SC 48	BOLD VENTURE	3,222 20	Pan	16/10/41	U 553	Cotton, steel, copper. 17 dead
SC 48	EMPIRE HERON	6,023 20	Br	15/10/41	U 568	7,673 tons sulphur. 42 dead
SC 48	ERVIKEN	6,595 21	Nor	16/10/41	U 558	9,303 tons rock phosphate. 28 dead
SC 48	EVROS	5,283 18	Gk	16/10/41	U 432	7,000 tons iron ore. 30 dead
SC 48	ILA	1,583 39	Nor	15/10/41	U 553	2,070 tons general. 14 dead
SC 48	RYM	1,369 19	Nor	16/10/41	U 558	570 standards timber. No dead
SC 48	SILVERCEDAR	4,354 24	Br	15/10/41	U 553	7,300 tons steel & general. 20 dead
SC 48	W C TEAGLE	9,552 17	Br	16/10/41	U 558	15,000 tons fuel oil. 48 dead

APPENDIX 3

Convoy	Ship's Name	GRT			Date of loss	Cause of loss	Comments
SC 52	EMPIRE ENERGY	6,589	23	Br	04/11/41	WRECKED	Maize. No dead
SC 52	EMPIRE GEMSBUCK	5,626	19	Br	03/11/41	U 203	6,200 tons general. No dead
SC 52	EVEROJA	4,830	10	Br	03/11/41	U 203	6,401 tons wheat. No dead
SC 52	FLYNDERBORG	2,022	30	Br	03/11/41	U 202	2,125 tons lumber. 3 dead
SC 52	GRETAVALE	4,586	28	Br	03/11/41	U 202	6,700 tons steel, MT. 42 dead
SC 52	MAROUKO PATERAS	4,269	17	Gk	03/11/41	WRECKED	Sugar. No dead
SC 53	EMPIRE DORADO	5,595	20	Br	22/11/41	COLLISION	Fruit, copper wire. No dead. Collision with THEDMITOR
SC 57	KIRNWOOD	3,829	28	Br	10/12/41	U 130	5,500 tons grain. 12 dead
SC 57	KURDISTAN	5,844	28	Br	10/12/41	U 130	4,256 tons foodstuffs, 2,100 tons metal. 10 dead
SC 57	STAR OF LUXOR	5,298	18	Eg	10/12/41	U 130	7,094 tons general & stores. 4 dead
SC 58	NIDARDAL	2,368	18	Nor	16/12/41	FOUNDERED	Sulphur, sank in approx 56.07N 21W
SC 67	HEINA	4,028	25	Nor	10/02/42	U 136	6,695 tons general. No dead
SC 73	INDEPENDENCE HALL	5,050	20	Amer	07/03/42	WRECKED	War stores. 10 dead
SC 79	EMPIRE LOTUS	3,696	20	Br	12/04/42	FOUNDERED	Cargo & casualties unknown
SC 94	ANNEBERG	2,537	02	Br	08/08/42	U 379	3,200 tons pulp No dead
SC 94	CAPE RACE	3,807	30	Br	10/08/42	U 660	3,979 tons lumber, 1,040 tons steel. No dead
SC 94	CONDYLIS	4,439	14	Gk	10/08/42	U 660 & U 438	6,924 tons grain & MT. 9 dead
SC 94	EMPIRE REINDEER	6,259	19	Br	10/08/42	U 660	5,950 tons general. No dead
SC 94	KAIMOKU	6,367	19	Amer	08/08/42	U 379	US Army stores. 4 dead
SC 94	KELSO	3,956	24	Br	08/08/42	U 176	2,618 tons general, 2,000 tons ammo. 3 dead
SC 94	MOUNT KASSION	7,914	18	Gk	08/08/42	U 176	9,700 tons general. No dead
SC 94	OREGON	6,008	20	Br	10/08/42	U 660 & U 438	8,107 tons general. 11 dead
SC 94	RADCHURCH	3,701	10	Br	09/08/42	U 176	Iron ore. No dead
SC 94	SPAR	3,616	24	Du	05/08/42	U 593	4,900 tons general. 3 dead
SC 94	TREHATA	4,817	28	Br	08/08/42	U 176	3,000 tons steel, 3,000 tons foodstuffs. 31 dead
SC 95	BALLADIER	3,279	19	Amer	15/08/42	U 705	Gen incl lumber. 11 dead
SC 97	BRONXVILLE	4,663	29	Nor	31/08/42	U 609	Gen & 530 tons explosives. No dead
SC 97	CAPIRA	5,265	20	Pan	31/08/42	U 609	Cargo unknown. 5 dead
SC 100	ATHELSULTAN	8,882	29	Br	22/09/42	U 617	13,000 tons molasses. 50 dead
SC 100	EMPIRE HARTEBEESTE	5,676	18	Br	20/09/42	U 596	7,000 tons steel, food & MT. 5 dead
SC 100	EMPIRE SOLDIER	4,539	28	Br	16/09/42	COLLISION	Collision F J WOLFE. General. No dead
SC 100	TENNESSEE	2,342	21	Br	22/09/42	U 617	3,438 tons wheat. 15 dead
SC 104	ASHWORTH	5,227	20	Br	13/10/42	U 221	7,300 tons bauxite. 49 dead
SC 104	EMPIRE MERSEY	5,791	20	Br	14/10/42	U 618	8,400 tons govt stores. 16 dead
SC 104	FAGERSTEN	2,342	21	Nor	13/10/42	U 221	Steel & lumber. 19 dead
SC 104	NELLIE	4,826	13	Gk	13/10/42	U 607	1,783 tons steel, lumber. 32 dead
SC 104	NIKOLINA MATKOVIC	3,672	18	Yug	13/10/42	U 661	Lumber & sugar. 14 dead
SC 104	SOUTHERN EMPRESS	12,398	14	Br	13/10/42	U 221	Fuel oil. 48 dead
SC 104	SUSANA	5,929	14	Amer	13/10/42	U 221	General & mails. 38 dead
SC 107	DALCROY	4,558	30	Br	02/11/42	U 402	1,809 tons steel, lumber. No dead
SC 107	DALEBY	4,640	29	Br	04/11/42	U 89	8,500 tons grain. No dead
SC 107	EMPIRE ANTELOPE	4,945	19	Br	02/11/42	U 402	5,560 tons general. No dead
SC 107	EMPIRE LEOPARD	5,676	17	Br	02/11/42	U 402	7,410 tons zinc concentrate. 37 dead
SC 107	EMPIRE LYNX	6,379	17	Br	03/11/42	U 132	7,850 tons general. No dead
SC 107	EMPIRE SUNRISE	7,459	41	Br	02/11/42	U 402 & U 84	10,000 tons steel & timber. No dead
SC 107	HAHIRA	6,855	20	Amer	03/11/42	U 521	8,985 tons fuel oil. 3 dead
SC 107	HARTINGTON	5,496	32	Br	02/11/42	U 522, U 521 & U 438	8,000 tons wheat, tanks. 24 dead
SC 107	HATIMURA	6,690	18	Br	03/11/42	U 132	Gen, ammo. 4 dead
SC 107	HOBBEMA	5,507	18	Du	03/11/42	U 132	7,000 tons gen & explosives. 28 dead
SC 107	JEYPORE	5,318	20	Br	03/11/42	U 89	6,200 tons gen & explosives. 1 dead
SC 107	MARITIMA	5,804	12	Br	02/11/42	U 522	7,167 tons gen & explosives. 32 dead
SC 107	MOUNT PELION	5,655	17	Gk	02/11/42	U 522	7,452 tons general & MT. 7 dead
SC 107	PARTHENON	3,189	08	Gk	02/11/42	U 522	General. 6 dead
SC 107	RINOS	4,649	19	Gk	02/11/42	U 402	6,151 general & MT, 8 dead
SC 109	BRILLIANT	9,132	30	Amer	18/11/42	U 43	13,500 tons fuels, lost in tow 25.1.43
SC 118	ADAMAS	4,144	18	Gk	08/02/43	COLLISION	Steel. No dead. Collision with SAMUEL HUNTINGTON
SC 118	AFRIKA	8,597	20	Br	07/02/43	U 402	7,000 tons gen, 4,000 tons steel. 23 dead
SC 118	DAGHILD	9,272	27	Nor	07/02/43	U 402, U 614 & U 608	13,000 tons dieso. No dead
SC 118	HARMALA	5,730	35	Br	07/02/43	U 614	8,500 tons iron ore. 53 dead
SC 118	HENRY R MALLORY	6,063	16	Amer	07/02/43	U 402	General & 383 passengers. 272 dead
SC 118	KALLIOPI	4,965	10	Gk	07/02/43	U 402	6,500 tons steel & lumber. 4 dead
SC 118	NEWTON ASH	4,625	25	Br	07/02/43	U 402	6,500 tons grain, stores & mail. 32 dead
SC 118	ROBERT E HOPKINS	6,625	21	Amer	07/02/43	U 402	8,500 tons fuel oil. No dead
SC 118	TOWARD	1,571	23	Br	07/02/43	U 402	Rescue ship. 58 dead
SC 121	BONNEVILLE	4,665	29	Nor	10/03/43	U 405	7,196 tons gen & explosives. 36 dead
SC 121	EGYPTIAN	2,868	20	Br	07/03/43	U 230	Oilseed, palm oil & tin ore. 44 dead
SC 121	EMPIRE IMPALA	6,116	20	Br	07/03/43	U 591	7,628 tons general. 48 dead

137

Convoy	Ship's Name	GRT		Date of loss	Cause of loss	Comments
SC 121	MALANTIC	3,837 29	Amer	09/03/43	U 409	8,000 tons ammunition. 25 dead
SC 121	MILOS	3,058 98	Sw	11/03/43	U 530	Steel & lumber. 30 dead
SC 121	NAILSEA COURT	4,946 36	Br	10/03/43	U 229	7,661 tons general. 45 dead
SC 121	ROSEWOOD	5,989 31	Br	09/03/43	U 409	Escort oiler. 42 dead
SC 122	ALDERAMIN	7,886 20	Du	17/03/43	U 338	10,000 tons oilseed & general. No dead
SC 122	CARRAS	5,234 18	Gk	19/03/43	U 666 & U 333	Wheat. No dead
SC 122	FORT CEDAR LAKE	7,134 42	Br	17/03/43	U 338 & U 665	General. No dead
SC 122	GRANVILLE	4,071 13	Pan	17/03/43	U 338	2,400 tons general, mails. 12 dead
SC 122	KING GRUFFYDD	5,072 19	Br	17/03/43	U 338	5,000 tons steel, 500 tons explosives. 22 dead
SC 122	KINGSBURY	4,898 37	Br	17/03/43	U 338	8,700 tons W African produce & bauxite. 4 dead
SC 122	PORT AUCKLAND	8,789 22	Br	18/03/43	U 305	7,000 tons frig meat, 1,000 tons general. 8 dead
SC 122	ZOUAVE	4,256 30	Br	17/03/43	U 305	7,100 tons iron ore. 13 dead
SC 129	ANTIGONE	4,545 28	Br	11/05/43	U 402	7,800 tons grain, gen & MT. 3 dead
SC 129	GRADO	3,082 18	Nor	11/05/43	U 402	1,000 tons steel, 3,000 tons lumber. No dead
SC 133	REIGH COUNT	4,657 07	Pan	05/06/43	COLLISION	Collision with CHAGRES. No dead
SC 143	YORKMAR	5,612 19	Amer	09/10/43	U 645	6,584 tons grain & general. 13 dead
SC 156	RUTH I	3,531 00	Nor	06/04/44	U 302	Steel & pitprops. 3 dead
SC 156	SOUTH AMERICA	6,246 31	Nor	06/04/44	U 302	Crude oil. No dead
SC 159	CHATEAUROUX	4,765 21	Br	02/11/44	WRECKED	Woodpulp. Wrecked after arrival. No dead
SC 167	KING EDGAR	4,536 27	Br	02/03/45	U 1302	Lumber, lead & zinc. 4 dead
SC 167	NOVASLI	3,204 20	Nor	02/03/45	U 1302	Lumber. No dead

SL and SL/MKS Convoy series 1939-1944

The SL convoy series was one of the early plans formulated by Trade Division. Just as there was no option but to commence Atlantic convoys from the Canadian seaboard so that the convoy could be organized and formed in a safe haven, some similar base had to be found for homeward bound vessels from the South Atlantic. The War Plan of the C-in-C, South Atlantic, therefore called for the establishment of a defended anchorage at the nearest suitable point on the western African coast to the UK. That point was Freetown, Sierra Leone; hence the designation SL, initially applied to the whole series.

While Freetown undoubtedly possessed a large, natural anchorage suitable for the assembly of convoys, that is where the suitability ceased. There was no port as such, cargo was handled by lighter and landed over the beach. There was little available space ashore, the land rising sharply to a ridge of hills. There was no accommodation available, the colonial administration and the few European residences occupied almost all the available land other than that containing the African population. This was nothing more than an oversize native village with neither sanitation, water supply, communications of any kind nor any facilities normally associated with a European settlement. Disease was endemic, the climate atrocious and particularly enervating to Europeans. Finally, despite an extremely high rainfall, there was a minimal fresh water supply in the coastal area, nor was there space to build even a small reservoir.

The problems faced by the C-in-C and his staff were therefore very considerable and only partially relieved by the allocation of an elderly Union Castle liner, EDINBURGH CASTLE built in 1910, as the static accommodation ship in the roadstead plus a hospital ship that lay as far out to seaward as was practicable to provide reasonably healthy conditions.

Initially oil and coal supplies had to be held afloat, detaining merchant tonnage at anchor for considerable periods. Coal had to be freighted from the UK, oil from the West Indies; all stores came from the UK (it took the civil side of Admiralty almost a year to provide basic furniture, equipment and stationery for the new base structure). Communications were also poor, the naval W/T station had to be built using materials, equipment and staff obtained from the UK; until then the only secure communication was by cable communication routed to the Colonial Secretariat. The C-in-C's War Diary records that, over a year after the outbreak of war, the delay in receipt of signalled communications was partly alleviated when the colonial authorities authorised funds for the purchase of a bicycle for the messenger. He had, up till then, conveyed messages by hand, walking from the Secretariat building to the Naval HQ. Such were the limitations of the land-based infrastructure.

The seaborne arrangements were little better. Convoy escort and all patrol work for the South Atlantic depended almost entirely on the use of armed merchant cruisers, and even these were in short supply initially. Eventually a basic local patrol force of trawlers was provided, again from the UK, and the few cruisers of the S Atlantic Station were also based on Freetown.

Due to the very varied nature of shipping that formed the convoys, fast refrigerated ships, fast cargo liners, tankers and the ubiquitous tramp, there was great disparity in speeds. The initial expedient that was resorted to was to sail convoys alternately, every other convoy being designated a Fast unit. All the convoys received an armed merchant cruiser escort from Freetown to a point in the Southwest Approaches to the UK where a destroyer escort took over, the AMC returning to Freetown. This system remained in force until the sailing of SL 14F on 27 Dec 1939. It must be stressed here that the local authority tended to suffix the F (and later S) designation to the code letters, not the convoy number. For the ease of computer produced lists the practice of appending the letter to the numeric characters has been used in this text.

Commencing with SL 15 sailing 1 Jan 1940, some of the Fast and Slow sections were ordered to rendezvous at the point where the A/S escort was to join, thus saving on escort vessels. It was found a difficult operation given the considerable distance traversed before the rendezvous position, and was heartily disliked by all concerned. However, the practice, and also the sailing of some convoys without any escort at all prior to the A/S rendezvous, had to be accepted. It was the end of Jan 1941 before duplicated convoy numbers, Fast or Slow, were abandoned and A/S escort throughout the passage could be provided.

In late 1942 the series was suspended as the route crossed the path of the US convoys for the North African invasion and passed far too close to the focal point of that operation. The last convoy to sail was SL 125, which suffered very heavy loss. Shipping after Oct 1942 was routed from Freetown to the Brazilian coast and then northward to Halifax, a system that remained in operation until mid March 1943 when SL 126 re-started the series.

With the sailing of SL 128 on 20 Apr 1943 it became possible to dovetail the dates of sailing so that the northbound SL convoy could meet and join with the homeward bound MKS convoy after the latter passed Gibraltar. The convoy so formed then adopted the title of BOTH convoys i.e. SL 128/MKS 12 etc.

The Commodore of one of the two convoys then became Commodore of the joint convoy, the other Commodore taking the junior position of Vice-Commodore.

"End to end" escort had been applied to the SL route from mid-1941 with an escort group bringing out the southbound ships in the OS series, turning round at Freetown and bringing back the next SL sailing after arrival of the OS convoy. There had also been established a small Freetown based escort force of elderly destroyers and corvettes. With the commencement of the joint SL/MKS convoys and the increasing numbers of long range escorts in 1943 that system gave way to the establishment of a proper Freetown based escort force. This force handled all the Freetown/Gibraltar traffic with the Gibraltar (and therefore from the SL/MKS rendezvous) to UK traffic being escorted by W Approaches groups which had escorted the southbound OS/KMS convoy.

As was stated much earlier, convoy was reactive to the threat, hence armed merchant cruiser escort was acceptable for the SL convoys until the establishment of U-boats and aircraft in Western France. When U-boats began to be directed further south in the Eastern Atlantic i.e. towards Freetown, which was a focal point for traffic, A/S escort throughout the route became essential. In the same way, the inability of BdU to maintain U-boat warfare south of Gibraltar by the end of 1944 led directly to the demise of the SL system, with the last convoy, SL 178, departing Freetown 25 Nov 1944. Thereafter ships sailed independently to either Casablanca or Gibraltar and joined the MKS convoy that formed at Gibraltar for the passage to the UK.

The first MKS convoys were the ships returning from the assault on North Africa, thereafter they were comprised of ships which had brought out the "follow up" stores from the UK under the designation KMS. As the North African coast was cleared both the outward and homeward series were extended eastward, eventually to Port Said when the Mediterranean was judged sufficiently safe for the passage of convoys.

The first MKS convoys were despatched to the UK as such, with no connection with any other series. As stated earlier, they were eventually routed to join the appropriate SL convoy at a point to the west of the

Gibraltar Strait, then assuming the dual designation of SL/MKS plus the appropriate convoy numbers.

In the listings appended, the Mediterranean passage of the MKS convoy appears under that designation. The passage from the Gibraltar Strait (the convoy did not usually enter Gibraltar itself) to the junction with the SL convoy is designated by "G" being suffixed to the convoy number. This is only to distinguish the two portions in this narrative; such a suffix did not appear in contemporary signals or documents.

The Trade Division statistics, once the convoys commenced their juncture west of Gibraltar, are most confusing. While separate figures are quoted for the SL and MKS portions during 1943 (the latter are shown in the purely MKS convoy data), from Jan 1944 only the total of the combined convoys appear in the figures. In order to lessen the confusion in the tables below, only this figure appears against the "SL/MKS" entry, the Freetown departure figure being left blank.

Courtesy Jack Tice

USCGC CAMPBELL photographed from HMCS MAYFLOWER in 1942. Built for extended North Atlantic patrols pre-war, she was one of a class of magnificent ships which served the Coast Guard for many years. She and her sisters were the mainstay of several US commanded Escort Groups in 1942, backed up by a miscellany of British, Canadian and Allied corvettes. In CAMPBELL's case, the group was A3 which included MAYFLOWER. As the photograph is undated except for the year, the convoy cannot be identified, but it was one of six trans-Atlantic convoys, HX 190, HX 196, SC 100, ON 102, ON 114 or ON 135.

SL and SL/MKS convoy data

CONVOY	DEP. PORT	DEP. DATE	ARRIVAL PORT	ARR. DATE	TDS	MV SUNK	MV DMGD
SL 1	FREETOWN	14/09/39	LIVERPOOL	01/10/39	8		
SL 1F	FREETOWN	20/09/39	LIVERPOOL	28/09/39	3		
SL 2	FREETOWN	21/09/39	LIVERPOOL	07/10/39	14		
SL 2F	FREETOWN	25/09/39	SOUTHEND	06/10/39	4		
SL 3	FREETOWN	28/09/39	LIVERPOOL	15/10/39	23		
SL 3F	FREETOWN	02/10/39	LIVERPOOL	13/10/39	2		
SL 4	FREETOWN	07/10/39	LIVERPOOL	26/10/39	19		
SL 4F	FREETOWN	12/10/39	LIVERPOOL	20/10/39	2		
SL 5	FREETOWN	15/10/39	LIVERPOOL	03/11/39	34		
SL 5F	FREETOWN	18/10/39	LONDON	30/10/39	3		
SL 6	FREETOWN	23/10/39	LIVERPOOL	10/11/39	31		
SL 7	FREETOWN	31/10/39	LIVERPOOL	16/11/39	39		
SL 8	FREETOWN	08/11/39	LIVERPOOL	24/11/39	28	1	
SL 9	FREETOWN	16/11/39	LIVERPOOL	02/12/39	11		
SL 9F	FREETOWN	17/11/39	LIVERPOOL	29/11/39	11		
SL 10	FREETOWN	24/11/39	LIVERPOOL	10/12/39	10		
SL 10F	FREETOWN	25/11/39	LIVERPOOL	08/12/39	7		
SL 11	FREETOWN	02/12/39	LIVERPOOL	18/12/39	22		
SL 11F	FREETOWN	03/12/39	LIVERPOOL	15/12/39	9		
SL 12	FREETOWN	10/12/39	LIVERPOOL	26/12/39	16		
SL 12F	FREETOWN	12/12/39	LIVERPOOL	25/12/39	6		
SL 13	FREETOWN	18/12/39	LIVERPOOL	06/01/40	10		
SL 13F	FREETOWN	19/12/39	LIVERPOOL	03/01/40	7		
SL 14	FREETOWN	26/12/39	LIVERPOOL	15/01/40	16		
SL 14F	FREETOWN	27/12/39	LIVERPOOL	11/01/40	8		
SL 15	FREETOWN	01/01/40	LIVERPOOL	19/01/40	7		
SL 15F	FREETOWN	05/01/40	RV WITH SL 15 IN 45N 13W	15/01/40	8		
SL 16	FREETOWN	08/01/40	LIVERPOOL	27/01/40	17		
SL 16F	FREETOWN	13/01/40	LIVERPOOL	27/01/40	12		
SL 17	FREETOWN	16/01/40	LIVERPOOL	04/02/40	12		
SL 17F	FREETOWN	20/01/40	DISPERSED	04/02/40	6		
SL 18	FREETOWN	24/01/40	LIVERPOOL	12/02/40	16		
SL 18F	FREETOWN	28/01/40	JOINED CONVOY SL 18	08/02/40	4		
SL 19	FREETOWN	01/02/40	JOINED SL 19F	16/02/40	21		
SL 19F	FREETOWN	05/02/40	LIVERPOOL	20/02/40	7		
SL 20	FREETOWN	10/02/40	JOINED SL 20F	25/02/40	17		
SL 20F	FREETOWN	14/02/40	LIVERPOOL	28/02/40	6		
SL 21	FREETOWN	18/02/40	LIVERPOOL	07/03/40	14		
SL 21F	FREETOWN	22/02/40	LIVERPOOL	07/03/40	7		
SL 22	FREETOWN	27/02/40	JOINED SL 22F	11/03/40	16		
SL 22F	FREETOWN	01/03/40	LIVERPOOL	15/03/40	7		
SL 23	FREETOWN	05/03/40	LIVERPOOL	22/03/40	13		
SL 23F	FREETOWN	09/03/40	RV WITH SL 23	19/03/40	4		
SL 24	FREETOWN	14/03/40	LIVERPOOL	31/03/40	16		
SL 25	FREETOWN	22/03/40	LIVERPOOL	08/04/40	20		
SL 26	FREETOWN	30/03/40	LIVERPOOL	15/04/40	18		
SL 27	FREETOWN	07/04/40	LIVERPOOL	24/04/40	18		
SL 28	FREETOWN	15/04/40	LIVERPOOL	01/05/40	22		

CONVOY	DEP. PORT	DEP. DATE	ARRIVAL PORT	ARR. DATE	TDS	MV SUNK	MV DMGD
SL 28F	FREETOWN	17/04/40	RV WITH SL 28	22/04/40	3		
SL 29	FREETOWN	23/04/40	LIVERPOOL	10/05/40	19		
SL 30	FREETOWN	01/05/40	LIVERPOOL	18/05/40	28		
SL 31	FREETOWN	09/05/40	LIVERPOOL	26/05/40	26		
SL 32	FREETOWN	17/05/40	LIVERPOOL	03/06/40	22		
SL 33	FREETOWN	23/05/40	LIVERPOOL	09/06/40	14		
SL 34	FREETOWN	31/05/40	LIVERPOOL	15/06/40	31	2	
SL 35	FREETOWN	08/06/40	LIVERPOOL	25/06/40	34		
SL 36	FREETOWN	15/06/40	LIVERPOOL	03/07/40	41	1	1
SL 37	FREETOWN	25/06/40	LIVERPOOL	12/07/40	49		
SL 38	FREETOWN	01/07/40	LIVERPOOL	20/07/40	30		
SL 38F	FREETOWN	04/07/40	LIVERPOOL	20/07/40	14		
SL 39	FREETOWN	09/07/40	LIVERPOOL	29/07/40	34		
SL 39F	FREETOWN	11/07/40	RV WITH SL 39	19/07/40	17		
SL 40	FREETOWN	16/07/40	LIVERPOOL	08/08/40	24		
SL 40F	FREETOWN	20/07/40	RV WITH SL 40	01/08/40	21		
SL 41	FREETOWN	25/07/40	RV WITH SL 41F	08/08/40	39		
SL 41F	FREETOWN	28/07/40	LIVERPOOL	14/08/40	22		
SL 42	FREETOWN	02/08/40	LIVERPOOL	21/08/40	53		
SL 43	FREETOWN	11/08/40	LIVERPOOL	31/08/40	47		
SL 44	FREETOWN	18/08/40	LIVERPOOL	07/09/40	29	1	1
SL 45	FREETOWN	26/08/40	LIVERPOOL	15/09/40	49	1	
SL 46	FREETOWN	03/09/40	LIVERPOOL	23/09/40	27		
SL 46S	FREETOWN	01/09/40	DISPERSED	13/09/40	32		
SL 47	FREETOWN	10/09/40	LIVERPOOL	28/09/40	39		3
SL 48	FREETOWN	19/09/40	LIVERPOOL	09/10/40	43		
SL 49	FREETOWN	27/09/40	LIVERPOOL	17/10/40	33		
SL 49S	FREETOWN	24/09/40	RV WITH SL 49	12/10/40	10		
SL 50	FREETOWN	03/10/40	LIVERPOOL	26/10/40	27		
SL 51	FREETOWN	12/10/40	OBAN	31/10/40	44		
SL 51S	FREETOWN	09/10/40	LIVERPOOL	31/10/40	17		
SL 52	FREETOWN	18/10/40	RV WITH SL 52F	05/11/40	11		
SL 52F	FREETOWN	22/10/40	LIVERPOOL	10/11/40	16	1	3
SL 53	FREETOWN	27/10/40	LIVERPOOL	18/11/40	24	1	1
SL 53S	FREETOWN	25/10/40	LIVERPOOL	18/11/40	6		
SL 54	FREETOWN	04/11/40	LIVERPOOL	26/11/40	25		
SL 54S	FREETOWN	01/11/40	LIVERPOOL	26/11/40	12		
SL 55	FREETOWN	12/11/40	LIVERPOOL	02/12/40	36		
SL 56	FREETOWN	21/11/40	LIVERPOOL	12/12/40	42		
SL 56S	FREETOWN	19/11/40	RV WITH SL 56	09/12/40	20		
SL 57	FREETOWN	28/11/40	LIVERPOOL	19/12/40	21		
SL 57S	FREETOWN	28/11/40	LIVERPOOL	22/12/40	11		1
SL 58	FREETOWN	07/12/40	LIVERPOOL	28/12/40	32		
SL 58S	FREETOWN	07/12/40	LIVERPOOL	02/01/41	10		2
SL 59	FREETOWN	15/12/40	LIVERPOOL	05/01/41	25		
SL 59S	FREETOWN	15/12/40	LIVERPOOL	07/01/41	12		
SL 60	FREETOWN	22/12/40	LIVERPOOL	13/01/41	31		
SL 60S	FREETOWN	22/12/40	LIVERPOOL	15/01/41	9		
SL 61	FREETOWN	01/01/41	LIVERPOOL	24/01/41	21		
SL 61S	FREETOWN	01/01/41	LIVERPOOL	26/01/41	23		

THE ALLIED CONVOY SYSTEM 1939-1945

CONVOY	DEP. PORT	DEP. DATE	ARRIVAL PORT	ARR. DATE	TDS	MV SUNK	MV DMGD
SL 62	FREETOWN	10/01/41	LIVERPOOL	03/02/41	32		
SL 63	FREETOWN	20/01/41	LIVERPOOL	09/02/41	29		
SL 63S	FREETOWN	18/01/41	LIVERPOOL	13/02/41	17		
SL 64	FREETOWN	30/01/41	LIVERPOOL	22/02/41	28		
SL 64S	FREETOWN	30/01/41	DISPERSED	12/02/41	19		1
SL 65	FREETOWN	10/02/41	LIVERPOOL	08/03/41	47		
SL 65S	FREETOWN	09/02/41	RV WITH SL 65	13/02/41	15		
SL 66	FREETOWN	18/02/41	LIVERPOOL	14/03/41	47		
SL 67	FREETOWN	01/03/41	LIVERPOOL	26/03/41	54	5	
SL 68	FREETOWN	13/03/41	DISPERSED	21/03/41	58	5	
SL 69	FREETOWN	23/03/41	LIVERPOOL	18/04/41	42	1	
SL 70	FREETOWN	29/03/41	LIVERPOOL	23/04/41	28		
SL 71	FREETOWN	08/04/41	LIVERPOOL	04/05/41	49		
SL 72	FREETOWN	17/04/41	LIVERPOOL	13/05/41	33	1	
SL 73	FREETOWN	27/04/41	LIVERPOOL	25/05/41	37	1	
SL 74	FREETOWN	10/05/41	LIVERPOOL	04/06/41	45		
SL 75	FREETOWN	17/05/41	LIVERPOOL	13/06/41	22		
SL 76	FREETOWN	30/05/41	LIVERPOOL	21/06/41	60	2	1
SL 77	FREETOWN	08/06/41	LIVERPOOL	03/07/41	15		
SL 78	FREETOWN	18/06/41	LIVERPOOL	12/07/41	25	4	
SL 79	FREETOWN	27/06/41	RV WITH HG 67	14/07/41	6		
SL 80	FREETOWN	03/07/41	LIVERPOOL	29/07/41	10		
SL 81	FREETOWN	15/07/41	LIVERPOOL	08/08/41	18	5	
SL 82	FREETOWN	24/07/41	LIVERPOOL	15/08/41	11		
SL 83	FREETOWN	05/08/41	LIVERPOOL	28/08/41	16		
SL 84	FREETOWN	15/08/41	LIVERPOOL	08/09/41	20		
SL 85	FREETOWN	25/08/41	LIVERPOOL	17/09/41	11	1	
SL 86	FREETOWN	04/09/41	LIVERPOOL	26/09/41	14		
SL 87	FREETOWN	14/09/41	LIVERPOOL	06/10/41	11	7	
SL 88	FREETOWN	24/09/41	RV WITH HG 74	08/10/41	15		
SL 89	FREETOWN	05/10/41	LIVERPOOL	26/10/41	23	2	
SL 90	FREETOWN	15/10/41	LIVERPOOL	06/11/41	21		
SL 91	FREETOWN	27/10/41	FORMED SL 91G	08/11/41	24		
SL 91G	GIBRALTAR	01/11/41	RV WITH SL 91	08/11/41	13		
SL 91G1	FORMED AT SEA	08/11/41	SPLIT	12/11/41			
SL 91GF	FORMED	12/11/41	LIVERPOOL	18/11/41			
SL 91GS	FORMED	12/11/41	LIVERPOOL	19/11/41			
SL 092	FREETOWN	06/11/41	LIVERPOOL	01/12/41	33		
SL 93	FREETOWN	19/11/41	LIVERPOOL	10/12/41	33		
SL 94	FREETOWN	30/11/41	LIVERPOOL	20/12/41	29		
SL 95	FREETOWN	12/12/41	LIVERPOOL	31/12/41	22		
SL 96	FREETOWN	26/12/41	DISPERSED	13/01/42	35		
SL 97	FREETOWN	04/01/42	LIVERPOOL	24/01/42	19		
SL 97G	GIBRALTAR	11/01/42	LIVERPOOL	24/01/42	11		
SL 98	FREETOWN	15/01/42	LIVERPOOL	05/02/42	26		
SL 99	FREETOWN	27/01/42	LIVERPOOL	16/02/42	40		
SL 100	FREETOWN	09/02/42	LIVERPOOL	04/03/42	32		
SL 100F	DET FROM SL 100	19/02/42	LIVERPOOL	28/02/42			
SL 101	FREETOWN	21/02/42	LIVERPOOL	15/03/42	52		
SL 102	FREETOWN	04/03/42	LIVERPOOL	26/03/42	39		
SL 103	FREETOWN	14/03/42	LIVERPOOL	02/04/42	39		
SL 103G	GIBRALTAR	22/03/42	JD SL 103	25/03/42	6		
SL 104	FREETOWN	23/03/42	LIVERPOOL	12/04/42	30		
SL 105	FREETOWN	03/04/42	LIVERPOOL	22/04/42	27		
SL 106	FREETOWN	09/04/42	LIVERPOOL	02/05/42	19		
SL 106F	DET FROM SL 106	24/04/42	LIVERPOOL	29/04/42			
SL 107	FREETOWN	16/04/42	LIVERPOOL	07/05/42	32		
SL 107F	DET FROM SL 107	04/05/42	LIVERPOOL	06/05/42			
SL 108	FREETOWN	26/04/42	LIVERPOOL	19/05/42	44		
SL 109	FREETOWN	04/05/42	LIVERPOOL	28/05/42	34	1	
SL 109F	DET FROM SL 109	19/05/42	LIVERPOOL	25/05/42			
SL 110	FREETOWN	13/05/42	LIVERPOOL	04/06/42	44		
SL 111	FREETOWN	24/05/42	LIVERPOOL	16/06/42	38		
SL 111F	DET FROM SL111	08/06/42	LIVERPOOL	13/06/42			
SL 112	FREETOWN	04/06/42	LIVERPOOL	23/06/42	54		
SL 113	FREETOWN	15/06/42	LIVERPOOL	05/07/42	41		
SL 114	FREETOWN	25/06/42	LIVERPOOL	17/07/42	40		
SL 115	FREETOWN	05/07/42	LIVERPOOL	26/07/42	27		
SL 116	FREETOWN	15/07/42	LIVERPOOL	04/08/42	33		
SL 117	FREETOWN	25/07/42	LIVERPOOL	15/08/42	34		
SL 118	FREETOWN	04/08/42	LIVERPOOL	26/08/42	34	4	
SL 119	FREETOWN	14/08/42	LIVERPOOL	04/09/42	29	2	
SL 120	FREETOWN	24/08/42	LIVERPOOL	15/09/42	25		
SL 120G	GIBRALTAR	02/09/42	RV WITH SL 120	08/09/42	3		
SL 121	FREETOWN	03/09/42	LIVERPOOL	21/09/42	27		
SL 122	FREETOWN	14/09/42	LIVERPOOL	06/10/42	34		
SL 123	FREETOWN	23/09/42	LIVERPOOL	14/10/42	27		
SL 124	FREETOWN	03/10/42	LIVERPOOL	22/10/42	29		
SL 124G	GIBRALTAR	12/10/42	JD SL 124	14/10/42	6		
SL 125	FREETOWN	16/10/42	LIVERPOOL	09/11/42	42	11	
SL 126	FREETOWN	12/03/43	LIVERPOOL	01/04/43	36	4	1
SL 127	FREETOWN	31/03/43	LIVERPOOL	23/04/43	21		
SL 127G	GIBRALTAR	13/04/43	RV WITH SL 127	14/04/43			
SL 128	FREETOWN	20/04/43	RV WITH MKS 12	04/05/43	32		
	SL 128/MKS 12	04/05/43	LIVERPOOL	14/05/43	52	1	
SL 129	FREETOWN	11/05/43	RV WITH MKS 13	24/05/43	46		
	SL 129/MKS 13	24/05/43	LIVERPOOL	01/06/43	79		
SL 130	FREETOWN	30/05/43	RV WITH MKS 14	11/06/43	37		
SL 130F	DET FROM SL130	18/06/43	LIVERPOOL	20/06/43			
	SL 130/MKS 14	11/06/43	LIVERPOOL	21/06/43			
SL 131	FREETOWN	13/06/43	RV WITH MKS 15	24/06/43	22		
	SL 131/MKS 15	24/06/43	LIVERPOOL	04/07/43	37		
SL 132	FREETOWN	28/06/43	RV WITH MKS 16	10/07/43	32		
	SL 132/MKS 16	10/07/43	SPLIT FAST & SLOW	17/07/43			1
SL 132F	CONVOY DIVIDED	17/07/43	LIVERPOOL	21/07/43			
SL 132S	CONVOY DIVIDED	17/07/43	LIVERPOOL	22/07/43			
SL 133	FREETOWN	13/07/43	RV WITH MKS 18	26/07/43	27		
	SL 133/MKS 18	26/07/43	LIVERPOOL	05/08/43			
SL 134	FREETOWN	28/07/43	LIVERPOOL	19/08/43	37		
SL 135	FREETOWN	14/08/43	RV WITH MKS 22	26/08/43	34		
	SL 135/MKS 22	26/08/43	LIVERPOOL	06/09/43			
SL 136	FREETOWN	03/09/43	RV WITH MKS 24	14/09/43	52		
SL 136F	DET FROM SL 136	21/09/43	LIVERPOOL	23/09/43			
	SL 136/MKS 24	14/09/43	LIVERPOOL	25/09/43			

APPENDIX 3

CONVOY	DEP. PORT	DEP. DATE	ARRIVAL PORT	ARR. DATE	TDS	MV SUNK	MV DMGD
SL 137	FREETOWN	23/09/43	RV WITH MKS 26	05/10/43	49		
	SL 137/MKS 26	05/10/43	LIVERPOOL	17/10/43			
SL 138	FREETOWN	13/10/43	RV WITH MKS 28	24/10/43	35		
	SL 138/MKS 28	24/10/43	LIVERPOOL	05/11/43		1	
SL 139	FREETOWN	02/11/43	RV WITH MKS 30	16/11/43	27		
	SL 139/MKS 30	16/11/43	LIVERPOOL	26/11/43			
SL 140	FREETOWN	12/11/43	RV WITH MKS 31	24/11/43	24		
	SL 140/MKS 31	24/11/43	LIVERPOOL	07/12/43			
SL 141	FREETOWN	23/11/43	RV WITH MKS 32	04/12/43	14		
	SL 141/MKS 32	04/12/43	LIVERPOOL	17/12/43			
SL 142	FREETOWN	02/12/43	RV WITH MKS 33	14/12/43	19		
	SL 142/MKS 33	14/12/43	LIVERPOOL	28/12/43			
SL 143	FREETOWN	11/12/43	RV WITH MKS 34	25/12/43			
	SL 143/MKS 34	25/12/43	LIVERPOOL	06/01/44	42		
SL 144	FREETOWN	22/12/43	GIBRALTAR	03/01/44	15		
	GIBRALTAR	06/01/44	LIVERPOOL	18/01/44	45		
SL 145	FREETOWN	01/01/44	RV WITH MKS 36	12/01/44			
	SL 145/MKS 36	12/01/44	LIVERPOOL	24/01/44	33		
SL 146	FREETOWN	12/01/44	RV WITH MKS 37	23/01/44			
	SL 146/MKS 37	23/01/44	LIVERPOOL	02/02/44	52		
SL 147	FREETOWN	22/01/44	RV WITH MKS 38	02/02/44			
	SL 147/MKS 38	02/02/44	LIVERPOOL	13/02/44	57		
SL 148	FREETOWN	01/02/44	RV WITH MKS 39	12/02/44			
	SL 148/MKS 39	12/02/44	LIVERPOOL	24/02/44	70		
SL 149	FREETOWN	11/02/44	RV WITH MKS 40	22/02/44			
	SL 149/MKS 40	22/02/44	LIVERPOOL	07/03/44	47		
SL 150	FREETOWN	21/02/44	RV WITH MKS 41	03/03/44			
	SL 150/MKS 41	03/03/44	LIVERPOOL	14/03/44	41		
SL 151	FREETOWN	02/03/44	RV WITH MKS 42	14/03/44			
	SL 151/MKS 42	14/03/44	LIVERPOOL	24/03/44	44		
SL 152	FREETOWN	13/03/44	RV WITH MKS 43	23/03/44			
	SL 152/MKS 43	23/03/44	LIVERPOOL	04/04/44	75		
SL 153	FREETOWN	22/03/44	RV WITH MKS 44	02/04/44			
	SL 153/MKS 44	02/04/44	LIVERPOOL	13/04/44	47		
SL 154	FREETOWN	01/04/44	RV WITH MKS 45	11/04/44			
	SL 154/MKS 45	11/04/44	LIVERPOOL	23/04/44	42		
SL 155	FREETOWN	11/04/44	RV WITH MKS 46	23/04/44			
	SL 155/MKS 46	23/04/44	LIVERPOOL	03/05/44	49		
SL 156	FREETOWN	21/04/44	RV WITH MKS 47	03/05/44			
	SL 156/MKS 47	03/05/44	LIVERPOOL	13/05/44	46		
SL 157	FREETOWN	01/05/44	RV WITH MKS 48	11/05/44			
	SL 157/MKS 48	11/05/44	LIVERPOOL	22/05/44	45		
SL 158	FREETOWN	11/05/44	RV WITH MKS 49	21/05/44			
	SL 158/MKS 49	21/05/44	LIVERPOOL	04/06/44	42		
SL 159	FREETOWN	17/05/44	RV WITH MKS 50	31/05/44			
	SL 159/MKS 50	31/05/44	LIVERPOOL	11/06/44	33		
SL 160	FREETOWN	31/05/44	RV WITH MKS 51	10/06/44			
	SL 160/MKS 51	10/06/44	LIVERPOOL	21/06/44	44		
SL 161	FREETOWN	11/06/44	RV WITH MKS 52	20/06/44			
	SL 161/MKS 52	20/06/44	LIVERPOOL	02/07/44	41		

CONVOY	DEP. PORT	DEP. DATE	ARRIVAL PORT	ARR. DATE	TDS	MV SUNK	MV DMGD
SL 162	FREETOWN	20/06/44	RV WITH MKS 53	30/06/44			
	SL 162/MKS 53	30/06/44	LIVERPOOL	12/07/44	36		
SL 163	FREETOWN	01/07/44	RV WITH MKS 54	11/07/44			
	SL 163/MKS 54	11/07/44	LIVERPOOL	22/07/44	42		
SL 164	FREETOWN	10/07/44	RV WITH MKS 55	21/07/44			
	SL 164/MKS 55	21/07/44	LIVERPOOL	02/08/44	33		
SL 165	FREETOWN	20/07/44	RV WITH MKS 56	30/07/44			
	SL 165/MKS 56	30/07/44	LIVERPOOL	10/08/44	35		
SL 166	FREETOWN	30/07/44	RV WITH MKS 57	09/08/44			
	SL 166/MKS 57	09/08/44	LIVERPOOL	20/08/44	31		
SL 167	FREETOWN	09/08/44	RV WITH MKS 58	19/08/44			
	SL 167/MKS 58	19/08/44	LIVERPOOL	29/08/44	29		
SL 168	FREETOWN	19/08/44	RV WITH MKS 59	30/08/44			
	SL 168/MKS 59	30/08/44	LIVERPOOL	07/09/44	33		
SL 169	FREETOWN	29/08/44	RV WITH MKS 60	10/09/44			
	SL 169/MKS 60	10/09/44	LIVERPOOL	17/09/44	40		
SL 170	FREETOWN	08/09/44	RV WITH MKS 61	18/09/44			
	SL 170/MKS 61	18/09/44	LIVERPOOL	26/09/44	39		
SL 171	FREETOWN	18/09/44	RV WITH MKS 62	30/09/44			
	SL 171/MKS 62	30/09/44	LIVERPOOL	08/10/44	17		
SL 172	FREETOWN	28/09/44	RV WITH MKS 63	09/10/44			
	SL 172/MKS 63	09/10/44	LIVERPOOL	16/10/44	23		
SL 173	FREETOWN	09/10/44	RV WITH MKS 64	19/10/44			
	SL 173/MKS 64	19/10/44	LIVERPOOL	28/10/44	38		
SL 174	FREETOWN	18/10/44	RV WITH MKS 65	30/10/44			
	SL 174/MKS 65	30/10/44	LIVERPOOL	07/11/44	44		
SL 175	FREETOWN	28/10/44	RV WITH MKS 66	08/11/44			
	SL 175/MKS 66	08/11/44	LIVERPOOL	15/11/44	38		
SL 176	FREETOWN	07/11/44	RV WITH MKS 67	18/11/44			
	SL 176/MKS 67	18/11/44	LIVERPOOL	24/11/44	28		
SL 177	FREETOWN	15/11/44	RV WITH MKS 68	26/11/44			
	SL 177/MKS 68	26/11/44	LIVERPOOL	05/12/44	35		
SL 178	FREETOWN	25/11/44	RV WITH MKS 69	06/12/44			
	SL 178/MKS 69	06/12/44	LIVERPOOL	15/12/44	39		

MKS convoy data

CONVOY	DEP. PORT	DEP. DATE	ARRIVAL PORT	ARR. DATE	TDS	MV SUNK	MV DMGD
MKS 1A	BOUGIE	13/11/42	GIBRALTAR	16/11/42			
MKS 10	ORAN	14/11/42	GIBRALTAR	15/11/42			
MKS 1X	ALGIERS	12/11/42	CLYDE	23/11/42	28	1	
MKS 1Y	GIBRALTAR	21/11/42	LIVERPOOL	30/11/42	17		
MKS 2	ALGIERS	21/11/42	LIVERPOOL	03/12/42	28		
MKS 2A	ALGIERS	23/11/42	LIVERPOOL	07/12/42	18		
MKS 3X	BONE	03/12/42	LIVERPOOL	19/12/42	42		
MKS 3Y	PHILIPPEVILLE	06/12/42	LIVERPOOL	23/12/42	24		
MKS 4	BONE	22/12/42	LIVERPOOL	06/01/43	55		
MKS 4Y	GIBRALTAR	01/01/43	LIVERPOOL	09/01/43	5		
MKS 5	PHILIPPEVILLE	05/01/43	LIVERPOOL	22/01/43	43		1
MKS 5X	BOUGIE	14/01/43	LIVERPOOL	25/01/43	10		
MKS 6	PHILIPPEVILLE	19/01/43	LIVERPOOL	01/02/43	36	1	1
MKS 7	ALGIERS	05/02/43	LIVERPOOL	17/02/43	65	3	
MKS 8	BONE	17/02/43	LIVERPOOL	01/03/43	48		1

THE ALLIED CONVOY SYSTEM 1939-1945

CONVOY	DEP. PORT	DEP. DATE	ARRIVAL PORT	ARR. DATE	TDS	MV SUNK	MV DMGD
MKS 9	BONE	04/03/43	LIVERPOOL	18/03/43	55		
MKS 10	BONE	23/03/43	LIVERPOOL	05/04/43	33	1	
MKS 11	BONE	10/04/43	LIVERPOOL	23/04/43	33		
MKS 12	BONE	22/04/43	RV WITH SL 128	04/05/43	22		
MKS 13	BOUGIE	14/05/43	GIBRALTAR	19/05/43			
MKS 13G	GIBRALTAR	22/05/43	RV WITH SL 129	24/05/43	31		
MKS 14	BONE	04/06/43	GIBRALTAR	09/06/43			
MKS 14G	GIBRALTAR	10/06/43	RV WITH SL 130	11/06/43	13		
MKS 15	ALEXANDRIA	11/06/43	GIBRALTAR	21/06/43			
MKS 15G	GIBRALTAR	23/06/43	RV WITH SL 131	24/06/43	17		
MKS 16	ALEXANDRIA	24/06/43	TRIPOLI, LIBYA	29/06/43			
MKS 16A	TRIPOLI, LIBYA	29/06/43	GIBRALTAR	06/07/43			
MKS 16G	GIBRALTAR	09/07/43	RV WITH SL 132	10/07/43	22		
MKS 18	TRIPOLI, LIBYA	17/07/43	GIBRALTAR	23/07/43			
MKS 18G	GIBRALTAR	23/07/43	RV WITH SL 133	26/07/43	18		
MKS 19	TRIPOLI, LIBYA	21/07/43	GIBRALTAR	28/07/43			
MKS 19Y	TRIPOLI	26/07/43	GIBRALTAR	31/07/43			
MKS 20	GIBRALTAR	31/07/43	LIVERPOOL	10/08/43	9		
MKS 21	ALEXANDRIA	03/08/43	GIBRALTAR	14/08/43			
MKS 21G	GIBRALTAR	14/08/43	CLYDE	25/08/43	32		
MKS 22	ALEXANDRIA	15/08/43	GIBRALTAR	25/08/43			
MKS 22G	GIBRALTAR	25/08/43	RV WITH SL 135	26/08/43	15		
MKS 23	ALEXANDRIA	25/08/43	GIBRALTAR	03/09/43			
MKS 23G	GIBRALTAR	04/09/43	LIVERPOOL	17/09/43	17		
MKS 24	ALEXANDRIA	04/09/43	GIBRALTAR	13/09/43			
MKS 24G	GIBRALTAR	13/09/43	RV WITH SL 136	14/09/43	17		
MKS 25	ALEXANDRIA	14/09/43	GIBRALTAR	25/09/43			
MKS 25G	GIBRALTAR	25/09/43	LIVERPOOL	08/10/43	31		
MKS 26	ALEXANDRIA	24/09/43	GIBRALTAR	04/10/43		2	
MKS 26G	GIBRALTAR	04/10/43	RV WITH SL 137	05/10/43	21		
MKS 27	ALEXANDRIA	04/10/43	GIBRALTAR	14/10/43			
MKS 27G	GIBRALTAR	14/10/43	LIVERPOOL	28/10/43	23		
MKS 28	ALEXANDRIA	14/10/43	GIBRALTAR	23/10/43		1	
MKS 28G	GIBRALTAR	23/10/43	RV WITH SL 138	24/10/43	23		
MKS 29	ALEXANDRIA	24/10/43	GIBRALTAR	03/11/43			
MKS 29G	GIBRALTAR	03/11/43	LIVERPOOL	18/11/43	28		
MKS 30	PORT SAID	02/11/43	GIBRALTAR	13/11/43			
MKS 30G	GIBRALTAR	13/11/43	RV WITH SL 139	16/11/43	30		
MKS 31	PORT SAID	13/11/43	GIBRALTAR	23/11/43			
MKS 31G	GIBRALTAR	23/11/43	RV WITH SL 140	24/11/43	28		
MKS 32	PORT SAID	22/11/43	GIBRALTAR	03/12/43			
MKS 32G	GIBRALTAR	03/12/43	RV WITH SL 141	04/12/43	24		
MKS 33	ALEXANDRIA	02/12/43	GIBRALTAR	13/12/43			
MKS 33G	GIBRALTAR	13/12/43	RV WITH SL 142	14/12/43	20		
MKS 34	PORT SAID	11/12/43	GIBRALTAR	24/12/43			
MKS 34G	GIBRALTAR	24/12/43	RV WITH SL 143	25/12/43	27		
MKS 35	PORT SAID	21/12/43	GIBRALTAR	01/01/44			
MKS 36	PORT SAID	31/12/43	GIBRALTAR	12/01/44			
MKS 36G	GIBRALTAR	11/01/44	RV WITH SL 145	12/01/44	20		
MKS 37	PORT SAID	10/01/44	GIBRALTAR	22/01/44			
MKS 37G	GIBRALTAR	22/01/44	RV WITH SL 146	23/01/44	25		
MKS 38	PORT SAID	21/01/44	GIBRALTAR	01/02/44			
MKS 38G	GIBRALTAR	01/02/44	RV WITH SL 147	02/02/44	29		
MKS 39	PORT SAID	30/01/44	GIBRALTAR	11/02/44			
MKS 39G	GIBRALTAR	11/02/44	RV WITH SL 148	12/02/44	44		
MKS 40	PORT SAID	09/02/44	GIBRALTAR	21/02/44			
MKS 40G	GIBRALTAR	21/02/44	RV WITH SL 149	22/02/44	28		
MKS 41	PORT SAID	19/02/44	GIBRALTAR	02/03/44			
MKS 41G	GIBRALTAR	02/03/44	RV WITH SL 150	03/03/44	24		
MKS 42	PORT SAID	29/02/44	GIBRALTAR	13/03/44			
MKS 42G	GIBRALTAR	13/03/44	RV WITH SL 151	14/03/44	21		
MKS 43	PORT SAID	10/03/44	GIBRALTAR	22/03/44			
MKS 43G	GIBRALTAR	22/03/44	RV WITH SL 152	23/03/44	38		
MKS 44	PORT SAID	20/03/44	GIBRALTAR	01/04/44			
MKS 44G	GIBRALTAR	01/04/44	RV WITH SL 153	02/04/44	22		
MKS 45	PORT SAID	30/03/44	RV WITH SL 154	11/04/44			
MKS 45G	GIBRALTAR	10/04/44	RV WITH SL 154	11/04/44	21		
MKS 46	PORT SAID	09/04/44	GIBRALTAR	21/04/44			
MKS 46G	GIBRALTAR	22/04/44	RV WITH SL 155	23/04/44	24		
MKS 47	PORT SAID	19/04/44	GIBRALTAR	01/05/44			
MKS 47G	GIBRALTAR	01/05/44	RV WITH SL 156	03/05/44	23		
MKS 48	PORT SAID	29/04/44	GIBRALTAR	10/05/44			
MKS 48G	GIBRALTAR	10/05/44	RV WITH SL 157	11/05/44	26		
MKS 49	PORT SAID	09/05/44	GIBRALTAR	20/05/44			
MKS 49G	GIBRALTAR	20/05/44	RV WITH SL 158	21/05/44	22		
MKS 50	PORT SAID	19/05/44	GIBRALTAR	31/05/44			
MKS 50G	GIBRALTAR	31/05/44	RV WITH SL 159	31/05/44	19		
MKS 51	PORT SAID	30/05/44	GIBRALTAR	09/06/44			
MKS 51G	GIBRALTAR	09/06/44	RV WITH SL 160	10/06/44	20		
MKS 52	PORT SAID	08/06/44	GIBRALTAR	20/06/44			
MKS 52G	GIBRALTAR	20/06/44	RV WITH SL 161	22/06/44	17		
MKS 53	PORT SAID	18/06/44	GIBRALTAR	29/06/44			
MKS 53G	GIBRALTAR	29/06/44	RV WITH SL 162	30/06/44	16		
MKS 54	PORT SAID	28/06/44	GIBRALTAR	10/07/44			
MKS 54G	GIBRALTAR	10/07/44	RV WITH SL 163	11/07/44	22		
MKS 55	PORT SAID	08/07/44	GIBRALTAR	20/07/44			
MKS 55G	GIBRALTAR	20/07/44	RV WITH SL 164	21/07/44	17		
MKS 56	PORT SAID	18/07/44	GIBRALTAR	29/07/44			
MKS 56G	GIBRALTAR	29/07/44	RV WITH SL 165	30/07/44	18		
MKS 57	PORT SAID	28/07/44	GIBRALTAR	08/08/44			
MKS 57G	GIBRALTAR	08/08/44	RV WITH SL 166	09/08/44	15		
MKS 58	PORT SAID	07/08/44	GIBRALTAR	17/08/44			
MKS 58G	GIBRALTAR	18/08/44	RV WITH SL 167	19/08/44	9		
MKS 59	PORT SAID	17/08/44	GIBRALTAR	28/08/44			
MKS 59G	GIBRALTAR	29/08/44	RV WITH SL 168	30/08/44	13		
MKS 60	PORT SAID	27/08/44	GIBRALTAR	07/09/44			
MKS 60G	GIBRALTAR	09/09/44	RV WITH SL 169	10/09/44	22		
MKS 61	PORT SAID	06/09/44	GIBRALTAR	17/09/44			

APPENDIX 3

CONVOY	DEP. PORT	DEP. DATE	ARRIVAL PORT	ARR. DATE	TDS	MV SUNK	MV DMGD
MKS 61G	GIBRALTAR	17/09/44	RV WITH SL 170	18/09/44	19		
MKS 62	PORT SAID	16/09/44	GIBRALTAR	27/09/44			
MKS 62G	GIBRALTAR	29/09/44	RV WITH SL 171	30/09/44	21		
MKS 63	PORT SAID	26/09/44	GIBRALTAR	08/10/44			
MKS 63G	GIBRALTAR	08/10/44	RV WITH SL 172	09/10/44	13		
MKS 64	PORT SAID	06/10/44	GIBRALTAR	18/10/44			
MKS 64G	GIBRALTAR	18/10/44	RV WITH SL 173	19/10/44	20		
MKS 65	PORT SAID	16/10/44	GIBRALTAR	28/10/44			
MKS 65G	GIBRALTAR	29/10/44	RV WITH SL 174	30/10/44	22		
MKS 66	PORT SAID	26/10/44	GIBRALTAR	06/11/44			
MKS 66G	GIBRALTAR	07/11/44	RV WITH SL 175	08/11/44	10		
MKS 67	PORT SAID	06/11/44	GIBRALTAR	16/11/44			
MKS 67G	GIBRALTAR	17/11/44	RV WITH SL 176	18/11/44	11		
MKS 68G	GIBRALTAR	25/11/44	RV WITH SL 177	26/11/44	18		
MKS 69G	GIBRALTAR	05/12/44	RV WITH SL 178	06/12/44	20		
MKS 70G	GIBRALTAR	11/12/44	LIVERPOOL	19/12/44	16		
MKS 71G	GIBRALTAR	16/12/44	LIVERPOOL	24/12/44	24	1	
MKS 72G	GIBRALTAR	21/12/44	LIVERPOOL	30/12/44	23		
MKS 73G	GIBRALTAR	26/12/44	LIVERPOOL	04/01/45	26		
MKS 74G	GIBRALTAR	31/12/44	LIVERPOOL	10/01/45	13		
MKS 75G	GIBRALTAR	05/01/45	LIVERPOOL	14/01/45	13		
MKS 76G	GIBRALTAR	10/01/45	LIVERPOOL	21/01/45	22		
MKS 77G	GIBRALTAR	15/01/45	LIVERPOOL	23/01/45	32		
MKS 78G	GIBRALTAR	21/01/45	LIVERPOOL	29/01/45	21		
MKS 79G	GIBRALTAR	26/01/45	LIVERPOOL	02/02/45	22		
MKS 80G	GIBRALTAR	31/01/45	LIVERPOOL	07/02/45	35		
MKS 81G	GIBRALTAR	05/02/45	LIVERPOOL	13/02/45	28		
MKS 82G	GIBRALTAR	09/02/45	LIVERPOOL	17/02/45	17		
MKS 83G	GIBRALTAR	14/02/45	LIVERPOOL	22/02/45	28		
MKS 84G	GIBRALTAR	19/02/45	LIVERPOOL	27/02/45	26		
MKS 85G	GIBRALTAR	24/02/45	LIVERPOOL	03/03/45	22		
MKS 86G	GIBRALTAR	01/03/45	LIVERPOOL	09/03/45	28		
MKS 87G	GIBRALTAR	06/03/45	LIVERPOOL	14/03/45	34		
MKS 88G	GIBRALTAR	11/03/45	LIVERPOOL	19/03/45	22		
MKS 89G	GIBRALTAR	16/03/45	LIVERPOOL	24/03/45	22		
MKS 90G	GIBRALTAR	21/03/45	LIVERPOOL	28/03/45	18		
MKS 91G	GIBRALTAR	26/03/45	LIVERPOOL	03/04/45	15		
MKS 92G	GIBRALTAR	31/03/45	LIVERPOOL	08/04/45	41		
MKS 93G	GIBRALTAR	05/04/45	LIVERPOOL	14/04/45	33		
MKS 94G	GIBRALTAR	10/04/45	LIVERPOOL	18/04/45	20		
MKS 95G	GIBRALTAR	15/04/45	LIVERPOOL	23/04/45	22		
MKS 96G	GIBRALTAR	20/04/45	LIVERPOOL	28/04/45	27		
MKS 97G	GIBRALTAR	25/04/45	LIVERPOOL	03/05/45	28		
MKS 98G	GIBRALTAR	30/04/45	LIVERPOOL	08/05/45	13		
MKS 99G	GIBRALTAR	05/05/45	LIVERPOOL	12/05/45	28		
MKS 100G	GIBRALTAR	10/05/45	LIVERPOOL	17/05/45	23		
MKS 101G	GIBRALTAR	15/05/45	LIVERPOOL	22/05/45	19		
MKS 102G	GIBRALTAR	20/05/45	LIVERPOOL	28/05/45	21		
MKS 103G	GIBRALTAR	25/05/45	LIVERPOOL	01/06/45	14		

Losses incurred in SL and SL/MKS convoy series, excluding stragglers

Convoy	Ship's Name	GRT			Date of loss	Cause of loss	Comments
SL 8	ROYSTON GRANGE	5,144	18	Br	25/11/39	U 28	Grain & general. Casualties unknown
SL 34	BARBARA MARIE	4,223	28	Br	12/06/40	U 46	7,200 tons iron ore. 32 dead
SL 34	WILLOWBANK	5,041	39	Br	12/06/40	U 46	8,750 tons maize. No dead
SL 36	AVELONA STAR	13,376	27	Br	30/06/40	U 43	5,630 tons meat, 1,000 tons oranges. 6 dead
SL 36	BEIGNON	5,218	39	Br	01/07/40	U 30	8,816 tons wheat. 3 dead
SL 42	CAPE ST GEORGE	5,112	28	Br	05/08/40	COLLISION	8,130 tons rice & maize. No dead
SL 44	ST GLEN	4,647	07	Br	06/09/40	AIRCRAFT	8,400 tons wheat, preserved meat, gen. 3 dead
SL 45	NAILSEA RIVER	5,548	17	Br	15/09/40	AIRCRAFT	7,000 tons wheat. No dead
SL 52F	NALON	7,222	15	Br	06/11/40	AIRCRAFT	3,000 tons copper, 2,805 tons gen. No dead
SL 53	APAPA	9,332	27	Br	15/11/40	AIRCRAFT	3,500 tons W African cargo, 95 pass. 23 dead
SL 60	BUITENZORG	7,073	16	Du	14/01/41	WRECKED	General. No dead
SL 62	HOMESIDE	4,617	24	Br	28/01/41	FOUNDERED	Iron ore. 37 dead
SL 64S	BORGESTAD	3,924	24	Nor	12/02/41	HIPPER	Cotton. 31 dead
SL 64S	DERRYNANE	4,896	38	Br	12/02/41	HIPPER	8,219 tons iron ore. 36 dead
SL 64S	OSWESTRY GRANGE	4,684	35	Br	12/02/41	HIPPER	7,368 tons general. 5 dead
SL 64S	PERSEUS	5,172	18	Gk	12/02/41	HIPPER	14 dead
SL 64S	SHREWSBURY	4,542	24	Br	12/02/41	HIPPER	3,250 tons linseed, 3,100 tons wheat. 20 dead
SL 64S	WARLABY	4,875	27	Br	12/02/41	HIPPER	7,400 tons general. 36 dead
SL 64S	WESTBURY	4,712	28	Br	12/02/41	HIPPER	8,100 tons cottonseed & cake. 5 dead
SL 67	HARMODIUS	5,229	19	Br	08/03/41	U 105	2,000 tons pigiron, 3,930 tons general. 11 dead
SL 67	HINDPOOL	4,897	28	Br	08/03/41	U 124	7,700 tons iron ore. 28 dead
SL 67	LAHORE	5,304	20	Br	08/03/41	U 124	General. No dead
SL 67	NARDANA	7,974	19	Br	08/03/41	U 124	General. 19 dead
SL 67	TIELBANK	5,084	37	Br	08/03/41	U 124	8,200 tons general. 4 dead
SL 68	ANDALUSIAN	3,082	18	Br	17/03/41	U 106	3,231 tons cocoa. No dead
SL 68	BENWYVIS	5,920	29	Br	21/03/41	U 105	Rice, lead, timber. 34 dead
SL 68	CLAN MACNAB	6,076	20	Br	18/03/41	COLLISION	Collision with STRIX on 17.3
SL 68	CLAN OGILVY	5,802	14	Br	21/03/41	U 105	Tea, pigiron, groundnuts. 61 dead
SL 68	JHELUM	4,038	36	Br	21/03/41	U 105	4,896 tons general. 8 dead
SL 68	MANDALIKA	7,750	30	Du	18/03/41	U 105	9,200 tons sugar. 3 dead
SL 68	TAPANOELI	7,031	24	Du	17/03/41	U 106	General. No dead
SL 69	SWEDRU	4,123	37	Br	16/04/41	AIRCRAFT	5,000 tons general. 24 dead
SL 72	SOMERSET	8,970	18	Br	11/05/41	AIRCRAFT	7,600 tons frig meat. No dead
SL 73	STARCROSS	4,662	36	Br	20/05/41	OTARIA. It S/M	7,458 tons general. No dead
SL 76	DJURDJURA	3,460	22	Br	13/06/41	BRIN. It S/M	5,000 tons iron ore. 33 dead
SL 76	EIRINI KYRIAKIDOU	3,781	22	Gk	13/06/41	BRIN. It S/M	Iron ore. All crew (31) dead
SL 78	EMPIRE ABILITY	7,603	31	Br	27/06/41	U 69	7,725 tons sugar, 675 tons gen. 2 dead
SL 78	OBERON	1,996	11	Du	27/06/41	U 123	Palm kernels & general. 6 dead

145

Convoy	Ship's Name	GRT			Date of loss	Cause of loss	Comments
SL 78	P.L.M.22	5,646	21	Br	27/06/41	U 123	7,600 tons ore. 32 dead
SL 78	RIVER LUGAR	5,423	37	Br	26/06/41	U 69	9,250 tons iron ore. 41 dead
SL 81	BELGRAVIAN	3,136	37	Br	05/08/41	U 372	4,000 tons W African produce. 2 dead
SL 81	CAPE RODNEY	4,512	40	Br	05/08/41	U 75	7,320 tons palm nuts. No dead
SL 81	HARLINGEN	5,415	33	Br	05/08/41	U 75	8,000 tons W Af produce. 2 dead
SL 81	KUMASIAN	4,922	35	Br	05/08/41	U 74	7,000 tons general. 1 dead
SL 81	SWIFTPOOL	5,205	29	Br	05/08/41	U 372	8,000 tons iron ore. 42 dead
SL 85	DARU	3,854	27	Br	15/09/41	AIRCRAFT	5,152 tons general. No dead
SL 87	DIXCOVE	3,790	27	Br	24/09/41	U 107	3,046 tons W African produce. 1 dead
SL 87	EDWARD BLYDEN	5,003	30	Br	22/09/41	U 103	5,525 tons general. No dead
SL 87	JOHN HOLT	4,975	38	Br	24/09/41	U 107	4,560 tons general. 1 dead
SL 87	LAFIAN	4,876	37	Br	24/09/41	U 107	6,853 tons general. No dead
SL 87	NICETO DE LARRINAGA	5,591	16	Br	22/09/41	U 103	8,300 tons ore, W African produce. 3 dead
SL 87	SILVERBELLE	5,302	27	Br	22/09/41	U 68	6,000 tons W African produce. No dead
SL 87	ST CLAIR II	3,753	29	Br	24/09/41	U 67	4,050 tons W African produce. 13 dead
SL 89	SERBINO	4,099	19	Br	21/10/41	U 82	3,500 tons general. 14 dead
SL 89	TREVERBYN	5,281	20	Br	21/10/41	U 82	6,900 tons iron ore. 48 dead
SL 109	DENPARK	3,491	28	Br	12/05/42	U 128	5,000 tons manganese ore. 21 dead
SL 110	ENSEIGNE MAURICE PREHAC	4,578	24	Br	27/05/42	FOUNDERED	Iron ore.
SL 118	BALINGKAR	6,318	21	Du	18/08/42	U 214	General. 2 dead
SL 118	CITY OF MANILA	7,452	16	Br	19/08/42	U 406	10,000 tons W African cargo 1 dead
SL 118	HATARANA	7,522	17	Br	18/08/42	U 214	8,300 tons general. No dead
SL 118	TRITON	6,607	30	Nor	17/08/42	U 566	Wool, wheat & general No dead
SL 119	CITY OF CARDIFF	5,661	18	Br	28/08/42	U 566	7,500 tons general. 21 dead
SL 119	ZUIDERKERK	8,424	22	Du	28/08/42	U 566	8,045 tons general. No dead
SL 125	BARON VERNON	3,642	29	Br	30/10/42	U 604	5,500 tons iron ore. No dead
SL 125	BRITTANY	4,772	28	Br	28/10/42	U 509	7,132 tons general. 14 dead
SL 125	BULLMOUTH	7,519	27	Br	30/10/42	U 409 & U 659	Ballast. 50 dead
SL 125	CORINALDO	7,131	21	Br	30/10/42	U 509, U 659 & U 203	5,141 tons frozen meat. 8 dead
SL 125	HOPECASTLE	5,178	37	Br	29/10/42	U 509 & U 203	5,500 tons general. 5 dead
SL 125	NAGPORE	5,283	20	Br	28/10/42	U 509	5,500 tons general, 1,500 tons copper. 19 dead
SL 125	PACIFIC STAR	7,591	20	Br	27/10/42	U 509	5,037 tons frig meat & general. No dead
SL 125	PRESIDENT DOUMER	11,898	34	Br	30/10/42	U 604	General, 63 passengers. 260 dead
SL 125	SILVERWILLOW	6,373	30	Br	30/10/42	U 409	9,000 tons general. 5 dead
SL 125	STENTOR	6,148	26	Br	27/10/42	U 509	6,000 tons W African produce. 44 dead
SL 125	TASMANIA	6,405	35	Br	31/10/42	U 659 & U 103	8,500 tons food & iron. 2 dead
SL 126	EMPIRE BOWMAN	7,031	42	Br	30/03/43	U 404	6,000 tons gen, 2,500 tons ore. 4 dead
SL 126	EMPIRE WHALE	6,159	19	Br	29/03/43	U 662	7,870 tons iron ore. 47 dead
SL 126	NAGARA	8,791	19	Br	28/03/43	U 404	6,069 tons meat. No dead
SL 126	UMARIA	6,852	42	Br	30/03/43	U 662	7,376 tons gen. No dead
SL 128MK	LACONIKOS	3,803	14	Gk	07/05/43	U 89	5,200 tons manganese ore. 23 dead
SL 135MK	URLANA	6,852	41	Br	05/09/43	WRECKED	Isle of Skye
SL 138MK	HALLFRIED	2,968	18	Nor	31/10/43	U 262	Iron ore. 31 dead

Note: BEIGNON of SL 36 was detached and does not appear in TDS statistical tables; she was acting as a Rescue Ship at the time of loss. The seven ships of SL 64S, sunk by HIPPER, do not appear in TDS statistical tables as the convoy was unescorted at the time. They are listed above however.

Losses incurred in MKS convoys, excluding stragglers

Convoy	Ship's Name	GRT			Date of loss	Cause of loss	Comments
MKS 1X	CLAN MACTAGGART	7,622	20	Br	16/11/42	U 92	Ballast. 3 dead
MKS 4	BARRISTER	6,348	39	Br	04/01/43	WRECKED	Ballast
MKS 6	HAMPTON LODGE	3,645	11	Br	20/01/43	AIRCRAFT	Ballast. No dead
MKS 7	BALTONIA	2,013	25	Br	08/02/43	MINED	1,215 tons oranges. 11 dead
MKS 7	EMPIRE MORDRED	7,024	42	Br	08/02/43	MINED	Ballast. 15 dead
MKS 7	MARY SLESSOR	5,027	30	Br	08/02/43	MINED	General. 32 dead
MKS 10	CITY OF PERTH	6,415	13	Br	26/03/43	U 431	Ballast. 2 dead
MKS 13	ALPERA	1,777	20	Br	22/05/43	AIRCRAFT	General, Axis PoWs MAIL. No dead
MKS 15	VOLTURNO	3,424	14	Br	23/06/43	AIRCRAFT	Potash, cork, general. 4 dead
MKS 15	SHETLAND	1,846	21	Br	23/06/43	AIRCRAFT	Potash, cork, general. 3 dead
MKS 21	FRANCIS W PETTYGROVE	7,176	43	Amer	13/08/43	AIRCRAFT	Towed to Gibraltar. CTL
MKS 26	EMPIRE COMMERCE	3,722	43	Br	30/09/43	U 410	Ballast. No dead
MKS 26	FORT HOWE	7,133	42	Br	30/09/43	U 410	Ballast. 2 dead
MKS 28	TIVIVES	4,596	11	Amer	21/10/43	AIRCRAFT	1,750 tons frig cargo. 2 dead
MKS 28	SALTWICK	3,775	29	Br	21/10/43	AIRCRAFT	Ballast & Red Cross mails. No dead
MKS 42	CLARK MILLS	7,176	42	Amer	09/03/44	MINED	Ballast. No dead
MKS 67	PALEMBANG	7,070	21	Du	06/11/44	WRECKED	Cotton. No dead
MKS 71	DUMFRIES	5,149	35	Br	23/12/44	U 772	8,258 tons iron ore. No dead
MKS 81	BLAIRNEVIS	4,155	30	Br	13/02/45	COLLISION	Iron ore, beached in Mersey. No dead. Collision with HMCS ORKNEY

Note: The ships listed above include HAMPTON LODGE, CITY OF PERTH, EMPIRE COMMERCE, FORT HOWE, TIVIVES, SALTWICK, CLARK MILLS and DUMFRIES lost in the Mediterranean.

OA convoy series 1939-1940

The OA series, together with the concurrent OB, were the first outward-bound oceanic convoys from the UK and were started very shortly after the outbreak of war. The OA series sailed initially from the Thames, with the main part of the convoy frequently forming in the Downs, then in use as a convoy anchorage.

The series was unusual for a variety of reasons, the principal one being that until mid-1940 the series was dual purpose, serving both as an oceanic and a coastal convoy with duplicate Commodores. When each convoy sailed from the Downs, it included oceangoing ships proceeding overseas, and oceangoing ships and coasters passing down Channel bound for South and West Coast ports between the Thames and the Clyde. Both sections of the convoy each had its own Commodore, and the portions divided when off Land's End with the ocean portion proceeding into the open sea, the coastal section turning north for the Bristol Channel and Irish Sea. There were frequently ships joining from the major ports of Southampton, Plymouth and Falmouth en route down Channel, and equally frequent departures to Channel ports of all sizes and to ports in the Bristol Channel and Irish Sea.

The oceanic section of the convoy then made a rendezvous in the Southwest Approaches with the OB convoy of the same number to continue as a joint convoy under the OB title and command to the appointed dispersal point. On a regular basis, usually every fifth OA/OB convoy, the merged convoy assumed a new title (in the OG series) and went southwards to Gibraltar. This practice ceased with convoy OA 177 (OG 36). (See the OG series notes for comments on this merger.)

Speeds of the ships using the OA series were much less than in the comparable eastbound HX convoys. The period of passage of an OA convoy was usually limited to a maximum of four days. It was provided with an A/S escort for most of that time and, because of the high number of small, old vessels and coasters coming forward for convoy on the route, convoy speed could be set as low as six knots for such a limited period. There were no serious losses during the Channel transit period until the French coast fell into German hands; after the losses to convoy OA 178 the series was operated from Methil Roads north around to the open ocean.

OA convoy data

CONVOY	DEP. PORT	DEP. DATE	ARRIVAL PORT	ARR. DATE	TDS	MV SUNK	MV DMGD
OA 1	DOWNS	07/09/39	DISPERSED	11/09/39	17		
OA 2	SOUTHEND	09/09/39	DISPERSED	12/09/39	20		
OA 3	SOUTHEND	11/09/39	DISPERSEDW	14/09/39	15		
OA 4	SOUTHEND	13/09/39	DISPERSED	16/09/39	31		
OA 4A	SOUTHEND	13/09/39	DISPERSED	17/09/39	9		
OA 5	SOUTHEND	15/09/39	DISPERSED	18/09/39	14		
OA 6	SOUTHEND	17/09/39	DISPERSED	20/09/39	30		
OA 7	SOUTHEND	19/09/39	DISPERSED	22/09/39	28		1
OA 8	SOUTHEND	21/09/39	DISPERSED	24/09/39	32		
OA 9	SOUTHEND	23/09/39	DISPERSED	26/09/39	31		
OA 10	SOUTHEND	25/09/39	DISPERSED	28/09/39	42		
OA 11	SOUTHEND	27/09/39	DISPERSED	30/09/39	29		
OA 12G	SOUTHEND	29/09/39	FORMED OG 1	02/10/39	20		
OA 13	SOUTHEND	01/10/39	DISPERSED	04/10/39	23		
OA 14	SOUTHEND	03/10/39	DISPERSED	06/10/39	6		
OA 15	SOUTHEND	05/10/39	DISPERSED	08/10/39	6		
OA 16G	SOUTHEND	07/10/39	FORMED OG 2	11/10/39	27		
OA 17	SOUTHEND	07/10/39	DISPERSED	11/10/39	11		
OA 18	SOUTHEND	11/10/39	DISPERSED	17/10/39	9		
OA 19	SOUTHEND	13/10/39	DISPERSED	17/10/39	13		
OA 20G	SOUTHEND	15/10/39	FORMED OG 3	17/10/39	21		
OA 21	SOUTHEND	17/10/39	DISPERSED	22/10/39	21		
OA 22	SOUTHEND	19/10/39	DISPERSED	23/10/39	9		
OA 23	SOUTHEND	21/10/39	DISPERSED	26/10/39	15		
OA 24G	SOUTHEND	23/10/39	FORMED OG 4	26/10/39	19		
OA 25	SOUTHEND	25/10/39	DISPERSED	28/10/39	19		
OA 26	SOUTHEND	27/10/39	DISPERSED	02/11/39	9		
OA 27	SOUTHEND	29/10/39	DISPERSED	02/11/39	16		
OA 28G	SOUTHEND	31/10/39	FORMED OG 5	03/11/39	15		
OA 29	SOUTHEND	02/11/39	DISPERSED	07/11/39	12		
OA 30	SOUTHEND	04/11/39	DISPERSED	07/11/39	12		
OA 31	SOUTHEND	06/11/39	DISPERSED	10/11/39	18		
OA 32G	SOUTHEND	08/11/39	FORMED OG 6	11/11/39	22		
OA 33	SOUTHEND	10/11/39	DISPERSED	15/11/39	12		
OA 34	SOUTHEND	12/11/39	DISPERSED	15/11/39	14		
OA 35	SOUTHEND	14/11/39	DISPERSED	19/11/39	6		
OA 36G	SOUTHEND	16/11/39	FORMED OG 7	17/11/39	19		
OA 37	SOUTHEND	18/11/39	DISPERSED	21/11/39	24		1
OA 38	SOUTHEND	20/11/39	DISPERSED	23/11/39	14		
OA 39	SOUTHEND	22/11/39	DISPERSED	25/11/39	4		
OA 40G	SOUTHEND	24/11/39	FORMED OG 8	26/11/39	20		
OA 41	SOUTHEND	25/11/39	DISPERSED	29/11/39	17		
OA 42	SOUTHEND	26/11/39	DISPERSED	30/11/39	8		
OA 43	SOUTHEND	28/11/39	DISPERSED	01/12/39	13		

THE ALLIED CONVOY SYSTEM 1939-1945

CONVOY	DEP. PORT	DEP. DATE	ARRIVAL PORT	ARR. DATE	TDS	MV SUNK	MV DMGD
OA 44	SOUTHEND	01/12/39	DISPERSED	03/12/39	19		
OA 45G	SOUTHEND	02/12/39	FORMED OG 9	05/12/39	24		
OA 46	SOUTHEND	03/12/39	DISPERSED	07/12/39	21		
OA 47	SOUTHEND	04/12/39	DISPERSED	08/12/39	9		
OA 48	SOUTHEND	06/12/39	DISPERSED	09/12/39	11		
OA 49	SOUTHEND	08/12/39	DISPERSED	11/12/39	11		
OA 50G	SOUTHEND	10/12/39	FORMED OG 10	13/12/39	36		
OA 51	SOUTHEND	11/12/39	DISPERSED	14/12/39	21		
OA 53	SOUTHEND	14/12/39	DISPERSED	16/12/39	28		
OA 54	SOUTHEND	16/12/39	DISPERSED	19/12/39	15		
OA 55G	SOUTHEND	18/12/39	FORMED OG 11	21/12/39	25		
OA 56	SOUTHEND	19/12/39	DISPERSED	21/12/39	18		
OA 57	SOUTHEND	20/12/39	DISPERSED	23/12/39	7		
OA 58	SOUTHEND	22/12/39	DISPERSED	25/12/39	15		
OA 60G	SOUTHEND	26/12/39	FORMED OG 12	28/12/39	9		
OA 61	SOUTHEND	27/12/39	DISPERSED	30/12/39	18		
OA 62	SOUTHEND	28/12/39	DISPERSED	31/12/39	8		
OA 63GF	SOUTHEND	30/12/39	FORMED OG 13F	01/01/40	21		
OA 64	SOUTHEND	01/01/40	DISPERSED	04/01/40	12		
OA 65G	SOUTHEND	03/01/40	FORMED OG 13	07/01/40	27		
OA 66	SOUTHEND	04/01/40	DISPERSED	08/01/40	17		
OA 67	SOUTHEND	05/01/40	DISPERSED	08/01/40	12		
OA 68GF	SOUTHEND	07/01/40	FORMED OG 14F	10/01/40	4		
OA 69	SOUTHEND	09/01/40	DISPERSED	11/01/40	19	1	
OA 70G	SOUTHEND	11/01/40	FORMED OG 14	14/01/40	18		
OA 71	SOUTHEND	12/01/40	DISPERSED	16/01/40	13		
OA 72	SOUTHEND	13/01/40	DISPERSED	17/01/40	5		
OA 73GF	SOUTHEND	16/01/40	FORMED OG 15F	18/01/40	11		
OA 74	SOUTHEND	17/01/40	DISPERSED	20/01/40	19		
OA 75G	SOUTHEND	19/01/40	FORMED OG 15	21/01/40	43		
OA 76	SOUTHEND	20/01/40	DISPERSED	23/01/40	12		
OA 77	SOUTHEND	21/01/40	DISPERSED	24/01/40	7		
OA 78GF	SOUTHEND	23/01/40	FORMED OG 16F	26/01/40	14		
OA 79	SOUTHEND	25/01/40	DISPERSED	28/01/40	12		
OA 80G	SOUTHEND	27/01/40	FORMED OG 16	31/01/40	27	2	
OA 81	SOUTHEND	28/01/40	DISPERSED	31/01/40	9		
OA 82	SOUTHEND	29/01/40	DISPERSED	01/02/40	6		
OA 83GF	SOUTHEND	31/01/40	FORMED OG 17F	03/02/40	9		
OA 84	SOUTHEND	02/02/40	DISPERSED	05/02/40	11	1	1
OA 85G	SOUTHEND	03/02/40	FORMED OG 17	06/02/40	11		
OA 86	SOUTHEND	05/02/40	DISPERSED	08/02/40	7		
OA 87	SOUTHEND	07/02/40	DISPERSED	09/02/40	23		
OA 88GF	SOUTHEND	08/02/40	FORMED OG 18F	11/02/40	13		
OA 89	SOUTHEND	10/02/40	DISPERSED	13/02/40	15		
OA 90G	SOUTHEND	12/02/40	FORMED OG 18	15/02/40	25		
OA 91	SOUTHEND	13/02/40	DISPERSED	16/02/40	7		
OA 92	SOUTHEND	15/02/40	DISPERSED	18/02/40	18		
OA 93GF	SOUTHEND	16/02/40	FORMED OG 19F	19/02/40	12		
OA 94	SOUTHEND	18/02/40	DISPERSED	21/02/40	22		
OA 095G	SOUTHEND	20/02/40	FORMED OG 19	23/02/40	10		
OA 96	SOUTHEND	21/02/40	DISPERSED	24/02/40	10		
OA 97	SOUTHEND	23/02/40	DISPERSED	26/02/40	17		
OA 98GF	SOUTHEND	24/02/40	FORMED OG 20F	27/02/40	19		
OA 99	SOUTHEND	27/02/40	DISPERSED	01/03/40	17		
OA 100G	SOUTHEND	28/02/40	FORMED OG 20	01/03/40	19		
OA 101	SOUTHEND	29/02/40	DISPERSED	03/03/40	7		
OA 102	SOUTHEND	02/03/40	DISPERSED	05/03/40	18		
OA 103GF	SOUTHEND	03/03/40	FORMED OG 21F	05/03/40	18		
OA 104	SOUTHEND	05/03/40	DISPERSED	08/03/40	8		
OA 105G	SOUTHEND	07/03/40	FORMED OG 21	11/03/40	25		
OA 106	SOUTHEND	08/03/40	DISPERSED	12/03/40	5		
OA 107	SOUTHEND	10/03/40	DISPERSED	13/03/40	20		
OA 108GF	SOUTHEND	11/03/40	FORMED OG 22F	13/03/40	12		
OA 109	SOUTHEND	13/03/40	DISPERSED	16/03/40	12		
OA 110G	SOUTHEND	15/03/40	FORMED OG 22	18/03/40	26		
OA 111	SOUTHEND	16/03/40	DISPERSED	19/03/40	5		
OA 112	SOUTHEND	18/03/40	DISPERSED	21/03/40	7		
OA 113GF	SOUTHEND	19/03/40	FORMED OG 23F	21/03/40	20		
OA 114	SOUTHEND	21/03/40	DISPERSED	24/03/40	22		
OA 115G	SOUTHEND	23/03/40	FORMED OG 23	25/03/40	33		
OA 116	SOUTHEND	24/03/40	DISPERSED	28/03/40	15		
OA 117	SOUTHEND	26/03/40	DISPERSED	29/03/40	13		
OA 118	SOUTHEND	27/03/40	FORMED OG 24F	29/03/40	19		
OA 119	SOUTHEND	28/03/40	DISPERSED	01/04/40	17		
OA 120G	SOUTHEND	31/03/40	RV OB 120	01/04/40	22		
OA 121	SOUTHEND	01/04/40	DISPERSED	04/04/40	6		
OA 122	SOUTHEND	02/04/40	DISPERSED	05/04/40	4		
OA 123GF	SOUTHEND	04/04/40	FORMED OG 25F	06/04/40	44		
OA 124	SOUTHEND	06/04/40	DISPERSED	09/04/40	15		
OA 125G	SOUTHEND	08/04/40	FORMED OG 25	10/04/40	38		
OA 126	SOUTHEND	09/04/40	DISPERSED	12/04/40	11		
OA 127	SOUTHEND	10/04/40	DISPERSED	13/04/40	10		
OA 128GF	SOUTHEND	12/04/40	FORMED OG 26F	14/04/40	39		
OA 129	SOUTHEND	14/04/40	DISPERSED	17/04/40	30		
OA 130G	SOUTHEND	16/04/40	FORMED OG 26	18/04/40	33		
OA 131	SOUTHEND	17/04/40	DISPERSED	20/04/40	20		
OA 133GF	SOUTHEND	20/04/40	FORMED OG 27F	22/04/40	37		
OA 134	SOUTHEND	22/04/40	DISPERSED	25/04/40	16		
OA 135G	SOUTHEND	24/04/40	FORMED OG 27	26/04/40	30		
OA 136	SOUTHEND	25/04/40	DISPERSED	27/04/40	14		
OA 137	SOUTHEND	27/04/40	DISPERSED	29/04/40	16		
OA 138GF	SOUTHEND	28/04/40	FORMED OG 28F	01/05/40	19		
OA 139	SOUTHEND	01/05/40	DISPERSED	04/05/40	42		
OA 140G	SOUTHEND	02/05/40	FORMED OG 28	05/05/40	25		
OA 141	SOUTHEND	03/05/40	DISPERSED	06/05/40	21		
OA 142	SOUTHEND	04/05/40	DISPERSED	07/05/40	7		
OA 143GF	SOUTHEND	06/05/40	FORMED OG 29F	09/05/40	28		
OA 144	SOUTHEND	08/05/40	DISPERSED	11/05/40	30		
OA 145G	SOUTHEND	10/05/40	FORMED OG 29	12/05/40	26		
OA 146	SOUTHEND	11/05/40	DISPERSED	15/05/40	18		
OA 147	SOUTHEND	12/05/40	DISPERSED	16/05/40	22		
OA 148GF	SOUTHEND	14/05/40	FORMED OG 30F	16/05/40	33		
OA 149	SOUTHEND	16/05/40	DETACHED	18/05/40	24		
OA 150G	SOUTHEND	18/05/40	FORMED OG 30	19/05/40	26		
OA 151	SOUTHEND	19/05/40	DISPERSED	22/05/40	11		
OA 152	SOUTHEND	20/05/40	DISPERSED	22/05/40	17		
OA 153GF	SOUTHEND	22/05/40	FORMED OG 31F	25/05/40	32		
OA 154	SOUTHEND	24/05/40	DISPERSED	27/05/40	16		

APPENDIX 3

CONVOY	DEP. PORT	DEP. DATE	ARRIVAL PORT	ARR. DATE	TDS	MV SUNK	MV DMGD	CONVOY	DEP. PORT	DEP. DATE	ARRIVAL PORT	ARR. DATE	TDS	MV SUNK	MV DMGD
OA 155G	SOUTHEND	26/05/40	FORMED OG 31	28/05/40	26			OA 198	METHIL	13/08/40	DISPERSED	18/08/40	10		
OA 156	SOUTHEND	27/05/40	DISPERSED	30/05/40	25			OA 199	METHIL	15/08/40	DISPERSED	20/08/40	29		1
OA 157	SOUTHEND	28/05/40	DISPERSED	31/05/40	18			OA 200	METHIL	16/08/40	DISPERSED	20/08/40	40		
OA 158GF	SOUTHEND	30/05/40	FORMED OG 32F	02/06/40	23			OA 201	METHIL	18/08/40	DISPERSED	22/08/40	27		
OA 159	SOUTHEND	01/06/40	DISPERSED	04/06/40	24			OA 202	METHIL	21/08/40	DISPERSED	25/08/40	40		
OA 160	SOUTHEND	02/06/40	DISPERSED	04/06/40	23			OA 203	METHIL	22/08/40	DISPERSED	26/08/40	11	2	1
OA 161G	SOUTHEND	03/06/40	FORMED OG 32	05/06/40	25			OA 204	METHIL	25/08/40	DISPERSED	29/08/40	43	2	1
OA 162	SOUTHEND	05/06/40	DISPERSED	07/06/40	13			OA 205	METHIL	27/08/40	DISPERSED	30/08/40	15		
OA 163GF	SOUTHEND	07/06/40	FORMED OG 33F	09/06/40	35			OA 206	METHIL	29/08/40	DISPERSED	02/09/40	48		1
OA 165	SOUTHEND	10/06/40	DISPERSED	12/06/40	29			OA 207	METHIL	31/08/40	DISPERSED	06/09/40	15	1	
OA 166G	SOUTHEND	11/06/40	FORMED OG 33	13/06/40	15			OA 208	METHIL	02/09/40	DISPERSED	06/09/40	43		3
OA 167	SOUTHEND	13/06/40	DISPERSED	16/06/40	40			OA 209	METHIL	04/09/40	DISPERSED	09/09/40	27		
OA 168GF	SOUTHEND	15/06/40	FORMED OG 34F	17/06/40	68			OA 210	METHIL	06/09/40	DISPERSED	10/09/40	35		
OA 169	SOUTHEND	17/06/40	DISPERSED	19/06/40	56			OA 211	METHIL	08/09/40	DISPERSED	12/09/40	25		
OA 170	SOUTHEND	18/06/40	DISPERSED	21/06/40	21			OA 212	METHIL	09/09/40	DISPERSED	13/09/40	14		
OA 171G	SOUTHEND	19/06/40	FORMED OG 34	21/06/40	22			OA 213	METHIL	12/09/40	DISPERSED	16/09/40	24		
OA 172	SOUTHEND	21/06/40	DISPERSED	25/06/40	56	2		OA 214	METHIL	14/09/40	DISPERSED	17/09/40	29		
OA 173G	SOUTHEND	24/06/40	FORMED OG 35	27/06/40	32			OA 215	METHIL	16/09/40	DISPERSED	20/09/40	3		
OA 174	SOUTHEND	25/06/40	DISPERSED	28/06/40	46			OA 216	METHIL	18/09/40	RV WITH OB 216	21/09/40	32		
OA 175	SOUTHEND	27/06/40	DISPERSED	01/07/40	48			OA 217	METHIL	19/09/40	DISPERSED	22/09/40	10		
OA 176	SOUTHEND	29/06/40	DISPERSED	02/07/40	35			OA 218	METHIL	22/09/40	DISPERSED	27/09/40	38		
OA 177G	SOUTHEND	01/07/40	FORMED OG 36	03/07/40	33	1		OA 219	METHIL	24/09/40	DISPERSED	28/09/40	17		
OA 178	SOUTHEND	03/07/40	DISPERSED	06/07/40	53	5	11	OA 220	METHIL	26/09/40	DISPERSED	28/09/40	44	1	1
OA 179	METHIL	08/07/40	DISPERSED	13/07/40	36	1		OA 221	METHIL	28/09/40	DISPERSED	02/10/40	22		
OA 182	METHIL	10/07/40	DISPERSED	14/07/40	37			OA 222	METHIL	30/09/40	RV WITH OB 222	03/10/40	33		
OA 183	METHIL	12/07/40	DISPERSED	15/07/40	15			OA 223	METHIL	01/10/40	DISPERSED	05/10/40	17		
OA 184	METHIL	14/07/40	DISPERSED	18/07/40	50			OA 224	METHIL	04/10/40	DISPERSED	08/10/40	26		
OA 186	METHIL	18/07/40	DISPERSED	21/07/40	39			OA 225	METHIL	06/10/40	DISPERSED	10/10/40	24		
OA 187	METHIL	20/07/40	DISPERSED	25/07/40	33			OA 226	METHIL	08/10/40	RV WITH OB 226	11/10/40	24		
OA 188	METHIL	22/07/40	DISPERSED	23/07/40	19			OA 227	METHIL	10/10/40	DISPERSED	14/10/40	12		
OA 190	METHIL	26/07/40	DISPERSED	29/07/40	49			OA 228	METHIL	12/10/40	DISPERSED	16/10/40	23	1	
OA 191	METHIL	28/07/40	DISPERSED	01/08/40	28			OA 229	METHIL	14/10/40	DISPERSED	18/10/40	13		
OA 192	METHIL	30/07/40	DISPERSED	03/08/40	18			OA 230	METHIL	16/10/40	RV WITH OB 230	20/10/40	9		
OA 193	METHIL	03/08/40	DISPERSED	07/08/40	35			OA 231	METHIL	18/10/40	DISPERSED	23/10/40	20		
OA 194	METHIL	05/08/40	DISPERSED	09/08/40	33			OA 232	METHIL	20/10/40	DISPERSED	26/10/40	27		1
OA 195	METHIL	07/08/40	DISPERSED	10/08/40	11			OA 233	METHIL	22/10/40	RV WITH OB 233	24/10/40	12		
OA 196	METHIL	09/08/40	DISPERSED	15/08/40	48			OA 234	METHIL	24/10/40	RV WITH OB 234	26/10/40	6		
OA 197	METHIL	11/08/40	DISPERSED	16/08/40	21										

Losses incurred in OA convoys, excluding stragglers

Convoy	Ship's Name	GRT			Date of loss	Cause of loss	Comments	Convoy	Ship's Name	GRT			Date of loss	Cause of loss	Comments
OA 69	DUNBAR CASTLE	10,002	30	Br	09/01/40	MINED	4,400 tons general. 9 dead	OA 178	ELMCREST	4,343	11	Br	04/07/40	S 20 (E BOAT)	Ballast. 16 dead
OA 80G	KERAMIAI	5,085	17	Gk	30/01/40	U 55	Ballast. No dead	OA 178	KOLGA	3,526	12	Est	04/07/40	AIRCRAFT	Ballast. 1 dead
OA 80G	VACLITE	5,026	28	Br	30/01/40	U 55	Ballast. No dead	OA 179	ALWAKI	4,533	22	Du	10/07/40	U 61	No data available
OA 84	BEAVERBURN	9,874	27	Br	05/02/40	U 41	General. 1 dead	OA 203	LLANISHEN	5,053	29	Br	23/08/40	AIRCRAFT	Ballast. 8 dead
OA 172	SARANAC	12,049	18	Br	25/06/40	U 51	Ballast. 4 dead	OA 203	MAKALLA	6,677	18	Br	23/08/40	AIRCRAFT	2,500 tons general. 12 dead
OA 172	WINDSORWOOD	5,395	36	Br	25/06/40	U 51	7,100 tons coal. No dead	OA 204	ASTRA II	2,393	23	Br	29/08/40	U 100	Ballast. 5 dead
OA 177G	AENEAS	10,058	10	Br	02/07/40	AIRCRAFT	General. 21 dead	OA 204	DALBLAIR	4,608	26	Br	28/08/40	U 100	Ballast. 24 dead
OA 178	BRITSUM	5,255	29	Du	04/07/40	AIRCRAFT	Ballast. Dead not known	OA 207	TITAN	9,035	06	Br	04/09/40	U 47	Ballast. 6 dead
OA 178	DALLAS CITY	4,952	35	Br	04/07/40	AIRCRAFT	Ammonium sulphate. No dead	OA 220	PORT DENISON	8,043	18	Br	27/09/40	AIRCRAFT	1,500 tons general. 16 dead
OA 178	DEUCALION	1,796	14	Du	04/07/40	AIRCRAFT	Ballast. 27 survivors	OA 228	HURUNUI	9,371	20	Br	14/10/40	U 98	Ballast. 2 dead

OB convoy series 1939-1941

The OB series commenced on 7 Sep 1939 from Liverpool, with the convoy routed south through St George's Channel to the open Atlantic. Like the contemporaneous OA series, ships for coastal routing were included, principally for the Welsh coal ports, but also for the Channel and London. Unlike the OA series, there was no coastal Commodore, and such ships were simply detached as independents off the Smalls LV or Land's End as appropriate.

Certain OB convoys amalgamated with the OA convoy of the same number and became OG for Gibraltar and ports south and eastward of that port. In each case the OB Commodore became Commodore of the joint convoy. Otherwise, the OA ships joined OB and the whole body proceeded to the open sea to disperse after some four days of passage. This pattern continued until the movement of the OA convoys northward (as already noted) and after OB 179 the OB series was re-routed through the North Channel from the Irish Sea to distance the route from French based aircraft.

Like the OA series, at first some of the OB convoys contained ships including numerous small coasters with a lower speed than the standard 9 knots. When this traffic reduced in July 1940, and with the increasing U-boat threat in Western Approaches, the 9-knot minimum was introduced.

OB convoys continued the standard pattern of dispersing to the west of the UK when outside the expected U-boat operating area. Experience showed the need to extend the dispersal points further west and, eventually, the escort problem was solved in 1941 with the introduction of mid-Atlantic escort and two new convoy series.

Initially OB convoys contained ships for North America and the Caribbean, the South American, Freetown and Cape trade being handled by the OG series. After July 1940, in the main, such ships were routed into the North Atlantic via the OB series and then detached as independents. It was accepted that this trade must, eventually, have its own convoy series and dedicated escorts but it was only in 1941 that such became available. Prior to that, certain OB convoys near the end of the series adopted a much more southerly course than usual, finally extending to calling at Freetown, detaching Caribbean and South American-bound ships en route as appropriate.

Towards the end of the series escort was already being extended to Canadian waters, and several convoys actually arrived in Halifax as formed units under escort.

The OB series finally ended with OB 349 which sailed 21 July 1941, thereafter the North Atlantic traffic was handled by the new ON series for North America and OS for Freetown and beyond.

Convoys OB 1 to 179 sailed via St George's Channel. Of these, OB 117 and OB 122 were cancelled to give 177 convoys comprising 2,470 ships. Of these, two convoys were attacked, each losing one ship to U-boats. OB 180 to 349 plus convoy OBA were intended to sail via the northern exit. As OB 185, 189, 247 & 342 were cancelled, a total of 168 convoys comprising 5,812 ships actually sailed. Of these, 23 convoys were attacked for the loss of 61 ships: 44 by U-boats, 1 mined and 16 by aircraft. These figures include some attacks made after the escort had left the convoy and these, plus the marine casualties and one ship mined, do not appear in the TDS figures shown in the convoy data below.

OB convoy data

CONVOY	DEP. PORT	DEP. DATE	ARRIVAL PORT	ARR. DATE	TDS	MV SUNK	MV DMGD
OB 1	LIVERPOOL	07/09/39	DISPERSED	10/09/39	10		
OB 2	LIVERPOOL	09/09/39	DISPERSED	14/09/39	9		
OB 3	LIVERPOOL	11/09/39	DISPERSED	16/09/39	6		
OB 4	LIVERPOOL	13/09/39	DISPERSED 48.28N 15.44W	16/09/39	9		
OB 5	LIVERPOOL	16/09/39	DISPERSED	19/09/39	8		
OB 6	LIVERPOOL	17/09/39	DISPERSED	20/09/39	8		
OB 7	LIVERPOOL	19/09/39	DISPERSED	23/09/39	13		
OB 8	LIVERPOOL	21/09/39	DISPERSED	25/09/39	11		
OB 9	LIVERPOOL	23/09/39	DISPERSED	26/09/39	23		
OB 10	LIVERPOOL	25/09/39	DISPERSED	28/09/39	13		
OB 11	LIVERPOOL	27/09/39	DISPERSED 49.52N 15.46W	30/09/39	17		
OB 12	LIVERPOOL	29/09/39	FORMED OG 1	02/10/39	24		
OB 13	LIVERPOOL	01/10/39	DISPERSED 50N 14.20W	04/10/39	31		
OB 14	LIVERPOOL	03/10/39	DISPERSED	06/10/39	6		
OB 15	LIVERPOOL	05/10/39	DISPERSED	08/10/39	11		
OB 16	LIVERPOOL	08/10/39	FORMED OG 2	11/10/39	20		
OB 17	LIVERPOOL	09/10/39	DISPERSED	12/10/39	11		
OB 18	LIVERPOOL	11/10/39	DISPERSED 48N 23W	17/10/39	9		

APPENDIX 3

CONVOY	DEP. PORT	DEP. DATE	ARRIVAL PORT	ARR. DATE	TDS	MV SUNK	MV DMGD
OB 19	LIVERPOOL	13/10/39	DISPERSED	18/10/39	9		
OB 20	LIVERPOOL	16/10/39	FORMED OG 3	17/10/39	20		
OB 21	LIVERPOOL	17/10/39	DISPERSED	22/10/39	14		
OB 22	LIVERPOOL	19/10/39	DISPERSED	22/10/39	18		
OB 23	LIVERPOOL	21/10/39	DISPERSED	26/10/39	20		
OB 24	LIVERPOOL	25/10/39	FORMED OG 4	27/10/39	24		
OB 25	LIVERPOOL	26/10/39	DISPERSED	30/10/39	19	1	
OB 26	LIVERPOOL	27/10/39	DISPERSED 48.30N 26.30W	01/11/39	18		
OB 27	LIVERPOOL	29/10/39	DISPERSED	03/11/39	19		
OB 28	LIVERPOOL	01/11/39	FORMED OG 5	03/11/39	25		
OB 29	LIVERPOOL	02/11/39	DISPERSED	07/11/39	21		
OB 30	LIVERPOOL	04/11/39	DISPERSED 48.07N 22.09W	09/11/39	20		
OB 31	LIVERPOOL	06/11/39	DISPERSED	11/11/39	8		
OB 32	LIVERPOOL	08/11/39	FORMED OG 6	11/11/39	18		
OB 33	LIVERPOOL	10/11/39	DISPERSED	15/11/39	33		
OB 34	LIVERPOOL	12/11/39	DISPERSED	18/11/39	17		
OB 35	LIVERPOOL	14/11/39	DISPERSED	19/11/39	14		
OB 36	LIVERPOOL	16/11/39	FORMED OG 7	17/11/39	30		
OB 37	LIVERPOOL	18/11/39	DISPERSED	21/11/39	27		
OB 38	LIVERPOOL	20/11/39	DISPERSED	23/11/39	13		
OB 39	LIVERPOOL	22/11/39	DISPERSED 49.58N 15.41W	25/11/39	9		
OB 40	LIVERPOOL	24/11/39	FORMED OG 8	26/11/39	34		
OB 41	LIVERPOOL	25/11/39	DISPERSED	27/11/39	4		
OB 42	LIVERPOOL	26/11/39	DISPERSED	01/12/39	11		
OB 43	LIVERPOOL	28/11/39	DISPERSED	04/12/39	9		
OB 44	LIVERPOOL	30/11/39	DISPERSED	03/12/39	13		
OB 45	LIVERPOOL	03/12/39	FORMED OG 9	05/12/39	30		
OB 46	LIVERPOOL	03/12/39	DISPERSED	07/12/39	7	1	
OB 47	LIVERPOOL	04/12/39	DISPERSED	08/12/39	20		
OB 48	LIVERPOOL	06/12/39	DISPERSED	10/12/39	13		
OB 49	LIVERPOOL	08/12/39	DISPERSED	12/12/39	12		
OB 50	LIVERPOOL	10/12/39	FORMED OG 10	13/12/39	27		
OB 51	LIVERPOOL	11/12/39	DISPERSED	14/12/39	8		
OB 52	LIVERPOOL	12/12/39	DISPERSED	17/12/39	14		
OB 53	LIVERPOOL	14/12/39	DISPERSED 48.50N 24W	19/12/39	13		
OB 54	LIVERPOOL	16/12/39	DISPERSED	19/12/39	12		
OB 55	LIVERPOOL	19/12/39	FORMED OG 11	20/12/39	34		
OB 56	LIVERPOOL	19/12/39	DISPERSED	21/12/39	7		
OB 57	LIVERPOOL	20/12/39	DISPERSED	23/12/39	20		
OB 58	LIVERPOOL	22/12/39	DISPERSED 47.51N 19.57W	26/12/39	21		
OB 59	LIVERPOOL	24/12/39	DISPERSED 47.17N 19.31W	28/12/39	24		
OB 60	LIVERPOOL	26/12/39	FORMED OG 12	28/12/39	31		
OB 62	LIVERPOOL	28/12/39	DISPERSED	31/12/39	14		
OB 63	LIVERPOOL	30/12/39	FORMED OG 13F	01/01/40	11		
OB 64	LIVERPOOL	01/01/40	DISPERSED	05/01/40	21		
OB 65	LIVERPOOL	03/01/40	FORMED OG 13	06/01/40	22		
OB 66	LIVERPOOL	04/01/40	DISPERSED	06/01/40	4		
OB 67	LIVERPOOL	05/01/40	DISPERSED	09/01/40	18		
OB 68	LIVERPOOL	07/01/40	FORMED OG 14F	10/01/40	27		
OB 69	LIVERPOOL	09/01/40	DISPERSED	13/01/40	16		
OB 70	LIVERPOOL	11/01/40	FORMED OG 14	14/01/40	37		
OB 71	LIVERPOOL	12/01/40	DISPERSED	16/01/40	8		
OB 71M	LIVERPOOL	12/01/40	DISPERSED	19/01/40	7		
OB 72	LIVERPOOL	16/01/40	DISPERSED 47.40N 09.45W	18/01/40	5		
OB 72M	LIVERPOOL	13/01/40	DISPERSED	18/01/40	7		
OB 73	LIVERPOOL	16/01/40	FORMED OG 15F	18/01/40	11		
OB 74	LIVERPOOL	17/01/40	DISPERSED	20/01/40	19	1	
OB 75	LIVERPOOL	19/01/40	FORMED OG 15	21/01/40	34		
OB 76	LIVERPOOL	20/01/40	DISPERSED	23/01/40	14		
OB 77	LIVERPOOL	21/01/40	DISPERSED	24/01/40	10		
OB 78	LIVERPOOL	24/01/40	DISPERSED	27/01/40	14		
OB 79	LIVERPOOL	25/01/40	DISPERSED	28/01/40	16		
OB 80	LIVERPOOL	27/01/40	FORMED OG 16	31/01/40	26		
OB 81	LIVERPOOL	28/01/40	DISPERSED	31/01/40	11		
OB 82	LIVERPOOL	29/01/40	DISPERSED	02/02/40	12		
OB 83	LIVERPOOL	01/02/40	FORMED OG 17F	03/02/40	22		
OB 84	LIVERPOOL	02/02/40	DISPERSED 49.48N 14.25W	05/02/40	20		
OB 85	LIVERPOOL	04/02/40	FORMED OG 17	06/02/40	12		
OB 86	LIVERPOOL	07/02/40	DISPERSED	10/02/40	27		
OB 87	LIVERPOOL	07/02/40	DISPERSED	10/02/40	8		
OB 88	LIVERPOOL	09/02/40	FORMED OG 18F	11/02/40	20		
OB 89	LIVERPOOL	10/02/40	DISPERSED	14/02/40	14		
OB 90	LIVERPOOL	13/02/40	FORMED OG 18	15/02/40	30		
OB 91	LIVERPOOL	13/02/40	DISPERSED 47.56N 15.10W	17/02/40	11		
OB 92	LIVERPOOL	15/02/40	DISPERSED	18/02/40	15		
OB 93	LIVERPOOL	17/02/40	FORMED OG 19F	19/02/40	21		
OB 94	LIVERPOOL	18/02/40	DISPERSED	22/02/40	25		
OB 95	LIVERPOOL	21/02/40	FORMED OG 19	23/02/40	27		
OB 96	LIVERPOOL	21/02/40	DISPERSED	24/02/40	11		
OB 97	LIVERPOOL	23/02/40	DISPERSED	27/02/40	15		
OB 98	LIVERPOOL	24/02/40	FORMED OG 20F	27/02/40	20		
OB 99	LIVERPOOL	26/02/40	DISPERSED	01/03/40	17		
OB 100	LIVERPOOL	28/02/40	FORMED OG 20	01/03/40	20		
OB 101	LIVERPOOL	29/02/40	DISPERSED	03/03/40	11		
OB 102	LIVERPOOL	02/03/40	DISPERSED 46.40N 20.40W	06/03/40	8		
OB 103	LIVERPOOL	03/03/40	FORMED OG 21F	05/03/40	26		
OB 104	LIVERPOOL	05/03/40	DISPERSED	08/03/40	26		
OB 105	LIVERPOOL	09/03/40	FORMED OG 21	11/03/40	20		
OB 106	LIVERPOOL	08/03/40	DISPERSED	11/03/40	19		
OB 107	LIVERPOOL	11/03/40	DISPERSED	15/03/40	14		
OB 108	LIVERPOOL	12/03/40	FORMED OG 22F	14/03/40	29		
OB 109	LIVERPOOL	13/03/40	DISPERSED	16/03/40	14		
OB 110	LIVERPOOL	16/03/40	FORMED OG 22	18/03/40	36		

◇ THE ALLIED CONVOY SYSTEM 1939-1945

CONVOY	DEP. PORT	DEP. DATE	ARRIVAL PORT	ARR. DATE	TDS	MV SUNK	MV DMGD
OB 111	LIVERPOOL	16/03/40	DISPERSED	20/03/40	16		
OB 112	LIVERPOOL	18/03/40	DISPERSED	23/03/40	15		
OB 113	LIVERPOOL	19/03/40	FORMED OG 23F	21/03/40	24		
OB 114	LIVERPOOL	21/03/40	DISPERSED 47.11N 18.59W	25/03/40	19		
OB 115	LIVERPOOL	23/03/40	FORMED OG 23	25/03/40	30		
OB 116	LIVERPOOL	24/03/40	DISPERSED 47.41N 15.33W	27/03/40	20		
OB 118	LIVERPOOL	27/03/40	FORMED OG 24F	29/03/40	12		
OB 119	LIVERPOOL	29/03/40	DISPERSED	01/04/40	20		
OB 120	LIVERPOOL	31/03/40	FORMED OG 24	03/04/40	35		
OB 121	LIVERPOOL	01/04/40	DISPERSED	04/04/40	14		
OB 123	LIVERPOOL	04/04/40	FORMED OG 25F	06/04/40	33		
OB 124	LIVERPOOL	06/04/40	DISPERSED	10/04/40	27		
OB 125	LIVERPOOL	08/04/40	FORMED OG 25	10/04/40	27		
OB 126	LIVERPOOL	09/04/40	DISPERSED	13/04/40	16		
OB 127	LIVERPOOL	10/04/40	DISPERSED	14/04/40	16		
OB 128	LIVERPOOL	13/04/40	FORMED OG 26F	14/04/40	35		
OB 129	LIVERPOOL	14/04/40	DISPERSED 47.20N 18.15W	18/04/40	32		
OB 130	LIVERPOOL	16/04/40	FORMED OG 26	18/04/40	26		
OB 131	LIVERPOOL	17/04/40	DISPERSED	21/04/40	16		
OB 132	LIVERPOOL	18/04/40	DISPERSED 48.15N 17.25W	22/04/40	13		
OB 133	LIVERPOOL	20/04/40	FORMED OG 27F	22/04/40	40		
OB 134	LIVERPOOL	22/04/40	DISPERSED 47N 19.30W	26/04/40	27		
OB 135	LIVERPOOL	24/04/40	FORMED OG 27	26/04/40	34		
OB 136	LIVERPOOL	25/04/40	DISPERSED	28/04/40	18		
OB 137	LIVERPOOL	26/04/40	DISPERSED	29/04/40	8		
OB 138	LIVERPOOL	28/04/40	FORMED OG 28F	01/05/40	28		
OB 139	LIVERPOOL	30/04/40	DISPERSED	03/05/40	22		
OB 140	LIVERPOOL	02/05/40	FORMED OG 28	05/05/40	28		
OB 141	LIVERPOOL	03/05/40	DISPERSED	06/05/40	16		
OB 142	LIVERPOOL	04/05/40	DISPERSED 46.28N 30.29W	08/05/40	13		
OB 143	LIVERPOOL	06/05/40	FORMED OG 29F	09/05/40	31		
OB 144	LIVERPOOL	08/05/40	DISPERSED 47N 19.08W	12/05/40	22		
OB 145	LIVERPOOL	10/05/40	FORMED OG 29	12/05/40	34		
OB 146	LIVERPOOL	11/05/40	DISPERSED	13/05/40	11		
OB 147	LIVERPOOL	12/05/40	DISPERSED	14/05/40	24		
OB 148	LIVERPOOL	14/05/40	FORMED OG 30F	15/05/40	23		
OB 149	LIVERPOOL	16/05/40	DISPERSED	17/05/40	18		
OB 150	LIVERPOOL	18/05/40	FORMED OG 30	20/05/40	24		
OB 151	LIVERPOOL	19/05/40	DISPERSED	22/05/40	23		
OB 152	LIVERPOOL	20/05/40	DISPERSED	24/05/40	8		
OB 153	LIVERPOOL	22/05/40	FORMED OG 31F	25/05/40	38		
OB 154	LIVERPOOL	24/05/40	DISPERSED 46.38N 20.20W	28/05/40	12		
OB 155	LIVERPOOL	26/05/40	FORMED OG 31	29/05/40	32		
OB 156	LIVERPOOL	27/05/40	DISPERSED	30/05/40	11		
OB 157	LIVERPOOL	28/05/40	DISPERSED	31/05/40	6		
OB 158	LIVERPOOL	30/05/40	FORMED OG 32F	02/06/40	31		
OB 159	LIVERPOOL	01/06/40	DISPERSED	04/06/40	23		
OB 160	LIVERPOOL	02/06/40	DISPERSED	05/06/40	14		
OB 161	LIVERPOOL	03/06/40	FORMED OG 32	05/06/40	24		
OB 162	LIVERPOOL	05/06/40	DISPERSED	08/06/40	29		
OB 163	LIVERPOOL	08/06/40	DISPERSED (OG 33F 9.6.40)	13/06/40	31		
OB 164	LIVERPOOL	09/06/40	DISPERSED 46.24N 19.58W	12/06/40	29		
OB 165	LIVERPOOL	10/06/40	DISPERSED	14/06/40	7		
OB 166	LIVERPOOL	11/06/40	FORMED OG 33	13/06/40	20		
OB 167	LIVERPOOL	13/06/40	DISPERSED	17/06/40	28		
OB 168	LIVERPOOL	15/06/40	FORMED OG 34F	17/06/40	24		
OB 169	LIVERPOOL	17/06/40	DISPERSED 46N 20.40W	22/06/40	32		
OB 170	LIVERPOOL	18/06/40	DISPERSED 46.25N 21W	23/06/40	15		
OB 171	LIVERPOOL	19/06/40	FORMED OG 34	21/06/40	15		
OB 172	LIVERPOOL	22/06/40	DISPERSED 46.55N 20.33W	26/06/40	50		
OB 173	LIVERPOOL	24/06/40	FORMED OG 35	27/06/40	9		
OB 174	LIVERPOOL	25/06/40	DISPERSED 47N 21W	30/06/40	64		
OB 175	LIVERPOOL	27/06/40	DISPERSED	30/06/40	42		
OB 176	LIVERPOOL	29/06/40	DISPERSED 48N 15.04W	02/07/40	28		
OB 177	LIVERPOOL	01/07/40	FORMED OG 36	03/07/40	21		
OB 178	LIVERPOOL	03/07/40	DISPERSED	07/07/40	49		
OB 179	LIVERPOOL	05/07/40	DISPERSED 46.40N 15.40W	09/07/40	29		
OB 180	LIVERPOOL	07/07/40	DISPERSED	10/07/40	47		
OB 181	LIVERPOOL	10/07/40	FORMED OG 37	12/07/40	19		
OB 182	LIVERPOOL	11/07/40	DISPERSED	14/07/40	34		
OB 183	LIVERPOOL	13/07/40	DISPERSED	17/07/40	43		
OB 184	LIVERPOOL	15/07/40	DISPERSED	18/07/40	43		
OB 186	LIVERPOOL	20/07/40	DISPERSED	22/07/40	54		
OB 187	LIVERPOOL	21/07/40	DISPERSED 53.43N 23.30W	25/07/40	37		
OB 188	LIVERPOOL	23/07/40	DISPERSED	27/07/40	37	2	
OB 190	LIVERPOOL	27/07/40	DISPERSED	31/07/40	63		
OB 191	LIVERPOOL	30/07/40	DISPERSED	02/08/40	29	1	3
OB 192	LIVERPOOL	31/07/40	DISPERSED 54.26N 20.16W	04/08/40	38		
OB 193	LIVERPOOL	04/08/40	DISPERSED	07/08/40	48	1	
OB 194	LIVERPOOL	06/08/40	DISPERSED 54.36N 18.02W	10/08/40	32		
OB 195	LIVERPOOL	08/08/40	DISPERSED	12/08/40	27		
OB 196	LIVERPOOL	10/08/40	DISPERSED	15/08/40	22		
OB 197	LIVERPOOL	13/08/40	DISPERSED	16/08/40	54	1	
OB 198	LIVERPOOL	15/08/40	DISPERSED 55.31N 16.55W	18/08/40	26		

◇ 152

APPENDIX 3

CONVOY	DEP. PORT	DEP. DATE	ARRIVAL PORT	ARR. DATE	TDS	MV SUNK	MV DMGD
OB 199	LIVERPOOL	16/08/40	DISPERSED 56N 20.14W	20/08/40	24		
OB 200	LIVERPOOL	18/08/40	DISPERSED	22/08/40	18		
OB 201	LIVERPOOL	20/08/40	DISPERSED	25/08/40	31		
OB 202	LIVERPOOL	22/08/40	DISPERSED	26/08/40	32	2	
OB 203	LIVERPOOL	24/08/40	DISPERSED 56.32N 21.26W	28/08/40	32		
OB 204	LIVERPOOL	26/08/40	DISPERSED	29/08/40	38		1
OB 205	LIVERPOOL	29/08/40	DISPERSED	30/08/40	33	1	2
OB 206	LIVERPOOL	31/08/40	DISPERSED	05/09/40	32	1	
OB 207	LIVERPOOL	01/09/40	DISPERSED	06/09/40	22		
OB 208	LIVERPOOL	03/09/40	DISPERSED	07/09/40	20		
OB 209	LIVERPOOL	05/09/40	DISPERSED	09/09/40	42		1
OB 210	LIVERPOOL	08/09/40	DISPERSED	10/09/40	30		
OB 211	LIVERPOOL	10/09/40	DISPERSED 56.30N 15.08W	13/09/40	20		
OB 212	LIVERPOOL	11/09/40	DISPERSED 53.30N 20.42W	16/09/40	22		
OB 213	LIVERPOOL	13/09/40	DISPERSED	18/09/40	20		
OB 214	LIVERPOOL	15/09/40	DISPERSED	18/09/40	29		
OB 215	LIVERPOOL	17/09/40	DISPERSED	21/09/40	25		
OB 216	LIVERPOOL	19/09/40	DISPERSED 53N 17.05W	23/09/40	27	4	
OB 217	LIVERPOOL	21/09/40	DISPERSED	25/09/40	38		
OB 218	LIVERPOOL	24/09/40	DISPERSED	29/09/40	25	2	1
OB 219	LIVERPOOL	25/09/40	DISPERSED 57.11N 29.32W	30/09/40	23		
OB 220	LIVERPOOL	27/09/40	DISPERSED	01/10/40	32		
OB 221	LIVERPOOL	29/09/40	DISPERSED 56.43N 20.29W	03/10/40	35		
OB 222	LIVERPOOL	01/10/40	DISPERSED	05/10/40	31		
OB 223	LIVERPOOL	03/10/40	DISPERSED 58.30N 25W	08/10/40	25		
OB 224	LIVERPOOL	05/10/40	DISPERSED 57.58N 24.25W	12/10/40	27		
OB 225	LIVERPOOL	07/10/40	DISPERSED	10/10/40	33		
OB 226	LIVERPOOL	09/10/40	DISPERSED	12/10/40	35		
OB 227	LIVERPOOL	11/10/40	DISPERSED	15/10/40	24		
OB 228	LIVERPOOL	13/10/40	DISPERSED	17/10/40	47	3	1
OB 229	LIVERPOOL	15/10/40	DISPERSED	18/10/40	35		
OB 230	LIVERPOOL	17/10/40	DISPERSED	20/10/40	24		1
OB 231	LIVERPOOL	19/10/40	DISPERSED	23/10/40	31		
OB 232	LIVERPOOL	21/10/40	DISPERSED 56.30N 26.50W	26/10/40	41		
OB 233	LIVERPOOL	23/10/40	DISPERSED	27/10/40	40		
OB 234	LIVERPOOL	24/10/40	DISPERSED	30/10/40	26		1
OB 235	LIVERPOOL	27/10/40	DISPERSED	31/10/40	35		
OB 236	LIVERPOOL	29/10/40	DISPERSED	02/11/40	34		
OB 237	LIVERPOOL	31/10/40	DISPERSED	02/11/40	36		
OB 238	LIVERPOOL	02/11/40	DISPERSED	05/11/40	31		
OB 239	LIVERPOOL	04/11/40	RETURNED TO OBAN	08/11/40	43		
OB 239/1	OBAN	10/11/40	DISPERSED	14/11/40	23		
OB 240	LIVERPOOL	08/11/40	DISPERSED	13/11/40	57		
OB 241	LIVERPOOL	09/11/40	DISPERSED	14/11/40	47		
OB 242	LIVERPOOL	11/11/40	DISPERSED	15/11/40	45		1
OB 243	LIVERPOOL	13/11/40	DISPERSED 54.10N 20.49W	18/11/40	26		
OB 244	LIVERPOOL	17/11/40	DISPERSED	22/11/40	46	3	
OB 245	LIVERPOOL	18/11/40	DISPERSED 56.35N 17.38W	22/11/40	42		
OB 246	LIVERPOOL	20/11/40	DISPERSED	24/11/40	22		
OB 248	LIVERPOOL	23/11/40	DISPERSED	26/11/40	44		2
OB 249	LIVERPOOL	24/11/40	DISPERSED 56.40N 17.21W	28/11/40	53		
OB 250	LIVERPOOL	26/11/40	DISPERSED	29/11/40	18		
OB 251	LIVERPOOL	28/11/40	DISPERSED	01/12/40	34		
OB 252	LIVERPOOL	30/11/40	DISPERSED	04/12/40	44		
OB 253	LIVERPOOL	02/12/40	DISPERSED	06/12/40	30		
OB 254	LIVERPOOL	04/12/40	DISPERSED	08/12/40	13		
OB 255	LIVERPOOL	07/12/40	DISPERSED	10/12/40	18		
OB 256	LIVERPOOL	08/12/40	DISPERSED 59.04N 15.30W	12/12/40	30		
OB 257	LIVERPOOL	10/12/40	DISPERSED	13/12/40	38		
OB 258	LIVERPOOL	12/12/40	DISPERSED	15/12/40	17		1
OB 259	LIVERPOOL	14/12/40	DISPERSED	17/12/40	35		1
OB 260	LIVERPOOL	16/12/40	DISPERSED	19/12/40	29		
OB 261	LIVERPOOL	19/12/40	DISPERSED	22/12/40	44		
OB 262	LIVERPOOL	20/12/40	DISPERSED	23/12/40	38		
OB 263	LIVERPOOL	23/12/40	DISPERSED	27/12/40	25	1	
OB 264	LIVERPOOL	24/12/40	DISPERSED	29/12/40	23		
OB 265	LIVERPOOL	26/12/40	DISPERSED	30/12/40	32		
OB 266	LIVERPOOL	28/12/40	DISPERSED	01/01/41	23		
OB 267	LIVERPOOL	30/12/40	DISPERSED 53.30N 18.10W	02/01/41	23		
OB 268	LIVERPOOL	01/01/41	DISPERSED	04/01/41	30		1
OB 269	LIVERPOOL	03/01/41	DISPERSED	06/01/41	26		
OB 270	LIVERPOOL	05/01/41	DISPERSED	08/01/41	16		
OB 271	LIVERPOOL	08/01/41	DISPERSED	12/01/41	25		
OB 272	LIVERPOOL	10/01/41	DISPERSED	14/01/41	28		
OB 273	LIVERPOOL	12/01/41	DISPERSED	16/01/41	33		
OB 274	LIVERPOOL	14/01/41	DISPERSED	19/01/41	38	2	
OB 275	LIVERPOOL	18/01/41	DISPERSED 60.56N 25W	23/01/41	39		1
OB 276	LIVERPOOL	20/01/41	DISPERSED	25/01/41	34		
OB 277	LIVERPOOL	22/01/41	DISPERSED	27/01/41	25		
OB 278	LIVERPOOL	24/01/41	DISPERSED	27/01/41	14		
OB 279	LIVERPOOL	28/01/41	DISPERSED 62N 23.10W	02/02/41	39		
OBA	OBAN	30/01/41	DISPERSED	03/02/41	6		1
OB 280	LIVERPOOL	31/01/41	DISPERSED	03/02/41	27		
OB 281	LIVERPOOL	01/02/41	DISPERSED	05/02/41	35		
OB 282	LIVERPOOL	03/02/41	DISPERSED	08/02/41	18		
OB 283	LIVERPOOL	08/02/41	DISPERSED	12/02/41	45		

THE ALLIED CONVOY SYSTEM 1939-1945

CONVOY	DEP. PORT	DEP. DATE	ARRIVAL PORT	ARR. DATE	TDS	MV SUNK	MV DMGD
OB 284	LIVERPOOL	09/02/41	DISPERSED	14/02/41	35		
OB 285	LIVERPOOL	11/02/41	DISPERSED	17/02/41	46		
OB 286	LIVERPOOL	13/02/41	DISPERSED 51.35N 21.35W	17/02/41	29		
OB 287	LIVERPOOL	16/02/41	DISPERSED	21/02/41	44	3	3
OB 288	LIVERPOOL	18/02/41	DISPERSED	22/02/41	46		2
OB 289	LIVERPOOL	20/02/41	DISPERSED	24/02/41	25	3	1
OB 290	LIVERPOOL	23/02/41	DISPERSED	27/02/41	41	10	6
OB 291	LIVERPOOL	27/02/41	DISPERSED	03/03/41	44		1
OB 292	LIVERPOOL	28/02/41	DISPERSED	06/03/41	42		
OB 293	LIVERPOOL	02/03/41	DISPERSED	08/03/41	37	3	2
OB 294	LIVERPOOL	05/03/41	DISPERSED 51.29N 20.30W	09/03/41	40		
OB 295	LIVERPOOL	08/03/41	DISPERSED	14/03/41	38		
OB 296	LIVERPOOL	10/03/41	DISPERSED	15/03/41	42		
OB 297	LIVERPOOL	12/03/41	DISPERSED 61.28N 21.59W	17/03/41	39		
OB 298	LIVERPOOL	16/03/41	DISPERSED	20/03/41	34	1	2
OB 299	LIVERPOOL	19/03/41	DISPERSED	25/03/41	38		
OB 300	LIVERPOOL	20/03/41	DISPERSED 58N 23.25W	26/03/41	28		
OB 301	LIVERPOOL	23/03/41	DISPERSED 53.59N 19.40W	27/03/41	33		
OB 302	LIVERPOOL	24/03/41	DISPERSED	30/03/41	31		
OB 303	LIVERPOOL	28/03/41	DISPERSED	03/04/41	51		
OB 304	LIVERPOOL	30/03/41	DISPERSED 62.20N 20.15W	04/04/41	41		
OB 305	LIVERPOOL	02/04/41	DISPERSED 54.30N 22.22W	06/04/41	39		
OB 306	LIVERPOOL	03/04/41	DISPERSED	09/04/41	18	1	
OB 307	LIVERPOOL	07/04/41	DISPERSED	13/04/41	24		
OB 308	LIVERPOOL	06/04/41	DISPERSED 66.21N 32.10W	13/04/41	30		
OB 309	LIVERPOOL	12/04/41	DISPERSED 50N 23.50W	19/04/41	47		
OB 310	LIVERPOOL	13/04/41	DISPERSED	18/04/41	48		
OB 311	LIVERPOOL	16/04/41	DISPERSED 61N 32.40W	25/04/41	39		
OB 312	LIVERPOOL	18/04/41	DISPERSED	25/04/41	25		
OB 313	LIVERPOOL	22/04/41	DISPERSED	28/04/41	38		
OB 314	LIVERPOOL	23/04/41	DISPERSED 61.05N 35.25W	30/04/41	33		
OB 315	LIVERPOOL	27/04/41	DISPERSED 58.30N 36.20W	04/05/41	34		
OB 316	LIVERPOOL	28/04/41	DISPERSED	05/05/41	20		
OB 317	LIVERPOOL	30/04/41	DISPERSED 51.50N 23.34W	06/05/41	23		
OB 318	LIVERPOOL	02/05/41	DISPERSED 60.12N 34.30W	10/05/41	38	5	2
OB 319	LIVERPOOL	07/05/41	DISPERSED 61N 35W	13/05/41	38		
OB 320	LIVERPOOL	08/05/41	DISPERSED	14/05/41	18		
OB 321	LIVERPOOL	11/05/41	DISPERSED	17/05/41	24	1	
OB 322	LIVERPOOL	12/05/41	DISPERSED	20/05/41	38		
OB 323	LIVERPOOL	17/05/41	DISPERSED	25/05/41	35		
OB 324	LIVERPOOL	18/05/41	DISPERSED 53N 29.30W	27/05/41	35	1	
OB 325	LIVERPOOL	21/05/41	DISPERSED	29/05/41	21		
OB 326	LIVERPOOL	22/05/41	DISPERSED 50.03N 30.37W	29/05/41	43		
OB 327	LIVERPOOL	28/05/41	DISPERSED 52.42N 22.18W	01/06/41	46		
OB 328	LIVERPOOL	29/05/41	DISPERSED	02/06/41	26		
OB 329	LIVERPOOL	31/05/41	DISPERSED 51.48N 20.48W	05/06/41	41		1
OB 330	LIVERPOOL	02/06/41	DISPERSED	07/06/41	40		
OB 331	LIVERPOOL	08/06/41	DISPERSED	19/06/41	47		
OB 332	LIVERPOOL	08/06/41	HALIFAX	23/06/41	43		
OB 333	LIVERPOOL	10/06/41	DISPERSED 40.20N 34.40W	21/06/41	46		
OB 334	LIVERPOOL	11/06/41	HALIFAX	25/06/41	51		
OB 335	LIVERPOOL	16/06/41	HALIFAX	02/07/41	41		
OB 336	LIVERPOOL	15/06/41	DISPERSED	25/06/41	24		
OB 337	LIVERPOOL	20/06/41	DISPERSED 48.17N 20.40W	28/06/41	51		
OB 338	LIVERPOOL	21/06/41	DISPERSED	03/07/41	50		
OB 339	LIVERPOOL	26/06/41	HALIFAX	12/07/41	49		
OB 340	LIVERPOOL	27/06/41	DISPERSED	13/07/41	36		
OB 341	LIVERPOOL	30/06/41	DISPERSED 48.30N 26.30W	06/07/41	35		
OB 341A	LIVERPOOL	02/07/41	HALIFAX	18/07/41	47		
OB 343	LIVERPOOL	06/07/41	DISPERSED 46N 55W	21/07/41	75		
OB 344	LIVERPOOL	07/07/41	DISPERSED 45.42N 54W	16/07/41	19		
OB 345	LIVERPOOL	11/07/41	HALIFAX	26/07/41	60		
OB 346	LIVERPOOL	14/07/41	FREETOWN	01/08/41	40		1
OB 347	LIVERPOOL	16/07/41	DISPERSED	31/07/41	64		
OB 348	LIVERPOOL	17/07/41	HALIFAX	31/07/41	50		
OB 349	LIVERPOOL	21/07/41	DISPERSED 50N 49W	01/08/41	44		

Courtesy K Macpherson

The original FLOWER corvette design. HMS GARDENIA, seen so early in her career that she still carries the M pennant number originally allocated, changed to K in mid-1940. The mainmast is stepped to provide longer W/T aerials hence greater transmission range, as she was intended for service on the Denmark Strait patrol.

Courtesy K Macpherson

HMS AURICULA in her "as built" state. Note that she still has the original minesweeping davits aft to handle wire sweep gear. No radar and only a quadruple 0.5 inch machine gun mounting as AA armament in the bandstand aft of the funnel.

Losses incurred in OB convoys, excluding stragglers

Convoy	Ship's Name	GRT			Date of loss	Cause of loss	Comments
OB 25	BRONTE	5,317	19	Br	30/10/39	U 34	General. No dead
OB 28	MERVYN	3,402	24	Br	01/11/39	COLLISION	Coal. No dead
OB 40	PEGU	8,106	21	Br	24/11/39	WRECKED	General. No dead
OB 46	NAVASOTA	8,795	17	Br	05/12/39	U 47	Ballast. 37 dead
OB 74	CAIRNROSS	5,494	21	Br	17/01/40	MINED	Coal. No dead
OB 188	ACCRA	9,337	26	Br	26/07/40	U 34	1,700 tons general. 2 dead
OB 188	SAMBRE	5,260	19	Br	27/07/40	U 34	1,500 tons general. No dead
OB 188	THIARA	10,364	39	Br	27/07/40	U 34	Ballast. 25 dead
OB 188	VINEMOOR	4,359	24	Br	26/07/40	U 34	Ballast. No dead
OB 191	JERSEY CITY	6,322	20	Br	31/07/40	U 99	Ballast. 2 dead
OB 193	BOMA	5,408	20	Br	05/08/40	U 56	1,000 tons coal. 3 dead
OB 197	HEDRUN	2,325	20	Sw	16/08/40	U 48	3,009 tons coal. 10 dead
OB 202	CUMBERLAND	10,939	19	Br	23/08/40	U 57	9,000 tons metal & general. 4 dead
OB 202	ST DUNSTAN	5,681	19	Br	23/08/40	U 57	Ballast. 14 dead
OB 205	SAN GABRIEL	4,943	20	Gk	30/08/40	U 59	Ballast. 2 dead. Towed in but CTL.
OB 206	THORNLEA	4,261	29	Br	02/09/40	U 46	6,400 tons coal. 3 dead
OB 213	CITY OF BENARES	11,081	36	Br	18/09/40	U 48	191 passengers. 253 dead
OB 213	MARINA	5,088	35	Br	18/09/40	U 48	5,700 tons general & coal. 2 dead
OB 216	BOKA	5,560	20	Pan	20/09/40	U 138	Coal. 8 dead
OB 216	CITY OF SIMLA	10,138	21	Br	21/09/40	U 138	3,000 tons general. 3 dead.
OB 216	EMPIRE ADVENTURE	5,145	21	Br	20/09/40	U 138	Ballast. 21 dead. Sank in tow 23.9
OB 216	NEW SEVILLA	13,802	00	Br	20/09/40	U 138	Whaling stores. 2 dead
OB 218	EMPIRE OCELOT	5,759	19	Br	28/09/40	U 32	Ballast. 2 dead
OB 218	MANCHESTER BRIGADE	6,042	18	Br	26/09/40	U 137	1,147 tons general. 58 dead
OB 218	STRATFORD	4,752	13	Br	26/09/40	U 137	Ballast. 2 dead
OB 228	BONHEUR	5,237	20	Br	15/10/40	U 138	5,200 tons general. No dead
OB 228	DOKKA	1,168	25	Nor	17/10/40	U 93	Ballast. 10 dead
OB 228	USKBRIDGE	2,700	40	Br	17/10/40	U 93	4,000 tons anthracite. 2 dead
OB 244	DAYDAWN	4,769	40	Br	21/11/40	U 103	6,860 tons coal. 2 dead
OB 244	KING IDWAL	5,115	20	Br	22/11/40	U 123	Ballast. 12 dead
OB 244	VICTORIA	6,085	19	Gk	21/11/40	U 103	Ballast. 27 survivors
OB 263	ARDANBHAN	4,980	29	Br	27/12/40	TAZZO LI (It S/M)	6,000 tons coal. 40 dead
OB 265	BODNANT	5,342	19	Br	30/12/40	COLLISION	General. No dead. Collision with CITY OF BEDFORD
OB 274	MEANDROS	4,581	19	Gk	16/01/41	AIRCRAFT	Ballast. No dead
OB 274	ONOBA	6,256	38	Du	16/01/41	AIRCRAFT	Ballast. No dead
OB 287	GRACIA	5,642	21	Br	19/02/41	AIRCRAFT	Ballast. No dead
OB 287	HOUSATONIC	5,559	19	Br	19/02/41	AIRCRAFT	Ballast. 3 dead
OB 287	SCOTTISH STANDARD	6,999	21	Br	21/02/41	AIRCRAFT	Ballast. 5 dead
OB 289	BRITISH GUNNER	6,894	22	Br	24/02/41	U 97	Ballast. 3 dead
OB 289	JONATHAN HOLT	3,793	38	Br	24/02/41	U 97	General. 52 dead
OB 289	MANSEPOOL	4,894	28	Br	24/02/41	U 97	Ballast. 2 dead
OB 290	AMSTELLAND	8,156	20	Du	26/02/41	AIRCRAFT	Ballast. 1 dead
OB 290	BEURSPLEIN	4,368	20	Du	26/02/41	AIRCRAFT	Ballast. 21 dead
OB 290	BORGLAND	3,636	18	Nor	26/02/41	U 47	Ballast, 6 aircraft. No dead
OB 290	KASONGO	5,254	18	Bel	27/02/41	U 47	General, ammunition. 6 dead
OB 290	KYRIAKOULA	4,340	18	Gk	26/02/41	AIRCRAFT	Ballast. No dead
OB 290	LLANWERN	4,966	28	Br	26/02/41	AIRCRAFT	Ballast. 27 dead
OB 290	MAHANADA	7,181	14	Br	26/02/41	AIRCRAFT	5,000 tons general. 3 dead
OB 290	RYDBOHOLM	3,197	33	Sw	26/02/41	AIRCRAFT	Ballast. 28 survivors
OB 290	SOLFERINO	2,580	18	Nor	26/02/41	AIRCRAFT	Ballast. 3 dead
OB 290	SWINBURNE	4,659	17	Br	26/02/41	AIRCRAFT	3,500 tons stores. No dead
OB 293	ATHELBEACH	6,568	31	Br	07/03/41	U 99	Ballast. 7 dead
OB 293	DUNAFF HEAD	5,258	18	Br	07/03/41	UA	Ballast. 5 dead
OB 293	TERJE VIKEN	20,638	36	Br	07/03/41	U 99 & U 47	Ballast. No dead. Sank 14/3
OB 298	BENVORLICH	5,193	19	Br	19/03/41	AIRCRAFT	6,000 tons general. 5 dead
OB 306	DUNSTAN	5,149	25	Br	06/04/41	AIRCRAFT	7,030 tons general. 2 dead
OB 318	BENGORE HEAD	2,609	22	Br	09/05/41	U 110	1,200 tons coal. 1 dead
OB 318	EASTERN STAR	5,658	20	Nor	07/05/41	U 94	General, 16 aircraft. No dead
OB 318	ESMOND	4,976	30	Br	09/05/41	U 110	Ballast. No dead
OB 318	GREGALIA	5,802	29	Br	09/05/41	U 201	Ballast. No dead
OB 318	IXION	10,263	12	Br	07/05/41	U 94	2,900 tons general. No dead
OB 321	KARLANDER	1,843	14	Nor	14/05/41	AIRCRAFT	Ballast. No dead
OB 334	BARON CARNEGIE	3,178	25	Br	11/06/41	AIRCRAFT	Ballast. 25 dead
OB 336	SCHIE	1,967	22	Du	24/06/41	U 203	Ballast. 29 dead
OB 336	KINROSS	4,956	35	Br	24/06/41	U 203	Ballast. No dead

ON convoy series 1941-1945

The successor to the OB series, these convoys were for ships destined for North America or the Caribbean from the UK. As an exception, during the suspension of the OS series over the period of the North African landings, ships for the Freetown area and beyond were included but dispersed in mid-Atlantic.

The ON convoys all sailed from Liverpool via the North Channel. Feeder convoys operated from Milford Haven with the Bristol Channel trade from Belfast, the Clyde, Oban and Loch Ewe, the latter two handling ships from the East Coast. The convoys were escorted from the UK, relieved by units from Iceland and, finally, from Newfoundland. There was therefore near continuous escort to Halifax NS, the usual terminal port.

By the end of 1941 the pattern of escort to EOMP, then MOMP and finally WOMP was superseded by a local UK escort, ocean escort to WOMP and a local Canadian escort to Halifax. In Aug 1942 the western terminal became NYC and this remained the case until the end of the European war.

To accommodate the slower ships, i.e. those capable of less than 9 knots, the expedient of designating alternate convoys as SLOW was introduced. Nevertheless the entire series continued as a strict numeric sequence and, in this narrative, convoys are simply referred to as ON. The true equivalent of the eastbound SC convoys was the ONS series referred to in the next note, established in 1943.

Convoys were routed well to the north rather than using the most economic Great Circle route. This was due to the need to remain as close as possible to air cover from Iceland, and the re-fuelling base there used by the escorts. With the introduction of escort carriers, MAC ships, additional VLR aircraft and the use of bases in the Azores, the Great Circle routes again became usable from late 1943. Eventually, in late 1944, the clearance of the enemy from northern France and his inability to use the Biscay Coast U-boat bases operationally, permitted the use of the Channel and the southern entrance to the Irish Sea on a regular basis for the first time since July 1940.

Some ON convoys included, from UK ports, ships for Iceland and also received ships from there for passage to North America. These ships were brought out from Iceland, usually by the US Escort Group based there, to ICOMP where ships for Iceland were detached and taken back by the same escort. When the western terminal became NYC, the ON convoys were routed via WOMP off St John's NF, where ships for that area were detached; the convoys then went on to HOMP, detaching Sydney CB ships en route. At HOMP a local escort from Halifax brought out any vessels for NYC and collected inward bound vessels for Halifax. Some ON convoys entered Cape Cod Bay, dispersing there to make passage to NYC via the Cape Cod Canal and East River, others rounded Cape Cod to enter NYC direct.

In late 1944, with the Channel once more being open for regular routing, ships sailed from the Thames to meet the Liverpool portion of the convoy off Land's End. A feeder convoy operated for ships from Antwerp to the Downs; East Coast port sailings were handled by the FN/FS coastal series. Clyde and Milford Haven sailings joined the Liverpool section with the united convoy sailing under control of the Commodore from Liverpool.

307 convoys sailed, ON 248 being a duplicated number suffixed F and S. ON 58 returned due to weather conditions, ON 185 was cancelled and an Iceland detachment proceeded as a separate convoy, totalling 307 convoys in all. 14,864 ships sailed in ON convoys of which 81 were lost by U-boat attack and a further 43 after straggling from the convoys. In addition to the direct losses in convoy to U-boats, ten warships were lost of the convoy escort; there were 23 marine casualties and three losses in ON 166 which may yet prove to be "in convoy" losses.

When the ON series commenced on 26 July 1941 the situation in the North Atlantic was favourable to the convoy rather than the U-boat. At that time signal decrypts were frequently available enabling timely diversion of convoys and the number of U-boats at sea had declined due to withdrawals for training purposes. In consequence only one ship was lost in direct attack on ON convoys up to the end of 1941. In 1942 only three ships were lost up to the end of April, the position then deteriorated and the balance swung in favour of the U-boat. This was principally due to two factors: the new construction and training program for U-boats and their crews was beginning to bear fruit, and the supply of signal intelligence had ceased and would not resume until the end of 1942. Additionally, with the introduction of convoy off the US coast in mid-1942 and consequent reduction in easy targets, attention once again turned to the oceanic Atlantic area.

ON convoy data

CONVOY	DEP. PORT	DEP. DATE	ARRIVAL PORT	ARR. DATE	TDS	MV SUNK	MV DMGD
ON 1	LIVERPOOL	26/07/41	DISPERSED 42.29N 45.45W	09/08/41	52		
ON 2	LIVERPOOL	27/07/41	DISPERSED	08/08/41	44		
ON 3	LIVERPOOL	31/07/41	DISPERSED	14/08/41	53		
ON 4	LIVERPOOL	06/08/41	DISPERSED 52.40N 47.26W	18/08/41	50		
ON 5	LIVERPOOL	06/08/41	DISPERSED 53.29N 37.35W	14/08/41	51		
ON 6	LIVERPOOL	11/08/41	DISPERSED	24/08/41	50		
ON 7	LIVERPOOL	15/08/41	DISPERSED 56.31N 42.39W	25/08/41	38		
ON 8	LIVERPOOL	16/08/41	DISPERSED 56.09N 44.32W	25/08/41	46		
ON 9	LIVERPOOL	20/08/41	DISPERSED	25/08/41	48		
ON 10	LIVERPOOL	27/08/41	DISPERSED	11/09/41	73		
ON 11	LIVERPOOL	30/08/41	DISPERSED	11/09/41	63		
ON 12	LIVERPOOL	01/09/41	DISPERSED 53.34N 36.14W	14/09/41	41		
ON 13	LIVERPOOL	05/09/41	DISPERSED 53.32N 26.16W	11/09/41	41		
ON 14	LIVERPOOL	07/09/41	DISPERSED 56.25N 24.50W	14/09/41	47		
ON 15	LIVERPOOL	11/09/41	DISPERSED 55.47N 30.40W	16/09/41	40		
ON 16	LIVERPOOL	13/09/41	DISPERSED	27/09/41	42		
ON 17	LIVERPOOL	17/09/41	DISPERSED 47.28N 40.57W	29/09/41	41		
ON 18	LIVERPOOL	19/09/41	DISPERSED 45.25N 50.25W	02/10/41	25		
ON 19	LIVERPOOL	21/09/41	DISPERSED	07/10/41	49		
ON 19A	REYKJAVIK	28/09/41	DISPERSED	04/10/41	3	1	
ON 20	LIVERPOOL	25/09/41	DISPERSED	09/10/41	52		1
ON 21	LIVERPOOL	28/09/41	DISPERSED 45.05N 52.37W	14/10/41	30		
ON 22	LIVERPOOL	02/10/41	DISPERSED	15/10/41	52		
ON 23	LIVERPOOL	04/10/41	HALIFAX	19/10/41	26		
ON 24	LIVERPOOL	08/10/41	DISPERSED 58N 28W	15/10/41	49		
ON 25	LIVERPOOL	10/10/41	DISPERSED	24/10/41	29		
ON 26	LIVERPOOL	14/10/41	DISPERSED	29/10/41	33		
ON 27	LIVERPOOL	16/10/41	DISPERSED	02/11/41	61		
ON 28	LIVERPOOL	20/10/41	DISPERSED 42.23N 58.44W	03/11/41	43		1
ON 29	LIVERPOOL	22/10/41	DISPERSED 51.17N 57.00W	05/11/41	31		
ON 30	LIVERPOOL	26/10/41	DISPERSED 43.10N 52.33W	09/11/41	48		
ON 31	LIVERPOOL	28/10/41	DISPERSED	15/11/41	37		
ON 32	LIVERPOOL	01/11/41	HALIFAX	16/11/41	49		
ON 33	LIVERPOOL	03/11/41	DISPERSED 43.30N 55.20W	23/11/41	49		
ON 34	LIVERPOOL	07/11/41	DISPERSED 46.18N 52.40W	21/11/41	44		
ON 35	LIVERPOOL	09/11/41	DISPERSED 46.09N 54.27W	27/11/41	29		
ON 36	LIVERPOOL	13/11/41	DISPERSED 49.24N 46.15W	25/11/41	41		
ON 37	LIVERPOOL	15/11/41	DISPERSED	30/11/41	43		
ON 38	LIVERPOOL	19/11/41	DISPERSED 54.30N 51.00W	30/11/41	33		
ON 39	LIVERPOOL	21/11/41	DISPERSED 53.34N 39.30W	04/12/41	35		
ON 40	LIVERPOOL	25/11/41	DISPERSED	04/12/41	28		
ON 41	LIVERPOOL	27/11/41	DISPERSED 47.44N 45.16W	11/12/41	37		
ON 42	LIVERPOOL	01/12/41	DISPERSED 47.44N 45.16W	14/12/41	49		
ON 43	LIVERPOOL	03/12/41	DISPERSED 54N 40W	15/12/41	18		
ON 44	LIVERPOOL	07/12/41	DISPERSED	15/12/41	34		
ON 45	LIVERPOOL	09/12/41	DISPERSED	16/12/41	16		
ON 46	LIVERPOOL	13/12/41	DISPERSED 55.39N 34W	21/12/41	28		
ON 47	LIVERPOOL	15/12/41	DISPERSED 58.42N 46W	23/12/41	23		
ON 48	LIVERPOOL	19/12/41	DISPERSED 43.59N 54.56W	31/12/41	49		
ON 49	LIVERPOOL	21/12/41	DISPERSED	05/01/42	26		
ON 50	LIVERPOOL	24/12/41	DISPERSED	03/01/42	35		
ON 51	LIVERPOOL	27/12/41	DISPERSED	11/01/42	25		
ON 52	LIVERPOOL	31/12/41	DISPERSED	11/01/42	42		
ON 53	LIVERPOOL	02/01/42	DISPERSED	19/01/42	26		
ON 54	LIVERPOOL	06/01/42	DISPERSED	17/01/42	34		
ON 55	LIVERPOOL	08/01/42	DISPERSED 44.25N 51.19W	26/01/42	28	2	
ON 56	LIVERPOOL	12/01/42	DISPERSED 59.00N 17.00W	16/01/42	36		
ON 57	LIVERPOOL	13/01/42	DISPERSED 43.20N 59.39W	07/02/42	15		
ON 58	LIVERPOOL	20/01/42	RETURNED	21/01/42			
ON 59	LIVERPOOL	23/01/42	DISPERSED 41.30N 52.53W	06/02/42	42		
ON 60	LIVERPOOL	26/01/42	HALIFAX	15/02/42	45	1	
ON 61	LIVERPOOL	27/01/42	DISPERSED	10/02/42	21		
ON 62	LIVERPOOL	01/02/42	DISPERSED 45.29N 58.28W	15/02/42	34		
ON 63	LIVERPOOL	02/02/42	DISPERSED 42.08N 55.20W	13/02/42	31		
ON 64	LIVERPOOL	07/02/42	HALIFAX	24/02/42	37		
ON 65	LIVERPOOL	08/02/42	DISPERSED 43.50N 47.45W	19/02/42	40		
ON 66	LIVERPOOL	13/02/42	DISPERSED OFF HALIFAX	26/02/42	19		
ON 67	LIVERPOOL	14/02/42	HALIFAX	01/03/42	37	7	1
ON 68	LIVERPOOL	19/02/42	DISPERSED	09/03/42	25		
ON 69	LIVERPOOL	20/02/42	DISPERSED OFF CAPE COD	06/03/42	31		
ON 70	LIVERPOOL	25/02/42	DISPERSED	15/03/42	30		
ON 71	LIVERPOOL	26/02/42	DISPERSED	08/03/42	42		

◇ THE ALLIED CONVOY SYSTEM 1939-1945

CONVOY	DEP. PORT	DEP. DATE	ARRIVAL PORT	ARR. DATE	TDS	MV SUNK	MV DMGD
ON 72	LIVERPOOL	03/03/42	HALIFAX	19/03/42	17		
ON 73	LIVERPOOL	05/03/42	DISPERSED 41.57N 60.15W	16/03/42	35		
ON 74	LIVERPOOL	09/03/42	HALIFAX	25/03/42	37		
ON 75	LIVERPOOL	10/03/42	DISPERSED	19/03/42	12		
ON 76	LIVERPOOL	15/03/42	HALIFAX	31/03/42	27		
ON 77	LIVERPOOL	17/03/42	DISPERSED 43.41N 59.12W	28/03/42	31		1
ON 78	LIVERPOOL	21/03/42	HALIFAX	09/04/42	27		
ON 79	LIVERPOOL	23/03/42	HALIFAX	07/04/42	29		
ON 80	LIVERPOOL	27/03/42	HALIFAX	15/04/42	26		
ON 81	LIVERPOOL	29/03/42	DISPERSED 38.30N 43.56W	09/04/42	13		
ON 82	LIVERPOOL	02/04/42	HALIFAX	18/04/42	30		
ON 83	LIVERPOOL	04/04/42	HALIFAX	17/04/42	31		
ON 84	LIVERPOOL	08/04/42	HALIFAX	25/04/42	23		
ON 85	LIVERPOOL	10/04/42	CAPE COD	23/04/42	15		
ON 86	LIVERPOOL	14/04/42	CAPE COD	29/04/42	45		
ON 87	LIVERPOOL	16/04/42	DISPERSED 36.03N 46.15W	26/04/42	25		
ON 88	LIVERPOOL	21/04/42	CAPE COD	08/05/42	46		
ON 89	LIVERPOOL	23/04/42	HALIFAX	05/05/42	49		
ON 90	LIVERPOOL	28/04/42	HALIFAX	15/05/42	47		
ON 91	LIVERPOOL	01/05/42	DISPERSED 42.18N 69.15W	15/05/42	31		
ON 92	LIVERPOOL	06/05/42	HALIFAX	21/05/42	42	7	
ON 93	LIVERPOOL	08/05/42	DISPERSED 38.55N 42.43W	17/05/42	25		
ON 94	LIVERPOOL	12/05/42	HALIFAX	25/05/42	30		
ON 95	LIVERPOOL	15/05/42	CAPE COD BAY	29/05/42	38		
ON 96	LIVERPOOL	19/05/42	HALIFAX	07/06/42	41		
ON 97	LIVERPOOL	22/05/42	HALIFAX	05/06/42	32		
ON 98	LIVERPOOL	26/05/42	NYC	12/06/42	30		
ON 99	LIVERPOOL	29/05/42	BOSTON	12/06/42	28		
ON 100	LIVERPOOL	02/06/42	CAPE COD	19/06/42	39	3	
ON 101	LIVERPOOL	05/06/42	BOSTON	18/06/42	20		
ON 102	LIVERPOOL	09/06/42	HALIFAX	25/06/42	47	1	
ON 103	LIVERPOOL	12/06/42	BOSTON	26/06/42	47		
ON 104	LIVERPOOL	16/06/42	BOSTON	02/07/42	36		
ON 105	LIVERPOOL	19/06/42	HALIFAX	30/06/42	36		
ON 106	LIVERPOOL	23/06/42	HALIFAX	08/07/42	32		
ON 107	LIVERPOOL	26/06/42	DISPERSED OFF HALIFAX	09/07/42	30		
ON 108	LIVERPOOL	30/06/42	BOSTON	18/07/42	37		
ON 109	LIVERPOOL	03/07/42	HALIFAX	18/07/42	25		
ON 110	LIVERPOOL	06/07/42	BOSTON	26/07/42	32		
ON 111	LIVERPOOL	10/07/42	DISPERSED 41.15N 71.25W	24/07/42	45		
ON 112	LIVERPOOL	13/07/42	CAPE COD	30/07/42	36		
ON 113	LIVERPOOL	17/07/42	HALIFAX	31/07/42	35	3	1
ON 114	LIVERPOOL	19/07/42	DISPERSED	04/08/42	32		
ON 115	LIVERPOOL	24/07/42	BOSTON	08/08/42	41	2	1
ON 116	LIVERPOOL	25/07/42	DISPERSED OFF BOSTON	12/08/42	36		
ON 117	LIVERPOOL	31/07/42	DISPERSED	15/08/42	44		
ON 118	LIVERPOOL	01/08/42	DISPERSED	20/08/42	33		
ON 119	LIVERPOOL	05/08/42	NYC	20/08/42	32		
ON 120	LIVERPOOL	08/08/42	DISPERSED	27/08/42	38		
ON 121	LIVERPOOL	12/08/42	DISPERSED	27/08/42	34		
ON 122	LIVERPOOL	15/08/42	DISPERSED	03/09/42	36	4	
ON 123	LIVERPOOL	21/08/42	BOSTON	03/09/42	39		
ON 124	LIVERPOOL	22/08/42	BOSTON	06/09/42	31		
ON 125	LIVERPOOL	28/08/42	NYC	12/09/42	28		
ON 126	LIVERPOOL	29/08/42	NYC	18/09/42	22		
ON 127	LIVERPOOL	04/09/42	NYC	20/09/42	34	6	4
ON 128	LIVERPOOL	05/09/42	NYC	24/09/42	22		
ON 129	LIVERPOOL	11/09/42	NYC	25/09/42	31		
ON 130	LIVERPOOL	12/09/42	NYC	30/09/42	31		
ON 131	LIVERPOOL	18/09/42	NYC	04/10/42	54		
ON 132	LIVERPOOL	19/09/42	NYC	08/10/42	37		
ON 133	LIVERPOOL	25/09/42	NYC	11/10/42	35		
ON 134	LIVERPOOL	26/09/42	NYC	17/10/42	42		
ON 135	LIVERPOOL	02/10/42	NYC	21/10/42	41		
ON 136	LIVERPOOL	03/10/42	NYC	26/10/42	36		
ON 137	LIVERPOOL	09/10/42	NYC	29/10/42	38		
ON 138	LIVERPOOL	11/10/42	NYC	03/11/42	57		1
ON 139	LIVERPOOL	16/10/42	NYC	01/11/42	38	2	
ON 140	LIVERPOOL	17/10/42	NYC	07/11/42	27		
ON 141	LIVERPOOL	24/10/42	NYC	10/11/42	59		
ON 142	LIVERPOOL	30/10/42	NYC	21/11/42	62		
ON 143	LIVERPOOL	01/11/42	NYC	16/11/42	26		
ON 144	LIVERPOOL	07/11/42	NYC	27/11/42	28	5	
ON 145	LIVERPOOL	09/11/42	NYC	25/11/42	35	1	2
ON 146	LIVERPOOL	15/11/42	NYC	08/12/42	38		
ON 147	LIVERPOOL	17/11/42	NYC	04/12/42	29		
ON 148	LIVERPOOL	23/11/42	NYC	13/12/42	23		
ON 149	LIVERPOOL	26/11/42	NYC	12/12/42	50		
ON 150	LIVERPOOL	01/12/42	NYC	25/12/42	42		
ON 151	LIVERPOOL	03/12/42	NYC	23/12/42	38		
ON 152	LIVERPOOL	09/12/42	NYC	31/12/42	15		
ON 153	LIVERPOOL	11/12/42	NYC	31/12/42	43	2	1
ON 154	LIVERPOOL	18/12/42	NYC	12/01/43	46	13	1
ON 155	LIVERPOOL	19/12/42	NYC	06/01/43	24		
ON 156	LIVERPOOL	24/12/42	NYC	17/01/43	19		
ON 157	LIVERPOOL	27/12/42	NYC	15/01/43	31		
ON 158	LIVERPOOL	02/01/43	NYC	23/01/43	35		
ON 159	LIVERPOOL	04/01/43	NYC	20/01/43	31		
ON 160	LIVERPOOL	11/01/43	NYC	04/02/43	25		
ON 161	LIVERPOOL	12/01/43	NYC	31/01/43	43		
ON 162	LIVERPOOL	23/01/43	NYC	11/02/43	58		
ON 163	LIVERPOOL	24/01/43	NYC	16/02/43	38		
ON 164	LIVERPOOL	01/02/43	NYC	19/02/43	35		
ON 165	LIVERPOOL	02/02/43	NYC	01/03/43	32		

APPENDIX 3

CONVOY	DEP. PORT	DEP. DATE	ARRIVAL PORT	ARR. DATE	TDS	MV SUNK	MV DMGD
ON 166	LIVERPOOL	11/02/43	NYC	03/03/43	48	11	1
ON 167	LIVERPOOL	14/02/43	NYC	08/03/43	27	2	
ON 168	LIVERPOOL	21/02/43	DISPERSED OFF CAPE COD	12/03/43	52		
ON 169	LIVERPOOL	22/02/43	NYC	21/03/43	36		
ON 170	LIVERPOOL	03/03/43	NYC	20/03/43	51		
ON 171	LIVERPOOL	04/03/43	HALIFAX	23/03/43	38		
ON 172	LIVERPOOL	09/03/43	NYC	27/03/43	16		
ON 173	LIVERPOOL	13/03/43	HALIFAX	29/03/43	37		
ON 174	LIVERPOOL	20/03/43	NYC	08/04/43	41		
ON 175	LIVERPOOL	24/03/43	NYC	16/04/43	36		
ON 176	LIVERPOOL	31/03/43	NYC	20/04/43	44	1	
ON 177	LIVERPOOL	06/04/43	NYC	23/04/43	20		
ON 178	LIVERPOOL	12/04/43	NYC	02/05/43	57	1	
ON 179	LIVERPOOL	18/04/43	NYC	06/05/43	51		
ON 180	LIVERPOOL	24/04/43	NYC	14/05/43	65		
ON 181	LIVERPOOL	30/04/43	NYC	18/05/43	44		
ON 182	LIVERPOOL	06/05/43	NYC	22/05/43	56		
ON 183	LIVERPOOL	10/05/43	NYC	25/05/43	32		
ON 184	LIVERPOOL	15/05/43	NYC	31/05/43	39		
ON 186	LIVERPOOL	24/05/43	NYC	07/06/43	44		
ON 187	LIVERPOOL	01/06/43	NYC	15/06/43	75		
ON 188	LIVERPOOL	10/06/43	NYC	26/06/43	56		
ON 189	LIVERPOOL	16/06/43	NYC	01/07/43	55		
ON 190	LIVERPOOL	24/06/43	NYC	09/07/43	87		
ON 191	LIVERPOOL	01/07/43	NYC	15/07/43	60		
ON 192	LIVERPOOL	09/07/43	NYC	22/07/43	85		
ON 193	LIVERPOOL	16/07/43	NYC	31/07/43	80		
ON 194	LIVERPOOL	24/07/43	NYC	07/08/43	82		
ON 195	LIVERPOOL	31/07/43	NYC	13/08/43	51		
ON 196	LIVERPOOL	08/08/43	NYC	21/08/43	78		
ON 197	LIVERPOOL	14/08/43	NYC	28/08/43	53		
ON 198	LIVERPOOL	21/08/43	NYC	04/09/43	52		
ON 199	LIVERPOOL	26/08/43	NYC	09/09/43	59		
ON 200	LIVERPOOL	02/09/43	NYC	18/09/43	55		
ON 201	LIVERPOOL	09/09/43	NYC	24/09/43	70		
ON 202	LIVERPOOL	15/09/43	NYC	01/10/43	38	5	1
ON 203	LIVERPOOL	22/09/43	NYC	10/10/43	66		
ON 204	LIVERPOOL	27/09/43	NYC	15/10/43	63		
ON 205	LIVERPOOL	05/10/43	NYC	23/10/43	66		
ON 206	LIVERPOOL	11/10/43	NYC	27/10/43	62		
ON 207	LIVERPOOL	18/10/43	NYC	04/11/43	52		
ON 208	LIVERPOOL	24/10/43	NYC	07/11/43	41		
ON 209	LIVERPOOL	31/10/43	NYC	17/11/43	59		
ON 210	LIVERPOOL	06/11/43	NYC	23/11/43	42		
ON 211	LIVERPOOL	13/11/43	NYC	29/11/43	49		
ON 212	LIVERPOOL	19/11/43	NYC	05/12/43	57		
ON 213	LIVERPOOL	26/11/43	NYC	14/12/43	60		
ON 214	LIVERPOOL	02/12/43	NYC	20/12/43	50		
ON 215	LIVERPOOL	09/12/43	NYC	28/12/43	58		
ON 216	LIVERPOOL	16/12/43	NYC	03/01/44	40		
ON 217	LIVERPOOL	24/12/43	NYC	10/01/44	70	1	
ON 218	LIVERPOOL	31/12/43	NYC	18/01/44	41		
ON 219	LIVERPOOL	08/01/44	NYC	27/01/44	61		
ON 220	LIVERPOOL	15/01/44	NYC	04/02/44	54		
ON 221	LIVERPOOL	24/01/44	NYC	11/02/44	63		
ON 222	LIVERPOOL	30/01/44	NYC	16/02/44	50		
ON 223	LIVERPOOL	07/02/44	NYC	24/02/44	54		
ON 224	LIVERPOOL	14/02/44	NYC	02/03/44	79		
ON 225	LIVERPOOL	22/02/44	NYC	08/03/44	59		
ON 226	LIVERPOOL	29/02/44	NYC	15/03/44	69		
ON 227	LIVERPOOL	08/03/44	NYC	22/03/44	61		
ON 228	LIVERPOOL	15/03/44	NYC	01/04/44	70		
ON 229	LIVERPOOL	23/03/44	NYC	07/04/44	61		
ON 230	LIVERPOOL	30/03/44	NYC	17/04/44	66		
ON 231	LIVERPOOL	07/04/44	NYC	24/04/44	89		
ON 232	LIVERPOOL	13/04/44	NYC	29/04/44	45		
ON 233	LIVERPOOL	20/04/44	NYC	09/05/44	111		
ON 234	LIVERPOOL	26/04/44	NYC	12/05/44	76		
ON 235	LIVERPOOL	04/05/44	NYC	18/05/44	65		
ON 236	LIVERPOOL	11/05/44	NYC	27/05/44	113		
ON 237	LIVERPOOL	19/05/44	NYC	03/06/44	64		
ON 238	LIVERPOOL	26/05/44	NYC	09/06/44	66		
ON 239	LIVERPOOL	03/06/44	NYC	22/06/44	97		
ON 240	LIVERPOOL	10/06/44	NYC	28/06/44	85		
ON 241	LIVERPOOL	18/06/44	NYC	02/07/44	96		
ON 242	LIVERPOOL	25/06/44	NYC	11/07/44	99		
ON 243	LIVERPOOL	03/07/44	NYC	18/07/44	89		
ON 244	LIVERPOOL	10/07/44	NYC	23/07/44	56		
ON 245	LIVERPOOL	18/07/44	NYC	02/08/44	101		
ON 246	LIVERPOOL	25/07/44	NYC	09/08/44	111		
ON 247	LIVERPOOL	02/08/44	NYC	15/08/44	89		
ON 248F	LIVERPOOL	06/08/44	NYC	20/08/44	52		
ON 248S	LIVERPOOL	12/08/44	NYC	27/08/44	102		
ON 249	LIVERPOOL	18/08/44	NYC	02/09/44	153		
ON 250	LIVERPOOL	24/08/44	NYC	07/09/44	76		
ON 251	LIVERPOOL	01/09/44	NYC	19/09/44	140	1	
ON 252	LIVERPOOL	07/09/44	NYC	22/09/44	81		
ON 253	LIVERPOOL	13/09/44	NYC	28/09/44	61		
ON 254	LIVERPOOL	16/09/44	NYC	05/10/44	82		
ON 255	LIVERPOOL	22/09/44	NYC	09/10/44	84		
ON 256	LIVERPOOL	28/09/44	NYC	12/10/44	73		
ON 257	LIVERPOOL	02/10/44	NYC	18/10/44	39		
ON 258	SOUTHEND	06/10/44	NYC	24/10/44	54		
ON 259	LIVERPOOL	12/10/44	NYC	29/10/44	37		
ON 260	SOUTHEND	15/10/44	HALIFAX	30/10/44	29		
ON 261	SOUTHEND	20/10/44	NYC	05/11/44	37		
ON 262	SOUTHEND	24/10/44	NYC	10/11/44	49		
ON 263	SOUTHEND	29/10/44	NYC	15/11/44	68		
ON 264	SOUTHEND	03/11/44	NYC	21/11/44	67		
ON 265	SOUTHEND	08/11/44	NYC	23/11/44	55		
ON 266	SOUTHEND	12/11/44	NYC	03/12/44	55		

◇ THE ALLIED CONVOY SYSTEM 1939-1945

CONVOY	DEP. PORT	DEP. DATE	ARRIVAL PORT	ARR. DATE	TDS	MV SUNK	MV DMGD	CONVOY	DEP. PORT	DEP. DATE	ARRIVAL PORT	ARR. DATE	TDS	MV SUNK	MV DMGD
ON 267	SOUTHEND	18/11/44	NYC	05/12/44	43			ON 288	SOUTHEND	02/03/45	NYC	19/03/45	108		
ON 268	SOUTHEND	23/11/44	NYC	10/12/44	59			ON 289	SOUTHEND	07/03/45	NYC	25/03/45	78		
ON 269	LIVERPOOL	29/11/44	NYC	15/12/44	59			ON 290	SOUTHEND	11/03/45	NYC	29/03/45	71		
ON 270	SOUTHEND	03/12/44	NYC	22/12/44	49			ON 291	SOUTHEND	17/03/45	NYC	06/04/45	71		
ON 271	SOUTHEND	08/12/44	NYC	28/12/44	69			ON 292	SOUTHEND	22/03/45	NYC	08/04/45	68		
ON 272	SOUTHEND	14/12/44	NYC	01/01/45	45			ON 293	SOUTHEND	27/03/45	NYC	15/04/45	82		
ON 273	SOUTHEND	18/12/44	NYC	04/01/45	64			ON 294	SOUTHEND	01/04/45	NYC	20/04/45	85		
ON 274	SOUTHEND	23/12/44	NYC	08/01/45	82			ON 295	LIVERPOOL	07/04/45	NYC	26/04/45	95		
ON 275	SOUTHEND	28/12/44	NYC	13/01/45	40			ON 296	LIVERPOOL	12/04/45	NYC	30/04/45	65		
ON 276	SOUTHEND	02/01/45	NYC	18/01/45	69			ON 297	LIVERPOOL	17/04/45	NYC	02/05/45	81		
ON 277	SOUTHEND	07/01/45	NYC	23/01/45	55	1		ON 298	SOUTHEND	21/04/45	NYC	07/05/45	70		
ON 278	SOUTHEND	12/01/45	NYC	31/01/45	47			ON 299	SOUTHEND	26/04/45	NYC	13/05/45	71		
ON 279	SOUTHEND	17/01/45	NYC	05/02/45	46			ON 300	LIVERPOOL	02/05/45	NYC	18/05/45	68		
ON 280	SOUTHEND	22/01/45	NYC	09/02/45	46			ON 301	SOUTHEND	06/05/45	NYC	22/05/45	65		
ON 281	SOUTHEND	26/01/45	NYC	12/02/45	41			ON 302	LIVERPOOL	12/05/45	DISPERSED 40.28N 70.16W	27/05/45	75		
ON 282	LIVERPOOL	01/02/45	NYC	19/02/45	55			ON 303	LIVERPOOL	17/05/45	DISPERSED, NYC ships arrived	02/06/45	81		
ON 283	SOUTHEND	05/02/45	NYC	27/02/45	58			ON 304	SOUTHEND	21/05/45	DISPERSED, NYC ships arrived	05/06/45	70		
ON 284	SOUTHEND	10/02/45	NYC	01/03/45	66			ON 305	SOUTHEND	27/05/45	Ships for FATHER POINT arrived	10/06/45	79		
ON 285	SOUTHEND	16/02/45	NYC	05/03/45	70										
ON 286	LIVERPOOL	21/02/45	NYC	09/03/45	55										
ON 287	SOUTHEND	25/02/45	NYC	14/03/45	90										

■ Courtesy K Macpherson

The CAPTAIN class frigate HMS STAYNER, probably running trials off Boston, in Jan 1944. An unusual propulsion system for RN ships, turbo-electric drive, gave this type a useful top speed of 24 knots. They were usually teamed with their slower diesel-electric counterparts, with the turbine ships operating as the Fast Division of the Group.

Thanks to their employment principally in the support role rather than close convoy escort, the class as a whole had an enviable success rate of U-Boats sunk. They also suffered heavy losses from counter-attacks by acoustic torpedo, a number of the class being sunk or finishing the war laid up with serious damage aft.

■ National Archives of Canada

A photograph of a diesel-electric version of the CAPTAIN class frigates. The original Archive caption is suspect–"N East of St John's NF on her maiden Atlantic crossing 25 Sept 1944." It is said to be HMS MANNERS, but she crossed the Atlantic from Bermuda to Belfast arriving on 7 March 1944, she was then under refit until the end of June.

If it is MANNERS, and was taken on 25 Sept, then she is serving with B6 Group and is on her way to join convoy HX 310 the following day.

The photograph has been censored, the light patch on the hull below and forward of A gun probably conceals a pennant number and a similar patch on her funnel may also obscure a Group insignia.

APPENDIX 3

Losses incurred in ON convoys, excluding stragglers

Convoy	Ship's Name	GRT			Date of loss	Cause of loss	Comments
ON 19A	TUVA	4,652	35	Du	02/10/41	U 575	Ballast. 1 dead
ON 23	WARKWORTH	4,941	24	Br	10/10/41	COLLISION	Ballast. No dead. Collision with SELUISTAN
ON 42	BENCLEUCH	5,562	19	Br	12/12/41	FIRE	General, stores 1 15" gun
ON 53	WIGRY	1,859	12	Pol	15/01/42	WRECKED	Ballast. 25 dead
ON 55	CHEPO	5,582	19	Pan	14/01/42	U 43	1,750 ton general. 17 dead
ON 55	EMPIRE SURF	6,641	41	Br	14/01/42	U 43	Ballast. 47 dead
ON 57	EMPIRE HOMER	6,993	41	Br	15/01/42	WRECKED	Ballast. No dead
ON 57	EUGENIE S EMBIRICOS	4,882	20	Gk	21/01/42	WRECKED	Ballast. Salved, CTL
ON 57	INGRID	2,606	20	Nor	19/01/42	WRECKED	Ballast. No dead
ON 57	LARISTAN	6,401	27	Br	15/01/42	WRECKED	Ballast. Salved as EMPIRE GULF
ON 57	R J CULLEN	6,993	19	Br	15/01/42	WRECKED	Ballast. No dead
ON 60	EMPIRE FUSILIER	5,408	21	Br	09/02/42	U 85	Ballast. 9 dead
ON 67	FINNANGER	9,551	28	Nor	24/02/42	U 158	Ballast. 39 dead
ON 67	ADELLEN	7,984	30	Br	22/02/42	U 155	Ballast. 36 dead
ON 67	ANADARA	8,009	35	Br	24/02/42	U 558, U 587 & U 558	Ballast. 62 dead
ON 67	EIDANGER	9,432	38	Nor	24/02/42	U 558 & U 158	Ballast. No dead
ON 67	EMPIRE CELT	8,032	41	Br	24/02/42	U 558	Ballast. 6 dead
ON 67	INVERARDER	5,578	19	Br	24/02/42	U 558	Ballast. No dead
ON 67	SAMA	1,799	37	Nor	22/02/42	U 155	1,000 tons china clay. 20 dead
ON 76	BRYNYMOR	4,771	36	Br	14/03/42	COLLISION	Ballast. No dead. Collision with EMPIRE HAWKSBILL
ON 92	BATNA	4,399	28	Br	13/05/42	U 94	4,988 tons coal. 1 dead
ON 92	COCLE	5,630	20	Pan	12/05/42	U 94	General. 4 dead
ON 92	CRISTALES	5,389	26	Br	12/05/42	U 124	General, china clay. No dead
ON 92	EMPIRE DELL	7,065	41	Br	12/05/42	U 124	Ballast. 2 dead. CAM ship
ON 92	LLANOVER	4,959	28	Br	12/05/42	U 124	Ballast. No dead
ON 92	MOUNT PARNES	4,371	17	Gk	12/05/42	U 124	Coal. No dead
ON 92	TOLKEN	4,471	22	Sw	13/05/42	U 94	Ballast. No dead
ON 94	ANNA MAZARAKI	5,411	13	Gk	24/05/42	WRECKED	Coal. No dead
ON 94	EMMY	3,895	14	Gk	25/05/42	WRECKED	Ballast. Wrecked in Morien Bay, CB
ON 100	DARTFORD	4,093	30	Br	11/06/42	U 124	Ballast. 30 dead
ON 100	EMPIRE CLOUGH	6,147	42	Br	10/06/42	U 94	Ballast. 5 dead
ON 100	RAMSAY	4,855	30	Br	10/06/42	U 94	Ballast. 40 dead
ON 102	SEATTLE SPIRIT	5,627	19	Amer	18/06/42	U 124	Ballast. 4 dead
ON 113	BROOMPARK	5,136	39	Br	25/07/42	U 552	Ballast. 4 dead. Sank in tow 1.8
ON 113	EMPIRE RAINBOW	6,942	41	Br	26/07/42	U 607	Ballast. No dead
ON 113	PACIFIC PIONEER	6,734	28	Br	29/07/42	U 132	Ballast. No dead
ON 115	BELGIAN SOLDIER	7,167	41	Bel	03/08/42	U 553 & U 607	Ballast. 21 dead
ON 115	LOCHKATRINE	9,419	22	Br	03/08/42	U 553	Ballast. 9 dead
ON 122	EMPIRE BREEZE	7,457	41	Br	25/08/42	U 176 or U 438	Ballast. 1 dead
ON 122	KATVALDIS	3,163	07	Br	25/08/42	U 605	Ballast. 3 dead
ON 122	SHEAF MOUNT	5,017	24	Br	25/08/42	U 605	Ballast. 31 dead
ON 122	TROLLA	1,598	23	Nor	25/08/42	U 438	Ballast. 5 dead
ON 127	ELISABETH VAN BELGIE	4,241	09	Bel	10/09/42	U 96	Ballast. 1 dead
ON 127	EMPIRE MOONBEAM	6,849	41	Br	12/09/42	U 211 & U 608	Ballast. 3 dead
ON 127	EMPIRE OIL	8,029	41	Br	11/09/42	U 659 & U 584	Ballast. 18 dead
ON 127	HEKTORIA	13,797	99	Br	12/09/42	U 211 & U 608	Ballast. 1 dead
ON 127	HINDANGER	4,884	29	Nor	11/09/42	U 583	Ballast. 1 dead
ON 127	SVEVE	6,313	30	Nor	10/09/42	U 96	Ballast. No dead
ON 132	MILCREST	5,283	19	Br	07/10/42	COLLISION	Ballast. 1 dead. Collision with EMPIRE LIGHTNING
ON 139	DONAX	8,036	38	Br	22/10/42	U 443	Ballast. No dead
ON 139	WINNIPEG II	8,379	18	Br	22/10/42	U 443	3,000 tons general, 68 pass. No dead
ON 144	MOUNT TAURUS	6,696	20	Gk	17/11/42	U 264	Ballast. 2 dead
ON 144	PARISMINA	4,732	08	Amer	18/11/42	U 624	Ballast. 22 dead
ON 144	PRESIDENT SERGENT	5,344	23	Br	18/11/42	U 624	Ballast. 20 dead
ON 144	WIDESTONE	3,192	20	Br	17/11/42	U 184	3,400 tons coal. 42 dead
ON 144	YAKA	5,432	20	Amer	18/11/42	U 624 & U522	Ballast. No dead.
ON 145	EMPIRE SAILOR	6,140	26	Br	21/11/42	U 518	2,500 tons gen, gas ammo. 22 dead
ON 152	MAIDEN CREEK	5,031	19	Amer	31/12/42	FOUNDERED	Zinc, copper concentrate. No dead
ON 152	OROPOS	4,474	13	Gk	19/12/42	FOUNDERED	Probably foundered 19-21.12.42. 34 dead
ON 153	EMILE FRANCQUI	5,859	20	Bel	16/12/42	U 664	634 tons stores. 46 dead
ON 153	BELLO	6,125	30	Nor	16/12/42	U 610	Ballast. 33 dead
ON 154	BARON COCHRANE	3,385	27	Br	28/12/42	U 406 & U 123	4,376 tons coal. 2 dead
ON 154	EMPIRE SHACKLETON	7,068	41	Br	29/12/42	U 406, U 123 & U 435	2,000 tons general, ammo & a/c. 37 dead
ON 154	EMPIRE UNION	5,952	24	Br	27/12/42	U 356	940 tons general. 6 dead
ON 154	EMPIRE WAGTAIL	4,893	19	Br	28/12/42	U 260	Cargo unknown. All (43) dead
ON 154	KING EDWARD	5,224	19	Br	27/12/42	U 356	Ballast. 23 dead
ON 154	LYNTON GRANGE	5,029	37	Br	29/12/42	U 406 & U 225	5,997 tons general. No dead
ON 154	MELMORE HEAD	5,273	18	Br	28/12/42	U 225	Ballast. 14 dead
ON 154	MELROSE ABBEY II	2,473	36	Br	27/12/42	U 411	3,403 tons coal. 7 dead
ON 154	NORSE KING	5,701	20	Nor	29/12/42	U 225 & U 435	5,453 tons coal. 35 dead
ON 154	PRESIDENT FRANCQUI	4,919	28	Bel	29/12/42	U 496, U 22 &, U 336	Ballast. 5 dead
ON 154	SOEKABOEMI	7,051	23	Du	27/12/42	U 441	5,000 tons general. 1 dead
ON 154	VILLE DE ROUEN	5,083	19	Br	28/12/42	U 225 & U 591	5,500 tons general. No dead
ON 154	ZARIAN	4,871	38	Br	29/12/42	U 406 & U 225	7,500 tons general. 4 dead
ON 158	ST SUNNIVA	1,368	31	Br	23/01/43	FOUNDERED	Rescue ship, detached. 64 dead
ON 160	VILLE DE TAMATAVE	6,276	31	Br	24/01/43	FOUNDERED	Ballast. All dead
ON 166	CHATTANOOGA CITY	5,687	21	Amer	22/02/43	U 606	Ballast. No dead
ON 166	EMPIRE REDSHANK	6,615	19	Br	22/02/43	U 606	Ballast. No dead
ON 166	EMPIRE TRADER	9,990	08	Br	23/02/43	U 92	985 tons chemicals. No dead
ON 166	EULIMA	6,207	37	Br	23/02/43	U 186	Ballast. 63 dead

◇ THE ALLIED CONVOY SYSTEM 1939-1945

Convoy	Ship's Name	GRT	Date of loss	Cause of loss	Comments
ON 166	EXPOSITOR	4,959 19 Amer	23/02/43	U 606 & U 303	Ballast. 6 dead
ON 166	GLITTRE	6,409 28 Nor	23/02/43	U 628 & U 603	Ballast. 3 dead
ON 166	HASTINGS	5,401 20 Amer	23/02/43	U 186	Ballast. 9 dead
ON 166	INGRIA	4,391 31 Nor	24/02/43	U 600 & U 628	Ballast. No dead
ON 166	JONATHAN STURGES	7,176 42 Amer	24/02/43	U 653	Ballast. 56 dead
ON 166	MANCHESTER MERCHANT	7,264 40 Br	25/02/43	U 628	Ballast. 36 dead
ON 166	N T NIELSEN ALONSO	9,348 00 Nor	22/02/43	U 92 & U 753	Ballast. 3 dead
ON 166	STIGSTAD	5,964 27 Nor	21/02/43	U 332 & U 603	Ballast. 3 dead
ON 166	STOCKPORT	1,683 11 Br	23/02/43	U 604	Rescue ship. 63 dead
ON 166	WINKLER	6,907 30 Pan	23/02/43	U 628 & U 223	Ballast. 20 dead
ON 167	H H ROGERS	8,807 16 Pan	21/02/43	U 664	Detached to UK.. Ballast. No dead
ON 167	ROSARIO	4,659 20 Amer	21/02/43	U 664	Detached to UK.. Ballast. 33 dead
ON 168	THOMAS HOOKER	7,176 42 Amer	07/03/43	FOUNDERED	Ballast. No dead

Convoy	Ship's Name	GRT	Date of loss	Cause of loss	Comments
ON 176	LANCASTRIAN PRINCE	1,914 40 Br	12/04/43	U 404	Ballast. 45 dead
ON 178	SCEBELI	3,025 37 Nor	21/04/43	U 191	Ballast. 2 dead
ON 202	FORT JEMSEG	7,134 43 Br	23/09/43	U 238	Ballast. 1 dead
ON 202	FREDERICK DOUGLASS	7,176 43 Amer	20/09/43	U 238 & U 654	Ballast. No dead
ON 202	OREGON EXPRESS	3,642 33 Nor	23/09/43	U 238	Ballast. 8 dead
ON 202	SKJELBRED	5,096 37 Nor	23/09/43	U 238	Ballast. No dead
ON 202	THEODORE DWIGHT WELD	7,176 43 Amer	20/09/43	U 238	Ballast. 33 dead
ON 217	EMPIRE HOUSMAN	7,359 43 Br	31/12/43	U 545 & U 744	Ballast. 1 dead. Sank 3/1/44
ON 218	JOSEPH SMITH	7,176 43 Amer	11/01/44	FOUNDERED	Ballast. No dead
ON 220	SAMUEL DEXTER	7,191 43 Amer	24/01/44	WRECKED	Ballast. No dead
ON 225	JOEL R POINSETT	7,176 43 Amer	04/03/44	FOUNDERED	Ballast. No dead
ON 251	FJORDHEIM	4,115 30 Nor	02/09/44	U 482	4,000 tons anthracite. 3 dead
ON 277	JONAS LIE	7,198 44 Amer	09/01/45	U 1055	Ballast. 2 dead. Sank 12.1
ON 294	PANAMA	6,650 15 Br	11/04/45	FOUNDERED	Ballast. 47 dead

■ Courtesy Murray Jones

HMCS COLLINGWOOD, an early Canadian version of the FLOWER design. This is a 1943 photograph as, while she still lacks the extended foc's'le and Hedgehog, she does have 271 radar abaft the bridge. This was fitted at Londonderry by the RN in Feb 1943 during a one month refit and work-up at Tobermory. At that time she was part of C4 Escort Group based at Londonderry.

ONS convoy series 1943-1945

From 1941, the westbound North Atlantic convoys received a new coding, ON (Outward North). As the speeds of ships using this route varied considerably, alternate convoys were designated for use by slower vessels and received the title ON (Slow), although continuing to be sequentially numbered. In consequence, there are many references to "ONS convoys" in signals and contemporary documents.

In 1943 a new series was commenced on 15 March 1943, numbered from 1, bearing the code letters ONS. This series continued with regular departures until 28 March 1944 (ONS 32) when it was suspended due to the withdrawal of Escort Groups in preparation for the Normandy invasion. Sailings resumed with ONS 33 on 29 Sept 1944 and continued until the end of European hostilities.

Convoys sailed from Liverpool with feeder convoys from Milford Haven, Belfast, the Clyde, Oban and Loch Ewe, and were routed to Halifax NS. Off Halifax the convoy divided, sending in to that port ships destined for Canada and receiving a small detachment of ships southbound from Halifax NS.

The convoy then assumed the title of XB (Halifax NS to Boston) and proceeded to Cape Cod Bay where it terminated. A few ships entered Boston but the main body proceeded via the Cape Cod Canal and the East River to New York City.

In all there were 51 convoys, of which only five suffered loss. Of these, one, ONS 5, was subjected to a major assault and lost eleven ships. Indeed this convoy action is regarded by many as the turning point of the Battle of the Atlantic. While the convoy losses were high, 6 U-boats were also sunk in action with the close escort. A second convoy, ONS 18, was involved in the last major convoy action of the North Atlantic in September 1943 when the U-boats endeavoured to re-assert their threat to trans-Atlantic trade. Although a hard fought action, ONS 18 lost only one merchant ship in the frequent attacks.

Total losses in the ONS series were 19 ships, three of which were stragglers lost out of convoy and unescorted.

ONS convoy data

CONVOY	DEP. PORT	DEP. DATE	ARRIVAL PORT	ARR. DATE	TDS	MV SUNK	MV DMGD
ONS 1	LIVERPOOL	15/03/43	HALIFAX	04/04/43	34		
ONS 2	LIVERPOOL	28/03/43	HALIFAX	19/04/43	31		
ONS 3	LIVERPOOL	05/04/43	HALIFAX	28/04/43	18	2	
ONS 4	LIVERPOOL	13/04/43	HALIFAX	05/05/43	32		
ONS 5	LIVERPOOL	21/04/43	HALIFAX	12/05/43	42	11	
ONS 6	LIVERPOOL	29/04/43	HALIFAX	17/05/43	31		
ONS 7	LIVERPOOL	07/05/43	HALIFAX	25/05/43	40	1	
ONS 8	LIVERPOOL	17/05/43	HALIFAX	01/06/43	52		
ONS 9	LIVERPOOL	28/05/43	HALIFAX	09/06/43	29		
ONS 10	LIVERPOOL	08/06/43	HALIFAX	27/06/43	54		
ONS 11	LIVERPOOL	19/06/43	HALIFAX	05/07/43	34		
ONS 12	LIVERPOOL	03/07/43	HALIFAX	18/07/43	75		
ONS 13	LIVERPOOL	14/07/43	HALIFAX	29/07/43	42		
ONS 14	LIVERPOOL	26/07/43	HALIFAX	09/08/43	50		
ONS 15	LIVERPOOL	06/08/43	HALIFAX	21/08/43	44		
ONS 16	LIVERPOOL	19/08/43	HALIFAX	01/09/43	25		
ONS 17	LIVERPOOL	31/08/43	HALIFAX	16/09/43	28		
ONS 18	LIVERPOOL	12/09/43	HALIFAX	29/09/43	27	1	
ONS 19	LIVERPOOL	26/09/43	HALIFAX	14/10/43	49		
ONS 20	LIVERPOOL	09/10/43	HALIFAX	26/10/43	50	1	
ONS 21	LIVERPOOL	22/10/43	HALIFAX	05/11/43	33		
ONS 22	LIVERPOOL	04/11/43	HALIFAX	22/11/43	26		
ONS 23	LIVERPOOL	17/11/43	HALIFAX	02/12/43	23		
ONS 24	LIVERPOOL	30/11/43	HALIFAX	18/12/43	29		
ONS 25	LIVERPOOL	15/12/43	HALIFAX	03/01/44	23		
ONS 26	LIVERPOOL	29/12/43	HALIFAX	18/01/44	31		
ONS 27	LIVERPOOL	13/01/44	HALIFAX	31/01/44	32		
ONS 28	LIVERPOOL	28/01/44	HALIFAX	15/02/44	29		
ONS 29	LIVERPOOL	12/02/44	HALIFAX	29/02/44	44		
ONS 30	LIVERPOOL	27/02/44	HALIFAX	13/03/44	29		
ONS 31	LIVERPOOL	13/03/44	HALIFAX	30/03/44	19		
ONS 32	LIVERPOOL	28/03/44	HALIFAX	18/04/44	48		
ONS 33	LIVERPOOL	29/09/44	HALIFAX	14/10/44	51		
ONS 34	LIVERPOOL	14/10/44	HALIFAX	01/11/44	45		
ONS 35	LIVERPOOL	29/10/44	HALIFAX	15/11/44	51		
ONS 36	LIVERPOOL	13/11/44	HALIFAX	03/12/44	55		
ONS 37	LIVERPOOL	28/11/44	HALIFAX	21/12/44	31		
ONS 38	LIVERPOOL	13/12/44	HALIFAX	02/01/45	26		
ONS 39	LIVERPOOL	28/12/44	HALIFAX	13/01/45	36		
ONS 40	LIVERPOOL	12/01/45	HALIFAX	30/01/45	32		
ONS 41	LIVERPOOL	29/01/45	HALIFAX	20/02/45	34		
ONS 42	LIVERPOOL	13/02/45	HALIFAX	05/03/45	33		
ONS 43	LIVERPOOL	27/02/45	HALIFAX	16/03/45	23		
ONS 44	LIVERPOOL	12/03/45	HALIFAX	31/03/45	21		
ONS 45	LIVERPOOL	22/03/45	HALIFAX	11/04/45	27		
ONS 46	LIVERPOOL	02/04/45	HALIFAX	20/04/45	24		
ONS 47	LIVERPOOL	11/04/45	HALIFAX	30/04/45	17		
ONS 48	LIVERPOOL	21/04/45	HALIFAX	04/05/45	21		
ONS 49	LIVERPOOL	02/05/45	HALIFAX	18/05/45	56		
ONS 50	LIVERPOOL	11/05/45	HALIFAX	29/05/45	17		
ONS 51	LIVERPOOL	21/05/45	HALIFAX	04/06/45	20		

Losses incurred in ONS convoys, excluding stragglers

Convoy	Ship's Name	GRT			Date of loss	Cause of loss	Comments
ONS 3	ASHANTIAN	4,917	35	Br	21/04/43	U 415	Ballast. 16 dead
ONS 3	WANSTEAD	5,486	28	Br	21/04/43	U 415 & U 413	Ballast. 1 dead
ONS 5	BONDE	1,570	36	Nor	05/05/43	U 266	1,891 tons coal. 5 dead
ONS 5	BRISTOL CITY	2,864	20	Br	05/05/43	U 358	2,500 tons china clay. 15 dead
ONS 5	DOLIUS	5,507	24	Br	05/05/43	U 638	Ballast. 4 dead
ONS 5	GHARINDA	5,306	19	Br	05/05/43	U 266	Ballast. No dead
ONS 5	HARBURY	5,081	33	Br	05/05/43	U 628	6,129 tons coal. 7 dead
ONS 5	HARPERLEY	4,586	30	Br	05/05/43	U 264	6,005 tons coal. 11 dead
ONS 5	MCKEESPORT	6,198	19	Amer	29/04/43	U 258	Ballast. 1 dead
ONS 5	SELVISTAN	5,136	24	Br	05/05/43	U 266	Ballast. 6 dead
ONS 5	WENTWORTH	5,212	19	Br	05/05/43	U 264	Ballast. 5 dead
ONS 5	WEST MADAKET	5,565	18	Amer	05/05/43	U 584	Ballast. No dead
ONS 5	WEST MAXIMUS	5,561	19	Amer	05/05/43	U 264 & U 628	Ballast. 5 dead
ONS 7	AYMERIC	5,196	19	Br	17/05/43	U 640	Ballast. 53 dead
ONS 18	STEEL VOYAGER	6,198	20	Amer	23/09/43	U 952	Ballast. No dead
ONS 20	ESSEX LANCE	6,625	18	Br	16/10/43	U 426	4,000 tons coal. No dead

OS and OS/KMS convoy series 1941-1945

The OS series, the southbound convoys that complemented the SL series, were started in mid-1941. Previously ships for the Caribbean and the South Atlantic had been included in the OB convoys, detaching en route as independents. The spread of the U-boat war southwards made the new series inevitable and, at the same time, "end to end" escort was provided on this route from the resources of W App Command.

The series continued until the end of Sept 1942 when, as with the northbound SL convoys, it was suspended during the run-up to the North African invasion. The last convoy to sail was OS 42, and the series resumed in mid-Feb 1943 with OS 43.

With the sailing of OS 46 on 15 April 1943, the series was amalgamated with the KMS convoy for Gibraltar and the Mediterranean, and bore the double title OS 46/KMS 13. The joint convoy separated when west of Gibraltar, the KMS portion proceeding to Gibraltar and into the Mediterranean and the OS section southward to Freetown. This practice continued until the final convoy, OS 131, sailing on 27 May 1945.

The joint convoys received their escort from W App Command until the dividing position; the W App Command escort then took the KMS portion on to Gibraltar. A Freetown based group, which had escorted a previous SL convoy northward to the rendezvous position with a MKS convoy, sailed from Gibraltar with ships requiring southbound passage to join and escort the OS convoy. A Mediterranean Fleet escort group undertook the Mediterranean passage of KMS ships.

The change in the pattern of U-boat operations from October 1944 affected this series. The nullifying of the French bases and the restriction of U-boat activities in Atlantic waters to the area within the continental shelf around the UK, i.e. within the 100 fathom line, effectively removed the risk of attack to this series of convoys once they were south of Ushant. Escort routine was then varied in that the majority of the escort and the Rescue Ship left the southbound convoy off the Portuguese coast and joined the appropriate northbound SL/MKS convoy. Only a token escort continued to Gibraltar, supplemented when needed by locally based ships from there. After the division of the convoy, the OS component continued for a period of hours before dispersing as independent ships for their respective destinations. There are therefore only two OS convoys (105 and 115) as discrete units after OS96/KMS 70.

LOSSES

In the tables which follow, for the OS, OS/KMS, KMSG and KMS convoys, the losses shown against the first two series are all for the Atlantic passage and total 22 ships lost by enemy action. The losses for the KMSG and KMS series, 28 ships lost by enemy action, are divided into 6 ships lost in the Atlantic passage ("G" suffix) and 22 ships lost in the Mediterranean.

APPENDIX 3

OS and OS/KMS convoy data

CONVOY	DEP. PORT	DEP. DATE	ARRIVAL PORT	ARR. DATE	TDS	MV SUNK	MV DMGD
OS 1	LIVERPOOL	24/07/41	FREETOWN	10/08/41	58	1	1
OS 2	LIVERPOOL	03/08/41	FREETOWN	22/08/41	17		
OS 3	LIVERPOOL	13/08/41	FREETOWN	01/09/41	36		
OS 4	LIVERPOOL	23/08/41	FREETOWN	11/09/41	33	5	
OS 5	LIVERPOOL	02/09/41	FREETOWN	21/09/41	26		
OS 6	LIVERPOOL	12/0/41	FREETOWN	03/10/41	29		
OS 7	LIVERPOOL	23/09/41	FREETOWN	14/10/41	41		
OS 8	LIVERPOOL	03/10/41	FREETOWN	26/10/41	46		
OS 9	LIVERPOOL	13/10/41	FREETOWN	01/11/41	33		
OS 9G	DET FROM OS 9	24/10/41	GIBRALTAR	28/10/41	12		
OS 10	LIVERPOOL	25/10/41	FREETOWN	18/11/41	33	1	
OS 11	LIVERPOOL	07/11/41	FREETOWN	28/11/41	41		
OS 12	LIVERPOOL	18/11/41	FREETOWN	11/12/41	55	1	
OS 13	LIVERPOOL	30/11/41	FREETOWN	20/12/41	45		
OS 14	LIVERPOOL	13/12/41	FREETOWN	03/01/42	25		
OS 15	LIVERPOOL	23/12/41	BATHURST	13/01/42	44		
OS 16	LIVERPOOL	05/01/42	FREETOWN	23/01/42	56		
OS 17	LIVERPOOL	18/01/42	FREETOWN	07/02/42	42		
OS 18	LIVERPOOL	30/01/42	FREETOWN	20/02/42	42		
OS 19	LIVERPOOL	11/02/42	FREETOWN	03/03/42	36		
OS 20	LIVERPOOL	22/02/42	FREETOWN	12/03/42	34		
OS 21	LIVERPOOL	04/03/42	FREETOWN	24/03/42	54		
OS 22	LIVERPOOL	13/03/42	FREETOWN	01/04/42	45		
OS 23	LIVERPOOL	24/03/42	FREETOWN	11/04/42	45		
OS 24	LIVERPOOL	02/04/42	FREETOWN	22/04/42	45		
OS 25	LIIVERPOOL	12/04/42	FREETOWN	29/04/42	39		
OS 26	LIVERPOOL	22/04/42	FREETOWN	09/05/42	41		
OS 27	LIVERPOOL	02/05/42	FREETOWN	19/05/42	45		
OS 28	LIVERPOOL	12/05/42	FREETOWN	30/05/42	37	2	
OS 29	LIVERPOOL	22/05/42	FREETOWN	11/06/42	44		
OS 30	LIVERPOOL	01/06/42	FREETOWN	19/06/42	48		
OS 31	LIVERPOOL	11/06/42	FREETOWN	30/06/42	31		
OS 32	LIVERPOOL	21/06/42	FREETOWN	08/07/42	45		
OS 33	LIVERPOOL	01/07/42	FREETOWN	20/07/42	40		
OS 34	LIVERPOOL	11/07/42	FREETOWN	30/07/42	35	2	
OS 35	LIVERPOOL	21/07/42	FREETOWN	10/08/42	51		
OS 36	LIVERPOOL	31/07/42	FREETOWN	18/08/42	31		
OS 37	LIVERPOOL	10/08/42	FREETOWN	29/08/42	32		
OS 38	LIVERPOOL	20/08/42	FREETOWN	07/09/42	33		
OS 39	LIVERPOOL	30/08/42	FREETOWN	18/09/42	28		
OS 40	LIVERPOOL	09/09/42	FREETOWN	27/09/42	16		
OS 41	LIVERPOOL	19/09/42	DISPERSED	01/10/42	20		
OS 42	LIVERPOOL	29/09/42	DISPERSED	09/10/42	22		
OS 43	LIVERPOOL	14/02/43	FREETOWN	04/03/43	34		
OS 44	LIVERPOOL	06/03/43	FREETOWN	24/03/43	46	4	
OS 45	LIVERPOOL	24/03/43	FREETOWN	14/04/43	42	2	
OS 46/KMS 13	LIVERPOOL	15/04/43	CONVOY SPLIT	24/04/43	69		
OS 46	EX OS 46/KMS 13	24/04/43	FREETOWN	03/05/43			
OS 47/KMS 14	LIVERPOOL	05/05/43	CONVOY SPLIT	16/05/43	80		
OS 47	EX OS 47/KMS 14	16/05/43	FREETOWN	25/05/43			
OS 48/KMS 15	LIVERPOOL	20/05/43	CONVOY SPLIT	29/05/43	57		
OS 48	EX OS 48/KMS 15	29/05/43	FREETOWN	07/06/43			
OS 49/KMS 16	LIVERPOOL	04/06/43	CONVOY SPLIT	13/06/43	76		
OS 49	EX OS 49/KMS 16	13/06/43	FREETOWN	23/06/43			
OS 50/KMS 17	LIVERPOOL	16/06/43	CONVOY SPLIT	27/06/43	57		
OS 50	EX OS 50/KMS 17	27/06/43	FREETOWN	08/07/43			
OS 51/KMS 20	LIVERPOOL	04/07/43	CONVOY SPLIT	13/07/43	57		
OS 51	EX OS 51/KMS 20	13/07/43	FREETOWN	23/07/43			
OS 52/KMS 21	LIVERPOOL	19/07/43	CONVOY SPLIT	28/07/43	65	2	1
OS 52	EX OS 52/KMS 21	28/07/43	FREETOWN	07/08/43			
OS 53/KMS 23	LIVERPOOL	08/08/43	CONVOY SPLIT	17/08/43	66	1	3
OS 53	EX OS 53/KMS 23	17/08/43	FREETOWN	27/08/43			
OS 54/KMS 25	LIVERPOOL	27/08/43	CONVOY SPLIT	08/09/43	52		
OS 54	EX OS 54/KMS 25	08/09/43	FREETOWN	17/09/43			
OS 55/KMS 27	LIVERPOOL	28/09/43	CONVOY SPLIT	28/09/43	82		
OS 55	EX OS 55/KMS 27	28/09/43	FREETOWN	08/10/43			
OS 56/KMS 29	LIVERPOOL	07/10/43	CONVOY SPLIT	18/10/43	77		
OS 56	EX OS 56/KMS 29	18/10/43	FREETOWN	29/10/43			
OS 57/KMS 31	LIVERPOOL	27/10/43	CONVOY SPLIT	09/11/43	78		
OS 57	EX OS 57/KMS 31	09/11/43	FREETOWN	19/11/43			
OS 58/KMS 32	LIVERPOOL	05/11/43	CONVOY SPLIT	18/11/43	46		
OS 58	EX OS 58/KMS 32	18/11/43	FREETOWN	28/11/43			
OS 59/KMS 33	LIVERPOOL	16/11/43	CONVOY SPLIT	28/11/43	46		
OS 59	EX OS 58/KMS 33	28/11/43	FREETOWN	08/12/43			
OS 60/KMS 34	LIVERPOOL	25/11/43	CONVOY SPLIT	07/12/43	47		
OS 60	EX OS 60/KMS 34	07/12/43	FREETOWN	18/12/43			
OS 61/KMS 35	LIVERPOOL	08/12/43	CONVOY SPLIT	20/12/43	42		
OS 61	EX OS 61/KMS 35	20/12/43	FREETOWN	29/12/43			
OS 62/KMS 36	LIVERPOOL	15/12/43	CONVOY SPLIT	02/01/44	40		
OS 62	EX OS 62/KMS 36	02/01/44	FREETOWN	11/01/44			
OS 063/KMS 37	LIVERPOOL	25/12/43	CONVOY SPLIT	07/01/44	50		
OS 63	EX OS 63/KMS 37	07/01/44	FREETOWN	17/01/44			
OS 064/KMS 38	LIVERPOOL	03/01/44	CONVOY SPLIT	16/01/44	38		
OS 064	EX OS 63/KMS 38	16/01/44	FREETOWN	26/01/44			
OS 65/KMS 39	LIVERPOOL	14/01/44	CONVOY SPLIT	26/01/44	50		
OS 65	EX OS 65/KMS 39	26/01/44	FREETOWN	06/02/44			
OS 66/KMS 40	LIVERPOOL	24/01/44	CONVOY SPLIT	05/02/44	41		
OS 66	EX OS 66/KMS 40	05/02/44	FREETOWN	15/02/44			
OS 67/KMS 41	LIVERPOOL	06/02/44	CONVOY SPLIT	15/02/44	60		
OS 67	EX OS 67/KMS 41	15/02/44	FREETOWN	26/02/44			
OS 68/KMS 42	LIVERPOOL	12/02/44	CONVOY SPLIT	23/02/44	54		
OS 68	EX OS 68/KMS 42	23/02/44	FREETOWN	05/03/44			
OS 69/KMS 43	LIVERPOOL	23/02/44	CONVOY SPLIT	05/03/44	47		
OS 69	EX OS 69/KMS 43	05/03/44	FREETOWN	15/03/44			
OS 70/KMS 44	LIVERPOOL	03/03/44	CONVOY SPLIT	15/03/44	44		
OS 70	EX OS 70/KMS 44	15/03/44	FREETOWN	25/03/44			
OS 71/KMS 45	LIVERPOOL	14/03/44	CONVOY SPLIT	25/03/44	42		
OS 71	EX OS 71/KMS 45	25/03/44	FREETOWN	04/04/44			
OS 72/KMS 46	LIVERPOOL	23/03/44	CONVOY SPLIT	05/04/44	41		
OS 72	EX OS 72/KMS 46	05/04/44	FREETOWN	14/04/44			

THE ALLIED CONVOY SYSTEM 1939-1945

CONVOY	DEP. PORT	DEP. DATE	ARRIVAL PORT	ARR. DATE	TDS	MV SUNK	MV DMGD
OS 73/KMS 47	LIVERPOL	03/04/44	CONVOY SPLIT	16/04/44	44		
OS 73	EX OS 73/KMS 47	16/04/44	FREETOWN	25/04/44			
OS 74/KMS 48	LIVERPOOL	12/04/44	CONVOY SPLIT	23/04/44	27		
OS 74	EX OS 74/KMS 48	23/04/44	FREETOWN	03/05/44			
OS 75/KMS 49	LIVERPOOL	23/04/44	CONVOY SPLIT	04/05/44	21		
OS 75	EX OS 75/KMS 49	04/05/44	FREETOWN	14/05/44			
OS 76/KMS 50	LIVERPOOL	02/05/44	CONVOY SPLIT	13/05/44	32		
OS 76	EX OS 76/KMS 50	13/05/44	FREETOWN	22/05/44			
OS 77/KMS 51	LIVERPOOL	13/05/44	CONVOY SPLIT	23/05/44	31		
OS 77	EX OS 77/KMS 51	23/05/44	FREETOWN	02/06/44			
OS 78/KMS 52	LIVERPOOL	22/05/44	CONVOY SPLIT	04/06/44	23		
OS 78	ES OS 78/KMS 52	04/06/44	FREETOWN	14/06/44			
OS 79/KMS 53	LIVERPOOL	02/06/44	CONVOY SPLIT	11/06/44	27		
OS 79	EX OS 79/KMS 53	11/06/44	FREETOWN	21/06/44			
OS 80/KMS 54	LIVERPOOL	11/06/44	CONVOY SPLIT	21/06/44	28		
OS 80	EX OS 80/KMS 54	21/06/44	FREETOWN	01/07/44			
OS 81/KMS 55	LIVERPOOL	22/06/44	CONVOY SPLIT	03/07/44	33		
OS 81	EX OS 81/KMS 55	03/07/44	FREETOWN	12/07/44			
OS 82/KMS 56	LIVERPOOL	01/07/44	CONVOY SPLIT	11/07/44	26		
OS 82	EX OS 82/KMS 56	11/07/44	FREETOWN	21/07/44			
OS 83/KMS 57	LIVERPOOL	12/07/44	CONVOY SPLIT	23/07/44	29		
OS 83	EX OS 84/KMS 57	23/07/44	FREETOWN	03/08/44			
OS 84/KMS 58	LIVERPOOL	21/07/44	CONVOY SPLIT	01/08/44	24		
OS 84	EX OS 84/KMS 58	01/08/44	FREETOWN	10/08/44			
OS 85/KMS 59	LIVERPOOL	01/08/44	CONVOY SPLIT	11/08/44	34		
OS 85	EX OS 85/KMS 59	11/08/44	FREETOWN	21/08/44			
OS 86/KMS 60	LIVERPOOL	10/08/44	CONVOY SPLIT	21/08/44	22		
OS 86	EX OS 86/KMS 60	21/08/44	FREETOWN	30/08/44			
OS 87/KMS 61	LIVERPOOL	25/08/44	COMVOY SPLIT	03/09/44	34		
OS 87	EX OS 87/KMS 61	03/09/44	FREETOWN	13/09/44			
OS 88/KMS 62	LIVERPOOL	04/09/44	CONVOY SPLIT	10/09/44	28		
OS 88	EX OS 88/KMS 62	10/09/44	FREETOWN	20/09/44			
OS 89/KMS 63	LIVERPOOL	15/09/44	CONVOY SPLIT	22/09/44	33		
OS 89	EX OS 89/KMS 63	22/09/44	FREETOWN	30/09/44			
OS 90/KMS 64	LIVERPOOL	24/09/44	CONVOY SPLIT	01/10/44	33		
OS 90	EX OS 90/KMS 64	01/10/44	FREETOWN	11/10/44			
OS 91/KMS 65	LIVERPOOL	04/10/44	CONVOY SPLIT	10/10/44	30		
OS 91	EX OS 91/KMS 65	10/10/44	FREETOWN	19/10/44			
OS 92/KMS 66	LIVERPOOL	15/10/44	CONVOY SPLIT	25/10/44	34	1	
OS 92	EX OS 92/KMS 66	25/10/44	FREETOWN	04/11/44			
OS 93/KMS 67	LIVERPOOL	24/10/44	CONVOY SPLIT	01/11/44	34		
OS 93	EX OS 93/KMS 67	01/11/44	CONVOY DISPERSED	02/11/44			
OS 94/KMS 68	LIVERPOOL	03/11/44	CONVOY SPLIT	07/11/44	34		
OS 94	EX OS 94/KMS 68	07/11/44	CONVOY DISPERSED	12/11/44			
OS 95/KMS 69	LIVERPOOL	13/11/44	CONVOY SPLIT	22/11/44	31		
OS 95	EX OS 95/KMS 69	22/11/44	CONVOY DISPERSED	26/11/44			
OS 96/KMS 70	LIVERPOOL	23/11/44	CONVOY SPLIT	26/11/44	40		

CONVOY	DEP. PORT	DEP. DATE	ARRIVAL PORT	ARR. DATE	TDS	MV SUNK	MV DMGD
OS 96	EX OS 96/KMS 70	26/11/44	CONVOY DISPERSED	27/11/44			
OS 97/KMS 71	LIVERPOOL	03/12/44	CONVOY SPLIT	07/12/44	29		
OS 97	EX OS 97/KMS 71	07/12/44	CONVOY DISPERSED	07/12/44			
OS 98/KMS 72	LIVERPOOL	13/12/44	CONVOY SPLIT	17/12/44	36		
OS 98	EX OS 98/KMS 72	17/12/44	CONVOY DISPERSED	17/12/44			
OS 99/KMS 73	LIVERPOOL	18/12/44	CONVOY SPLIT	21/12/44	21		
OS 99	EX OS 99/KMS 73	21/12/44	CONVOY DISPERSED	21/12/44			
OS 100/KMS74	LIVERPOOL	23/12/44	CONVOY SPLIT	26/12/44	28		
OS 100	EX OS 100/KMS 74	26/12/44	CONVOY DISPERSED	26/12/44			
OS 101/KMS 75	LIVERPOOL	28/12/44	CONVOY SPLIT	31/12/44	14		
OS 101	EX OS 101/KMS 75	31/12/44	CONVOY DISPERSED	31/12/44			
OS 102/KMS 76	LIVERPOOL	02/01/45	GIBRALTAR	10/01/45	16		
OS 102	DID NOT FORM		NO FREETOWN SHIPS				
OS 103/KMS 77	LIVERPOOL	07/01/45	CONVOY SPLIT	10/01/45	21		
OS 103	EX OS 103/KMS 77	10/01/45	CONVOY DISPERSED	10/01/45			
OS 104/KMS 78	LIVERPOOL	12/01/45	CONVOY SPLIT	15/01/45	19		
OS 104	EX OS 104/KMS 78	15/01/45	CONVOY DISPERSED	15/01/45			
OS 105/KMS 79	LIVERPOOL	17/01/45	CONVOY SPLIT	22/01/45	16		
OS 105	EX OS 105/KMS 79	22/01/45	CONVOY DISPERSED	26/01/45			
OS 106/KMS 80	LIVERPOOL	22/01/45	CONVOY SPLIT	25/01/45	27		
OS 106	EX OS 106/KMS 80	25/01/45	CONVOY DISPERSED	25/01/45			
OS 107/KMS 81	LIVERPOOL	27/01/45	CONVOY SPLIT	30/01/45	8		
OS 107	EX OS 107/KMS 81	30/01/45	CONVOY DISPERSED	30/01/45			
OS 108/KMS 82	LIVERPOOL	01/02/45	CONVOY SPLIT	05/02/45	21		
OS 108	DID NOT FORM						
OS 109/KMS 83	LIVERPOOL	06/02/45	CONVOY SPLIT	10/02/45	20		
OS 109	DID NOT FORM						
OS 110/KMS 84	LIVERPOOL	11/02/45	CONVOY SPLIT	15/02/45	21		
OS 110	DID NOT FORM						
OS 111/KMS 85	LIVERPOOL	17/02/45	CONVOY SPLIT	21/02/45	17		
OS 111	DID NOT FORM						
OS 112/KMS 86	LIVERPOOL	22/02/45	CONVOY DISPERSED	24/02/45	22		
OS 112	DID NOT FORM						
OS 113/KMS 87	LIVERPOOL	26/02/45	CONVOY SPLIT	01/03/45	20		
OS 113	DID NOT FORM						
OS 114/KMS 88	LIVERPOOL	03/03/45	CONVOY SPLIT	07/03/45	24		
OS 114	DID NOT FORM						
OS 115/KMS 89	LIVERPOOL	09/03/45	CONVOY SPLIT	14/03/45	24	1	
OS 115	EX OS 115/KMS 89	14/03/45	CONVOY DISPERSED	22/03/45			

APPENDIX 3

CONVOY	DEP. PORT	DEP. DATE	ARRIVAL PORT	ARR. DATE	TDS	MV SUNK	MV DMGD
OS 116/KMS 90	LIVERPOOL	13/03/45	CONVOY SPLIT	17/03/45	24		
OS 116	DID NOT FORM						
OS 117/KMS 91	LIVERPOOL	18/03/45	GIBRALTAR	26/03/45	25		
OS 117	DID NOT FORM						
OS 118/KMS 92	LIVERPOOL	23/03/45	CONVOY SPLIT	29/03/45	29		
OS 118	DID NOT FORM						
OS 119/KMS 93	LIVERPOOL	28/03/45	CONVOY SPLIT	04/04/45	16		
OS 119	DID NOT FORM						
OS 120/KMS 94	LIVERPOOL	02/04/45	CONVOY SPLIT	07/04/45	21		
OS 120	DID NOT FORM						
OS 121/KMS 95	LIVERPOOL	07/04/45	CONVOY SPLIT	14/04/45	22		
OS 121	DID NOT FORM						
OS 122/KMS 96	LIVERPOOL	12/04/45	CONVOY SPLIT	18/04/45	13		
OS 122	DID NOT FORM						
OS 123/KMS 97	LIVERPOOL	17/04/45	CONVOY SPLIT	23/04/45	20		
OS 123	DID NOT FORM						
OS 124/KMS 98	LIVERPOOL	22/04/45	CONVOY SPLIT	27/04/45	20		
OS 124	DID NOT FORM						
OS 125/KMS 99	LIVERPOOL	27/04/45	CONVOY DISPERSED	01/05/45	23		
OS 125	DID NOT FORM						
OS 126/KMS 100	LIVERPOOL	02/05/45	CONVOY DISPERSED	08/05/45	20		
OS 126	DID NOT FORM						
OS 127/KMS 101	LIVERPOOL	07/05/45	CONVOY DISPERSED	13/05/45	15		
OS 127	DID NOT FORM						
OS 128/KMS 102	LIVERPOOL	11/05/45	CONVOY DISPERSED	15/05/45	7		
OS 128	DID NOT FORM						
OS 129/KMS 103	LIVERPOOL	17/05/45	CONVOY DISPERSED	21/05/45	16		
OS 129	DID NOT FORM						
OS 130/KMS 104	LIVERPOOL	22/05/45	CONVOY DISPERSED	24/05/45	25		
OS 130	DID NOT FORM						
OS 131/KMS 105	LIVERPOOL	27/05/45	CONVOY DISPERSED	30/05/45	13		
OS 131	DID NOT FORM						

Courtesy National Archives of Canada

A very sparsely equipped ST CROIX on 28 June 1942 probably en route to join convoy SC 89 which sailed from Sydney CB two days before. She has three of her four original 4-inch guns, no close range armament other than a 12pdr HA aft and one set of RN type 21-inch torpedo tubes mounted on the centre line in lieu of her original four sets. Her sole radar is the early Canadian SW1C at the foremast.

ST CROIX saw extensive North Atlantic service with 21st Escort Group of Newfoundland Command, sinking U 90 on 24 July 1942 and sharing U 87 with SHEDIAC on 4 Mar 1943. Her end was tragic, during the early part of the ON 202/ONS 18 action in Sept 1943 she was sunk by an acoustic torpedo from U 305. Her survivors were picked up by the frigate ITCHEN, as were those from the corvette POLYANTHUS. ITCHEN was then hit by U 666, also with an acoustic torpedo, which exploded her magazine. Only three men survived from the three ships' companies.

KMS convoy series 1942-1945

The landings in French North Africa in November 1942 caused the start of two new convoy series KMF and KMS. Each coding had its own numeric sequence and the lettering was derived from United Kingdom to Mediterranean Fast and Slow.

The Fast series were operational convoys, KMF 1 being the transports of the initial landing force. Thereafter the series continued being used for the reinforcement convoys and, eventually, for personnel ship convoys for Italy and Port Said. The return of personnel ships to the UK carried the reversal code MKF. There are separate notes and tables for both these series.

The Slow series were trade convoys, KMS 1 being the supply and MT ships to support the troops carried in KMF 1. Thereafter the series was used for all freight ships proceeding on the UK/Mediterranean route thus supplanting the previous OG series. Ships returning to the UK from the Mediterranean carried the reversal code MKS, which therefore replaced the old HG coding.

Both the Fast and Slow series were progressively extended eastwards as the Mediterranean was re-opened to convoys, Port Said eventually becoming the eastern terminal.

The early KMS and MKS convoys did not effect a juncture with any other series; they will be apparent in the listings in that they have named terminal ports. In early 1943 the sailings of the OS and SL series were adjusted so that those convoys arrived at a convenient point west of Gibraltar where Slow ships for and from the Mediterranean detached and joined. From that time therefore convoys carried a dual title OS/KMS and SL/MKS; there was no similar dual titling for the KMF/MKF series.

In the listings that follow it will be noted that the KMS series contains convoys with the suffix G to the numerals. This is to indicate 1) those convoys which did not join an OS convoy but proceeded as a separate unit; 2) to indicate the KMS portion of a joint OS/KMS convoy between leaving the OS/KMS convoy and arrival at or passing Gibraltar. The KMS prefix is used only for the Mediterranean portion of a convoy passage. The suffix G did NOT appear in signals or other documents of the time.

In the table of KMS convoys that appears below, losses which occurred in the Atlantic are listed against the convoys suffixed "G." Losses incurred in the Mediterranean, i.e. east of Gibraltar, position 36.08N 05.22W, appear against the convoys with the plain KMS designation. In the summary of losses incurred, which follows the convoy data tables, Mediterranean losses appear separately as it is very difficult indeed to produce meaningful figures for numbers of ships in convoy within the Mediterranean, a matter already discussed in the preamble to APPENDIX 2.

KMS convoy data

CONVOY	DEP. PORT	DEP. DATE	ARRIVAL PORT	ARR. DATE	TDS	MV SUNK	MV DMGD
KMS 1G	CLYDE	22/10/42	GIBRALTAR	07/11/42	46		
KMS 1	GIBRALTAR	07/11/42	ALGIERS	08/11/42			
KMS 2G	LOCH EWE	25/10/42	GIBRALTAR	10/11/42	51		
KMS 2	GIBRALTAR	10/11/42	ALGIERS	12/11/42		1	
KMS 3G	LIVERPOOL	07/11/42	GIBRALTAR	22/11/42	56	2	
KMS 3	GIBRALTAR	22//11/42	BONE	26/11/42		1	
KMS 4G	CLYDE	26/11/42	GIBRALTAR	08/12/42	60		
KMS 4	GIBRALTAR	08/12/42	BONE	13/12/42			
KMS 5G	CLYDE	11/12/42	GIBRALTAR	24/1/2/42	39		
KMS 5	GIBRALTAR	24/12/42	BONE	27/12/42			
KMS 6G	CLYDE	24/12/42	GIBRALTAR	04/01/43	49		1
KMS 6	GIBRALTAR	04/01/43	BONE	08/01/43		2	
KMS 7G	CLYDE	07/01/43	GIBRALTAR	18/01/43	49		1
KMS 7	GIBRALTAR	18/01/43	BONE	22/01/43		1	
KMS 8G	CLYDE	21/01/43	GIBRALTAR	06/02/43	54		1
KMS 8	GIBRALTAR	06/02/43	BONE	08/02/43		2	
KMS 9G	CLYDE	06/02/43	GIBRALTAR	16/02/43	48		
KMS 9	GIBRALTAR	16/02/43	BONE	20/02/43			
KMS 10G	CLYDE	26/02/43	GIBRALTAR	07/03/43	57	1	3
KMS 10	GIBRALTAR	07/03/43	BONE	11/03/43			
KMS 11G	CLYDE	14/03/43	GIBRALTAR	24/03/43	61	1	
KMS 11	GIBRALTAR	24/03/43	BONE	28/03/43		2	
KMS 12G	CLYDE	31/03/43	GIBRALTAR	12/04/43	40		
KMS 12	GIBRALTAR	12/04/43	BONE	15/04/43			
KMS 13G	EX OS 46/KMS 13	24/04/43	GIBRALTAR	26/04/43	44		1
KMS 13	GIBRALTAR	26/04/43	BONE	29/04/43			
KMS 14G	EX OS 47/KMS 14	16/05/43	GIBRALTAR	17/05/43	40		
KMS 14	GIBRALTAR	17/05/43	BONE	21/05/43		1	1
KMS 14X	GIBRALTAR	17/05/43	ALEXANDRIA	26/05/43			
KMS 15G	EX OS 48/KMS 15	29/05/43	GIBRALTAR	30/05/43	26		
KMS 15	GIBRALTAR	31/05/43	PORT SAID	14/06/43			
KMS 16G	EX OS 49/KMS 16	13/06/43	GIBRALTAR	15/06/43	46		
KMS 16	GIBRALTAR	16/06/43	PORT SAID	28/06/43			
KMS 17G	EX OS 50/KMS 17	27/06/43	GIBRALTAR	29/06/43	34		
KMS 17	GIBRALTAR	30/06/43	SFAX	06/07/43			
KMS 18AG	CLYDE	20/06/43	GIBRALTAR	29/06/43	10		
KMS 18BG	CLYDE	24/06/43	PASSED GIBRALTAR	03/07/43	20		

APPENDIX 3

CONVOY	DEP. PORT	DEP. DATE	ARRIVAL PORT	ARR. DATE	TDS	MV SUNK	MV DMGD
KMS 18B	PASSED GIBRALTARGIB	03/07/43	OP HUSKY	10/07/43		3	
KMS 19G	CLYDE	25/06/43	PASSED GIBRALTAR	06/07/43	36		
KMS 19	PASSED GIBRALTAR	06/07/43	OP HUSKY	16/07/43			
KMS 19A	AUGUSTA	21/07/43	MALTA	22/07/43			
KMS 19M	MALTA	17/07/43	AUGUSTA	18/07/43			
KMS 19T	MALTA	23/07/43	TRIPOLI, LIBYA	24/07/43			
KMS 19Y	ALGIERS	14/07/43	OP HUSKY	20/07/43			
KMS 20G	EX OS 51/KMS 20	13/07/43	GIBRALTAR	14/07/43	34		
KMS 20	GIBRALTAR	18/07/43	ALGIERS	20/07/43			
KMS 21G	EX OS 52/KMS 21	28/07/43	GIBRALTAR	29/07/43	42		
KMS 21	GIBRALTAR	29/07/43	PORT SAID	09/08/43		1	
KMS 22G	LIVERPOOL	28/07/43	GIBRALTAR	09/08/43	35		
KMS 22	GIBRALTAR	09/08/43	PORT SAID	20/08/43			
KMS 23G	EX OS 53/KMS 23	17/08/43	GIBRALTAR	18/08/43	46		
KMS 23	GIBRALTAR	18/08/43	PORT SAID	30/08/43			
KMS 24G	LIVERPOOL	17/08/43	GIBRALTAR	30/08/43	33		
KMS 24	GIBRALTAR	30/08/43	PORT SAID	10/09/43			
KMS 25G	EX OS 54/KMS 25	08/09/43	GIBRALTAR	10/09/43	41		
KMS 25	GIBRALTAR	10/09/43	PORT SAID	21/09/43			
KMS 26G	LIVERPOOL	05/09/43	GIBRALTAR	18/09/43	42		
KMS 26	GIBRALTAR	18/09/43	PORT SAID	29/09/43			
KMS 27G	EX OS 55/KMS 27	28/09/43	GIBRALTAR	29/09/43	54		
KMS 27	GIBRALTAR	29/09/43	PORT SAID	11/10/43		1	
KMS 28G	LIVERPOOL	26/09/43	GIBRALTAR	07/10/43	64		
KMS 28	GIBRALTAR	07/10/43	PORT SAID	19/10/43			
KMS 29G	EX OS 56/KMS 29	18/10/43	GIBRALTAR	20/10/43	52		
KMS 29	GIBRALTAR	20/10/43	PORT SAID	31/10/43			
KMS 30G	LIVERPOOL	17/10/43	GIBRALTAR	31/10/43	40		
KMS 30	GIBRALTAR	31/10/43	PORT SAID	11/11/43		1	
KMS 31G	EX OS 57/KMS 31	09/11/43	GIBRALTAR	10/11/43	50		
KMS 31	GIBRALTAR	10/11/43	PORT SAID	21/11/43		4	2
KMS 32G	EX OS 58/KMS 32	18/11/43	GIBRALTAR	19/11/43	39		
KMS 32	GIBRALTAR	19/11/43	PORT SAID	30/11/43			
KMS 33G	EX OS 59/KMS 33	28/11/43	GIBRALTAR	29/11/43	35		
KMS 33	GIBRALTAR	29/11/43	PORT SAID	09/12/43			
KMS 34G	EX OS 60/KMS 34	07/12/43	GIBRALTAR	09/12/43	41		
KMS 34	GIBRALTAR	09/12/43	PORT SAID	20/12/43			
KMS 35G	EX OS 61/KMS 35	19/12/43	GIBRALTAR	19/12/43	38		
KMS 35	GIBRALTAR	19/12/43	PORT SAID	01/01/44			
KMS 36G	EX OS 62/KMS 36	02/01/44	GIBRALTAR	03/01/44	44		
KMS 36	GIBRALTAR	03/01/44	PORT SAID	13/01/44			
KMS 37G	EX OS 63/KMS 37	07/01/44	GIBRALTAR	07/01/44	40		
KMS 37	GIBRALTAR	07/01/44	PORT SAID	20/01/44		2	
KMS 38G	EX OS 64/KMS 38	15/01/44	GIBRALTAR	17/01/44	35		
KMS 38	GIBRALTAR	17/01/44	PORT SAID	27/01/44			
KMS 39G	EX OS 65/KMS 39	26/01/44	GIBRALTAR	28/01/44	41		
KMS 39	GIBRALTAR	28/01/44	PORT SAID	07/02/44			
KMS 40G	EX OS 66/KMS 40	05/02/44	GIBRALTAR	07/02/44	41		
KMS 40	GIBRALTAR	07/02/44	PORT SAID	18/02/44			
KMS 41G	EX OS 67/KMS 41	15/02/44	GIBRALTAR	17/02/44	46		
KMS 41	GIBRALTAR	17/02/44	PORT SAID	27/02/44			
KMS 42G	EX OS 68/KMS 42	23/02/44	GIBRALTAR	25/02/44	45		
KMS 42	GIBRALTAR	25/02/44	PORT SAID	06/03/44			
KMS 43G	EX OS 69/KMS 43	05/03/44	GIBRALTAR	06/03/44	36		
KMS 43	GIBRALTAR	06/03/44	PORT SAID	16/03/44			
KMS 44G	EX OS 70/KMS 44	15/03/44	GIBRALTAR	17/03/44	38		
KMS 44	GIBRALTAR	17/03/44	PORT SAID	27/03/44			
KMS 45G	EX OS 71/KMS 45	25/03/44	GIBRALTAR	27/03/44	34		
KMS 45	GIBRALTAR	27/03/44	PORT SAID	06/04/44			
KMS 45A	GIBRALTAR	31/03/44	AUGUSTA	04/04/44			
KMS 46G	EX OS 72/KMS 46	05/04/44	GIBRALTAR	06/04/44	26		
KMS 46	GIBRALTAR	06/04/44	PORT SAID	16/04/44			
KMS 47G	EX OS 73/KMS 47	16/04/44	GIBRALTAR	17/04/44	32		
KMS 47	GIBRALTAR	17/04/44	PORT SAID	27/04/44			
KMS 48G	EX OS 74/KMS 48	23/04/44	GIBRALTAR	25/04/44	19		
KMS 48	GIBRALTAR	25/04/44	PORT SAID	05/05/44			
KMS 48A	GIBRALTAR	01/05/44	AUGUSTA	06/05/44			
KMS 49G	EX OS 75/KMS 49	04/05/44	GIBRALTAR	06/05/44	13		
KMS 49	GIBRALTAR	06/05/44	PORT SAID	16/05/44			
KMS 50G	EX OS 76/KMS 50	13/05/44	GIBRALTAR	15/05/44	23		
KMS 50	GIBRALTAR	15/05/44	PORT SAID	25/05/44			
KMS 51G	EX OS 77/KMS 51	23/05/44	GIBRALTAR	25/05/44	23		
KMS 51	GIBRALTAR	28/05/44	PORT SAID	09/06/44		1	
KMS 52G	EX OS 78/KMS 52	04/06/44	GIBRALTAR	06/06/44	18		
KMS 52	GIBRALTAR	06/06/44	PORT SAID	16/06/44			
KMS 53G	EX OS 79/KMS 53	11/06/44	GIBRALTAR	13/06/44	18		
KMS 53	GIBRALTAR	14/06/44	PORT SAID	24/06/44			
KMS 54G	EX OS 80/KMS 54	21/06/44	GIBRALTAR	23/06/44	18		
KMS 54	GIBRALTAR	23/06/44	PORT SAID	03/07/44			
KMS 55G	EX OS 81/KMS 55	02/07/44	GIBRALTAR	04/07/44	23		
KMS 55	GIBRALTAR	04/07/44	PORT SAID	14/07/44			
KMS 56G	EX OS 82/KMS 56	11/07/44	GIBRALTAR	13/07/44	20		
KMS 56	GIBRALTAR	13/07/44	PORT SAID	23/07/44			
KMS 57G	EX OS 83/KMS 57	23/07/44	GIBRALTAR	25/07/44	22		
KMS 57	GIBRALTAR	25/07/44	PORT SAID	04/08/44			
KMS 58G	EX OS 84/KMS 58	31/07/44	GIBRALTAR	02/08/44	20		
KMS 58	GIBRALTAR	02/08/44	PORT SAID	12/08/44			
KMS 59G	EX OS 85/KMS 59	11/08/44	GIBRALTAR	13/08/44	26		
KMS 59	GIBRALTAR	13/08/44	PORT SAID	23/08/44			
KMS 60G	EX OS 86/KMS 60	21/08/44	GIBRALTAR	23/08/44	16		
KMS 60	GIBRALTAR	23/08/44	PORT SAID	02/09/44			
KMS 61G	EX OS 87/KMS 61	03/09/44	GIBRALTAR	04/09/44	26		
KMS 61	GIBRALTAR	04/09/44	PORT SAID	14/09/44			
KMS 62G	EX OS 88/KMS 62	10/09/44	GIBRALTAR	12/09/44	16		
KMS 62	GIBRALTAR	12/09/44	PORT SAID	22/09/44			
KMS 63G	EX OS 89/KMS 63	22/09/44	GIBRALTAR	23/09/44	28		
KMS 63	GIBRALTAR	23/09/44	PORT SAID	03/10/44			
KMS 64G	EX OS 90/KMS 64	01/10/44	GIBRALTAR	02/10/44	26		
KMS 64	GIBRALTAR	02/10/44	PORT SAID	12/10/44			

◇ THE ALLIED CONVOY SYSTEM 1939-1945

CONVOY	DEP. PORT	DEP. DATE	ARRIVAL PORT	ARR. DATE	TDS	MV SUNK	MV DMGD
KMS 65G	EX OS 91/KMS 65	10/10/44	GIBRALTAR	11/10/44	23		
KMS 65	GIBRALTAR	11/10/44	PORT SAID	21/10/44			
KMS 66G	EX OS 92/KMS 66	25/10/44	GIBRALTAR	26/10/44	30		
KMS 66	GIBRALTAR	26/10/44	PORT SAID	05/11/44			
KMS 67G	EX OS 93/KMS 67	01/11/44	GIBRALTAR	02/11/44	22		
KMS 67	GIBRALTAR	02/11/44	PORT SAID	12/11/44			
KMS 68G	EX OS 94/KMS 68	10/11/44	GIBRALTAR	13/11/44	23		
KMS 68	GIBRALTAR	13/11/44	PORT SAID	22/11/44			
KMS 69G	EX OS 95/KMS 69	22/11/44	GIBRALTAR	23/11/44	23		
KMS 69	GIBRALTAR	23/11/44	DISPERSED 1800Z OFF MALTA	27/11/44			
KMS 70G	EX OS 96/KMS 70	26/11/44	DISPERSED	27/11/44	32		
KMS 71G	EX OS 97/KMS 71	07/12/44	DISPERSED	07/12/44	23		
KMS 73G	EX OS 99/KMS 72	21/12/44	GIBRALTAR	26/12/44	17		
KMS 74G	EX OS 100/KMS 74	26/12/44	GIBRALTAR	31/12/44	19		
KMS 75G	EX OS 101/KMS 75	31/12/44	GIBRALTAR	05/01/45	13		
KMS 76G	LIVERPOOL	02/01/45	GIBRALTAR	10/01/45	16	1	
KMS 77G	EX OS 103/KMS 77	10/01/45	GIBRALTAR	15/01/45	19		
KMS 78G	EX OS 104/KMS 78	15/01/45	GIBRALTAR	19/01/45	18		
KMS 79G	EX OS 105/KMS 79	22/01/45	DISPERSED	22/01/45	14		
KMS 80G	EX OS 106/KMS 80	22/01/45	GIBRALTAR	30/01/45	23		
KMS 81G	EX OS 107/KMS 81	30/01/45	GIBRALTAR	05/02/45	7		
KMS 82G	EX OS 108/KMS 82	05/02/45	GIBRALTAR	09/02/45	20		
KMS 83G	EX OS 109/KMS 83	10/02/45	GIBRALTAR	16/02/45	12		
KMS 84G	EX OS 110 KMS 84	15/02/45	GIBRALTAR	19/02/45	22		
KMS 85G	EX OS 111/KMS 85	21/02/45	GIBRALTAR	25/02/45	15		
KMS 086G	EX OS 112/KMS 86	24/02/45	DISPERSED	25/02/45	20		
KMS 087G	EX OS 113/KMS 87	01/03/45	GIBRALTAR	06/03/45	13		
KMS 88G	EX OS 114/KMS 88	07/03/45	GIBRALTAR	11/03/45	19		
KMS 89G	EX OS 115/KMS 89	10/03/45	GIBRALTAR	16/03/45	19	1	
KMS 90G	EX OS 116/KMS 90	17/03/45	GIBRALTAR	21/03/45	20		
KMS 91G	EX OS 117/KMS 91	25/03/45	GIBRALTAR	26/03/45	15		
KMS 92G	EX OS 118/KMS 92	29/03/45	GIBRALTAR	01/04/45	25		
KMS 93G	EX OS 119/KMS 93	04/04/45	DISPERSED	06/04/45	13		
KMS 94G	EX OS 120/KMS 94	07/04/45	DISPERSED	11/04/45	18		
KMS 95G	EX OS 121/KMS 95	14/04/45	GIBRALTAR	16/04/45	20		
KMS 96G	EX OS 122/KMS 96	18/04/45	DISPERSED	18/04/45	12		
KMS 97G	EX OS 123/KMS 9	23/04/45	GIBRALTAR	24/04/45	18		
KMS 98G	EX OS 124/KMS 9	27/04/45	GIBRALTAR	01/05/45	17		

Losses incurred in OS and OS/KMS convoys, excluding stragglers

Convoy	Ship's Name	GRT			Date of loss	Cause of loss	Comments
OS 1	BOTWEY	5,106	16	Br	26/07/41	U 141	Ballast. No dead.
OS 4	EMBASSAGE	4,954	35	Br	27/08/41	U 557	8,540 tons general incl a/c & MT. 39 dead
OS 4	SAUGOR	6,303	28	Br	27/08/41	U 557	General, a/c. 59 dead
OS 4	TREMODA	4,736	28	Br	27/08/41	U 557	General & military stores. 32 dead
OS 4	SEGUNDO	4,414	25	Nor	27/08/41	U 557	Ballast. 7 dead
OS 4	OTAIO	10,298	30	Br	28/08/41	U 558	General, stores. 26 dead
OS 7	BEREBY	5,248	19	Br	24/09/41	WRECKED	Stores. No dead
OS 10	BENNEKOM	5,998	17	Du	31/10/41	U 96	900 tons gen, 300 tons stores. 8 dead
OS 12	THORNLIEBANK	5,569	39	Br	29/11/41	U 43	General. All (75) dead
OS 17	FLORISTAN	5,478	28	Br	19/01/42	WRECKED	General. No dead
OS 17	MOBEKA	6,111	37	Bel	19/01/42	WRECKED	Cargo unknown. No dead
OS 28	MONTENOL	2,646	17	Br	21/05/42	U 159	Ballast. 3 dead
OS 28	NEW BRUNSWICK	6,529	19	Br	21/05/42	U 159	5,895 tons stores & general, 20 a/c. 3 dead
OS 34	EMPIRE HAWKSBILL	5,724	20	Br	19/07/42	U 564	Cargo unknown. All (46) dead
OS 34	LAVINGTON COURT	5,372	40	Br	19/07/42	U 564	6,000 tons military cargo. 6 dead
OS 41	DEFOE	6,245	40	Br	24/09/42	FIRE	Stores, explosives. 16 dead
OS 44	CLAN ALPINE	5,442	18	Br	13/03/43	U 107	7,317 tons gen, 4,000 tons stores. 26 dead
OS 44	DJAMBI	6,984	19	Du	13/03/43	COLLISION	Cargo unknown. No dead. Collision with SILVERBEECH
OS 44	MARCELLA	4,592	38	Br	13/03/43	U 107	6,800 tons stores, 500 tons general. 44 dead
OS 44	OPORTO	2,352	28	Br	13/03/43	U 107	1,500 tons general. 43 dead
OS 44	SEMBILANGAN	4,990	23	Du	13/03/43	U 107	4,657 tons general. 86 dead, 1 survivor
OS 45	GOGRA	5,190	19	Br	02/04/43	U 124	6,000 tons stores, 1,000 tons ammo. 82 dead
OS 45	KATHA	4,357	38	Br	02/04/43	U 124	7,000 tons stores, 16 a/c. 6 dead
OS 52KM	HALIZONES	5,298	20	Br	27/07/43	AIRCRAFT	2,834 tons general. No dead
OS 52KM	EL ARGENTINO	9,501	28	Br	26/07/43	AIRCRAFT	Ballast. 4 dead
OS 58/KM	WARFIELD	6,070	17	Br	15/08/43	AIRCRAFT	3,600 tons ammo & gas bombs. 2 dead
OS 97KM	P.L.M.21	5,417	21	Fr	03/12/44	WRECKED	Coal. No dead
OS 115KM	LORNASTON	4,934	25	Br	08/03/45	U 275	6,002 tons coal. No dead
OS 119	ANTONIO	5,225	18	Br	28/03/45	COLLISION	No details available

Losses incurred in KMS convoys, excluding stragglers

Convoy	Ship's Name	GRT	Date of loss	Cause of loss	Comments
KMS 2	BROWNING	5,332 19 Br	11/11/42	U 593	US Army stores. 1 dead
KMS 3G	GRANGEPARK	5,132 19 Br	20/11/42	U 263	2,000 tons stores. 3 dead
KMS 3G	PRINS HARALD	7,244 42 Nor	20/11/42	U 263	War stores. 3 dead
KMS 3	TRENTBANK	5,060 29 Br	24/11/42	AIRCRAFT	3,000 tons stores. 2 dead.
KMS 6	AKABAHRA	1,524 29 Nor	07/01/43	AIRCRAFT	Cargo unknown. No dead
KMS 6	BENALBANACH	7,153 40 Br	07/01/43	AIRCRAFT	Explosives, MT, petrol, 389 troops. 417 dead
KMS 7	JEAN JADOT	5,859 29 Bel	20/01/43	U 453	Stores, 323 troops. 6 dead
KMS 8	EMPIRE BANNER	6,699 42 Br	07/02/43	U 77	3,800 tons AFVs & MT. No dead
KMS 8	EMPIRE WEBSTER	7,043 42 Br	07/02/43	U 77	3,000 tons coal, stores. 4 dead
KMS 10G	FORT BATTLE RIVER	7,133 42 Br	06/03/43	U 410	3,000 tons stores. No dead
KMS 11G	CITY OF CHRIST CHURCH	6,009 15 Br	21/03/43	AIRCRAFT	6,900 tons stores, ammo. No dead
KMS 11	EMPIRE ROWAN	9,462 22 Br	27/03/43	AIRCRAFT	4,500 tons coal, stores. 3 dead
KMS 11	PRINS WILLEM III	1,524 39 Du	26/03/43	AIRCRAFT	Cargo unknown. 11 dead
KMS 14	EMPIRE EVE	5,979 41 Br	18/05/43	U 414	6,500 tons coal, lub oil. 5 dead
KMS 18B	CITY OF VENICE	8,762 24 Br	04/07/43	U 375	700 tons stores, 11 dead
KMS 18B	DEVIS	6,054 38 Br	05/07/43	U 593	4,000 tons stores. 52 dead
KMS 18B	ST ESSYLT	5,634 41 Br	04/07/43	U 375	900 tons stores. 1 dead
KMS 26	RICHARD OLNEY	7,191 43 Amer	22/09/43	MINED	Towed Bizerta, CTL. 2 dead
KMS 27	STANMORE	4,970 40 Br	02/10/43	U 223	2,500 tons stores. No dead
KMS 30	MONT VISO	4,531 21 Fr	03/11/43	U 593	Cargo & dead unknown.
KMS 31	BIRCHBANK	5,151 24 Br	11/11/43	AIRCRAFT	9,000 tons general & stores. 2 dead
KMS 31	CARLIER	7,217 15 Bel	11/11/43	AIRCRAFT	6,200 tons general & stores. 72 dead
KMS 31	INDIAN PRINCE	6,376 26 Br	11/11/43	AIRCRAFT	5,900 tons stores. 1 dead
KMS 31	NIVOSE	8,500 32 Fr	11/11/43	AIRCRAFT	11,000 tons FFO. Dead unknown
KMS 37	DANIEL WEBSTER	7,176 43 Amer	10/01/44	AIRCRAFT	Army stores. No dead.
KMS 37	OCEAN HUNTER	7,178 42 Br	10/01/44	AIRCRAFT	Gen & stores. No dead
KMS 51	NORDEFLINGE	2,873 42 Br	30/05/44	AIRCRAFT	3,682 tons coal. 12 dead
KMS 76G	BLACKHEATH	4,637 36 Br	10/01/45	U 870	General, stores. No dead

Courtesy National Archives of Canada

HMCS KAPUSKASING, a unit of the "ALGERINE" class minesweeper type. RCN vessels of this class were widely employed in the Western Escort Force out of St John's NF and Halifax southward to New York. This photograph is titled by NAC "with convoy June 1945." This is unlikely, the ships are light and therefore westbound, and the last westbound escort duty by KAPUSKASING was with ONS 46 in April 1945, and onwards to Boston in the appropriate XB convoy.

◇ THE ALLIED CONVOY SYSTEM 1939-1945

The KMF/MKF convoy series 1942-1945

The assault convoy taking personnel ships to the Algerian coast for the Operation Torch landings in October 1942 was titled KMF 1 and, when separated into two sections for the Oran and Algiers landings, assumed the suffix O and A as appropriate. Subsequent KMF convoys contained personnel ships and fast MT ships carrying reinforcements for the initial landings.

As the campaign in North Africa proceeded, finally resulting in the surrender of Axis forces in Africa, personnel ships under the KMF designation were able to proceed further east. Eventually the reduced risk from attack following the enemy defeat in North Africa became acceptable, and loaded personnel ships passed through the area to Port Said. This resulted in the suspension of the WS series and the inclusion in KMF convoys of ships for India.

It was quite normal for convoys within the Mediterranean passage to be joined by vessels in transit between North African ports. The numbers of ships in convoy quoted in the following table relates, therefore, only to the North Atlantic passage to the Gibraltar Strait.

The convoy code for the entire passage remained KMF; the ships named in the table of losses that follows the convoy data were all lost in the Mediterranean.

Troopships returning from the initial landings, and subsequent reinforcement, adopted the reversal code MKF. When convoys began to operate direct to Port Said, this code was used for personnel ships from the Indian Ocean and within the Mediterranean, generally when returning to the UK; this included part passages within the Mediterranean. As noted in the preceding paragraph, the suffix "G" has been added to denote losses in the Atlantic, otherwise they may be assumed to be in the Mediterranean.

▪ Courtesy Air Historical Branch, MoD (Crown Copyright)

Convoy KMF 1 en route to the invasion of North Africa in Nov 1942. An interesting photograph of one of the larger troop convoys of World War II, and one which escaped the notice of both German Intelligence, BdU and the U-boats at sea. Only one attack was made, on the day prior to the assault, in which the troopship THOMAS STONE was damaged.

◇ 172

KMF convoy data

CONVOY	DEP. PORT	DEP. DATE	ARRIVAL PORT	ARR. DATE	TDS	MV SUNK	MV DMGD
KMF 1	CLYDE	26/10/42	ORAN	08/11/42	39	1	
KMF 2	CLYDE	01/11/42	ALGIERS	12/11/42	17		
KMF 3	CLYDE	14/11/42	ALGIERS	23/11/42	18		1
KMF 4	CLYDE	27/11/42	BONE	07/12/42	26		
KMF 5	CLYDE	12/12/42	GIBRALTAR	20/12/42	12		
KMF 5A	GIBRALTAR	20/12/42	ALGIERS	22/12/42		1	
KMF 6	CLYDE	26/12/42	ALGIERS	03/01/43	9		
KMF 7	CLYDE	08/01/43	ALGIERS	17/01/43	10		
KMF 8	CLYDE	24/01/43	ALGIERS	01/02/43	8		
KMF 9	CLYDE	08/02/43	ALGIERS	16/02/43	5		
KMF 10A	CLYDE	25/02/43	ALGIERS	04/03/43	6		
KMF 10B	CLYDE	02/03/43	ALGIERS	09/03/43	8		
KMF 11	CLYDE	15/03/43	ALGIERS	23/03/43	9	1	
KMF 11X	ALGIERS	24/03/43	BONE	25/03/43			
KMF 13	CLYDE	16/04/43	ALGIERS	23/04/43	11		
KMF 15	CLYDE	19/05/43	ALGIERS	28/05/43	12		
KMF 7	CLYDE	18/06/43	ALGIERS	27/06/43	8		
KMF 18	CLYDE	28/06/43	SICILY, OP HUSKY	11/07/43	13		
KMF 19	CLYDE	01/07/43	ALGIERS	09/07/43	8		
KMF 19A	ALGIERS	09/07/43	MALTA	13/07/43			
KMF 20	CLYDE	19/07/43	ALGIERS	28/07/43	8		
KMF 20A	ALGIERS	28/07/43	JD GTX 4	31/07/43			
KMF 20B	ALGIERS	29/07/43	PHILIPEVILLE	30/07/43			
KMF 22	CLYDE	18/08/43	PORT SAID	29/08/43	20		
KMF 24	CLYDE	15/09/43	ALEXANDRIA	29/09/43	14		
KMF 25	LIVERPOOL	16/10/43	ALEXANDRIA	30/10/43	11		
KMF 25A	LIVERPOOL	27/10/43	ALEXANDRIA	11/11/43	23		
KMF 26	CLYDE	15/11/43	ALEXANDRIA	30/11/43	18		
KMF 27	CLYDE	16/12/43	PORT SAID	30/12/43	16		
KMF 28	CLYDE	15/01/44	PORT SAID	30/01/44	23		
KMF 28A	CLYDE	01/02/44	ALGIERS	08/02/44	1		
KMF 29	CLYDE	21/02/44	ALEXANDRIA	05/03/44	19		
KMF 29A	CLYDE	03/03/44	ALEXANDRIA	17/03/44	1		
KMF 29B	CLYDE	14/03/44	ORAN	22/03/44	3		
KMF 30	CLYDE	29/03/44	PORT SAID	12/04/44	26		
KMF 31	CLYDE	05/05/44	PORT SAID	19/05/44	17		
KMF 32	CLYDE	11/06/44	PORT SAID	24/06/44	12		
KMF 33	CLYDE	18/07/44	PORT SAID	31/07/44	17		
KMF 34	CLYDE	24/08/44	PORT SAID	07/09/44	14		
KMF 35	CLYDE	01/10/44	PORT SAID	11/10/44	16		
KMF 35A	CLYDE	20/10/44	PORT SAID	31/10/44	6		
KMF 36	CLYDE	06/11/44	ALEXANDRIA	19/11/44	20		
KMF 37	CLYDE	16/12/44	GIBRALTAR	21/12/44	15		
KMF 37A	CLYDE	20/12/44	GIBRALTAR	24/12/44	1		
KMF 38	CLYDE	05/01/45	GIBRALTAR	10/01/45	10		
KMF 38A	CLYDE	16/01/45	GIBRALTAR	23/01/45	1		
KMF 39	CLYDE	28/01/45	GIBRALTAR	04/02/45	17		
KMF 40	LIVERPOOL	18/02/45	GIBRALTAR	24/02/45	12		
KMF 41	CLYDE	10/03/45	GIBRALTAR	17/03/45	16		
KMF 42	CLYDE	31/03/45	GIBRALTAR	07/04/45	16		
KMF 43	CLYDE	17/04/45	GIBRALTAR	23/04/45	13		
KMF 44	CLYDE	05/05/45	GIBRALTAR	11/05/45	10		
KMF 45	CLYDE	23/05/45	DISPERSED 47.56N 08.39W	24/05/45	14		

Author's collection

The USN transport THOMAS STONE was a unit of convoy KMF 1, intended to land her troops at Algiers in the first wave of the assault. However, during the approach she was torpedoed on 7 Nov 1942 and disabled. The commander of the US troops onboard, determined to take his appointed part in the landings, requested that the landing craft (the ship carried 24 LCAs) be lowered and ordered his troops to embark. They set off on a 140 mile journey escorted by the frigate HMS SPEY, unfortunately heavy seas and breakdowns caused all except two to be sunk. The troops were embarked in SPEY and finally arrived at Algiers some hours behind schedule, tired, no doubt seasick, but triumphant.

THOMAS STONE was taken in tow by the destroyer HMS WISHART and eventually beached off Algiers where she is seen in this photograph. She was the only actual casualty prior to the initial landings; eventually handed over to the French Navy in 1943 she was utilised as a hulk at Algiers.

Losses incurred in KMF convoys, excluding stragglers

Convoy	Ship's Name	GRT			Date of loss	Cause of loss	Comments
KMF 1	THOMAS STONE	7,191	42	Amer	07/11/42	AIRCRAFT	800 troops. No dead. CTL
KMF 5A	STRATHALLAN	23,722	38	Br	22/12/42	U 562	4,691 troops. 6 crew dead
KMF 11	WINDSOR CASTLE	19,141	22	Br	22/03/43	AIRCRAFT	2,699 troops. 1 crew dead
KMF 25A	SANTA ELENA	9,135	33	Amer	06/11/43	AIRCRAFT	1,965 troops & nurses. 4 dead

Convoy	Ship's Name	GRT			Date of loss	Cause of loss	Comments
KMF 25A	MARNIX VAN ST ALDEGONDE	19,335	30	Du	06/11/43	AIRCRAFT	2,924 troops. No dead
KMF 26	ROHNA	8,602	26	Br	26/11/43	AIRCRAFT	2,000 US troops. 1,149 dead

Note: All KMF losses sustained in the Mediterranean.

MKF convoy data

CONVOY	DEP. PORT	DEP. DATE	ARRIVAL PORT	ARR. DATE	TDS	MV SUNK	MV DMGD
MKF 1	ALGIERS	12/11/42	GIBRALTAR	15/11/42			
MKF 1A	ALGIERS	13/11/42	GIBRALTAR	14/11/42			
MKF 10	ORAN	13/11/42	GIBRALTAR	14/11/42			
MKF 1X	GIBRALTAR	12/11/42	CLYDE	19/11/42	11	1	
MKF 1Y	GIBRALTAR	14/11/42	CLYDE	20/11/42	8	1	
MKF 2	ALGIERS	15/11/42	CLYDE	23/11/42	15		
MKF 3	ALGIERS	23/11/42	CLYDE	03/12/42	16		
MKF 4	ALGIERS	10/12/42	CLYDE	18/12/42	15		
MKF 4Y	BONE	11/12/42	CLYDE	24/12/42	6		
MKF 5	ALGIERS	24/12/42	CLYDE	31/12/42	8		
MKF 6	PHILIPEVILLE	05/01/43	CLYDE	14/01/43	7		
MKF 7	ALGIERS	18/01/43	DISPERSED	25/01/43	9		
MKF 8	ALGIERS	02/02/43	CLYDE	09/02/43	7		
MKF 9	ALGIERS	17/02/43	CLYDE	24/02/43	5		
MKF 10A	ALGIERS	06/03/43	CLYDE	14/03/42	10		
MKF 10B	ALGIERS	10/03/43	CLYDE	17/03/43	4		
MKF 11	BONE	26/03/43	CLYDE	05/04/43	11		
MKF 11A	GIBRALTAR	05/04/43	LIVERPOOL	12/04/43	4		
MKF 13	ALGIERS	24/04/43	CLYDE	02/05/43	14		
MKF 15	ALGIERS	28/05/43	CLYDE	05/06/43	19		
MKF 17	ALGIERS	28/06/43	GIBRALTAR	30/06/43			
MKF 17A	PORT SAID	05/07/43	GIBRALTAR	17/07/43			
MKF 18	SICILY	10/07/43	CLYDE	23/07/43	13		
MKF 19	GIBRALTAR	24/07/43	CLYDE	30/07/43	11		
MKF 19Y	MALTA	20/07/43	GIBRALTAR	23/07/43			
MKF 20	ALGIERS	31/07/43	CLYDE	11/08/43	4		
MKF 22	PORT SAID	19/08/43	CLYDE	09/09/43	9		
MKF 24	PORT SAID	17/09/43	CLYDE	07/10/43	12		
MKF 24A	GIBRALTAR	12/10/43	LOCH EWE	18/10/43	2		
MKF 25	PORT SAID	17/10/43	CLYDE	04/11/43	25		
MKF 25A	PORT SAID	31/10/43	CLYDE	24/11/43	21		
MKF 26	PORT SAID	17/11/43	LIVERPOOL	09/12/43	25		
MKF 27	PORT SAID	16/12/43	LIVERPOOL	04/01/44	12		
MKF 27A	PORT SAID	15/01/44	LIVERPOOL	27/01/44	2		
MKF 28	PORT SAID	20/01/44	LIVERPOOL	07/02/44	13		
MKF 28A	PORT SAID	03/02/44	LIVERPOOL	20/02/44	3		
MKF 29	PORT SAID	02/03/44	LIVERPOOL	16/03/44	22		
MKF 29A	GIBRALTAR	23/03/44	CLYDE	29/03/44	5		
MKF 29B	ALGIERS	08/04/44	LIVERPOOL	17/04/44	1		
MKF 30	PORT SAID	08/04/44	LIVERPOOL	21/04/44	10		
MKF 31	PORT SAID	15/05/44	LIVERPOOL	29/05/44	15		
MKF 32	PORT SAID	21/06/44	LIVERPOOL	04/07/44	13		
MKF 33	PORT SAID	28/07/44	LIVERPOOL	11/08/44	16		
MKF 34	PORT SAID	03/09/44	LIVERPOOL	14/09/44	17		
MKF 35	PORT SAID	10/10/44	LIVERPOOL	21/10/44	17		
MKF 35A	MARSEILLES	20/10/44	LIVERPOOL	02/11/44	1		
MKF 36	PORT SAID	16/11/44	LIVERPOOL	30/11/44	15		
MKF 36A	GIBRALTAR	24/12/44	LIVERPOOL	29/12/44	1		
MKF 37	GIBRALTAR	01/01/45	LIVERPOOL	06/01/45	14		
MKF 38	GIBRALTAR	21/01/45	CLYDE	27/01/45	7		
MKF 39	GIBRALTAR	14/02/45	LIVERPOOL	20/02/45	17		
MKF 40	GIBRALTAR	06/03/45	LIVERPOOL	12/03/45	13		
MKF 41	GIBRALTAR	25/03/45	LIVERPOOL	30/03/45	11		
MKF 42	GIBRALTAR	12/04/45	LIVERPOOL	17/04/45	14		
MKF 43	GIBRALTAR	29/04/45	LIVERPOOL	05/05/45	15		
MKF 44	GIBRALTAR	17/05/45	LIVERPOOL	22/05/45	13		
MKF 45	GIBRALTAR	04/06/45	LIVERPOOL	08/06/45	11		

Losses incurred in MKF convoys, excluding stragglers

Convoy	Ship's Name	GRT			Date of loss	Cause of loss	Comments
MKF 1XG	WARWICK CASTLE	20,107	30	Br	14/11/42	U 413	Red Ensign LSI(L) in ballast. 62 dead

Convoy	Ship's Name	GRT			Date of loss	Cause of loss	Comments
MKF 1YG	ETTRICK	11,279	38	Br	15/11/42	U 155	Red Ensign LSI(L) in ballast. 24 dead

Note: Both MKF losses sustained in the Atlantic.

OG convoy series 1939-1943

The OG series was a hybrid; originally it was formed southwest of Land's End by the junction of OA and OB convoys of the same number (or significant portions thereof), which then proceeded to Gibraltar. At first these convoys included ships for the Iberian Peninsula, the Mediterranean and Ports beyond Suez and, for part of the voyage, ships for the Caribbean and South America, which detached en route.

As the speed of many of the smaller vessels in the Iberian trade did not approach the 9-knot minimum limit, it was the practice to sail Fast convoys alternately; these were suffixed F. The system ceased after OB 37 when the series became almost exclusively for Gibraltar and adjacent ports due to the entry of Italy to the war and also the German occupation of northern and western France.

Up to this time the escort of both OG and HG convoys was also hybrid. After the juncture of the OA and OB portions of the convoy, the escort of one of the two original convoys continued southward with OG, the other returning to its base or joining an inward bound convoy. The OG escort was relieved south of Ushant by French vessels, which took the convoy on to the vicinity of Gibraltar, where a local escort from the Flotilla stationed there joined. Not infrequently the French ships remained with the convoy to Gibraltar itself.

After OG 37, when the use of the Channel and the southern exit from the Irish Sea ceased, OG convoys formed and sailed as such from Liverpool via the North Channel. The series ceased in August 1942, prior to Operation Torch (the North African invasion), and briefly resumed in 1943. However, these few late OG convoys sailed in conjunction with either KMS or KX convoys and were simply the Gibraltar contingent of them. While they are listed in the tables that follow so far as dates are concerned, their statistics are included in the relevant KX and KMS convoys. The relevant KX and KMS numbers are suffixed to OG in the table.

After July 1940, the sailings from Liverpool occasionally included ships for North America; such vessels detached early in the passage as they made use of the convoy protection for only a few days.

Considering that most of the convoys passage was within the operational range of French based aircraft and the convoys speed frequently below that of even the slowest Atlantic convoy, it is remarkable how small the number of losses was. Only two convoys incurred in excess of five ships sunk, but they did include heavy passenger losses.

OG convoy data

CONVOY	DEP. PORT	DEP. DATE	ARRIVAL PORT	ARR. DATE	TDS	MV SUNK	MV DMGD
OG 1	FORMED AT SEA	02/10/39	GIBRALTAR	08/10/39	37		
OG 2	FORMED AT SEA	11/10/39	GIBRALTAR	17/10/39	34		
OG 3	FORMED AT SEA	17/10/39	GIBRALTAR	23/10/39	30		
OG 4	FORMED AT SEA	26/10/39	PORT SAID	08/11/39	41		
OG 5	FORMED AT SEA	03/11/39	GIBRALTAR	09/11/39	34		
OG 6	FORMED AT SEA	11/11/39	GIBRALTAR	16/11/39	32		
OG 7	FORMED AT SEA	17/11/39	GIBRALTAR	24/11/39	38		
OG 8	FORMED AT SEA	26/11/39	GIBRALTAR	03/12/39	42		
OG 9	FORMED AT SEA	05/12/39	GIBRALTAR	11/12/39	50		
OG 10	FORMED AT SEA	13/12/39	GIBRALTAR	18/12/39	56		
OG 11	FORMED AT SEA	21/12/39	GIBRALTAR	26/12/39	43		
OG 12	FORMED AT SEA	28/12/39	GIBRALTAR	04/01/40	37		
OG 13	FORMED AT SEA	06/01/40	GIBRALTAR	12/01/40	37		
OG 13F	MILFORD HAVEN	01/01/40	GIBRALTAR	07/01/40	23		
OG 14	FORMED AT SEA	14/01/40	GIBRALTAR	19/01/40	42		
OG 14F	FORMED AT SEA	10/01/40	GIBRALTAR	15/01/40	23		
OG 15	FORMED AT SEA	21/01/40	GIBRALTAR	27/01/40	50		
OG 15F	FORMED AT SEA	18/01/40	GIBRALTAR	23/01/40	20		
OG 16	FORMED AT SEA	31/01/40	GIBRALTAR	05/02/40	37	1	
OG 16F	FORMED AT SEA	26/01/40	GIBRALTAR	01/02/40	23		
OG 17	FORMED AT SEA	06/02/40	GIBRALTAR	13/02/40	23		
OG 17F	FORMED AT SEA	03/02/40	GIBRALTAR	09/02/40	26		
OG 18	FORMED AT SEA	15/02/40	GIBRALTAR	22/02/40	45	1	
OG 18F	FORMED AT SEA	11/02/40	GIBRALTAR	17/02/40	30		
OG 19	FORMED AT SEA	23/02/40	GIBRALTAR	29/02/40	34		
OG 19F	FORMED AT SEA	19/02/40	GIBRALTAR	25/02/40	34	1	
OG 20	FORMED AT SEA	01/03/40	GIBRALTAR	07/03/40	32		
OG 20F	FORMED AT SEA	27/02/40	GIBRALTAR	04/03/40	38		
OG 21	FORMED AT SEA	11/03/40	GIBRALTAR	17/03/40	29		
OG 21F	FORMED AT SEA	05/03/40	GIBRALTAR	11/03/40	45		
OG 22	FORMED AT SEA	18/03/40	GIBRALTAR	24/03/40	49		
OG 22F	FORMED AT SEA	13/03/40	GIBRALTAR	19/03/40	30		
OG 23	FORMED AT SEA	25/03/40	GIBRALTAR	31/03/40	51		
OG 23F	FORMED AT SEA	21/03/40	GIBRALTAR	28/03/40	40		
OG 24	FORMED AT SEA	03/04/40	GIBRALTAR	08/04/40	54		
OG 24F	FORMED AT SEA	29/03/40	GIBRALTAR	04/04/40	28		
OG 25	FORMED AT SEA	10/04/40	GIBRALTAR	16/04/40	49		
OG 25F	FORMED AT SEA	06/04/40	GIBRALTAR	12/04/40	57		
OG 26	FORMED AT SEA	18/04/40	GIBRALTAR	25/04/40	55		
OG 26F	FORMED AT SEA	14/04/40	GIBRALTAR	20/04/40	54		
OG 27	FORMED AT SEA	26/04/40	GIBRALTAR	03/05/40	51		
OG 27F	FORMED AT SEA	22/04/40	GIBRALTAR	28/04/40	60		
OG 28	FORMED AT SEA	05/05/40	GIBRALTAR	10/05/40	51		
OG 28F	FORMED AT SEA	01/05/40	GIBRALTAR	06/05/40	46		
OG 29	FORMED AT SEA	12/05/40	GIBRALTAR	18/05/40	50		
OG 29F	FORMED AT SEA	09/05/40	GIBRALTAR	14/05/40	56		

CONVOY	DEP. PORT	DEP. DATE	ARRIVAL PORT	ARR. DATE	TDS	MV SUNK	MV DMGD	CONVOY	DEP. PORT	DEP. DATE	ARRIVAL PORT	ARR. DATE	TDS	MV SUNK	MV DMGD
OG 30	FORMED AT SEA	19/05/40	GIBRALTAR	26/05/40	40			OG 63	LIVERPOOL	25/05/41	GIBRALTAR	07/06/41	39	3	
OG 30F	FORMED AT SEA	16/05/40	GIBRALTAR	22/05/40	44			OG 64	LIVERPOOL	04/06/41	GIBRALTAR	18/06/41	52		
OG 31	FORMED AT SEA	28/05/40	GIBRALTAR	03/06/40	40			OG 65	LIVERPOOL	14/06/41	GIBRALTAR	28/06/41	64		
OG 31F	FORMED AT SEA	25/05/40	GIBRALTAR	30/05/40	55			OG 66	LIVERPOOL	24/06/41	GIBRALTAR	08/07/41	55		
OG 32	FORMED AT SEA	05/06/40	GIBRALTAR	11/06/40	37			OG 67	LIVERPOOL	04/07/41	GIBRALTAR	20/07/41	51		
OG 32F	FORMED AT SEA	02/06/40	GIBRALTAR	07/06/40	42			OG 68	LIVERPOOL	12/07/41	GIBRALTAR	26/07/41	33		
OG 33	FORMED AT SEA	13/06/40	GIBRALTAR	19/06/40	31			OG 69	LIVERPOOL	20/07/41	GIBRALTAR	01/08/41	27	7	
OG 33F	FORMED AT SEA	09/06/40	GIBRALTAR	14/06/40	53		1	OG 70	LIVERPOOL	30/07/41	GIBRALTAR	12/08/41	30		
OG 34	FORMED AT SEA	21/06/40	GIBRALTAR	03/07/40	28			OG 71	LIVERPOOL	13/08/41	GIBRALTAR	25/08/41	21	7	
OG 34F	FORMED AT SEA	17/06/40	GIBRALTAR	24/06/40	33			OG 72	LIVERPOOL	19/08/41	GIBRALTAR	01/09/41	14		
OG 35	FORMED AT SEA	27/06/40	GIBRALTAR	01/07/40	15			OG 73	LIVERPOOL	29/08/41	GIBRALTAR	13/09/41	21		
OG 36	FORMED AT SEA	03/07/40	GIBRALTAR	09/07/40	34			OG 74	LIVERPOOL	12/09/41	GIBRALTAR	27/09/41	22	3	
OG 37	FORMED AT SEA	12/07/40	GIBRALTAR	17/07/40	15			OG 75	LIVERPOOL	27/09/41	GIBRALTAR	13/10/41	21		
OG 38	LIVERPOOL	17/07/40	GIBRALTAR	29/07/40	20			OG 76	LIVERPOOL	28/10/41	GIBRALTAR	11/11/41	22		
OG 39	LIVERPOOL	26/07/40	GIBRALTAR	06/08/40	21			OG 77	LIVERPOOL	25/11/41	GIBRALTAR	13/12/41	22		
OG 40	LIVERPOOL	03/08/40	GIBRALTAR	14/08/40	21			OG 78	LIVERPOOL	10/01/42	GIBRALTAR	24/01/42	26		
OG 41	LIVERPOOL	19/08/40	GIBRALTAR	02/09/40	30			OG 79	LIVERPOOL	26/01/42	GIBRALTAR	07/02/42	21		
OG 42	LIVERPOOL	04/09/40	GIBRALTAR	16/09/40	51			OG 80	LIVERPOOL	23/02/42	GIBRALTAR	08/03/42	28		
OG 43	LIVERPOOL	20/09/40	GIBRALTAR	03/10/40	46			OG 81	LIVERPOOL	17/03/42	GIBRALTAR	29/03/42	22		
OG 44	LIVERPOOL	11/10/40	GIBRALTAR	24/10/40	36			OG 82	LIVERPOOL	08/04/42	GIBRALTAR	20/04/42	17		
OG 45	LIVERPOOL	30/10/40	GIBRALTAR	11/11/40	27			OG 83	LIVERPOOL	30/04/42	GIBRALTAR	11/05/42	23		
OG 46	LIVERPOOL	18/11/40	GIBRALTAR	05/12/40	39	1		OG 84	LIVERPOOL	21/05/42	GIBRALTAR	02/06/42	21		
OG 47	LIVERPOOL	09/12/40	GIBRALTAR	25/12/40	30	1		OG 85	LIVERPOOL	13/06/42	GIBRALTAR	25/06/42	22		
OG 48	LIVERPOOL	29/12/40	GIBRALTAR	09/01/41	29			OG 86	LIVERPOOL	02/07/42	GIBRALTAR	14/07/42	20		
OG 49	LIVERPOOL	07/01/41	GIBRALTAR	21/01/41	5			OG 87	LIVERPOOL	20/07/42	GIBRALTAR	03/08/42	15		
OG 50	LIVERPOOL	16/01/41	GIBRALTAR	31/01/41	12			OG 88	LIVERPOOL	11/08/42	GIBRALTAR	24/08/42	21		
OG 51	LIVERPOOL	26/01/41	GIBRALTAR	08/02/41	19		1	OG 89	LIVERPOOL	31/08/42	GIBRALTAR	14/09/42	20		
OG 52	LIVERPOOL	05/02/41	GIBRALTAR	21/02/41	45			OG 90/KX 10	LIVERPOOL	20/05/43	GIBRALTAR	31/05/43			
OG 53	LIVERPOOL	15/02/41	GIBRALTAR	01/03/41	44			OG 91/KMS 22	LIVERPOOL	28/07/43	GIBRALTAR	09/08/43			
OG 54	LIVERPOOL	25/02/41	GIBRALTAR	14/03/41	43			OG 92/KMS 24	LIVERPOOL	17/08/43	GIBRALTAR	30/08/43			
OG 55	LIVERPOOL	07/03/41	GIBRALTAR	21/03/41	42			OG 93/KMS 26	LIVERPOOL	05/09/43	GIBRALTAR	19/09/43			
OG 56	LIVERPOOL	17/03/41	GIBRALTAR	02/04/41	35			OG 94/KMS 28	LIVERPOOL	26/09/43	GIBRALTAR	09/10/43			
OG 57	LIVERPOOL	27/03/41	GIBRALTAR	11/04/41	37			OG 95/KMS 30	LIVERPOOL	17/10/43	GIBRALTAR	01/11/43			
OG 58	LIVERPOOL	06/04/41	GIBRALTAR	21/04/41	47										
OG 59	LIVERPOOL	15/04/41	GIBRALTAR	28/04/41	44										
OG 60	LIVERPOOL	26/04/41	GIBRALTAR	10/05/41	35										
OG 61	LIVERPOOL	05/05/41	GIBRALTAR	19/05/41	42										
OG 62	LIVERPOOL	15/05/41	GIBRALTAR	29/05/41	31										

Losses incurred in OG convoys, excluding stragglers

Convoy	Ship's Name	GRT			Date of loss	Cause of loss	Comments
OG 16	ARMANISTAN	6,805	37	Br	03/02/40	U 25	8,300 tons general. No dead
OG 18	PYRRHUS	7,418	14	Br	17/02/40	U 37	4,000 tons general. 8 dead
OG 19F	BRITISH ENDEAVOUR	4,580	27	Br	22/02/40	U 50	Ballast. 5 dead
OG 45	GARTBRATTAN	1,811	31	Br	05/11/40	COLLISION	Coal. No dead. Collision with MELROSE PARK
OG 46	JEANNE M	2,465	19	Br	02/12/40	U 37	3,200 tons coal. 7 dead
OG 47	MANGEN	1,253	22	Sw	20/12/40	MOCENIGO. It S/M	1,396 tons coal. 8 dead
OG 53	JESSMORE	4,099	21	Br	21/02/41	COLLISION	General. No dead

Convoy	Ship's Name	GRT			Date of loss	Cause of loss	Comments
OG 63	BARON LOVAT	3,395	26	Br	06/06/41	MARCONI. It S/M	3,245 tons coke. No dead
OG 63	GLEN HEAD	2,011	09	Br	06/06/41	AIRCRAFT	600 tons coal, 200 tons general. 27 dead
OG 63	TABERG	1,392	20	Sw	06/06/41	MARCONI. It S/M	Ballast. 15 dead
OG 69	ERATO	1,335	23	Br	27/07/41	U 126	1,200 tons stores, 732 tons gen. 9 dead
OG 69	HAWKINGE	2,475	24	Br	27/07/41	U 203	2,806 tons coal. 15 dead
OG 69	INGA I	1,304	21	Nor	27/07/41	U 126	1,670 tons coal & coke. 3 dead

Convoy	Ship's Name	GRT			Date of loss	Cause of loss	Comments
OG 69	KELLWYN	1,459	20	Br	27/07/41	U 79	1,100 tons coke. 14 dead
OG 69	LAPLAND	1,330	36	Br	28/07/41	U 203	950 tons tinplate & general. No dead
OG 69	NORITA	1,615	24	Sw	28/07/41	U 203	1,500 tons coke & general. 2 dead
OG 69	WROTHAM	1,884	27	Br	28/07/41	U 561	Ballast. No dead
OG 71	AGUILA	3,255	17	Br	19/08/41	U 201	1,288 tons general & 91 pass. 156 dead
OG 71	ALDERGROVE	1,974	18	Br	22/08/41	U 201	2,650 tons patent fuel. 1 dead
OG 71	ALVA	1,584	34	Br	19/08/41	U 559	2,300 tons coal. 16 dead
OG 71	CISCAR	1,808	19	Br	19/08/41	U 201	1,400 tons general & stores. 18 dead
OG 71	CLONLARA	1,203	26	Br	22/08/41	U 564	1,000 tons coal. 11 dead
OG 71	EMPIRE OAK	482	41	Br	22/08/41	U 564	Tug. 14 dead +9 survivors from ALVA
OG 71	STORK	787	37	Br	23/08/41	U 201	Petrol. 19 dead
OG 74	BALTALLINN	1,303	20	Br	20/09/41	U 124	442 tons stores. 8 dead plus 10 more in WALMER CASTLE
OG 74	CITY OF WATERFORD	1,017	79	Br	19/09/41	COLLISION	Coal. 5 dead in WALMER CASTLE. Collision with THAMES
OG 74	EMPIRE MOAT	2,922	41	Br	20/09/41	U 124	Ballast. 5 dead in WALMER CASTLE.
OG 74	WALMER CASTLE	906	36	Br	21/09/41	AIRCRAFT	11 plus 20 survivors dead

HG convoy series 1939-1942

The HG series was also a hybrid. Anticipating that Italy would follow its German partner in declaring war in 1939, the C-in-C Mediterranean had instituted convoy from Port Said to Gibraltar, these being titled "GREEN" and numbered. This practice ceased in November 1939 and the next three convoys took the HG sequence of numbers as HG 7 to HG 9, their predecessors HG 1 to HG 6 having sailed from Gibraltar. Convoy then ceased in the Mediterranean, the HG series thereafter again originated at Gibraltar starting with HG 10.

At first the convoys divided off Ushant with the Thames and East Coast portion proceeding to the Downs; the balance entered the Irish Sea via St George's Channel. This practice ceased with the surrender of France in June 1940; thereafter the whole convoy went west of Ireland and used the North Channel entrance to the Irish Sea. Ships for the East Coast were detached to Oban and joined the coastal convoy system there.

Alternate convoys were suffixed F and sailed as Fast convoys, the practice ceasing when the Mediterranean was closed to traffic after June 1940. On certain occasions additional convoys, under the title SL numeral G, were sailed from Gibraltar to meet and proceed with an SL convoy. Indeed, sometimes they absorbed the SL ships and proceeded under their SLG designation.

As with the OG convoys, the HG series until June 1940 was frequently escorted from Gibraltar by French warships until the vicinity of Ushant, when British escorts took over. 13th Destroyer Flotilla, based at Gibraltar, also escorted during the early stage of the passage. After the French collapse, an all British escort accompanied the convoys throughout their passage. The series ceased prior to the North African invasion and did not restart; instead the newly introduced MKS series handled the post Operation Torch Mediterranean to the UK traffic.

The curious use of HG 34F for a convoy designation in August 41, when that number had already been used in its correct sequence in June 1940, should be noted. For record purposes it has been designated here as 34FA. The reason for the odd duplication is unknown. It may have been allocated by the NCS staff at Gibraltar who might, due to relief of personnel, not have been aware of its previous use.

HG convoy data

CONVOY	DEP. PORT	DEP. DATE	ARRIVAL PORT	ARR. DATE	TDS	MV SUNK	MV DMGD
HG 1	GIBRALTAR	26/09/39	LIVERPOOL	06/10/39	28		
HG 1F	GIBRALTAR	26/09/39	LIVERPOOL	01/10/39	4		
HG 2	GIBRALTAR	05/10/39	UK PORTS	13/10/39	13		
HG 2F	GIBRALTAR	05/10/39	LIVERPOOL	09/10/39	2		
HG 3	GIBRALTAR	13/10/39	LIVERPOOL	21/10/39	25		
HG 4	GIBRALTAR	22/10/39	UK PORTS	29/10/39	41		
HG 5	GIBRALTAR	29/10/39	UK PORTS	06/11/39	40		
HG 6	GIBRALTAR	06/11/39	UK PORTS	14/11/39	36		
HG 7	PORT SAID	03/11/39	LIVERPOOL	22/11/39	32		
HG 8	PORT SAID	11/11/39	LIVERPOOL	30/11/39	38		
HG 9	PORT SAID	19/11/39	LIVERPOOL	08/12/39	52		
HG 10	GIBRALTAR	08/12/39	LIVERPOOL	16/12/39	62		
HG 11	GIBRALTAR	16/12/39	LIVERPOOL	24/12/39	52		
HG 12	GIBRALTAR	24/12/39	LIVERPOOL	02/01/40	48		
HG 13	GIBRALTAR	31/12/39	LIVERPOOL	10/01/40	28		
HG 13F	GIBRALTAR	29/12/39	LIVERPOOL	05/01/40	10		
HG 14	GIBRALTAR	08/01/40	LIVERPOOL	17/01/40	33		
HG 14F	GIBRALTAR	05/01/40	LIVERPOOL	15/01/40	15		

◇ THE ALLIED CONVOY SYSTEM 1939-1945

CONVOY	DEP. PORT	DEP. DATE	ARRIVAL PORT	ARR. DATE	TDS	MV SUNK	MV DMGD
HG 15	GIBRALTAR	16/01/40	LIVERPOOL	25/01/40	37		
HG 15F	GIBRALTAR	13/01/40	LIVERPOOL	22/01/40	13		
HG 16	GIBRALTAR	24/01/40	LIVERPOOL	03/02/40	42		
HG 16F	GIBRALTAR	21/01/40	LIVERPOOL	28/01/40	15		
HG 17	GIBRALTAR	01/02/40	LIVERPOOL	11/02/40	20		
HG 17F	GIBRALTAR	29/01/40	LIVERPOOL	07/02/40	25		
HG 18	GIBRALTAR	09/02/40	LIVERPOOL	19/02/40	36		
HG 18F	GIBRALTAR	06/02/40	LIVERPOOL	15/02/40	32		
HG 19	GIBRALTAR	17/02/40	LIVERPOOL	27/02/40	36		
HG 19F	GIBRALTAR	14/02/40	LIVERPOOL	23/02/40	25		
HG 20	GIBRALTAR	25/02/40	LIVERPOOL	06/03/40	37		
HG 20F	GIBRALTAR	22/02/40	LIVERPOOL	03/03/40	30		
HG 21	GIBRALTAR	04/03/40	LIVERPOOL	13/03/40	36		
HG 21F	GIBRALTAR	01/03/40	LIVERPOOL	10/03/40	36		
HG 22	GIBRALTAR	12/03/40	LIVERPOOL	22/03/40	38		
HG 22F	GIBRALTAR	09/03/40	LIVERPOOL	18/03/40	30		
HG 23	GIBRALTAR	20/03/40	LIVERPOOL	30/03/40	36		
HG 23F	GIBRALTAR	17/03/40	LIVERPOOL	26/03/40	30		
HG 24	GIBRALTAR	28/03/40	LIVERPOOL	07/04/40	41		
HG 24F	GIBRALTAR	25/03/40	LIVERPOOL	03/04/40	22		
HG 25	GIBRALTAR	05/04/40	LIVERPOOL	15/04/40	37		
HG 25F	GIBRALTAR	02/04/40	LIVERPOOL	11/04/40	23		
HG 26	GIBRALTAR	13/04/40	LIVERPOOL	23/04/40	33		
HG 26F	GIBRALTAR	10/04/40	LIVERPOOL	19/04/40	17		
HG 27	GIBRALTAR	21/04/40	DOWNS	01/05/40	31		
HG 27F	GIBRALTAR	18/04/40	LIVERPOOL	27/04/40	26		
HG 28	GIBRALTAR	29/04/40	LIVERPOOL	09/05/40	25		
HG 28F	GIBRALTAR	26/04/40	LIVERPOOL	05/05/40	40		
HG 29	GIBRALTAR	07/05/40	LIVERPOOL	17/05/40	45		
HG 29F	GIBRALTAR	04/05/40	LIVERPOOL	13/05/40	47		
HG 30	GIBRALTAR	15/05/40	LIVERPOOL	25/05/40	27		
HG 30F	GIBRALTAR	12/05/40	LIVERPOOL	20/05/40	42		
HG 31	GIBRALTAR	23/05/40	LIVERPOOL	02/06/40	22	1	
HG 31F	GIBRALTAR	20/05/40	LIVERPOOL	29/05/40	29		
HG 32	GIBRALTAR	31/05/40	LIVERPOOL	10/06/40	24		
HG 32F	GIBRALTAR	28/05/40	LIVERPOOL	06/06/40	32		
HG 33	GIBRALTAR	08/06/40	LIVERPOOL	18/06/40	23		
HG 33F	GIBRALTAR	05/06/40	LIVERPOOL	14/06/40	41		
HG 34	GIBRALTAR	16/06/40	LIVERPOOL	26/06/40	15		
HG 34F	GIBRALTAR	13/06/40	LIVERPOOL	22/06/40	21	3	
HG 35	GIBRALTAR	21/06/40	LIVERPOOL	01/07/40	20		
HGZ	GIBRALTAR	24/06/40	JOINED SL 36	01/07/40	24		
HG 36	GIBRALTAR	28/06/40	LIVERPOOL	08/07/40	12		
HGY	GIBRALTAR	02/07/40	LIVERPOOL	14/07/40	27		
HG 37	GIBRALTAR	07/07/40	LIVERPOOL	16/07/40	22		
HG 38	GIBRALTAR	10/07/40	LIVERPOOL	27/07/40	5		
HG 39	GIBRALTAR	21/07/40	LIVERPOOL	05/08/40	18		
HG 40	GIBRALTAR	30/07/40	LIVERPOOL	14/08/40	24		
HG 40F	GIBRALTAR	27/07/40	LIVERPOOL	03/08/40	3		
HG 41	GIBRALTAR	11/08/40	LIVERPOOL	26/08/40	45		
HG 42	GIBRALTAR	20/08/40	LIVERPOOL	03/09/40	17		

CONVOY	DEP. PORT	DEP. DATE	ARRIVAL PORT	ARR. DATE	TDS	MV SUNK	MV DMGD
HG 43	GIBRALTAR	04/09/40	LIVERPOOL	18/09/40	21		
HG 44	GIBRALTAR	19/09/40	LIVERPOOL	04/10/40	28		1
HG 45	GIBRALTAR	09/10/40	LIVERPOOL	27/10/40	49		
HG 46	GIBRALTAR	31/10/40	LIVERPOOL	19/11/40	51		
HG 47	GIBRALTAR	20/11/40	LIVERPOOL	04/12/40	30		
HG 48	GIBRALTAR	09/12/40	LIVERPOOL	23/12/40	19		
HG 49	GIBRALTAR	29/12/40	LIVERPOOL	15/01/41	22	1	
HG 50	GIBRALTAR	08/01/41	LIVERPOOL	26/01/41	10	1	2
HG 51	GIBRALTAR	18/01/41	LIVERPOOL	03/02/41	14		
HG 52	GIBRALTAR	27/01/41	LIVERPOOL	15/02/41	30		
HG 53	GIBRALTAR	06/02/41	LIVERPOOL	24/02/41	21	8	
HG 54	GIBRALTAR	20/02/41	LIVERPOOL	12/03/41	25		
HG 55	GIBRALTAR	03/03/41	LIVERPOOL	22/03/41	9		
HG 56	GIBRALTAR	15/03/41	LIVERPOOL	02/04/41	25		
HG 57	GIBRALTAR	25/03/41	LIVERPOOL	11/04/41	24		
HG 58	GIBRALTAR	03/04/41	LIVERPOOL	21/04/41	24		1
HG 59	GIBRALTAR	15/04/41	LIVERPOOL	01/05/41	19		
HG 60	GIBRALTAR	24/04/41	LIVERPOOL	12/05/41	15		
HG 61	GIBRALTAR	06/05/41	LIVERPOOL	20/05/41	23	1	
HG 62	GIBRALTAR	14/05/41	LIVERPOOL	02/06/41	18		
HG 63	GIBRALTAR	25/05/41	LIVERPOOL	09/06/41	29		
HG 064	GIBRALTAR	04/06/41	LIVERPOOL	19/06/41	24		
HG 65	GIBRALTAR	14/06/41	LIVERPOOL	29/06/41	14		
HG 66	GIBRALTAR	24/06/41	LIVERPOOL	09/07/41	16		
HG 67	GIBRALTAR	08/07/41	LIVERPOOL	24/07/41	27		
HG 68	GIBRALTAR	18/07/41	LIVERPOOL	02/08/41	18		
HG 69	GIBRALTAR	28/07/41	LIVERPOOL	11/08/41	13		
HG 34FA	GIBRALTAR	06/08/41	LIVERPOOL	14/08/41	4		
HG 70	GIBRALTAR	09/08/41	LIVERPOOL	23/08/41	24		
HG 71	GIBRALTAR	18/08/41	LIVERPOOL	02/09/41	13		
HG 72	GIBRALTAR	02/09/41	LIVERPOOL	17/09/41	17		
HG 73	GIBRALTAR	17/09/41	LIVERPOOL	01/10/41	25	9	
HG 74	GIBRALTAR	02/10/41	LIVERPOOL	18/10/41	22		
HG 75	GIBRALTAR	22/10/41	LIVERPOOL	03/11/41	17	4	
HG 76	GIBRALTAR	14/12/41	LIVERPOOL	30/12/41	32	2	
HG 77	GIBRALTAR	31/12/41	LIVERPOOL	12/01/42	13		
HG 78	GIBRALTAR	02/02/42	LIVERPOOL	14/02/42	4		
HG 78A	GIBRALTAR	11/02/42	LIVERPOOL	23/02/42	2		
HG 79	GIBRALTAR	22/02/42	LIVERPOOL	06/03/42	28		
HG 80	GIBRALTAR	14/03/42	LIVERPOOL	26/03/42	14		
HG 81	GIBRALTAR	05/04/42	LIVERPOOL	15/04/42	17		
HG 82	GIBRALTAR	27/04/42	LIVERPOOL	08/05/42	29		
HG 83	GIBRALTAR	22/05/42	LIVERPOOL	03/06/42	20		
HG 84	GIBRALTAR	10/06/42	LIVERPOOL	20/06/42	23	5	
HG 85	GIBRALTAR	30/06/42	LIVERPOOL	12/07/42	20		
HG 86	GIBRALTAR	22/07/42	LIVERPOOL	01/08/42	17		
HG 87	GIBRALTAR	07/08/42	LIVERPOOL	18/08/42	23		
HG 88	GIBRALTAR	29/08/42	LIVERPOOL	09/09/42	24		
HG 89	GIBRALTAR	19/09/42	LIVERPOOL	30/09/42	19		

APPENDIX 3

Losses incurred in HG convoys, excluding stragglers

Convoy	Ship's Name	GRT			Date of loss	Cause of loss	Comments
HG 1	MAHRATTA	6,690	17	Br	06/10/39	WRECKED	Pigiron, jute, general
HG 3	CITY OF MANDALAY	7,028	25	Br	17/10/39	U 46	General. 7 dead
HG 3	CLAN CHISHOLM	7,256	37	Br	17/10/39	U 48	8,500 tons general. 4 dead
HG 3	YORKSHIRE	10,183	20	Br	17/10/39	U 37	General. 58 dead
HG 15	GLENEDEN	4,772	09	Br	25/01/40	WRECKED	3,000 tons maize. No dead
HG 31	ORANGEMOOR	5,775	23	Br	31/05/40	U 101	8,150 tons iron ore. 18 dead
HG 34F	BARON LOUDON	3,164	25	Br	19/06/40	U 48	5,050 tons iron ore. 3 dead
HG 34F	BRITISH MONARCH	5,661	23	Br	19/06/40	U 48	8,200 tons iron ore. All (40) dead
HG 34F	OTTERPOOL	4,876	26	Br	20/06/40	U 30	8,180 tons iron ore. 22 dead
HG 34F	TUDOR	6,607	30	Nor	19/06/40	U 48	4,500 tons steel. 1 dead
HG 49	BEACHY	1,600	36	Br	11/01/41	AIRCRAFT	Rescue ship. 5 dead
HG 50	MOSTYN	1,859	09	Br	23/01/41	AIRCRAFT	2,060 tons pitwood. 2 dead
HG 53	BRANDENBURG	1,473	10	Br	10/02/41	U 37	1,800 tons pyrites, sulphur. 23 dead
HG 53	BRITANNIC	2,490	18	Br	09/02/41	AIRCRAFT	3,300 tons iron ore. 1 dead
HG 53	COURLAND	1,325	32	Br	09/02/41	U 37	1,395 tons general. All (30) dead
HG 53	DAGMAR I	2,471	03	Br	09/02/41	AIRCRAFT	1,100 tons oranges & oxide. 5 dead
HG 53	ESTRELLANO	1,982	20	Br	09/02/41	U 37	2.000 tons general. 6 dead
HG 53	JURA	1,759	29	Br	09/02/41	AIRCRAFT	2,800 tons pyrites. 17 dead
HG 53	TEJO	967	16	Nor	09/02/41	AIRCRAFT	General. 4 dead
HG 53	VARNA	1,514	24	Br	09/02/41	AIRCRAFT	2,000 tons pitwood. No dead
HG 61	EMPIRE RIDGE	2,911	41	Br	19/05/41	U 96	3,500 tons iron ore. 31 dead
HG 73	AVOCETA	3,442	23	Br	26/09/41	U 203	469 tons general, 88 passengers. 123 dead
HG 73	CERVANTES	1,810	19	Br	26/09/41	U 201	500 tons potash, 400 tons cork. 8 dead
HG 73	CORTES	1,374	19	Br	26/09/41	U 124	General. 31 dead
HG 73	EMPIRE STREAM	2,911	41	Br	25/09/41	U 124	3,500 tons potash. 8 dead
HG 73	LAPWING	1,348	20	Br	26/09/41	U 203	750 tons pyrites & cork. 24 dead
HG 73	MARGARETA	3,103	04	Br	27/09/41	U 201	400 tons general. No dead
HG 73	PETREL	1,354	20	Br	26/09/41	U 124	405 tons general. 22 dead
HG 73	SIREMALM	2,468	06	Nor	27/09/41	U 201	Iron ore. All crew (27) dead
HG 73	VARANGBERG	2,842	15	Nor	26/09/41	U 203	4,100 tons iron ore. 21 dead
HG 75	ALHAMA	1,352	38	Br	24/10/41	U 563	1,940 tons general. No dead
HG 75	ARIOSTO	2,176	40	Br	24/10/41	U 564	590 tons general. 6 dead
HG 75	CARSBRECK	3,670	36	Br	24/10/41	U 564	6,000 tons iron ore. 23 dead
HG 75	ULEA	1,574	36	Br	28/10/41	U 432	2,393 tons copper pyrites. 19 dead
HG 76	ANNAVORE	3,324	21	Nor	21/12/41	U 567	4,800 tons iron pyrites. 34 dead
HG 76	RUCKINGE	2,869	39	Br	19/12/41	U 108	2,150 tons general. 2 dead
HG 82	CRESSADO	1,228	13	Br	08/05/42	COLLISION	Cork & general. No dead. Collision with HMS PALOMARES
HG 84	CITY OF OXFORD	2,759	26	Br	15/06/42	U 552	2,000 tons ore, 300 tons cork. 1 dead
HG 84	ETRIB	1,943	19	Br	15/06/42	U 552	2,014 tons fruit pulp, 260 tons general. 4 dead
HG 84	PELAYO	1,345	27	Br	15/06/42	U 552	755 tons stores, scrap iron. 16 dead
HG 84	SLEMDAL	7,374	31	Nor	15/06/42	U 552	Fuel oil. No dead
HG 84	THURSO	2,436	19	Br	15/06/42	U 552	850 tons general, PoW mails. 13 dead
HG 88	PRIMER ENRIQUE	101	29	Br	03/09/42	FOUNDERED	Fishing vessel in tow for UK
HG 88	SEGUNDO ENRIQUE	113	30	Br	03/09/42	FOUNDERED	Fishing vessel in tow for UK

UG convoy series 1942-1945

Like the British organized KM convoys, these two US series commenced as a result of the invasion of French North Africa, Operation Torch. There was a slight difference in that the initial US assault convoy, coded UGF 1 (United States to Gibraltar Fast), contained both the personnel and the stores ships for the assault; there was therefore no comparable Slow convoy with the coding UGS 1. To preserve uniformity, the first slow stores convoy that sailed to backup the landings was coded UGS 2.

The US assault was on the Atlantic coast of Morocco at Casablanca, the British landings on the Mediterranean coast of Algeria at Algiers and Oran. This division avoided the necessity of the convoys crossing each other's route. After the landings and the securing of Casablanca, the whole Moroccan coast was designated the Moroccan Sea Frontier, ensuring that control and responsibility rested with the 10th Fleet, a shore based USN organization in Washington DC. Control of the UG and GU series was therefore wholly a USN responsibility.

The convoys formed in Hampton Roads, south of New York, but it was not unusual for some ships to sail from New York City and join the convoy directly after its sailing. Hampton Roads would not therefore appear in those ships' voyage records. There are also occasional oddities in the early convoys in the Mediterranean, and there are occasions where the UGS convoy amalgamated with a KMS convoy for some part of the passage

While Casablanca remained the nominal eastern terminal, the gradual opening of the Mediterranean to shipping and the eastward progress of the land forces, caused the extension of the series eastward. The Fast series ceased in June 1943, being resumed in May 1944, the Slow series continued until the end of the European war with its eastern terminal at Port Said until the end of 1944, when UGS 60 reverted to Oran as its terminal.

THE ALLIED CONVOY SYSTEM 1939-1945

Escorts were entirely a USN responsibility in the Atlantic with the escorts turning round at Casablanca. The convoy escort was supported by a USN escort oiler in almost every case and, a support group formed around a USN escort carrier, provided mid-Atlantic air cover to supplement the aircraft based in the Azores. British escorts were provided from Mediterranean Fleet resources, from a point west of Gibraltar to the eastern terminal. Eventually, the need to land US supplies nearer to the recipient forces diverted an increasing amount of the UGS shipping to Oran, the US escort then continuing to that port where RN escorts took over. The final change was that the USN escort continued to Cape Bon in Tunisia, which became the changeover position from USN to RN escorts. In December 1944, with the removal of both submarine and aerial menace to the convoy routes in the Mediterranean, the UGS series terminated at Oran.

Ships northbound for southern French ports after termination of convoys can sometimes be recorded in signals with UGS codings; however, this is an irregular occurrence and they do not appear to have been escorted.

Only three ships, other than stragglers, were lost during the trans-Atlantic passage of UGS convoys by enemy action. This loss occurred in UGS 6; all other losses were in the Mediterranean. There was no loss to the UGF series.

UGS convoy data

CONVOY	DEP. PORT	DEP. DATE	ARRIVAL PORT	ARR. DATE	TDS	MV SUNK	MV DMGD
UGS 2	HAMPTON ROADS	13/11/42	CASABLANCA	01/12/42	45		
UGS 3	HAMPTON ROADS	12/12/42	ORAN	01/01/43	40		
UGS 4	HAMPTON ROADS	13/01/43	CASABLANCA	02/02/43	48		
UGS 5	HAMPTON ROADS	07/02/43	ORAN	26/02/43	43		
UGS 5A	HAMPTON ROADS	18/02/43	ORAN	06/03/43	16		
UGS 6	HAMPTON ROADS	04/03/43	ORAN	22/03/43	45	3	
UGS 6A	HAMPTON ROADS	19/03/43	RV WITH KMS 12	13/04/43	22		
UGS 7	HAMPTON ROADS	01/04/43	BONE	22/04/43	45		
UGS 7A	HAMPTON ROADS	14/04/43	BONE	07/05/43	46		
UGS 08	HAMPTON ROADS	28/04/43	ALGIERS	21/05/43	58		
UGS 8A	HAMPTON ROADS	14/05/43	TRIPOLI	08/06/43	80		
UGS 9	NYC	28/05/43	ORAN	15/06/43	73		
UGS 10	HAMPTON ROADS	13/06/43	ORAN	03/07/43	69		
UGS 11	HAMPTON ROADS	27/06/43	ORAN	18/07/43	59		
UGS 12	HAMPTON ROADS	12/07/43	JOINED KMS 21	29/07/43	77		
UGS 13	HAMPTON ROADS	27/07/43	PORT SAID	24/08/43	82		
UGS 14	HAMPTON ROADS	07/08/43	PORT SAID	02/09/43	67		
UGS 15	HAMPTON ROADS	16/08/43	PORT SAID	12/09/43	50		
UGS 16	HAMPTON ROADS	27/08/43	PORT SAID	24/09/43	79		
UGS 17	HAMPTON ROADS	06/09/43	PORT SAID	03/10/43	66		
UGS 18	HAMPTON ROADS	15/09/43	PORT SAID	13/10/43	65		
UGS 19	HAMPTON ROADS	25/09/43	PORT SAID	22/10/43	56		
UGS 20	HAMPTON ROADS	05/10/43	PORT SAID	01/11/43	64		
UGS 21	HAMPTON ROADS	15/10/43	PORT SAID	11/11/43	67		
UGS 22	HAMPTON ROADS	25/10/43	PORT SAID	22/11/43	64		
UGS 23	HAMPTON ROADS	04/11/43	PORT SAID	01/12/43	51		
UGS 24	HAMPTON ROADS	14/11/43	PORT SAID	12/12/43	69		
UGS 25	HAMPTON ROADS	24/11/43	PORT SAID	21/12/43	59		
UGS 26	HAMPTON ROADS	05/12/43	PORT SAID	30/12/43	78		
UGS 27	HAMPTON ROADS	15/12/43	PORT SAID	11/01/44	71		
UGS 28	HAMPTON ROADS	25/12/43	PORT SAID	21/01/44	68		
UGS 29	HAMPTON ROADS	05/01/44	PORT SAID	31/01/44	44		
UGS 30	HAMPTON ROADS	14/01/44	PORT SAID	10/02/44	66		
UGS 31	HAMPTON ROADS	25/01/44	PORT SAID	21/02/44	72		
UGS 32	HAMPTON ROADS	03/02/44	PORT SAID	01/03/44	76		
UGS 33	HAMPTON ROADS	13/02/44	PORT SAID	12/03/44	4		
UGS 33A	HAMPTON ROADS	18/02/44	GIBRALTAR	29/02/44	74		
UGS 34	HAMPTON ROADS	23/02/44	PORT SAID	20/03/44	64		
UGS 35	HAMPTON ROADS	04/03/44	PORT SAID	31/03/44	61		
UGS 36	HAMPTON ROADS	14/03/44	PORT SAID	09/04/44	79		
UGS 37	HAMPTON ROADS	24/03/44	PORT SAID	19/04/44	73		
UGS 38	HAMPTON ROADS	03/04/44	PORT SAID	28/04/44	85		
UGS 39	HAMPTON ROADS	13/04/44	PORT SAID	09/05/44	88		
UGS 40	HAMPTON ROADS	23/04/44	PORT SAID	19/05/44	77		
UGS 41	HAMPTON ROADS	03/05/44	PORT SAID	30/05/44	70		
UGS 42	HAMPTON ROADS	13/05/44	PORT SAID	08/06/44	86		
UGS 43	HAMPTON ROADS	23/05/44	PORT SAID	18/06/44	79		
UGS 44	HAMPTON ROADS	02/06/44	PORT SAID	28/06/44	74		
UGS 45	HAMPTON ROADS	12/06/44	PORT SAID	07/07/44	74		
UGS 46	HAMPTON ROADS	24/06/44	PORT SAID	20/07/44	69		
UGS 47	HAMPTON ROADS	04/07/44	PORT SAID	29/07/44	67		
UGS 48	HAMPTON ROADS	14/07/44	PORT SAID	08/08/44	65		
UGS 49	HAMPTON ROADS	24/07/44	PORT SAID	19/08/44	66		
UGS 50	HAMPTON ROADS	03/08/44	PORT SAID	29/08/44	66		
UGS 51	HAMPTON ROADS	13/08/44	PORT SAID	08/09/44	65		
UGS 52	HAMPTON ROADS	23/08/44	PORT SAID	17/09/44	59		
UGS 53	HAMPTON ROADS	02/09/44	PORT SAID	28/09/44	62		
UGS 54	HAMPTON ROADS	12/09/44	PORT SAID	10/10/44	60		
UGS 55	HAMPTON ROADS	22/09/44	PORT SAID	17/10/44	69		
UGS 55B	HAMPTON ROADS	27/09/44	CASABLANCA	13/10/44	19		
UGS 56	HAMPTON ROADS	01/10/44	PORT SAID	28/10/44	69		
UGS 57	HAMPTON ROADS	12/10/44	PORT SAID	09/11/44	86		
UGS 58	HAMPTON ROADS	22/10/44	PORT SAID	18/11/44	83		
UGS 59	HAMPTON ROADS	01/11/44	PORT SAID	27/11/44	86		
UGS 60	HAMPTON ROADS	11/11/44	GIBRALTAR	26/11/44	75		
UGS 61	HAMPTON RDS	21/11/44	GIBRALTAR	07/12/44	77		
UGS 62	HAMPTON ROADS	01/12/44	GIBRALTAR	17/12/44	93		
UGS 63	HAMPTON ROADS	11/12/44	GIBRALTAR	27/12/44	91		

APPENDIX 3

CONVOY	DEP. PORT	DEP. DATE	ARRIVAL PORT	ARR. DATE	TDS	MV SUNK	MV DMGD	CONVOY	DEP. PORT	DEP. DATE	ARRIVAL PORT	ARR. DATE	TDS	MV SUNK	MV DMGD
UGS 64	HAMPTON ROADS	19/12/44	GIBRALTAR	04/01/45	70			UGS 80	HAMPTON ROADS	14/03/45	DISPERSED	29/03/45	48		
UGS 65	HAMPTON ROADS	29/12/44	GIBRALTAR	15/01/45	74			UGS 81	HAMPTON ROADS	19/03/45	GIBRALTAR	03/04/45	44		
UGS 66	HAMPTON ROADS	03/01/45	GIBRALTAR	19/01/45	33			UGS 82	HAMPTON ROADS	24/03/45	GIBRALTAR	07/04/45	43		
UGS 67	HAMPTON ROADS	08/01/45	GIBRALTAR	26/01/45	48			UGS 83	HAMPTON ROADS	29/03/45	GIBRALTAR	14/04/45	51		
UGS 68	HAMPTON ROADS	13/01/45	GIBRALTAR	27/01/45	37			UGS 84	HAMPTON ROADS	03/04/45	GIBRALTAR	17/04/45	47		
UGS 69	HAMPTON ROADS	18/01/45	GIBRALTAR	01/02/45	47			UGS 85	HAMPTON ROADS	08/04/45	GIBRALTAR	23/04/45	49		
UGS 70	HAMPTON ROADS	23/01/45	GIBRALTAR	07/02/45	54			UGS 86	HAMPTON ROADS	13/04/45	GIBRALTAR	28/04/45	55		
UGS 71	HAMPTON ROADS	28/01/45	SOUTHERN FRANCE	16/02/45	36			UGS 87	HAMPTON ROADS	18/04/45	GIBRALTAR	03/05/45	43		
UGS 72	HAMPTON ROADS	02/02/45	GIBRALTAR	17/02/45	46			UGS 88	HAMPTON ROADS	23/04/45	DISPERSED	08/05/45	40		
UGS 73	HAMPTON ROADS	07/02/45	GIBRALTAR	23/02/45	38			UGS 89	HAMPTON ROADS	28/04/45	DISPERSED	12/05/45	36		
UGS 74	HAMPTON ROADS	12/02/45	ORAN	01/03/45	43			UGS 0	HAMPTON ROADS	03/05/45	DISPERSED	18/05/45	43		
UGS 75	HAMPTON ROADS	17/02/45	GIBRALTAR	04/03/45	57			UGS 91	HAMPTON ROADS	08/05/45	DISPERSED	23/05/45	46		
UGS 76	HAMPTON ROADS	22/02/45	GIBRALTAR	10/03/45	41			UGS 92	HAMPTON ROADS	13/05/45	DISPERSED	27/05/45	44		
UGS 77	HAMPTON ROADS	27/02/45	GIBRALTAR	14/03/45	34			UGS 93	HAMPTON ROADS	18/05/45	ORAN	04/06/45	30		
UGS 78	HAMPTON ROADS	04/03/45	GIBRALTAR	18/03/45	45			UGS 94	HAMPTON ROADS	23/05/45	GIBRALTAR	07/06/45	51		
UGS 79	HAMPTON ROADS	09/03/45	CASABLANCA	23/03/45	43			UGS 95	HAMPTON ROADS	28/05/45	DISPERSED	29/05/45	28		

Losses incurred in UGS convoys, excluding stragglers

Convoy	Ship's Name	GRT			Date of loss	Cause of loss	Comments
UGS 3	ARTHUR MIDDLETON	7,176	42	Amer	01/01/43	U 73	Explosives & mail. All (66) crew dead
UGS 5	PAN ROYAL	5,627	18	Amer	09/02/43	COLLISION	Cargo unknown. No dead
UGS 6	WYOMING	8,062	30	Fr	15/03/43	U 524	5,500 tons gen. 30 pass. No dead
UGS 6	BENJAMIN HARRISON	7,191	42	Amer	16/03/43	U 172	Stores etc. 3 dead
UGS 6	MOLLY PITCHER	7,200	43	Amer	17/03/43	U 167 & U 521	Food, stores etc. 4 dead
UGS 7	SIDI-BEL-ABBES	4,392	29	Fr	20/04/43	U 565	1,000 French troops. Approx 611 dead
UGS 7	MICHIGAN	5,594	19	Amer	20/04/43	U 565	7,400 tons general. No dead
UGS 10	LOT	4,220	39	Fr	22/06/43	U 572	6,000 tons fuel oil. 23 dead. French naval tanker
UGS 13	EMPIRE KESTREL	2,674	19	Br	16/08/43	AIRCRAFT	1,600 tons stores. 11 dead
UGS 14	JOHN BELL	7,242	43	Amer	26/08/43	U 410	Stores. 1 dead
UGS 14	RICHARD HENDERSON	7,194	43	Amer	26/08/43	U 410	Stores, expl. No dead

Convoy	Ship's Name	GRT			Date of loss	Cause of loss	Comments
UGS 17	CHRISTIAN MICHELSON	7,176	43	Amer	26/09/43	U 410	10,000 tons ammo & oil. 47 dead
UGS 18	FORT FITZGERALD	7,133	43	Br	04/10/43	AIRCRAFT	Stores, ammo. 5 dead
UGS 30	EDWARD BATES	7,176	43	Amer	01/02/44	AIRCRAFT	Flour. 1 dead
UGS 33	DANIEL CHESTER FRENCH	7,176	42	Amer	06/03/44	MINED	Allied field. General & ammo. 37 dead
UGS 33	VIRGINIA DARE	7,176	42	Amer	06/03/44	MINED	Allied field. Cargo & dead unknown
UGS 37	MEYER LONDON	7,210	44	Amer	16/04/44	U 407	Stores. No dead
UGS 37	THOMAS G MASARYK	7,176	43	Amer	16/04/44	U 407	General. Dead unknown. CTL
UGS 38	ROYAL STAR	7,900	19	Br	20/04/44	AIRCRAFT	5,650 ton frig meat. 1 dead
UGS 38	PAUL HAMILTON	7,177	42	Amer	20/04/44	AIRCRAFT	Explosives. 504 troops. All dead
UGS 57	JOHN BANVARD	7,191	42	Amer	31/10/44	WRECKED	Azores, salved, CTL, bu in USA
UGS 72	REGENT LION	9,551	37	Br	17/02/45	U 300	12,440 tons petrol. 3 dead. CTL

UGF convoy data

CONVOY	DEP. PORT	DEP. DATE	ARRIVAL PORT	ARR. DATE	TDS	MV SUNK	MV DMGD	CONVOY	DEP. PORT	DEP. DATE	ARRIVAL PORT	ARR. DATE	TDS	MV SUNK	MV DMGD
UGF 1	HAMPTON ROADS	24/10/42	CASABLANCA	08/11/42	31			UGF 12	HAMPTON ROADS	01/07/44	NAPLES	15/07/44	24		
UGF 2	HAMPTON ROADS	02/11/42	CASABLANCA	18/11/42	22			UGF 13	HAMPTON ROADS	28/07/44	NAPLES	12/08/44	14		
UGF 3	HAMPTON ROADS	13/12/42	CASABLANCA	24/12/42	17			UGF 14	HAMPTON ROADS	24/08/44	NAPLES	08/09/44	10		
UGF 4	HAMPTON ROADS	14/01/43	ORAN	27/01/43	21			UGF 15	HAMPTON ROADS	20/09/44	NAPLES	04/10/44	10		
UGF 5	HAMPTON ROADS	08/02/43	ORAN	21/02/43	20			UGF 15B	HAMPTON ROADS	06/10/44	MARSEILLES	20/10/44	19		
UGF 6	HAMPTON ROADS	05/03/43	ORAN	19/03/43	22			UGF 16	HAMPTON ROADS	14/10/44	NAPLES	28/10/44	10		
UGF 7	HAMPTON ROADS	02/04/43	ORAN	13/04/43	16			UGF 17	HAMPTON ROADS	13/11/44	NAPLES	26/11/44	6		
UGF 8	HAMPTON ROADS	29/04/43	ORAN	11/05/43	24			UGF 17B	HAMPTON ROADS	25/11/44	MARSEILLES	08/12/44	12		
UGF 8A	HAMPTON ROADS	10/05/43	ORAN	23/05/43	14			UGF 18	HAMPTON ROADS	10/12/44	NAPLES	24/12/44	10		
UGF 9	HAMPTON ROADS	08/06/43	ORAN	22/06/43	24			UGF 19	HAMPTON ROADS	06/01/45	NAPLES	18/01/45	6		
UGF 9A	HAMPTON ROADS	10/06/43	ORAN	21/06/43	11			UGF 20	HAMPTON ROADS	09/02/45	NAPLES	19/02/45	3		
UGF 10	HAMPTON ROADS	21/08/43	ORAN	02/09/43	25			UGF 21	HAMPTON ROADS	01/03/45	NAPLES	14/03/45	4		
UGF 11	HAMPTON ROADS	17/05/44	NAPLES	31/05/44	5			UGF 22	HAMPTON ROADS	28/03/45	ORAN	08/04/45	2		

◇ THE ALLIED CONVOY SYSTEM 1939-1945

GU convoy series

As there had been no UGS 1 convoy, the GUS series conformed by numbering the first convoy GUS 2. Convoys sailed from Casablanca and the US terminal was the Hampton Roads anchorage. It was not unusual however for some ships to be detached direct to New York City with their arrival date being one day prior to the Hampton Roads date.

As with the UGS convoys, North Atlantic escort was a USN responsibility, the RN providing escort within the Mediterranean and westward from the Gibraltar Strait to the Casablanca rendezvous. As the series formed at ports to the east of Oran, that port (and later Cape Bon), became the eastern limit of USN responsibility. Mediterranean escort finally ceased in late 1944 with the destruction of the last U-boat in that sea and the restriction of German held airfields to Northern Italy.

There were no war losses to Fast series GUF, in either the Mediterranean or the North Atlantic. GUS losses appear below the convoy data for that series.

GUS convoy data

CONVOY	DEP. PORT	DEP. DATE	ARRIVAL PORT	ARR. DATE	TDS	MV SUNK	MV DMGD
GUS 2	ORAN	21/12/42	HAMPTON ROADS	13/01/43	40		
GUS 3	ORAN	18/01/43	HAMPTON ROADS	07/02/43	40		
GUS 4	ORAN	20/02/43	HAMPTON ROADS	11/03/43	49		
GUS 5	ORAN	13/03/43	HAMPTON ROADS	01/04/43	42		
GUS 5A	ORAN	23/03/43	HAMPTON ROADS	15/04/43	28		
GUS 5B	ORAN	27/03/43	HAMPTON ROADS	18/04/43	6		
GUS 6	ORAN	10/04/43	HAMPTON ROADS	28/04/43	45		
GUS 6A	ALGIERS	21/04/43	HAMPTON ROADS	08/05/43	30		
GUS 7	ALGIERS	06/05/43	HAMPTON ROADS	26/05/43	35		
GUS 7A	ORAN	24/05/43	HAMPTON ROADS	08/06/43	44		
GUS 8	ORAN	07/06/43	HAMPTON ROADS	27/06/43	65		
GUS 8A	ORAN	20/06/43	HAMPTON ROADS	11/07/43	42		
GUS 9	ORAN	06/07/43	HAMPTON ROADS	23/07/43	43		
GUS 10	BIZERTA	18/07/43	HAMPTON ROADS	09/08/43	40		
GUS 10X	TRIPOLI, LIBYA	21/07/43	HAMPTON ROADS	13/08/43	25		
GUS 11	ALEXANDRIA	28/07/43	HAMPTON ROADS	26/08/43	56		
GUS 12	ALEXANDRIA	10/08/43	HAMPTON ROADS	06/09/43	40		
GUS 13	ALEXANDRIA	20/08/43	HAMPTON ROADS	14/09/43	36		
GUS 14	ALEXANDRIA	30/08/43	HAMPTON ROADS	26/09/43	42		
GUS 15	ALEXANDRIA	09/09/43	HAMPTON ROADS	04/10/43	37		
GUS 16	ALEXANDRIA	19/09/43	HAMPTON ROADS	15/10/43	69		
GUS 17	ALEXANDRIA	29/09/43	HAMPTON ROADS	27/10/43	36		
GUS 18	ALEXANDRIA	09/10/43	HAMPTON ROADS	06/11/43	52		
GUS 19	ALEXANDRIA	19/10/43	HAMPTON ROADS	15/11/43	61		
GUS 20	ALEXANDRIA	29/10/43	HAMPTON ROADS	24/11/43	78		
GUS 21	PORT SAID	07/11/43	HAMPTON ROADS	05/12/43	49		
GUS 22	PORT SAID	17/11/43	HAMPTON ROADS	17/12/43	57		
GUS 23	PORT SAID	27/11/43	HAMPTON ROADS	25/12/43	44		
GUS 24	PORT SAID	06/12/43	HAMPTON ROADS	03/01/44	60		
GUS 25	PORT SAID	16/12/43	HAMPTON ROADS	17/01/44	56		
GUS 26	PORT SAID	26/12/43	HAMPTON ROADS	24/01/44	53		
GUS 27	PORT SAID	05/01/44	HAMPTON ROADS	04/02/44	52		
GUS 28	PORT SAID	15/01/44	HAMPTON ROADS	15/02/44	66		
GUS 29	PORT SAID	25/01/44	HAMPTON ROADS	22/02/44	51		
GUS 30	PORT SAID	04/02/44	HAMPTON ROADS	08/03/44	73		
GUS 31	PORT SAID	14/02/44	HAMPTON ROADS	18/03/44	103		
GUS 32	PORT SAID	24/02/44	HAMPTON ROADS	23/03/44	91		
GUS 33	PORT SAID	05/03/44	HAMPTON ROADS	04/04/44	98		
GUS 34	PORT SAID	15/03/44	HAMPTON ROADS	14/04/44	81		
GUS 35	PORT SAID	25/03/44	HAMPTON ROADS	22/04/44	61		
GUS 36	PORT SAID	04/04/44	HAMPTON ROADS	02/05/44	90		
GUS 37	PORT SAID	14/04/44	HAMPTON ROADS	11/05/44	92		
GUS 38	PORT SAID	24/04/44	HAMPTON ROADS	22/05/44	107		
GUS 39	PORT SAID	04/05/44	HAMPTON ROADS	29/05/44	94		
GUS 40	PORT SAID	14/05/44	HAMPTON ROADS	09/06/44	80		
GUS 41	PORT SAID	24/05/44	HAMPTON ROADS	19/06/44	70		
GUS 42	PORT SAID	03/06/44	HAMPTON ROADS	29/06/44	75		
GUS 43	PORT SAID	13/06/44	HAMPTON ROADS	10/07/44	53		
GUS 44	PORT SAID	24/06/44	HAMPTON ROADS	18/07/44	34		
GUS 45	PORT SAID	04/07/44	HAMPTON ROADS	29/07/44	41		
GUS 46	PORT SAID	14/07/44	HAMPTON ROADS	08/08/44	56		
GUS 47	PORT SAID	24/07/44	HAMPTON ROADS	18/08/44	52		
GUS 48	PORT SAID	03/08/44	HAMPTON ROADS	28/08/44	62		
GUS 49	PORT SAID	13/08/44	HAMPTON ROADS	08/09/44	35		
GUS 50	PORT SAID	23/08/44	HAMPTON ROADS	18/09/44	81		
GUS 51	PORT SAID	02/09/44	HAMPTON ROADS	28/09/44	107		
GUS 52	PORT SAID	11/09/44	HAMPTON ROADS	08/10/44	70		
GUS 53	PORT SAID	22/09/44	HAMPTON ROADS	17/10/44	64		
GUS 54	PORT SAID	02/10/44	HAMPTON ROADS	28/10/44	52		
GUS 55	PORT SAID	12/10/44	HAMPTON ROADS	06/11/44	73		
GUS 55B	ORAN	20/10/44	HAMPTON ROADS	07/11/44	13		
GUS 56	PORT SAID	22/10/44	HAMPTON ROADS	19/11/44	68		
GUS 57	PORT SAID	01/11/44	HAMPTON ROADS	30/11/44	76		
GUS 58	PORT SAID	11/11/44	ORAN	20/11/44			
GUS 59	ORAN	22/11/44	HAMPTON ROADS	10/12/44	98		
GUS 60	ORAN	03/12/44	HAMPTON ROADS	22/12/44	120		
GUS 61	ORAN	12/12/44	HAMPTON ROADS	29/12/44	68		
GUS 62	ORAN	22/12/44	HAMPTON ROADS	10/01/45	106		
GUS 63	ORAN	02/01/45	HAMPTON ROADS	20/01/45	76		
GUS 64	ORAN	06/01/45	HAMPTON ROADS	24/01/45	21		
GUS 65	ORAN	12/01/45	HAMPTON ROADS	02/02/45	41		
GUS 66	ORAN	17/01/45	HAMPTON ROADS	06/02/45	45		
GUS 67	ORAN	22/01/45	HAMPTON ROADS	14/02/45	49		
GUS 68	ORAN	27/01/45	HAMPTON ROADS	14/02/45	42		

APPENDIX 3

CONVOY	DEP. PORT	DEP. DATE	ARRIVAL PORT	ARR. DATE	TDS	MV SUNK	MV DMGD
GUS 69	ORAN	01/02/45	HAMPTON ROADS	19/02/45	54		
GUS 70	ORAN	06/02/45	HAMPTON ROADS	24/02/45	57		
GUS 71	ORAN	11/02/45	HAMPTON ROADS	28/02/45	47		
GUS 72	ORAN	16/02/45	HAMPTON ROADS	06/03/45	47		
GUS 73	ORAN	21/02/45	HAMPTON ROADS	11/03/45	34		
GUS 74	ORAN	26/02/45	HAMPTON ROADS	16/03/45	43		
GUS 75	ORAN	03/03/45	HAMPTON ROADS	20/03/45	45		
GUS 76	ORAN	08/03/45	HAMPTON ROADS	24/03/45	38		
GUS 77	ORAN	13/03/45	HAMPTON ROADS	30/03/45	52		
GUS 78	ORAN	18/03/45	HAMPTON ROADS	04/04/45	45		
GUS 79	ORAN	23/03/45	HAMPTON ROADS	09/04/45	43		
GUS 80	ORAN	28/03/45	HAMPTON ROADS	13/04/45	35		
GUS 81	ORAN	02/04/45	HAMPTON ROADS	21/04/45	45		
GUS 82	ORAN	07/04/45	HAMPTON ROADS	26/04/45	38		
GUS 83	ORAN	12/04/45	HAMPTON ROADS	30/04/45	46		
GUS 84	ORAN	17/04/45	HAMPTON ROADS	05/05/45	58		
GUS 85	ORAN	22/04/45	HAMPTON ROADS	09/05/45	39		
GUS 86	ORAN	27/04/45	HAMPTON ROADS	14/05/45	42		
GUS 87	ORAN	02/05/45	HAMPTON ROADS	18/05/45	38		
GUS 88	ORAN	07/05/45	HAMPTON ROADS	23/05/45	46		
GUS 89	ORAN	12/05/45	HAMPTON ROADS	29/05/45	42		
GUS 90	ORAN	17/05/45	HAMPTON ROADS	02/06/45	46		
GUS 91	ORAN	22/05/45	HAMPTON ROADS	08/06/45	23		
GUS 92	ORAN	27/05/45	HAMPTON ROADS	11/06/45	nk		

Losses incurred in GUS convoys, excluding stragglers

Convoy	Ship's Name	GRT		Date of loss	Cause of loss	Comments
GUS 18	JAMES RUSSELL LOWELL	7,176	42 Amer	15/10/43	U 371	Ballast. No dead
GUS 25	ALPHERAT	5,759	28 Br	21/12/43	AIRCRAFT	7,000 tons general. No dead
GUS 31	GEORGE CLEEVE	7,176	43 Amer	22/02/44	U 969	Scrap. 1 dead
GUS 63	HENRY MILLER	7,207	43 Amer	03/01/45	U 870	Towed Gibraltar, CTL. No dead

GUF convoy data

CONVOY	DEP. PORT	DEP. DATE	ARRIVAL PORT	ARR. DATE	TDS	MV SUNK	MV DMGD
GUF 2	CASABLANCA	29/11/42	HAMPTON ROADS	11/12/42	18		
GUF 2A	CASABLANCA	12/12/42	HAMPTON ROADS	25/12/42	12		
GUF 3	ORAN	30/12/42	HAMPTON ROADS	13/01/43	21		
GUF 4	ORAN	31/01/43	HAMPTON ROADS	13/02/43	29		
GUF 5	ORAN	26/02/43	HAMPTON ROADS	11/03/43	22		
GUF 6	ORAN	24/03/43	HAMPTON ROADS	07/04/43	15		
GUF 7	ORAN	18/04/43	HAMPTON ROADS	30/04/43	10		
GUF 8	ORAN	18/05/43	HAMPTON ROADS	31/05/43	15		
GUF 9	ORAN	21/07/43	HAMPTON ROADS	03/08/43	18		
GUF 10	ORAN	09/09/43	HAMPTON ROADS	21/09/43	20		
GUF 11	ORAN	03/06/44	HAMPTON ROADS	14/06/44	7		
GUF 12	NAPLES	21/07/44	HAMPTON ROADS	04/08/44	15		
GUF 13	NAPLES	18/08/44	HAMPTON ROADS	31/08/44	13		
GUF 14	NAPLES	13/09/44	HAMPTON ROADS	26/09/44	16		
GUF 15	NAPLES	10/10/44	HAMPTON ROADS	23/10/44	10		
GUF 15B	MARSEILLES	22/10/44	HAMPTON ROADS	07/11/44	29		
GUF 16	MARSEILLES	02/11/44	HAMPTON ROADS	17/11/44	19		
GUF 17	NAPLES	01/12/44	HAMPTON ROADS	14/12/44	7		
GUF 17B	ORAN	13/12/44	HAMPTON ROADS	23/12/44	8		
GUF 18	ORAN	31/12/44	HAMPTON ROADS	11/01/45	9		
GUF 19	ORAN	23/01/45	HAMPTON ROADS	05/02/45	4		
GUF 20	ORAN	01/03/45	HAMPTON ROADS	12/03/45	5		
GUF 21	ORAN	21/03/45	HAMPTON ROADS	01/04/45	9		
GUF 22	ORAN	16/04/45	HAMPTON ROADS	28/04/45	4		

No losses were incurred in the GUF series convoys

CU convoy series 1943-1945

Following the North African landings and the resultant high expenditure of fuel from UK stocks, it was requested that additional supplies should be shipped to the UK. There was some reluctance to do this on the US side but eventually 9 convoys totalling 159 ships, of which 145 were tankers, took place during 1943.

The demands for fuel escalated towards the end of 1943 and the convoy series was reorganized accordingly. The fast tanker tonnage was now utilised on the New York to UK route, oil supplies being freighted from the Caribbean fields in older, slower vessels. The frequency of convoys was also increased so that 1944 saw 43 convoys totalling 1,364 ships of which 802 were tankers.

The convoys were entirely a USN responsibility and had a passage speed of 14 knots. In consequence they were found useful for the passage of freighters and liners whose speeds were greater than that of the standard HX series; this accounts for the considerable increase in 1944 of non-tanker vessels. Such convoys were sometimes designated by the prefix "T" (for "troopship") to the CU alpha code; they retained the numeric sequence however.

After the Normandy landings, increasing numbers of ships from these convoys were routed to French ports to discharge cargo and personnel, returning to the UK to join the westbound UC convoy.

Submarine activity in the North Atlantic was greatly reduced during the period of this series, and the escort provided was also strong, as evidenced by the loss of only three ships from a total of 2,255 sailings.

CU convoy data

CONVOY	DEP. PORT	DEP. DATE	ARRIVAL PORT	ARR. DATE	TDS	MV SUNK	MV DMGD
CU 1	CURACAO	20/03/43	LIVERPOOL	01/04/43	9		
CU 2	CURACAO	21/05/43	LIVERPOOL	05/06/43	15		
CU 3	CURACAO	11/07/43	CLYDE	24/07/43	23		
CU 4	CURACAO	26/08/43	LIVERPOOL	09/09/43	22		
CU 5	NYC	13/10/43	LIVERPOOL	24/10/43	19		
CU 6	CURACAO	26/10/43	LIVERPOOL	12/11/43	19		
CU 7	NYC	20/11/43	LIVERPOOL	01/12/43	17		
CU 8	NYC	02/12/43	LIVERPOOL	13/12/43	18		
CU 9	NYC	15/12/43	LIVERPOOL	26/12/43	17		
CU 10	NYC	26/12/43	LIVERPOOL	06/01/44	16		
CU 11	NYC	09/01/44	LIVERPOOL	20/01/44	20		
CU 12	NYC	19/01/44	LIVERPOOL	30/01/44	23		
CU 13	NYC	01/02/44	LIVERPOOL	13/02/44	23		
CU 14	NYC	12/02/44	LIVERPOOL	24/02/44	21		
CU 15	NYC	22/02/44	LIVERPOOL	06/03/44	19		
CU 16	NYC	01/03/44	LIVERPOOL	12/03/44	27		
CU 17	NYC	10/03/44	LIVERPOOL	20/03/44	23	1	
CU 18	NYC	19/03/44	LIVERPOOL	29/03/44	24		
CU 19	NYC	28/03/44	LIVERPOOL	08/04/44	26		
CU 20	NYC	06/04/44	LIVERPOOL	18/04/44	27		
CU 21	NYC	16/04/44	LIVERPOOL	26/04/44	25	1	
CU 22	NYC	24/04/44	LIVERPOOL	06/05/44	31		
CU 23	NYC	03/05/44	LIVERPOOL	14/05/44	44		
CU 24	NYC	12/05/44	LIVERPOOL	23/05/44	44		
CU 24B	NYC	14/05/44	LIVERPOOL	25/05/44	13		
CU 25	NYC	21/05/44	LIVERPOOL	31/05/44	39		
CU 26	NYC	30/05/44	LIVERPOOL	11/06/44	34		
CU 27	NYC	08/06/44	LIVERPOOL	20/06/44	22		
CU 28	NYC	16/06/44	LIVERPOOL	27/06/44	37		
CU 29	NYC	24/06/44	LIVERPOOL	05/07/44	30		
CU 30	NYC	02/07/44	LIVERPOOL	12/07/44	38		
CU 31	NYC	10/07/44	LIVERPOOL	22/07/44	33		
CU 32	NYC	18/07/44	LIVERPOOL	29/07/44	42		
CU 33	NYC	26/07/44	LIVERPOOL	05/08/44	33		
CU 34	NYC	03/08/44	LIVERPOOL	13/08/44	33		
CU 35	NYC	11/08/44	LIVERPOOL	22/08/44	51		
CU 36	NYC	19/08/44	LIVERPOOL	31/08/44	31	1	
CU 37	NYC	27/08/44	LIVERPOOL	07/09/44	49		
CU 38	NYC	04/09/44	LIVERPOOL	15/09/44	40		
CU 39	NYC	12/09/44	LIVERPOOL	23/09/44	45		
CU 40	NYC	20/09/44	LIVERPOOL	01/10/44	28		
CU 41	NYC	29/09/44	LIVERPOOL	10/10/44	43		
CU 42	NYC	06/10/44	LIVERPOOL	17/10/44	31		
CU 43	NYC	15/10/44	LIVERPOOL	25/10/44	23		
CU 44	NYC	22/10/44	LIVERPOOL	02/11/44	46		
CU 45	NYC	30/10/44	LIVERPOOL	10/11/44	32		
CU 46	NYC	07/11/44	LIVERPOOL	18/11/44	33		
CU 47	NYC	15/11/44	LIVERPOOL	26/11/44	34		
CU 48	NYC	23/11/44	LIVERPOOL	05/12/44	29		
CU 49	NYC	01/12/44	LIVERPOOL	12/12/44	36		
CU 50	NYC	09/12/44	LIVERPOOL	20/12/44	35		
CU 51	NYC	17/12/44	LIVERPOOL	27/12/44	31		
CU 52	NYC	26/12/44	LIVERPOOL	07/01/45	29		
CU 53	NYC	03/01/45	LIVERPOOL	14/01/45	33		
CU 54	NYC	10/01/45	LIVERPOOL	22/01/45	35		
CU 55	NYC	18/01/45	LIVERPOOL	28/01/45	39		
CU 56	NYC	26/01/45	LIVERPOOL	05/02/45	39		
CU 57	NYC	05/02/45	LIVERPOOL	16/02/45	39		
CU 58	NYC	11/02/45	LIVERPOOL	22/02/45	25		
CU 59	NYC	19/02/45	LIVERPOOL	01/03/45	38		
CU 60	NYC	27/02/45	LIVERPOOL	11/03/45	24		
CU 61	NYC	08/03/45	LIVERPOOL	18/03/45	36		
CU 62	NYC	15/03/45	LIVERPOOL	27/03/45	46		
CU 63	NYC	23/03/45	LIVERPOOL	03/04/45	44		
CU 64	NYC	31/03/45	LIVERPOOL	12/04/45	35		
CU 65	NYC	08/04/45	LIVERPOOL	19/04/45	37		1
CU 66	NYC	16/04/45	LIVERPOOL	28/04/45	49		
CU 67	NYC	24/04/45	LIVERPOOL	05/05/45	46		
CU 68	NYC	02/05/45	LIVERPOOL	14/05/45	37		
CU 69	NYC	10/05/45	LIVERPOOL	20/05/45	31		
CU 70	NYC	15/05/45	LIVERPOOL	25/05/45	24		
CU 71	NYC	20/05/45	LIVERPOOL	30/05/45	21		
CU 72	NYC	25/05/45	LIVERPOOL	03/06/45	23		
CU 73	NYC	30/05/45	LIVERPOOL	08/06/45	2		

Losses incurred in CU convoys, excluding stragglers

Convoy	Ship's Name	GRT			Date of loss	Cause of loss	Comments
CU 15	EL COSTON	7,286	24	Pan	26/02/44	COLLISION	With MURFREESBORO, cargo unknown
CU 17	SEAKAY	10,342	42	Amer	19/03/44	U 311	14,000 tons vap oil, 14 a/c. 1 dead
CU 21	PAN-PENNSYLVANIA	11,017	43	Amer	16/04/44	U 550	140,000 barrels petrol. 25 dead
CU 36	JACKSONVILLE	10,448	44	Amer	30/08/44	U 482	14,300 tons petrol. 76 dead
CU 65	ST MIHIEL	10,296	45	Amer	09/04/45	COLLISION	With NASHBULK. Avgas. Dead unknown

UC convoys 1943-1945

CONVOY	DEP. PORT	DEP. DATE	ARRIVAL PORT	ARR. DATE	TDS	MV SUNK	MV DMGD
UC 1	LIVERPOOL	15/02/43	CURACAO	06/03/43	32	2	
UC 2	LIVERPOOL	09/04/43	CURACAO	23/04/43	11		
UC 3	LIVERPOOL	10/06/43	CURACAO	26/06/43	15		
UC 3A	LIVERPOOL	30/07/43	CURACAO	10/08/43	22		
UC 4	LIVERPOOL	15/09/43	CURACAO	27/09/43	22		
UC 5	LIVERPOOL	29/10/43	NYC	09/11/43	18		
UC 6	LIVERPOOL	18/11/43	NYC	27/11/43	24		
UC 7	LIVERPOOL	08/12/43	NYC	20/12/43	18		
UC 8	LIVERPOOL	18/12/43	NYC	02/01/44	17		
UC 9	LIVERPOOL	31/12/43	NYC	10/01/44	22		
UC 10	LIVERPOOL	12/01/44	NYC	25/01/44	20		
UC 11	LIVERPOOL	27/01/44	NYC	07/02/44	18		
UC 12	LIVERPOOL	07/02/44	NYC	18/02/44	24		
UC 13	LIVERPOOL	18/02/44	NYC	27/02/44	27		
UC 14	LIVERPOOL	01/03/44	NYC	11/03/44	21		
UC 15	LIVERPOOL	12/03/44	NYC	22/03/44	29		
UC 16	LIVERPOOL	17/03/44	NYC	28/03/44	24		
UC 17	LIVERPOOL	27/03/44	NYC	07/04/44	23		
UC 18	LIVERPOOL	05/04/44	NYC	17/04/44	19		
UC 19	LIVERPOOL	13/04/44	NYC	24/04/44	28		
UC 20	LIVERPOOL	24/04/44	NYC	03/05/44	23		
UC 21	LIVERPOOL	02/05/44	NYC	12/05/44	25		
UC 22	LIVERPOOL	10/05/44	NYC	20/05/44	25		
UC 23	LIVERPOOL	18/05/44	NYC	28/05/44	40		
UC 24	LIVERPOOL	29/05/44	NYC	09/06/44	46		
UC 25	LIVERPOOL	05/06/44	NYC	16/06/44	33		
UC 26	LIVERPOOL	15/06/44	NYC	27/06/44	43		
UC 27	LIVERPOOL	23/06/44	NYC	04/07/44	27		
UC 28	LIVERPOOL	01/07/44	NYC	12/07/44	32		
UC 29	LIVERPOOL	09/07/44	NYC	19/07/44	29		
UC 30	LIVERPOOL	16/07/44	NYC	27/07/44	50		
UC 31	LIVERPOOL	25/07/44	NYC	05/08/44	31		
UC 32	LIVERPOOL	03/08/44	NYC	14/08/44	44		
UC 33	LIVERPOOL	09/08/44	NYC	20/08/44	38		
UC 34	LIVERPOOL	17/08/44	NYC	28/08/44	35		
UC 35	LIVERPOOL	26/08/44	NYC	05/09/44	52		
UC 36	LIVERPOOL	04/09/44	NYC	15/09/44	30		
UC 37	LIVERPOOL	12/09/44	NYC	23/09/44	53		
UC 38A	LIVERPOOL	19/09/44	NYC	30/09/44	30		
UC 38B	LIVERPOOL	23/09/44	NYC	03/10/44	15		
UC 39A	LIVERPOOL	27/09/44	NYC	08/10/44	36		
UC 39B	LIVERPOOL	30/09/44	NYC	10/10/44	16		
UC 40A	LIVERPOOL	06/10/44	NYC	16/10/44	29		
UC 40B	LIVERPOOL	10/10/44	NYC	20/10/44	6		
UC 41A	LIVERPOOL	14/10/44	NYC	25/10/44	29		
UC 41B	LIVERPOOL	17/10/44	DISPERSED IN FULL GALE	28/10/44	6		
UC 42A	LIVERPOOL	21/10/44	NYC	01/11/44	32		
UC 42B	LIVERPOOL	25/10/44	NYC	05/11/44	9		
UC 43A	LIVERPOOL	29/10/44	NYC	09/11/44	25		
UC 43B	LIVERPOOL	02/11/44	NYC	12/11/44	5		
UC 44A	LIVERPOOL	06/11/44	NYC	16/11/44	29		
UC 44B	LIVERPOOL	10/11/44	NYC	21/11/44	18		
UC 45A	LIVERPOOL	14/11/44	NYC	26/11/44	32		
UC 45B	LIVERPOOL	18/11/44	NYC	30/11/44	12		
UC 46A	LIVERPOOL	22/11/44	NYC	03/12/44	16		
UC 46B	LIVERPOOL	26/11/44	NYC	08/12/44	17		
UC 47A	LIVERPOOL	01/12/44	NYC	12/12/44	33		
UC 47B	LIVERPOOL	04/12/44	NYC	17/12/44	5		
UC 48A	LIVERPOOL	08/12/44	NYC	22/12/44	32		
UC 48B	LIVERPOOL	12/12/44	NYC	24/12/44	6		
UC 49A	LIVERPOOL	16/12/44	NYC	27/12/44	21		
UC 49B	LIVERPOOL	20/12/44	NYC	31/12/44	12		
UC 50A	LIVERPOOL	24/12/44	NYC	04/01/45	26		
UC 50B	LIVERPOOL	28/12/44	NYC	08/01/45	7		
UC 51A	LIVERPOOL	01/01/45	NYC	12/01/45	19		
UC 51B	LIVERPOOL	05/01/45	NYC	15/01/45	18		
UC 52A	LIVERPOOL	10/01/45	NYC	21/01/45	24		
UC 52B	LIVERPOOL	12/01/45	NYC	23/01/45	12		
UC 53A	LIVERPOOL	19/01/45	NYC	02/02/45	31		
UC 53B	LIVERPOOL	21/01/45	NYC	04/02/45	12		
UC 54A	LIVERPOOL	28/01/45	NYC	09/02/45	32		
UC 55A	LIVERPOOL	02/02/45	NYC	14/02/45	26		
UC 55B	LIVERPOOL	06/02/45	NYC	18/02/45	9		
UC 56A	LIVERPOOL	11/02/45	NYC	23/02/45	30		
UC 56B	LIVERPOOL	14/02/45	NYC	25/02/45	7		
UC 57A	LIVERPOOL	20/02/45	NYC	05/03/45	34		
UC 057B	LIVERPOOL	23/02/45	NYC	05/03/45	11		
UC 58A	LIVERPOOL	26/02/45	NYC	09/03/45	19		
UC 58B	LIVERPOOL	02/03/45	NYC	12/03/45	13		
UC 59A	LIVERPOOL	06/03/45	NYC	17/03/45	28		
UC 59B	LIVERPOOL	10/03/45	NYC	21/03/45	25		
UC 60A	LIVERPOOL	14/03/45	NYC	25/03/45	20		
UC 60B	LIVERPOOL	18/03/45	NYC	29/03/45	13		
UC 61A	LIVERPOOL	21/03/45	NYC	01/04/45	25		
UC 61B	LIVERPOOL	25/03/45	NYC	04/04/45	9		
UC 62A	LIVERPOOL	31/03/45	NYC	11/04/45	41		
UC 62B	LIVERPOOL	02/04/45	NYC	13/04/45	10		
UC 63A	LIVERPOOL	07/04/45	NYC	19/04/45	32		
UC 63B	LIVERPOOL	11/04/45	NYC	23/04/45	13		
UC 64A	LIVERPOOL	16/04/45	NYC	28/04/45	26		
UC 64B	LIVERPOOL	19/04/45	NYC	30/04/45	19		
UC 65A	LIVERPOOL	23/04/45	NYC	05/05/45	34		
UC 65B	LIVERPOOL	27/04/45	NYC	07/05/45	10		
UC 66A	LIVERPOOL	02/05/45	NYC	13/05/45	40		
UC 66B	LIVERPOOL	04/05/45	NYC	15/05/45	8		
UC 67A	LIVERPOOL	09/05/45	NYC	19/05/45	37		
UC 67B	LIVERPOOL	13/05/45	NYC	23/05/45	12		
UC 68A	LIVERPOOL	17/05/45	NYC	28/05/45	28		
UC 68B	LIVERPOOL	19/05/45	NYC	29/05/45	11		
UC 69	LIVERPOOL	24/05/45	NYC	03/06/45	25		
UC 70A	LIVERPOOL	29/05/45	NYC	08/06/45	4		
UC 70B	LIVERPOOL	05/06/45	DISPERSED	06/06/45	2		
UC 71	LIVERPOOL	03/06/45	DISPERSED	04/06/45	6		

Losses incurred in UC convoys

Convoy	Ship's Name	GRT	Date of loss	Cause of loss	Comments
UC 1	ATHELPRINCESS	8,882 29 Br	23/02/43	U 186	Ballast. 1 dead

Convoy	Ship's Name	GRT	Date of loss	Cause of loss	Comments
UC 1	EMPIRE NORSEMAN	9,811 42 Br	23/02/43	U 202 & U 558	Ballast. No dead

Courtesy K Macpherson

Manned by the RCN, HMCS ANNAN on 25 Sept 1944, shortly after her completion in a British yard, the RCN having agreed to provide crews for seven RIVER class frigates owing to a RN manning shortage. The second of the name, her predecessor became USS NATCHEZ prior to completion in Canada. ANNAN served from June 1944 in the RCN in the North Atlantic. A typical British RIVER class design similar to earlier construction for the RN. Later Canadian built vessels of this type mounted a twin 4-inch in the "B" position and a 12pdr HA in "X." While serving with 6th Escort Group, in the support role, ANNAN sank U 1006 on 16 Oct 1944 with depth charges and gunfire and took 44 prisoners. Returned to the RN post-war, she was sold to the Royal Danish Navy as NIELS EBBESEN in Nov 1945.

Courtesy K Macpherson

The RIVER design frigate HMCS PENETANG at sea in March 1945. The twin 4-inch mounting fitted in the majority of RCN frigates is clearly shown and contrasts with the single mountings in British built ships. The aft gun position accommodated a single 12pdr in the Canadian built ships. The Hedgehog mounting in A position, with its box like weather cover, is also very apparent. The HF/DF aerial is mounted at the masthead and 271 radar at the after end of the bridge.

APPENDIX 4

CONVOY OPERATIONS SUPPORTING NORTH RUSSIA AND MALTA

All the convoy series already discussed were either trade convoys, i.e. convoys engaged on the normal wartime trade routes with cargo for overseas destinations or in ballast to collect imports, or operational convoys transporting troops. The political necessity of supporting Russia post-June 1941, and the desperate need to ensure the survival of Malta as an operational base and to feed its population, led to operational convoys whose escort frequently involved major Fleet operations and a command structure not usual to convoys.

The usual criteria for Trade Division figures of ships involved cannot be applied as statistics are either not available or the figures involved are obtained in a different way from that for normal convoys. In the tables which follow, the total number of ships carrying supplies to, or returning from, both Russia and Malta are shown. The figures include vessels which were forced, for whatever reason, to abort their passage: Convoy Rescue Ships, RFA oilers (whether freighting or supplying the escort), and RN-manned cargo carrying ships.

The losses incurred during these operations are listed by ship name, and include vessels lost in North Russia and Malta during their enforced stay in those ports, all of which were in very close proximity to enemy air bases. Marine cause losses, of whatever nature, are also included as these deprived the intended recipient of supplies. Finally "own goals," where ships were lost due to British minefields, are also included.

RUSSIAN OPERATIONS

The Russian operations, with numerous convoys and ships involved, suffered large losses on specific occasions although the overall loss was not significantly higher than North Atlantic convoys. The true nature of the operation has been somewhat obscured by the scale of losses in two convoys, in one of which almost all were suffered after a flawed decision to scatter the convoy had been taken in the Admiralty in London. It is therefore difficult to quantify the losses between "convoy attacks" and "independent ships" so that a complete list of losses in North Russian operations is given.

The purpose behind the efforts to take supplies to North Russia was also political, not strategic. The volume shipped was considerable in tonnage, but amounted to only approximately a quarter of all supplies to Russia in 1941-45. The greatest amount, some 70% in all, was shipped from the US to Russia via the Persian Gulf while a small quantity went in neutral Russian ships from the west coast of the US to Vladivostok. Russia did not enter the war against Japan until 9 Aug 1945, shortly before the surrender of that country.

Politically important though the northern route was, and costly in terms of merchantmen sunk and lives lost, it is questionable whether there would have been a significant, strategic effect on the outcome of the war if the summer convoys of 1942 had been suspended. That there would have been political dissent between the Russian and other Allied leaders, possibly of great significance, is undoubted.

Forty-two convoys and one major unescorted, independent operation by merchantmen were undertaken to North Russia for a total of 848 ships sailed of which 65 were lost. Thirty-six convoys and one major unescorted, independent westward passage were made for a total of 735 ships of which 40 were lost, a grand total in both directions of 1,583 ships, of which 105 were lost.

The decision to sail Russian convoys was a political one, general orders being issued by the Admiralty to the C-in-C Home Fleet to carry out the specific operation. The SOE of the escort and the Convoy Commodore exercised convoy command in the usual way. As enemy opposition increased, surface cover had to be provided against possible enemy action by major forces, and the escort then included a cruiser or cruisers in the vicinity of the convoy under the command of a Flag Officer who held overall tactical authority. Eventually, escort involved substantial elements of the Home Fleet: a cruiser squadron in close proximity to the convoy, one or two escort carriers, the convoy escort plus escort groups in support. The whole force came under the orders of the C-in-C Home Fleet, or his immediate deputy, with the Flag at sea in one of the heavy units.

◇ THE ALLIED CONVOY SYSTEM 1939-1945

In the tables below, the term "Kola Inlet" is used when ships either left an eastbound convoy for Archangel or joined a westbound convoy from that port. For the majority of ships, Murmansk or anchorages within Kola Inlet were the usual eastern terminus for convoys. Murmansk is, of course, an ice-free port while Archangel is icebound and unusable by shipping for several months during the winter.

■ Author's collection

The troopship EMPRESS OF AUSTRALIA entering Kola Fjord on 6 Nov 1944 at the end of the passage of convoy JW 61A to North Russia. She, with the other ship of the convoy SCYTHIA, conveyed some 11,000 Russian nationals captured in Normandy fighting for the German Army. This was the start of a general return of such prisoners, some 5,000 via the Gulf port of Basra, over 50,000 by British and Allied transports from South France to Odessa, and a figure reported as 60,000 returned by British troops after May 1945 from the Italo-Yugoslav border. Over 40,000 British, Commonwealth and Allied released prisoners of war were brought back from Odessa in the return voyages.

Eastbound PQ and JW convoy data, and independant passages

CONVOY	DEP. PORT	DEP. DATE	ARRIVAL PORT	ARR. DATE	TDS	MV SUNK	MV DMGD
DERVISH	LIVERPOOL	12/08/41	ARCHANGEL	31/08/41	7		
PQ 1	HVALFJORD	29/09/41	ARCHANGEL	11/10/41	11		
PQ 2	LIVERPOOL	13/10/41	ARCHANGEL	30/10/41	6		
PQ 3	HVALFJORD	09/11/41	ARCHANGEL	22/11/41	8		
PQ 4	HVALFJORD	17/11/41	ARCHANGEL	28/11/41	8		
PQ 5	HVALFJORD	27/11/41	ARCHANGEL	13/12/41	7		
PQ 6	HVALFJORD	08/12/41	MURMANSK	20/12/41	8		
PQ 7A	HVALFJORD	26/12/41	MURMANSK	12/01/42	2		
Escort did not meet convoy, ships independent							
PQ 7B	HVALFJORD	31/12/41	MURMANSK	11/01/42	9		
PQ 8	HVALFJORD	08/01/42	ARCHANGEL	17/01/42	8		
First eastbound convoy which was attacked							
PQ 9	REYKJAVIK	01/02/42	MURMANSK	10/02/42	10		
Convoy not attacked							
PQ 10	LOCH EWE	26/01/42	REYKJAVIK	31/01/42			
Ships formed part of PQ 9 for passage to Russia							

CONVOY	DEP. PORT	DEP. DATE	ARRIVAL PORT	ARR. DATE	TDS	MV SUNK	MV DMGD
PQ 11	KIRKWALL	14/02/42	MURMANSK	22/02/42	13		
Convoy not attacked							
PQ 12	REYKJAVIK	01/03/42	MURMANSK	12/03/42	17		
Convoy searched for but not attacked							
PQ 13	LOCH EWE	10/03/42	MURMANSK	31/03/42	19		
PQ 14	OBAN	26/03/42	MURMANSK	19/04/42	8		
Many ships returned due to ice and fog							
PQ 15	OBAN	10/04/42	MURMANSK	05/05/42	26		
PQ 16	REYKJAVIK	21/05/42	MURMANSK	30/05/42	36		
First heavily attacked convoy, 7 freighters sunk							
PQ 17	REYKJAVIK	27/06/42	DISPERSED	04/07/42	39		
Dispersed by Admiralty order, many losses							
PQ 18	LOCH EWE	02/09/42	ARCHANGEL	21/09/42	44		
Heavy air attacks, and losses							
JW 51A	LOCH EWE	15/12/42	KOLA INLET	25/12/42	16		
Undetected by the enemy							

◇ 188

CONVOY	DEP. PORT	DEP. DATE	ARRIVAL PORT	ARR. DATE	TDS	MV SUNK	MV DMGD
JW 51B	LOCH EWE	22/12/42	KOLA INLET	04/01/43	15		
	Attacked by enemy surface ships, no convoy loss						
JW 52	LOCH EWE	17/01/43	KOLA INLET	27/01/43	14		
	Minor attacks, no losses						
JW 53	LOCH EWE	15/02/43	KOLA INLET	27/02/43	29		
	No attacks due mainly to appalling weather						
JW 54A	LOCH EWE	15/11/43	KOLA INLET	24/11/43	19		
	Undetected passage						
JW 54B	LOCH EWE	22/11/43	ARCHANGEL	03/12/43	15		
	Undetected passage						
JW 55A	LOCH EWE	12/12/43	ARCHANGEL	22/12/43	19		
	Unmolested passage, battleship escort						
JW 55B	LOCH EWE	20/12/43	ARCHANGEL	30/12/43	19		
	Resulted in sinking of SCHARNHORST						
JW 56A	LOCH EWE	12/01/44	KOLA INLET	28/01/44	20		
	Three losses to U-Boat attack						
JW 56B	LOCH EWE	22/01/44	KOLA INLET	01/02/44	17		
	Many U-Boat attacks, no merchant losses						
JW 57	LOCH EWE	20/02/44	KOLA INLET	28/02/44	43		
	No merchant losses						
JW 58	LOCH EWE	27/03/44	KOLA INLET	04/04/44	50		
	No merchant losses						
JW 59	LOCH EWE	15/08/44	KOLA INLET	25/08/44	34		
	Russian warships in company on way to Russia						

CONVOY	DEP. PORT	DEP. DATE	ARRIVAL PORT	ARR. DATE	TDS	MV SUNK	MV DMGD
JW 60	LOCH EWE	15/09/44	KOLA INLET	23/09/44	31		
	No attacks or losses						
JW 61	LOCH EWE	20/10/44	KOLA INLET	28/10/44	30		
	No attacks or losses, three carriers in escort						
JW 61A	LIVERPOOL	31/10/44	MURMANSK	06/11/44	2		
	Carrying Russians captured in German service						
JW 62	LOCH EWE	29/11/44	KOLA INLET	07/12/44	31		
	Unscathed passage						
JW 63	LOCH EWE	30/12/44	KOLA INLET	08/01/45	38		
	Undetected passage						
JW 64	CLYDE	03/02/45	KOLA INLET	15/02/45	28		
JW 65	CLYDE	11/03/45	KOLA INLET	21/03/45	26		
JW 66	CLYDE	16/04/45	KOLA INLET	25/04/45	27		
JW 67	CLYDE	12/05/45	KOLA INLET	20/05/45	26		
	Post-war escorted sailing						

Operations FB, the unescorted passage of merchant ships to North Russia from Iceland, took place between 29 Oct and 2 Nov 1942. Thirteen merchant ships: six British, six American and one Russian, sailed at twelve-hour intervals. Three ships returned to Iceland, five were sunk and five arrived in North Russia.

Westbound QP and RA convoy data and independent passages

CONVOY	DEP. PORT	DEP. DATE	ARRIVAL PORT	ARR. DATE	TDS	MV SUNK	MV DMGD
QP 1	ARCHANGEL	28/09/41	SCAPA FLOW	10/10/41	14		
QP 2	ARCHANGEL	03/11/41	KIRKWALL	17/11/41	12		
QP 3	ARCHANGEL	27/11/41	DISPERSED	03/12/41	10		
	Arrived Seidisfjord						
QP 4	ARCHANGEL	29/12/41	DISPERSED	09/01/42	13		
QP 5	MURMANSK	13/01/42	DISPERSED	19/01/42	4		
QP 6	MURMANSK	24/01/42	DISPERSED	28/01/42	6		
QP 7	MURMANSK	12/02/42	DISPERSED	15/02/42	8		
	Arrived Seidisfjord						
QP 8	MURMANSK	01/03/42	REYKJAVIK	11/03/42	15		
QP 9	KOLA INLET	21/03/42	REYKJAVIK	03/04/42	18		
QP 10	KOLA INLET	10/04/42	REYKJAVIK	21/04/42	15		
QP 11	MURMANSK	28/04/42	REYKJAVIK	07/05/42	13		
QP 12	KOLA INLET	21/05/42	REYKJAVIK	29/05/42	14		
QP 13	ARCHANGEL	26/06/42	REYKJAVIK	07/07/42	35		
QP 14	ARCHANGEL	13/09/42	LOCH EWE	26/09/42	20		
QP 15	KOLA INLET	17/11/42	LOCH EWE	30/11/42	31		
RA 51	KOLA INLET	30/12/42	LOCH EWE	11/01/43	14		
RA 52	KOLA INLET	29/01/43	LOCH EWE	09/02/43	10		
RA 53	KOLA INLET	01/03/43	LOCH EWE	14/03/43	30		
RA 54A	KOLA INLET	01/11/43	LOCH EWE	14/11/43	13		
RA 54B	ARCHANGEL	26/11/43	LOCH EWE	09/12/43	10		

CONVOY	DEP. PORT	DEP. DATE	ARRIVAL PORT	ARR. DATE	TDS	MV SUNK	MV DMG
RA 55A	KOLA INLET	22/12/43	LOCH EWE	01/01/44	23		
RA 55B	KOLA INLET	31/12/43	LOCH EWE	08/01/44	8		
RA 56	KOLA INLET	03/02/44	LOCH EWE	11/02/44	39		
RA 57	KOLA INLET	02/03/44	LOCH EWE	10/03/44	33		
RA 58	KOLA INLET	07/04/44	LOCH EWE	14/04/44	38		
RA 59	KOLA INLET	28/04/44	LOCH EWE	06/05/44	43		
RA 59A	KOLA INLET	28/08/44	LOCH EWE	05/09/44	9		
RA 60	KOLA INLET	28/09/44	LOCH EWE	05/10/44	32		
RA 61	KOLA INLET	02/11/44	LOCH EWE	09/11/44	37		
RA 61A	KOLA INLET	11/11/44	LOCH EWE	17/11/44	2		
RA 62	KOLA INLET	10/12/44	LOCH EWE	19/12/44	29		
RA 63	KOLA INLET	11/01/45	LOCH EWE	21/01/45	31		
RA 64	KOLA INLET	17/02/45	LOCH EWE	28/02/45	33		
RA 65	KOLA INLET	23/03/45	LOCH EWE	01/04/45	26		
RA 66	KOLA INLET	29/04/45	CLYDE	08/05/45	27		
RA 67	KOLA INLET	23/05/45	CLYDE	30/05/45	25		

In addition to the convoys listed above, between 29 Oct 1942 and 24 Jan 1943 twenty-five Russian merchant ships made independent unescorted passage westwards from North Russia. Three ships, DONBASS, KRASNY PARTIZAN and UFA were lost, all the others arrived safely.

THE ALLIED CONVOY SYSTEM 1939-1945

Losses incurred in Russian convoys, independent passages and in Russian ports.

Ship's Name	GRT			Date of loss	Cause of loss	Convoy	Comments
WAZIRISTAN	5,135	24	Br	02/01/42	U 134	PQ 7A	General. 47 dead
IJORA	2,815	21	Russ	07/03/42	IHN	QP 8	Timber. Casualties unknown
RACELAND	4,807	10	Pan	28/03/42	AIRCRAFT	PQ 13	9,000 tons stores & general. 7 dead
EMPIRE RANGER	7,008	42	Br	28/03/42	AIRCRAFT	PQ 13	War material. 1 dead in PoW camp
BATEAU	4,687	26	Pan	29/03/42	Z 26	PQ 13	War material. 39 dead
EFFINGHAM	6,421	19	Amer	30/03/42	U 435	PQ 13	General & war material. No dead
INDUNA	5,086	25	Br	30/03/42	U 376	PQ 13	2,700 tons stores & cased petrol. 31 dead
EMPIRE STARLIGHT	6,850	41	Br	03/04/42	AIRCRAFT	IN PORT	At Murmansk, 1 dead. Salved postwar
NEW WESTMINSTER CITY	4,747	29	Br	03/04/42	AIRCRAFT	IN PORT	At Murmansk. 2 dead. Salved postwar
EMPIRE COWPER	7,164	41	Br	11/04/42	AIRCRAFT	QP 10	Pitprops & chrome ore. 19 dead
HARPALION	5,486	32	Br	11/04/42	AIRCRAFT	QP 10	600 tons manganese ore. No dead
EL OCCIDENTE	6,008	10	Pan	13/04/42	U 435	QP 10	210 tons chrome ore. 20 dead
KIEV	5,823	17	Russ	13/04/42	U 435	QP 10	No details available
LANCASTER CASTLE	5,172	37	Br	14/04/42	AIRCRAFT	IN PORT	At Murmansk. 10 dead
EMPIRE HOWARD	6,985	41	Br	16/04/42	U 403	PQ 14	2,000 tons war material. 25 dead
TSIOLKOVSKY	2,847	35	Russ	01/05/42	Z 24 & Z 25	QP 11	Cargo unknown. 27 dead
JUTLAND	6,153	28	Br	02/05/42	AIRCRAFT	PQ 15	1,560 tons stores, 800 t ammo. 1 dead
CAPE CORSO	3,807	29	Br	02/05/42	AIRCRAFT	PQ 15	Munitions. 50 dead
BOTAVON	5,848	12	Br	03/05/42	AIRCRAFT	PQ 15	2,600 tons stores. 21 dead
SYROS	6,191	20	Amer	26/05/42	U 703	PQ 16	War material. 12 dead
CITY OF JOLIET	6,167	20	Amer	27/05/42	AIRCRAFT	PQ 16	7,000 tons stores. No dead
MORMACSUL	5,481	20	Amer	27/05/42	AIRCRAFT	PQ 16	War material. Dead unknown
ALAMAR	5,689	16	Amer	27/05/42	AIRCRAFT	PQ 16	War material. No dead
LOWTHER CASTLE	5,171	37	Br	27/05/42	AIRCRAFT	PQ 16	4,800 tons stores. 1 dead
EMPIRE LAWRENCE	7,457	41	Br	27/05/42	AIRCRAFT	PQ 16	5,000 tons stores. 19 dead
EMPIRE PURCELL	7,049	42	Br	27/05/42	AIRCRAFT	PQ 16	1,500 tons stores & general. 8 dead
STEEL WORKER	5,685	20	Amer	03/06/42	MINED IN PORT		At Murmansk after arrival
ALCOA CADET	4,823	19	Amer	21/06/42	MINED IN PORT		At Kola inlet. 1 dead
CHRISTOPHER NEWPORT	7,191	42	Amer	04/07/42	AIRCRAFT	PQ 17	8,144 tons stores. 3 dead
WILLIAM HOOPER	7,177	42	Amer	04/07/42	AIRCRAFT	PQ 17	8,486 tons stores. 3 dead
NAVARINO	4,841	37	Br	04/07/42	AIRCRAFT	PQ 17	2,750 tons war stores. 4 dead
DANIEL MORGAN	7,177	42	Amer	05/07/42	U 88	PQ 17	8,539 tons war stores. 3 dead
RIVER AFTON	5,479	35	Br	05/07/42	U 703	PQ 17	3,479 tons stores. 22 dead
EARLSTON	7,195	41	Br	05/07/42	U 334	PQ 17	3,000 tons war stores. Dead unknown
HONOMU	6,977	19	Amer	05/07/42	U 456	PQ 17	7,704 tons war stores. No dead
PAULUS POTTER	7,168	42	Du	05/07/42	AIRCRAFT	PQ 17	Cargo unknown. No dead
WASHINGTON	5,564	19	Amer	05/07/42	AIRCRAFT	PQ 17	5,819 tons stores. No dead
BOLTON CASTLE	5,203	39	Br	05/07/42	AIRCRAFT	PQ 17	5,000 tons war cargo. No dead
PAN KRAFT	5,644	19	Amer	05/07/42	AIRCRAFT	PQ 17	5,000 tons a/c & spares. 2 dead
PETER KERR	6,476	20	Amer	05/07/42	AIRCRAFT	PQ 17	6,600 tons stores. No dead
FAIRFIELD CITY	5,686	21	Amer	05/07/42	AIRCRAFT	PQ 17	7,207 tons war stores. 8 dead
ZAAFARAN	1,559	21	Br	05/07/42	AIRCRAFT	PQ 17	Rescue ship. 1 dead
CARLTON	5,127	20	Amer	05/07/42	U 88	PQ 17	5,000 tons general. 3 dead
EMPIRE BYRON	6,645	41	Br	05/07/42	U 703	PQ 17	3,500 tons war stores. 7 dead
EXTERMINATOR	6,115	24	Pan	05/07/42	MINED	QP 13	Ballast. No dead. Salved, bu 1943 in USA
RODINA	4,441	22	Russ	05/07/42	MINED	QP 13	No dead
MASSMAR	5,828	20	Amer	05/07/42	MINED	QP 13	No dead
HEFFRON	7,611	19	Amer	05/07/42	MINED	QP 13	No dead
JOHN RANDOLPH	7,191	41	Amer	05/07/42	MINED	QP 13	No dead, forepart salved, bu postwar
HYBERT	6,120	20	Amer	05/07/42	MINED	QP 13	No dead
PAN ATLANTIC	5,411	19	Amer	06/07/42	AIRCRAFT	PQ 17	6,129 tons war stores. 26 dead
JOHN WITHERSPOON	7,191	42	Amer	06/07/42	U 255	PQ 17	8,555 tons war stores. 1 dead
ALDERSDALE	8,402	37	Br	07/07/42	U 457	PQ 17	Escort oiler. Dead not known
HARTLEBURY	5,082	34	Br	07/07/42	U 355	PQ 17	3,200 tons war stores. 38 dead
ALCOA RANGER	5,116	19	Amer	07/07/42	U 255	PQ 17	5,093 tons stores. No dead
OLOPANA	6,069	20	Amer	08/07/42	U 255	PQ 17	6,532 tons war stores. 6 dead
HOOSIER	5,060	20	Amer	10/07/42	U 376	PQ 17	War stores. No dead
EL CAPITAN	5,255	17	Pan	10/07/42	U 251	PQ 17	War stores. No dead
SUKHONA	3,124	18	Russ	13/09/42	AIRCRAFT	PQ 18	No information available
JOHN PENN	7,177	42	Amer	13/09/42	AIRCRAFT	PQ 18	7,500 tons war stores. 3 dead
EMPIRE STEVENSON	6,209	41	Br	13/09/42	AIRCRAFT	PQ 18	War stores. All (59) dead

Ship's Name	GRT			Date of loss	Cause of loss	Convoy	Comments
STALINGRAD	3,559	31	Russ	13/09/42	U 408	PQ 18	No information available
MACBETH	4,941	20	Pan	13/09/42	AIRCRAFT	PQ 18	6,072 tons general. No dead
AFRICANDER	5,441	21	Pan	13/09/42	AIRCRAFT	PQ 18	Machinery, tanks, a/c. No dead
OLIVER ELLSWORTH	7,191	42	Amer	13/09/42	U 408	PQ 18	7,447 tons general. 1 dead
EMPIRE BEAUMONT	7,044	42	Br	13/09/42	AIRCRAFT	PQ 18	4,000 tons stores. 6 dead
OREGONIAN	4,862	17	Amer	13/09/42	AIRCRAFT	PQ 18	War stores. 28 dead
WACOSTA	5,432	20	Amer	13/09/42	AIRCRAFT	PQ 18	Cargo unknown. 49 survivors, dead unknown
ATHELTEMPLAR	8,992	30	Br	14/09/42	U 457	PQ 18	9,400 tons FFO. 3 dead
MARY LUCKENBACH	5,049	19	Amer	14/09/42	AIRCRAFT	PQ 18	5,219 tons war stores. Dead unknown
KENTUCKY	5,446	21	Amer	18/09/42	AIRCRAFT	PQ 18	Ashore. No dead. Part cargo salved
SILVER SWORD	4,937	19	Amer	20/09/42	U 255	QP 14	Chrome ore, asbestos etc. 1 dead
BELLINGHAM	5,345	20	Amer	22/09/42	U 435	QP 14	Chrome ore & general. No dead
OCEAN VOICE	7,174	41	Br	22/09/42	U 435	QP 14	Timber. No dead
GRAY RANGER	3,313	41	Br	22/09/42	U 435	QP 14	RFA escort oiler. 21 survivors
EMPIRE GILBERT	6,640	41	Br	02/11/42	U 586	OP FB	War stores. 63 dead
DEKABRIST	7,363	03	Russ	04/11/42	AIRCRAFT	OP FB	Cargo & casualties unknown
WILLIAM CLARK	7,176	42	Amer	04/11/42	U 354	OP FB	6,256 tons stores. 30 dead
EMPIRE SKY	7,455	41	Br	06/11/42	U 625	OP FB	Stores. No survivors
DONBASS	7,925	35	Russ	07/11/42	Z 27	INDEP	No survivors
CHULMLEIGH	5,445	38	Br	16/11/42	U 625	OP FB	Stores. Dead unknown
GOOLISTAN	5,851	29	Br	23/11/42	U 625	QP 15	No survivors
KUZNETZ LESOV	3,974	33	Russ	23/11/42	U 601	QP 15	No data available
BALLOT	6,131	22	Pan	02/01/43	WRECKED	JW 51B	War material, dead unknown
UFA	1,892	17	Russ	26/01/43	U 255	INDEP	No data available
KRASNY PARTIZAN	2,418	27	Russ	29/01/43	U 255	INDEP	No data available
GREYLOCK	7,460	21	Amer	03/02/43	U 255	RA 52	1,200 tons calcium phosphate. No dead.
EXECUTIVE	4,978	20	Amer	05/03/43	U 255	RA 53	1,520 tons potassium chlorate. 9 dead.
RICHARD BLAND	7,191	42	Amer	05/03/43	U 255	RA 53	1,140 tons lumber. 3 dead
J L M CURRY	7,167	42	Amer	07/03/43	FOUNDERED	RA 53	Hull defects, ballast. No dead
PUERTO RICAN	6,076	19	Amer	09/03/43	U 586	RA 53	Ore. 61 dead, 1 survivor
OCEAN FREEDOM	7,173	42	Br	13/03/43	AIRCRAFT	IN PORT	Lost at Murmansk. No dead
PENELOPE BARKER	7,177	42	Amer	25/01/44	U 278	JW 56A	7,850 tons war stores. 16 dead
ANDREW G CURTIN	7,200	43	Amer	25/01/44	U 716	JW 56A	9,000 tons war stores. 3 dead
FORT BELLINGHAM	7,153	43	Br	26/01/44	U 360 & U 957	JW 56A	4,800 tons war stores. 39 dead
EMPIRE TOURIST	7,062	43	Br	04/03/44	U 703	RA 57	1,100 tons lumber, 600 tons coal. No dead
WILLIAM S THAYER	7,176	43	Amer	30/04/44	U 711	RA 59	Ballast, 165 passengers. 33 dead
SAMSUVA	7,219	44	Br	29/09/44	U 310	RA 60	Pitprops. 3 dead
EDWARD H CROCKETT	7,176	44	Amer	29/09/44	U 310	RA 60	1,659 tons chrome ore. 1 dead
HORACE GRAY	7,200	43	Amer	14/02/45	U 711	BK 3	2,400 tons potash. No dead. To join RA 64
NORFJELL	8,129	42	Nor	14/02/45	U 968	BK 3	Ballast. 2 dead. To join RA 64
THOMAS SCOTT	7,176	42	Amer	17/02/45	U 968	RA 64	Ballast, 40 passengers. No dead
HENRY BACON	7,177	42	Amer	23/02/45	AIRCRAFT	RA 64	Ballast. 22 dead
HORACE BUSHNELL	7,176	43	Amer	20/03/45	U 995	JW 65	6,500 tons stores. 5 dead
THOMAS DONALDSON	7,210	44	Amer	20/03/45	U 968	JW 65	7,679 tons war stores. 4 dead

THE MALTA CONVOYS AND OPERATIONS

The ability of Malta to resist attack and to remain an operational base was entirely dependent upon the supplies taken to the island between June 1940 and Dec 1942 by the Royal and Merchant Navies acting jointly in complete accord. Had these supplies been prevented from reaching Malta, or even a convoy delayed for a short interval, the surrender of the island would have become inevitable, so limited were the reserves of food available in Malta.

The Malta operations can be divided into five separate and discrete aspects:

1. The supply of fighter aircraft for the defence of the island, carried out in a series of operations by aircraft carriers and ships of the Home Fleet, Force H, local Gibraltar based escorts and, on two notable occasions, a US carrier.
2. The supply of high value, i.e. medical and urgent war stores, concentrated food and the like, and the transport of essential personnel by operational, surface warships.
3. Similar supply by submarines, both operational craft and those converted to a dedicated stores role.

4. The attempted transport of bulk stores by covert, unescorted passage of merchantmen.
5. Major Fleet operations, from both east and west, to force through the passage of convoys of merchantmen carrying bulk supplies.

Only the last two categories are germane to this book. They were far more important to the island, its population and garrison, and the outcome of the global conflict than the North Russian counterpart, but were on a much smaller scale. There were a total of 209 ship passages to and from Malta, resulting in 30 merchant ships being lost. The total of warship losses in these two operational categories was far higher than in the comparable Russian series.

In the list of convoy data, it should be remembered that in most cases, the OPERATION name is far better known than the appropriate convoy title. Control of the merchant ships of the convoys was also totally different from the usual chain of command: there was no Commodore, direct command of the convoy was vested in the Senior Officer of the close escort and each merchantman carried a Naval Officer as adviser to the Master. The control of the entire operation, frequently involving almost the entire strength of the Mediterranean Fleet or major portions of the Home Fleet and Force H, rested with a senior Flag Officer afloat.

Statistics of merchant ship sailings to and from Malta in the period 21 June 1940 to 31 December 1942

OP NAME/ CONVOY	DEP. PORT	SAILED	ARRIVAL PORT	ARR. DATE	TOTAL	LOST SHIPS
MF 1	MALTA	09/07/40	ALEXANDRIA	11/07/40	3	
MS 1	MALTA	10/07/40	ALEXANDRIA	14/07/40	5	
MF 2	ALEXANDRIA	29/08/40	MALTA	02/09/40	3	
MF 3	ALEXANDRIA	08/10/40	MALTA	11/10/40	4	
MF 4	MALTA	11/10/40	ALEXANDRIA	16/10/40	3	
MW 3	ALEXANDRIA	04/11/40	MALTA	10/11/40	5	
ME 3	MALTA	10/11/40	ALEXANDRIA	13/11/40	4	
MW 4	ALEXANDRIA	23/11/40	MALTA	26/11/40	4	
Op COLLAR	GIBRALTAR	25/11/40	MALTA	26/11/40	2	
ME 4	MALTA	26/11/40	ALEXANDRIA	29/11/40	5	
MW 5A	ALEXANDRIA	16/12/40	MALTA	20/12/40	2	
MW 5B	ALEXANDRIA	18/12/40	MALTA	20/12/40	5	
ME 5A	MALTA	20/12/40	ALEXANDRIA	23/12/40	4	
MG 1	MALTA	20/12/40	GIBRALTAR	24/12/40	2	
Op EXCESS	GIBRALTAR	06/01/41	MALTA	10/01/41	1	
MW 5.5	ALEXANDRIA	07/01/41	MALTA	10/01/41	2	
ME 5.5	MALTA	10/01/41	ALEXANDRIA	13/01/41	2	
ME 6	MALTA	10/01/41	ALEXANDRIA	13/01/41	7	
Op MC 8	MALTA	20/02/41	ALEXANDRIA	22/02/41	2	
MW 6	ALEXANDRIA	19/03/41	MALTA	23/03/41	4	
Op MD 2	ALEXANDRIA	18/04/41	MALTA	21/04/41	1	
ME 7	MALTA	19/04/41	ALEXANDRIA	22/04/41	4	
Op TEMPLE	GIBRALTAR	28/04/41	MALTA	-	1	1
Op MD 3	MALTA	28/04/41	ALEXANDRIA	30/04/41	1	
Op TIGER	GIBRALTAR	06/05/41	ALEXANDRIA	12/05/41	5	1
MW 7A	ALEXANDRIA	06/05/41	MALTA	10/05/41	4	
MW 7B	ALEXANDRIA	05/05/41	MALTA	10/05/41	2	
GM 1	GIBRALTAR	21/07/41	MALTA	24/07/41	6	
MG 1	MALTA	23/07/41	GIBRALTAR	26/07/41	7	
Op PROPELLER	GIBRALTAR	13/09/41	MALTA	19/09/41	1	
Op HALBERD, GM 2	GIBRALTAR	25/09/41	MALTA	29/09/41	9	1
Op HALBERD, MG 2	MALTA	26/09/41	GIBRALTAR	29/09/41	1	
INDEPENDENT	MALTA	27/09/41	GIBRALTAR	30/09/41	2	
INDEPENDENT	MALTA	16/10/41	GIBRALTAR	19/10/41	1	
INDEPENDENT	MALTA	22/10/41	GIBRALTAR	27/10/41	3	1
Op ASTROLOGER	GIBRALTAR	12/11/41	MALTA	-	1	1
Op ASTROLOGER	GIBRALTAR	14/11/41	MALTA	-	1	1
Untitled operation	MALTA	05/12/41	ALEXANDRIA	08/12/41	1	
Untitled operation	ALEXANDRIA	15/12/41	MALTA	18/12/41	1	
ME 8	MALTA	26/12/41	ALEXANDRIA	29/12/41	4	
Op MF 2	ALEXANDRIA	06/01/42	MALTA	08/01/42	1	
Op MF 2	MALTA	06/01/42	ALEXANDRIA	08/01/42	1	
Op MF 3/MW 8/8A	ALEXANDRIA	16/01/42	MALTA	19/01/42	4	1
Op MF 4	ALEXANDRIA	24/01/42	MALTA	27/01/42	1	
Op MF 4	MALTA	25/01/42	ALEXANDRIA	28/01/42	2	
Op MF 5, MW 9	ALEXANDRIA	12/02/42	MALTA	15/02/42	3	2
ME 10	MALTA	13/02/42	ALEXANDRIA	16/02/42	3	
MW 10	ALEXANDRIA	20/03/42	MALTA	23/03/42	4	4
Op HARPOON	GIBRALTAR	11/06/42	MALTA	15/06/42	5	4
Op VIGOROUS	ALEXANDRIA	12/06/42	MALTA	17/06/42	12	2
Op PEDESTAL	GIBRALTAR	10/08/42	MALTA	14/08/42	14	9
INDEPENDENT	ALEXANDRIA	01/11/42	MALTA	03/11/42	1	
Op CRUPPER	GIBRALTAR	08/11/42	MALTA	-	2	2
MW 13	ALEXANDRIA	17/11/42	MALTA	20/11/42	4	
MW 14	PORT SAID	01/12/42	MALTA	05/12/42	5	
MW 15	PORT SAID	06/12/42	MALTA	10/12/42	2	
ME 11	MALTA	07/12/42	PORT SAID	11/12/42	9	
MW 16	ALEXANDRIA	11/12/42	MALTA	14/12/42	3	
ME 12	MALTA	17/12/42	PORT SAID	20/12/42	4	
MW 17	ALEXANDRIA	17/12/42	MALTA	21/12/42	2	
MW 18	ALEXANDRIA	28/12/42	MALTA	31/12/42	2	
Total					209	30

Losses incurred in Malta operations

Convoy/Operation	Ship's name	GRT	Yr	Flag	Date of loss	Cause of loss	Cargo. casualties
TEMPLE	PARRACOMBE	4,702	28	Br	02/05/41	MINE	Stores. 29 dead
TIGER	EMPIRE SONG	9,228	4	Br	09/05/41	MINE	Stores. 18 dead
HALBERD	IMPERIAL STAR	12,427	35	Br	27/09/41	AIRCRAFT	Stores. No dead
ASTROLOGER	EMPIRE DEFENDER	5,649	10	Br	15/11/41	AIRCRAFT	Stores. 4 dead
ASTROLOGER	EMPIRE PELICAN	6,463	19	Br	14/11/41	AIRCRAFT	Stores. 1 dead
MW 8A	THERMOPYLAE	6,655	30	Nor	19/01/42	AIRCRAFT	Stores, troops. 3 dead
MW 9	CLAN CHATTAN	7,262	37	Br	14/02/42	AIRCRAFT	Stores. No dead
MW 9	ROWALLAN CASTLE	7,793	39	Br	14/02/42	AIRCRAFT	Stores. No dead
MW 10	BRECONSHIRE	9,776	39	Br	26/03/42	AIRCRAFT	Fuels, stores
MW 10	CLAN CAMPBELL	7,255	37	Br	23/03/42	AIRCRAFT	Stores. 10 dead
MW 10	PAMPAS	5,415	41	Br	26/03/42	AIRCRAFT	Stores. No dead
MW 10	TALABOT	6,798	36	Nor	26/03/42	AIRCRAFT	Stores. No dead
HARPOON	TANIMBAR	8,169	30	Du	14/06/42	AIRCRAFT	Stores. 23 dead
HARPOON	CHANT	5,601	38	Amer	15/06/42	AIRCRAFT	Stores. 4 dead
HARPOON	KENTUCKY	9,308	42	Amer	15/06/42	AIRCRAFT	Fuels. No dead
HARPOON	BURDWAN	6,069	28	Br	15/06/42	AIRCRAFT	Stores. 3 dead
VIGOROUS	BHUTAN	6,104	29	Br	14/06/42	AIRCRAFT	Stores, avgas. 6 dead
VIGOROUS	AAGTEKERK	6,811	34	Du	14/06/42	AIRCRAFT	Stores. 48 dead
PEDESTAL	DEUCALION	7,516	30	Br	12/08/42	AIRCRAFT	Stores. 1 dead
PEDESTAL	EMPIRE HOPE	12,688	41	Br	12/08/42	AIRCRAFT	Stores. No dead
PEDESTAL	CLAN FERGUSON	7,347	38	Br	12/08/42	AIRCRAFT	Stores. 18 dead
PEDESTAL	ALMERIA LYKES	7,773	40	Amer	13/08/42	MAS 554	Stores. No dead
PEDESTAL	GLENORCHY	8,982	39	Br	13/08/42	MS 31	Stores. 7 dead
PEDESTAL	SANTA ELISA	8,379	41	Amer	13/08/42	S 36	Stores. 4 dead
PEDESTAL	WAIRANGI	12,436	35	Br	13/08/42	MAS 557	Stores. No dead
PEDESTAL	WAIMARAMA	12,843	38	Br	13/08/42	AIRCRAFT	Stores. 83 dead
PEDESTAL	DORSET	13,041	34	Br	13/08/42	AIRCRAFT	Stores. No dead
PEDESTAL	OHIO	9,514	40	Br	15/08/42	AIRCRAFT	Fuels. 2 dead
CRUPPER	ARDEOLA	2,609	12	Br	10/11/42	CAPTURED	Stores. No dead
CRUPPER	TADORNA	1,947	28	Br	10/11/42	CAPTURED	Stores. No dead

Notes:
1. OHIO was towed in to Malta and, despite sinking on arrival, over 90% of her cargo of 13,500 tons of varied fuels was recovered.
2. A small quantity of fuel was recovered from the wreck of BRECONSHIRE after her sinking off Malta.
3. A small and unknown quantity of cargo was removed from PAMPAS and TALABOT prior to their sinking. Later other cargo was recovered from the two sunken wrecks, quantity unknown.

Author's collection

The North African theatre, the Middle East generally and India all had to be supplied with personnel and their equipment from the UK via the Cape of Good Hope. Here ships of convoy WS 12, which sailed from the Clyde 30 Sept 1941, are seen.

From left to right in the picture DOMINION MONARCH, CLAN LAMONT (distant and making smoke) SAMARIA (in the foreground) and HIGHLAND PRINCESS.

APPENDIX 5

THE WS CONVOYS

Mention of this series of highly important troop convoys appears in the main text. The complexity of the convoys, which sailed from up to four ports in the UK to form the convoy off Oversay in the North Channel, makes it difficult to prepare a meaningful tabular listing as has been done for the other series.

The problem is accentuated by the frequency with which individual convoys divided and re-formed, the use of two ports in South Africa for fuelling and watering, and the sub-division of the main convoy body into two or more sub-sections with differing destinations when in the Indian Ocean. The abridged information in the table that follows will, it is hoped, identify the individual convoys sufficiently to guide researchers to the appropriate documents in the PRO at Kew. So far as the author is aware that repository is the sole source of official information on this series of convoys.

The number of ships shown as being in each convoy is that of merchant ships which formed the convoy on departure from the UK. The figure does not include warships that formed part of the convoy for passage overseas nor merchant ships that returned to the UK for any reason.

Readers wishing to identify a convoy in which they or a family member proceeded overseas, should note that the embarkation of personnel took place up to three days prior to the sailing from the embarkation port. The final sailing of the convoy, i.e. its departure from the Clyde OR its formation off Oversay, could be several days after departure from a port of embarkation. In at least one case, personnel ships lay in Moelfre Bay for several days prior to the Clyde portion sailing. As convoys sailed at approximately four-week intervals, it should not be difficult to isolate the basic details of a specific convoy for research purposes.

APPENDIX 5

Convoy	Sailed/Formed	Ships	Comment
WS 1	29/06/40	3	AQUITANIA, MAURETANIA and QUEEN MARY from UK to Ceylon, arrived 29/07/40, where troops were transferred to smaller ships for passage to Suez under a different designation
WS 2	05/08/40	16	Sailed from Liverpool and Clyde to S Africa. Twelve ships went on to Suez;, dispersing 14/09/40. Three, plus an additional ship, went to Bombay arriving 15/09/40
WS 3A SLOW	03/10/40	5	Sailed from Liverpool, finally joined WS 3B FAST on 03/11/40
WS 3B FAST	07/10/40	6	Sailed Liverpool and the Clyde, and was joined on 03/11/40 by WS 3A SLOW arriving at Suez 16/11/40
WS 3C	01/11/40	2	Formed at Capetown for Suez. At Aden joined convoy BN 8 to arrive Suez 23/11/40
WS 4	02/11/40	17	Formed off Oversay, dividing into Fast and Slow sections 11/11/40, re-forming 17/11/40 at Freetown and arriving at Suez 22 and 23/12/40
WS 4B	18/11/40	10	Sailed as a single convoy and arrived Suez 28/12/40
WS 5A	18/12/40	25	FAST section sailed 19/12/40, combined at sea. Attacked by HIPPER 25/12/40, no loss. Convoy scattered, 5 ships for Gibraltar arrived there, remainder proceeded to Freetown where convoy re-formed. Finally arrived Suez 16/02/41
WS 5B	12/01/41	20	Delayed in Moelfre Bay 8 to 11/01/41. Arrived Suez 03/03/41
WS 5BX	24/02/41	4	4 ships of WS 5B sailing from Mobasa to Bombay arriving 03/03/41. Then two further ships but under the same designation, from Bombay on 05/03/41 to Singapore arriving 11/03/41
WS 6A	09/02/41	29	Joined by WS 6B at Freetown, finally dispersing off Perim 15/04/41 to arrive Suez as independent ships
WS 6B	17/02/41	4	Sailed to join WS 6A at Freetown
WS 7	24/03/41	21	Convoy divided off Mombasa, Suez ships dispersing off Perim to arrive at Suez 06/05/41
WS 7X	01/05/41	4	Detached from WS 7 on this date, to arrive Bombay 05/05/41
WS 8A	26/04/41	15	Included five ships for Malta in Op TIGER. All other ships arrived Suez 13/06/41
WS 8B	22/05/41	7	Dispersed off Aden 04/07/41 for Suez
WS 8X	31/05/41	3	Finally dispersed off Aden 11/07/41 to arrive Suez 15/07/41
WS 8C	09/08/41	19	Azores invasion convoy. Sailed Clyde to Scapa Flow, returning Clyde 13/08/41 on cancellation of operation
WS 9A	03/06/41	15	Some ships detached as WS 9AX, remainder dispersed off Aden 21/07/41 for Suez.
WS 9AX	18/07/41	3	Ships detached from WS 9A for Bombay arriving 22/07/41. Then onward to Colombo arriving 30/07/41 and Singapore arriving 05/08/41
WS 9A2	11/07/41	3	Formed at Durban from ILE DE FRANCE, MAURETANIA and NIEUW AMSTERDAM, dispersed off Aden 18/07 for Suez
WS 9B	30/06/41	12	Some ships detached as WS 9BX, remainder dispersed off Aden 14/08/41 for Suez.
WS 9BX	13/08/41	2	Ships detached from WS 9B for Bombay, arriving 16/08/41
WS 9C	13/07/41	9	Principally ships for Malta in Operation SUBSTANCE, arriving Gibraltar 20/07/41
WS 10	03/08/41	19	Divided in S Africa with Suez ships dispersing 23/09/41 off Aden
WS 10B	06/09/41	5	Bombay ships sailing from S Africa after detaching from WS 10. Arrived Bombay 20/09/41
WS 10X	16/08/41	6	Dispersed off Aden 27/09/41 for Suez
WS 11	31/08/41	19	Divided Fast and Slow after sailing, re-formed at Freetown. Convoy dispersed off Aden 19/10/41 for Suez
WS 11X	17/10/41	12	Twelve ships that detached from WS 11 on 17/10/41 to arrive at Bombay 22/10/41. 6 ships then went on to Colombo arriving 31/10, the convoy then went on to Singapore arriving 06/11/41
WS 11X	17/09/41	15	Using the same designation as above, consisted of ships for Malta in Operation HALBERD, and small LSIs for Gibraltar arriving 25/09/41
WS 12	01/10/41	24	Detaching some ships in the Indian Ocean, Suez ships dispersed off Aden 20/11/41
WS 12J	17/11/41	3	Three ships detached from WS 12 to arrive Colombo 23/11/41
WS 12V	24/11/41	2	Two ships from Colombo to Singapore arriving 28/11/41.
WS 12X	10/11/41	6	Six USN transports that embarked British troops at Halifax NS for Suez. Sailed via Trinidad with USN escort to arrive Capetown 09/12/41. Sailed with a RN escort 13/12/41 for Bombay arriving 27/12/41
WS 12Z	13/11/41	16	Divided into three parts in the Indian Ocean
WS 12ZA		3	Three ships from WS 12Z for Suez, dispersing off Aden 04/01/42
WS 12ZB		8	Eight ships from WS 12Z for Bombay, arriving 06/01/42
DM 1		4	Four ships from WS 12Z for Singapore arriving 13/01/42
WS 14	09/12/41	28	Divided into three parts off S Africa on 19/01/42
WS 14A	19/01/42		Suez ships which dispersed off Aden 22/01/42
WS 14B	19/01/42		Bombay ships which arrived 28/01/42
DM 2	19/01/42		Batavia ships which arrived 03/02/42
WS 15	12/01/42	23	Divided into three parts in Indian Ocean 26/02/42
WS 15A	26/02/42		Suez ships which dispersed off Aden 01/03/42
WS 15B	26/02/42		Bombay ships which arrived 04/03/42
DM 3	26/02/42		Singapore ships which were diverted to Colombo and some then to Bombay to arrive 04/03/42 and 06/03/42 respectively
WS 16	17/02./42	21	Divided in Indian Ocean l03/04/42 into two sections
WS 16A	03/04/42	3	Ships for Suez dispersing off Aden 06/04/42

◇ THE ALLIED CONVOY SYSTEM 1939-1945

Convoy	Sailed/Formed	Ships	Comment
WS 16B	03/04/42	11	Ships for Bombay arriving 08/04/42
WS 17	23/03/42	32	Divided at Freetown, re-formed in S Africa. Convoy divided 11/05/42
WS 17A	11/05/42	4	Four ships detached for Suez, dispersing off Aden 14/05/42
WS 17B	11/05/42	9	Nine ships detached for Bombay, arriving 16/05/42
WS 17BZ	10/05/42	7	Convoy formed at Mombasa, sailing as shown for Bombay arriving there 19/05/42
WS 18	15/04/42	20	Plus naval repair ship HECLA which was damaged, and freighter SOUDAN sunk, by mines 15/05/42. Convoy divided 02/06/42 when 3 ships detached for Suez, dispersing off Aden 04/06/42, remainder to Bombay arriving 07/06/42
WS 19	10/05/42	17	Convoy divided 27/06/42 with Suez ships dispersing off Aden 30/06/42 and Bombay detachment arriving 01/07/42
WS 19P	01/06/42	23	An unusual repetition of a number for an individual convoy, which divided when leaving S Africa into WS 19P and WS 19L
WS 19PA	08/07/42	11	Eleven of the original 19P convoy, which detached 17/07/42 for Suez, dispersing off Aden 20/07/42
WS 19PB	08/07/42	6	Six of the original 19P convoy detached 17/07/42 for Bombay arriving 23/07/42
WS 19L	07/07/42	10	Convoy formed off Durban from the original WS 19P, for Suez dispersing off Aden 17/07/42
WS 19W	23/05/42	1	Single ship unescorted passage by QUEEN MARY to Suez arriving 22/06/42
WS 19Z	05/06/42	5	Ships for Malta in Op HARPOON, entering Mediterranean 12/06/42
WS 19Q		1	AQUITANIA, detached from WS 19P as a single, unescorted, ship for Suez arriving 08/07/42
WS 19Y	17/06/42	1	Single ship, unescorted passage by QUEEN ELIZABETH to Suez arriving 18/07/42
WS 20	21/06/42	22	After leaving S Africa, convoy divided on 01/08/42
WS 20A			Ships for Suez, dispersing off Aden 06/08/42
WS 20B			Ships for Bombay arriving 09/08/42
WS 21	29/7/42	12	Convoy divided on 10/09/42, after leaving S Africa
WS 21A		6	Ships for Suez, dispersing off Aden 16/09/42
WS 21B		6	Ships for Bombay arriving 19/09/42
WS 21P	17/07/42	13	Another repetitive use of a number. Convoy total includes eight ships sailing from the USA as AS 4 which joined at sea on 05/08/42. Only 10 ships sailed from S Africa 16/08/42 all for Suez, dispersing off Aden 29/08/42
WS 21PG		3	Three ships from WS 21P which formed a separate convoy off Durban 19/08 for the Persian Gulf, dispersing off Hormuz 01/09/42
WS 21S	02/08/42	14	Ships for Malta in Op PEDESTAL, passed Gibraltar Strait 10/08/42
WS 22	29/08/42	20	Convoy divided in Indian Ocean with 2 ships arriving Mombasa 12/10
WS 22A		4	Suez ships from WS 22 dispersing off Aden 16/10/42
WS 22B		6	Bombay ships from WS 22 arriving 17/10/42
WS 23	04/10/42	8	Delayed departure with ships watering in Belfast Lough prior to 04/10/42. Divided in Indian Ocean
WS 23A	17/11/42	4	Suez ships of WS 23, dispersed off Aden 21/11/42
WS 23B	17/11/42	4	Bombay ships of WS 23 arriving 24/11/42
WS 24	31/10/42	7	Routed from UK to Bahia, Brazil to avoid the Op Torch convoys, divided when leaving Durban, to which all ships went.
WS 24A	13/12/42	1	ARAWA, in company with convoy CM 36, arrived Aden 28/12/42 for Suez
WS 24B	06/12/42	2	Bombay ships from WS 24 arriving 17/12/42
WS 25	18/12/42	9	Arrived Durban, final destination, 18/10/43
WS 25W	23/12/42	1	Single, unescorted, passage by QUEEN MARY to Suez arriving 18/01/43
WS 26	23/01/43	17	Sailed in company with KMF 8. Detached as WS 26 29/01/43. Divided in the Indian Ocean 11/03/43
WS 26A	11/03/43	7	Suez ships from WS 26, dispersing off Aden 15/03/43
WS 26B	11/03/43	6	Bombay ships from WS 26 arriving 17/03/43
WS 27	27/02/43	6	Sailed with KMF 10A, dividing on 02/03/43 with 6 ships in WS convoy. Convoy dispersed off Aden 09/04/43
WS 28	16/03/43	15	Sailed with KMF 11, dividing 21/03/43 with 15 ships in WS convoy. Convoy dispersed off Aden 30/04/43 for Suez.
WS 29	16/04/43	13	Sailed with KMF 12, dividing with 13 ships in WS convoy, arriving at Freetown 28/04/43
WS 29A	20/04/43	2	Small convoy arriving at Freetown 04/05/43
WS 29	06/05/43		Combined WS 29 and WS 29A from Freetown, dividing again in the Indian Ocean after leaving S Africa
WS 29A	02/06/43		Seven Aden ships for Suez dispersing off Aden 08/06/43
WS 29B	02/06/43		Six Bombay ships, arriving there 10/08/43
WS 30	21/05/43	7	Sailed with KMF 15 dividing 25/05/43 with 7 ships in WS convoy. Final arrivals 1 detached 03/07/43 independent for Colombo, 2 detached independent 04/07/43 for Aden and Suez and 2 ships to Bombay arriving 09/07/43
WS 31	21/06/43	7	Sailed with KMF 17, dividing 26/06/43 with 7 ships in WS convoy. Final, reduced, convoy sailed Capetown for Bombay arriving 13/08/43
WS 32	20/07/43	8	Sailed with KMF 20, dividing 25/07/43 with 8 ships in WS convoy. Convoy arrived Bombay 10/09/43, STRATHMORE having detached independent for Suez on 06/09/43
WS 33	17/08/43	17	Sailed with KMF 22 all ships proceeding to Gibraltar. 6 WS ships sailed Gibraltar 03/09/43. Divided in the Indian Ocean with DUCHESS OF RICHMOND proceeding to Aden for Suez. Remaining ships assumed title of CM 46 to Bombay arriving 04/11/43.

APPENDIX 6

SOURCES

Information regarding convoys of the 1939-45 period rests primarily in three locations: London, Ottawa and Washington DC. The three nations have varying legislation regarding custody of and access to Government records but in all cases the end result is the same: they are each in a single national location.

In the case of British records, they are held at the Public Record Office, Ruskin Avenue, Kew, in southwest London and have been accessible since 1972. They appear in three main series of records: ADM (for Admiralty) 199, 217 and 237. Of these, the 199 series provides the greater part of available information.

In Ottawa the Directorate of History and Heritage, National Defence HQ, holds some surviving Canadian records which, apart from covering the local Canadian coastal convoy system, included many documents concerning the North Atlantic where the Royal Canadian Navy played such a prominent role throughout the war.

In Washington DC, the United States Navy Historical Centre in Washington Navy Yard holds certain convoy records. However the main body, including all remaining convoy signals and papers in US custody (a massive archive with a great deal of information on the North Atlantic convoys as well as the purely American organized series, both local and oceanic), have passed to the National Archives and Records Administration, 700 Pennsylvania Avenue NW, Washington DC 20408-0001, USA.

The British, Canadian and US repositories all permit personal visitors but under varying restrictions, and none will conduct research on behalf of correspondents in the normal course. The National Archives in the USA will, at a fee, supply requested photostats but under strictly limited conditions.

A researcher unable to attend personally at the British archive at the Public Record Office must appoint a representative to do his research.

The Canadian authorities limit visits to the Directorate of History to Tuesday and Wednesday of each week; otherwise, by prior arrangements made in writing. Brief, written questions are dealt with; otherwise, the services of a private research agent is necessary for which the individual must make their own arrangements, including costs.

Many Canadian naval records, including log books and suchlike, have been transferred to the National Archives of Canada, 395 Wellington Street, Ottawa, Canada K1A 0N3, to which office application for research facilities must be made. The actual division, and therefore location, of 1939-45 Canadian naval records is uncertain, and prior application for assistance is therefore advisable to one or other of the departments referred to.

Writing from forty years' experience of research into convoys, it can be stated categorically that there are no known alternative sources giving information of worth on convoys, other than those referred to in the following passage.

With specialised knowledge and experience of the convoy systems, use can be made of such records as library copies of Lloyd's List of Confidential Movements 1939-45, Voyage Record Cards of Lloyd's of London and casualty returns, both war loss and marine cause. The two volumes of *Lloyd's War Losses, the Second World War* are also of great value. This last publication is still in print and is held by most major reference libraries; the Guildhall Library also holds the originals. All the sources referred to can be accessed at the Guildhall Library, in the City of London. While access is freely granted by the custodians, personal research must be undertaken; except for minor enquiries, researchers must rely upon their own efforts.

British records of convoys fall into two categories: reports and papers prepared by the Commodores relating to the passage of a specific convoy, and Reports of Proceedings (RoPs) prepared by the Senior Officer of the Escort (SOE) relating to his command's activities during a specific period, these may cover one or more convoys.

Due to the differing times of rendering reports, and to the original Admiralty filing system, such reports usually appear in separate volumes in the ADM 199 series, each volume containing a number of reports on convoys of one or more series. It is usual therefore for at least two volumes to have to be consulted to cover a single convoy, sometimes more. The PRO maintains an adequate card index system of individual convoy numbers, each card annotated with the relevant ADM references.

Additional to the ADM 199 series, which usually contains only the Commodore's Report and a few supporting documents, or the Report of Proceedings, there is the ADM 217 series, which contains ONLY RoPs for a limited period of the war. Some convoys may however be covered by this series only.

Finally, there is the ADM 237 series that is the remnant of an original archive of files, one for each individual convoy. Such files may be bulky, up to six inches thick, some consist only of one or two pieces of paper. At best, the file contains both the Commodore's Report and the RoP plus copies of the signal traffic relating to the specific convoy. In the main, only North Atlantic and UK coastal convoy are covered by this series.

There are few files for any convoys with codes beginning with a letter before O. Initially, the Admiralty filing system contained all available Commodores' reports and RoPs, and these were casebound within the Admiralty Record Office. It is these files, in their original docket covers which bear the comments made during circulation in Admiralty, that appear in ADM 199. There are gaps in the sequence of convoys, and it must be remembered that outward convoys' reports were made at an overseas port, and that a number of reports may have been lost at sea in transit to Britain. Similarly no filing system is foolproof and some may have been discarded or mislaid in the very early days. It is known that many reports, held at the original Western Approaches HQ in Devonport, were lost in severe air raids there prior to the HQ move to Liverpool.

The ADM 237 systems used to be much more complete; for example, a complete set of files is known to have been sent to Admiralty from Liverpool in late 1945, some 1,200 parcels. Nevertheless, of 358 HX files only 12 survive! This is due to wholesale destruction to clear archive space some thirty years ago (600 shelf feet of files were destroyed) authorised by the then Admiralty Librarian on the grounds that the ADM 199 series adequately covered the matter.

In Canada, likewise, there are major gaps. Here the loss of primary documents is accidental; an error by junior staff and contractors destroyed numerous original records complete with their staff comments, principally RoPs of Canadian warships.

American records, at both the Washington Navy Yard and at the National Archive, are much more complete but suffer from a lack of preservation and consequent deterioration. The bulk of material is so great that the cost of microfilming or the like is prohibitive and there are doubts as to the ability to use many of the records without causing serious damage as they decay with age.

It is an unfortunate fact that the preservation of very large quantities of paper records, especially when not originally intended to be other than ephemeral, is expensive in finance, personnel and space. The large bulk of convoy papers and their very limited value except to a small number of enthusiasts, plus the fact that they are not revenue producing, makes major expenditure on them by national governments unlikely. Similarly, any effort to charge fees for access, even if expended on preservation and storage, would probably place the cost far beyond the means of the amateur researchers who are almost the sole users of the archive.

Amongst published works on the subject of convoy there are two, both official, which are essential for researchers. The first, issued by the Naval Staff as a Restricted document on 1 Oct 1945, is a chronological list of all British and foreign (excluding enemy) merchant ships lost and damaged by the enemy during 1939-45. Known by its title of BR 1337, its value lies principally in the thirty pages of text, graphs and charts that precede the ship loss listings. These listings are those which were made publicly available in 1947 and have since been commercially reprinted, but without any amendment whatever. They are, inevitably, of dubious accuracy due to their hurried preparation so soon after the end of hostilities, with inadequate time to consult all records. They give an accurate listing of ships lost, but the information as to date can be inaccurate and positions far too general, such as "North Atlantic." The two volume *Lloyd's War Losses*, already referred to, is a more accurate and therefore preferable source.

The second source is the two volume *Defeat of the Enemy Attack on Shipping 1939-1945* issued as a Confidential Book CB 3304 in two volumes in 1957. These volumes are available since 1988 in the Public Record Office under references ADM 239/415 and 416. They have also been made available in mid-1998, in facsimile, by the Naval Records Society from whose publishers copies may be obtained. It is also probable that major libraries will hold copies of the 1998 volume.

These sources, with their detailed analyses and statistics, are vital to research into the subject of convoy and are strongly recommended to students of the subject.

CONFIDENTIAL.

Commodore A. J. Baxter in S.S. ARDEOLA for Gibraltar/Lisbon.
Vice " Master of S.S. TADORNA for Seville.
Rear " " of S.S. BLAIRATHOL for Gibraltar.

CRUISING ORDER : MERCANTILE CONVOY

CONVOY O.G. 79   Date. 26/...

Columns to be 3 Day & 5 Night cables apart
Ships in column to be 2 cables apart
Normal cruising speed of the Convoy 8 knots
Commodore of the Convoy (Guide) in
S.S. ARDEOLA
Vice-Commodore in S.S. TADORNA
Rear-Commodore in S.S. BLAIRATHOL

OCEAN ESCORT.

Name.	
H.M.S. BLACK SWAN	S/O
LA MALOUINE	
CARNATION	
BLUEBELL	
MYOSOTIS	
~~CAMPION~~	
STONECROP	
~~FOWEY~~	
MALLOW	

CALL SIGNS.

Commodore (individual).............YDD1
Vice-Commodore (individual)........YDD2
Whole Convoy......................YDD3
Commodore's Portion of Convoy.....YDD4
Vice-Commodore's Portion of Convoy..YDD5
Senior Officer, Local Escort......YDD6
Rear Commodore Portion   YDD7
Oban Portion   YDD8

PORT.   CRUISING ORDER.

Column Number	1	2 Vice Commodore	3	4 Commodore	5	6 Rear Commodore	7
Distinguishing Signal and Convoy Call Sign of each column.	01	02	03	04	05	06	07
Name	L CAM 11 EMPIRE FOAM Gyc.	L CL 21 TADORNA	L M/F 31 BARON RAMSEY	L CL 41 ARDEOLA	G CL 51 SHUNA	O 61 BLAIRATHOL	L CAM 71 EMPIRE DARWIN
Height, After Masthead to Waterline	(9) 60 feet	(5) 70 feet	(5) 90 feet	(7) 91 feet	(7) 58 feet	84 feet	feet
Name	M CL 12 TINTERN ABBEY	M 22 BLAIRESK	L CL X 32 EMPIRE SNIPE	L P 42 LAGO (NOR)	G CL 52 WALLSEND	O CL 62 ~~SALTWICK~~	O 72 GLAISDALE
Height, After Masthead to Waterline	(5) 68 feet	(5) 86 feet	(5) 78 feet	(7) 75 feet	(7) 66 feet	90 feet	86 feet
Name	M 13 CARA	M CL 23 L.R. POLO	M 33 LYNCHAUG (NOR)	O X 43 BRITISH COAST	G CL S 53 INNESMOOR	G CL S 63 M/F ~~EMPIRE CAMERON~~ L.R.	O CL 73 ~~RUNSWICK~~
Height, After Masthead to Waterline	(5) 60 feet	(5) 70 feet	(5) 90 feet	(6) feet	(6) 87 feet	feet	81 feet
Name	O 14 CISNEROS	M 24 OTTINGE	M 34 SHETLAND	G CL S 44 EMPIRE IMPALA	G 54 ~~FINLAND~~	O 64 CITY OF OXFORD	O 74 HOLMBURY
Height, After Masthead to Waterline	84 feet	(10) 72 feet	(6) 55 feet	(7) 100 feet	feet	85 feet	80 feet
Name	15	25	35	M 45 ADJUTANT	55	65	75
Height, After Masthead to Waterline	feet	feet	feet	(5) 66 feet	feet	feet	feet

54. 62. 63. 73 These vessels did not sail.

L = Liverpool Ships
M = Milford "
G = Clyde "
O = Oban "
CAM = Catapult Ship
L.R. = Light Repeating Ship.

(-) = Number of Guns.
X = Quantity of Explosives.
P = Passengers
S = Special
M/F = D/F Guard.
Gyc. = Gyro Compass.

NAVAL CONTROL
28 JAN 1942
LIVERPOOL

APPENDIX 7

Convoy form A.1.

Amongst the papers delivered to the assembled Masters and other officers at the Convoy Conference that preceded every convoy was the Convoy Form A 1. A facsimile of such a form, for convoy OG 79, is shown after this text.

The preamble to the form contains the distances between ships and columns in this early 1942 convoy, still variable, with column distances being 3 cables (600 yards) apart during daylight and 5 cables (1,000 yards) at night. Ships were to keep station 2 cables (400 yards) astern of their next ahead. The names of the Ocean Escort are then given, followed by the call signs both individual and collective, for the convoy.

The Commodore, Vice Commodore and Rear Commodore ships are all indicated with a rubber stamped representation of the appropriate pennant flown by those ships, in the appropriate colours on the original. Commodore and Rear Commodore pennant was white and blue, Vice Commodore red.

Ships' names are shown in the numbered squares that indicate the number of the position and therefore the pennant number of the ship for the period of the convoy. For the information of all, a series of code letters and figures then appear within the relevant square for each ship.

Taking pennant 11, EMPIRE FOAM as an example, the upper line contains the letters "L" and "CAM" indicating that she was a CAM ship sailing from Liverpool. The letters that appear in the top left-hand corner of other squares, "M," "G" and "O" indicate Milford Haven, Glasgow and Oban as sailing ports. An ON convoy of this period would also have shown "LE" Loch Ewe, Gibraltar convoys rarely included ships from that port. Other letters also appearing in the top line, centrally or in the right hand corner, are "CL" Coloured lights (for night signalling purposes), "M/F" indicating Medium Frequency Radio Guard, "X" Explosives onboard, "P" carrying passengers and "S" special cargo. EMPIRE FOAM's name also has "Gyc" typed below it, indicating that she was fitted with a gyro compass. The magnetic compass was the standard item fitted in almost all merchant ships of that era

Immediately above the ship's name in square 23 appears "LR" signifying Light Repeating, i.e. SS POLO was obliged to repeat all Coloured Light signals observed.

The final line shows, on the left, a figure enclosed in brackets indicating the number of guns mounted and a numeric value preceding the printed word "feet." This last item indicated the height of the ship's mainmast so that this, in conjunction with a sextant, could be used to maintain the correct interval between ships in the same column.

All ships are British unless stated; foreign ships have their (abbreviated) nationality shown after their names, as in LAGO and LYNGHAUG.

Courtesy K Macpherson

At Halifax, NS at the end of Sept 1945. Two Type IXC/40 U-boats, U 889 outboard and U 190 inboard, lie alongside three RCN frigates, HMCS JOLIETTE, THETFORD MINES and ST CATHARINES. The last named, the inboard ship, had undergone a long refit since Sept 1944 to fit her for Pacific service. Note that she has lost the HF/DF aerial at the masthead, replacing it with a USN radar; her bridge has been altered and she no longer has the 271 radar mounted in the other frigates.

U 889 was passed to the USN and sunk as a target 20 Nov 1947, U 190 remained in Canadian service for trials and was finally sunk by RCN vessels 21 Oct 1947.

INDEX OF SHIP LOSSES

SHIP NAME	CONVOY	LOSS DATE	PGE
AAGTEKERK	VIGOROUS	14/06/42	193
ACCRA	OB 188	26/07/40	155
ADAMAS	SC 118	08/02/43	137
ADELLEN	ON 67	22/02/42	161
AENEAS	OA 177G	02/07/40	149
AFRICANDER	PQ 18	13/09/42	191
AFRIKA	SC 118	07/02/43	137
AGUILA	OG 71	19/08/41	177
AIKATERINI	SC 19	29/01/41	136
AKABAHRA	KMS 6	07/01/43	171
ALAMAR	PQ 16	27/05/42	190
ALCOA CADET	MINED IN PORT	21/06/42	190
ALCOA RANGER	PQ 17	07/07/42	190
ALDERAMIN	SC 122	17/03/43	138
ALDERGROVE	OG 71	22/08/41	177
ALDERPOOL	SC 26	03/04/41	136
ALDERSDALE	PQ 17	07/07/42	190
ALEXANDROS	SC 3	15/09/40	136
ALHAMA	HG 75	24/10/41	179
ALMA DAWSON	SC 11	24/11/40	136
ALMERIA LYKES	PEDESTAL	13/08/42	193
ALPERA	MKS 13	22/05/43	146
ALPHERAT	GUS 25	21/12/43	183
ALVA	OG 71	19/08/41	177
ALWAKI	OA 179	10/07/40	149
AMERIKA	HX 234	22/04/43	132
AMSTELLAND	OB 290	26/02/41	155
ANADARA	ON 67	24/02/42	161
ANDALUSIAN	SL 68	17/03/41	145
ANDERSON	HX 174	10/02/42	132
ANDREA F LUCKENBACH	HX 228	10/03/43	132
ANDREW G CURTIN	JW 56A	25/01/44	191
ANNA MAZARAKI	ON 94	24/05/42	161
ANNAVORE	HG 76	21/12/41	179
ANNEBERG	SC 94	08/08/42	137
ANTHEA	HX 93	08/12/40	131
ANTIGONE	SC 129	11/05/43	138
ANTONIO	OS 119	28/03/45	170
APAPA	SL 53	15/11/40	145
APPALACHEE	HX 90	01/12/40	131
ARDANBHAN	OB 263	27/12/40	155
ARDEOLA	CRUPPER	10/11/42	193
ARIOSTO	HG 75	24/10/41	179
ARMANISTAN	OG 16	03/02/40	176
ARTHUR MIDDLETON	UGS 3	01/01/43	181
ASHANTIAN	ONS 3	21/04/43	164
ASHWORTH	SC 104	13/10/42	137
ASSYRIAN	SC 7	19/10/40	136
ASTRA II	OA 204	29/08/40	149
ATHELBEACH	OB 293	07/03/41	155
ATHELCREST	HX 65	25/08/40	131
ATHELPRINCESS	UC 1	23/02/43	186
ATHELSULTAN	SC 100	22/09/42	137
ATHELTEMPLAR	PQ 18	14/09/42	191
AVELONA STAR	SL 36	30/06/40	145
AVOCETA	HG 73	26/09/41	179
AYMERIC	ONS 7	17/05/43	164
BALINGKAR	SL 118	18/08/42	146
BALLADIER	SC 95	15/08/42	137
BALLOT	JW 51B	02/01/43	191

SHIP NAME	CONVOY	LOSS DATE	PGE
BALTALLINN	OG 74	20/09/41	177
BALTONIA	MKS 7	08/02/43	146
BARBARA MARIE	SL 34	12/06/40	145
BARBRO	SC 44	20/09/41	136
BARFONN	SC 48	16/10/41	136
BARNBY	HX 126	22/05/41	132
BARON CARNEGIE	OB 334	11/06/41	155
BARON COCHRANE	ON 154	28/12/42	161
BARON LOUDON	HG 34F	19/06/40	179
BARON LOVAT	OG 63	06/06/41	176
BARON PENTLAND	SC 42	10/09/41	136
BARON VERNON	SL 125	30/10/42	146
BARRISTER	MKS 4	04/01/43	146
BARRWHIN	HX 212	29/10/42	132
BATEAU	PQ 13	29/03/42	190
BATNA	ON 92	13/05/42	161
BEACHY	HG 49	11/01/41	179
BEATUS	SC 7	18/10/40	136
BEAVERBURN	OA 84	05/02/40	149
BEAVERFORD	HX 84	05/11/40	131
BEDUIN	HX 112	16/03/41	131
BEIGNON	SL 36	01/07/40	145
BELGIAN SOLDIER	ON 115	03/08/42	161
BELGRAVIAN	SL 81	05/08/41	146
BELLINGHAM	QP 14	22/09/42	191
BELLO	ON 153	16/12/42	161
BENALBANACH	KMS 6	07/01/43	171
BENCLEUCH	ON 42	12/12/41	161
BENGORE HEAD	OB 318	09/05/41	155
BENJAMIN HARRISON	UGS 6	16/03/43	181
BENNEKOM	OS 10	31/10/41	170
BENVORLICH	OB 298	19/03/41	155
BENWYVIS	SL 68	21/03/41	145
BEREBY	OS 7	24/09/41	170
BERURY	SC 42	11/09/41	136
BEURSPLEIN	OB 290	26/02/41	155
BHUTAN	VIGOROUS	14/06/42	193
BILDERDIJK	HX 79	19/10/40	131
BIRCHBANK	KMS 31	11/11/43	171
BLACKHEATH	KMS 76G	10/01/45	171
BLAIRANGUS	HX 72	21/09/40	131
BLAIRMORE	SC 1	24/08/40	136
BLAIRNEVIS	MKS 81	13/02/45	146
BODNANT	OB 265	30/12/40	155
BOEKELO	SC 7	19/10/40	136
BOKA	OB 216	20/09/40	155
BOLD VENTURE	SC 48	16/10/41	136
BOLTON CASTLE	PQ 17	05/07/42	190
BOMA	OB 193	05/08/40	155
BONDE	ONS 5	05/05/43	164
BONHEUR	OB 228	15/10/40	155
BONNEVILLE	SC 121	10/03/43	137
BORGESTAD	SL 64S	12/02/41	145
BORGLAND	OB 290	26/02/41	155
BOTAVON	PQ 15	03/05/42	190
BOTWEY	OS 1	26/07/41	170
BRADFYNE	SC 11	23/11/40	136
BRANDANGER	HX 77	11/10/40	131
BRANDENBURG	HG 53	10/02/41	179
BRANT COUNTY	HX 228	11/03/43	132

SHIP NAME	CONVOY	LOSS DATE	PGE
BRECONSHIRE	MW 10	26/03/42	193
BRILLIANT	SC 109	18/11/42	137
BRISTOL CITY	ONS 5	05/05/43	164
BRITANNIC	HG 53	09/02/41	179
BRITISH ARDOUR	HX 231	05/04/43	132
BRITISH ENDEAVOUR	OG 19F	22/02/40	176
BRITISH GUNNER	OB 289	24/02/41	155
BRITISH MONARCH	HG 34F	19/06/40	179
BRITISH RELIANCE	SC 26	02/04/41	136
BRITISH SECURITY	HX 126	20/05/41	132
BRITSUM	OA 178	04/07/40	149
BRITTANY	SL 125	28/10/42	146
BROCKLEY HILL	HX 133	24/06/41	132
BRONTE	OB 25	30/10/39	155
BRONXVILLE	SC 97	31/08/42	137
BROOMPARK	ON 113	25/07/42	161
BROWNING	KMS 2	11/11/42	171
BRUSE	SC 11	23/11/40	136
BRYNYMOR	ON 76	14/03/42	161
BUITENZORG	SL 60	14/01/41	145
BULLMOUTH	SL 125	30/10/42	146
BULYSSES	SC 42	10/09/41	136
BURDWAN	HARPOON	15/06/42	193
BUSSUM	SC 11	23/11/40	136
CADILLAC	HX 109	01/03/41	131
CAIRNROSS	OB 74	17/01/40	155
CALEDONIA	HX 121	28/04/41	131
CANADIAN STAR	HX 229	18/03/43	132
CANONESA	HX 72	21/09/40	131
CAPE CORSO	PQ 15	02/05/42	190
CAPE RACE	SC 94	10/08/42	137
CAPE RODNEY	SL 81	05/08/41	146
CAPE ST GEORGE	SL 42	05/08/40	145
CAPE YORK	HX 65	26/08/40	131
CAPIRA	SC 97	31/08/42	137
CAPRELLA	HX 79	20/10/40	131
CAPULET	HX 121	28/04/41	131
CARLIER	KMS 31	11/11/43	171
CARLTON	PQ 17	05/07/42	190
CARRAS	SC 122	19/03/43	138
CARSBRECK	HG 75	24/10/41	179
CASTLEMOOR	HX 20	25/02/40	130
CERVANTES	HG 73	26/09/41	179
CHANCELLOR	HXF 11	02/12/39	133
CHANT	HARPOON	15/06/42	193
CHARLES L D	HX 217	09/12/42	132
CHATEAUROUX	SC 159	02/11/44	138
CHATTANOOGA CITY	ON 166	22/02/43	161
CHELSEA	HX 66	30/08/40	131
CHEPO	ON 55	14/01/42	161
CHRISTIAN MICHELSON	UGS 17	26/09/43	181
CHRISTOPHER NEWPORT	PQ 17	04/07/42	190
CHULMLEIGH	OP FB	16/11/42	191
CISCAR	OG 71	19/08/41	177
CITY OF BEDFORD	HX 97	30/12/40	131
CITY OF BENARES	OB 213	18/09/40	155
CITY OF CARDIFF	SL 119	28/08/42	146
CITY OF CHRIST CHURCH	KMS 11G	21/03/43	171
CITY OF JOLIET	PQ 16	27/05/42	190
CITY OF MANDALAY	HG 3	17/10/39	179

THE ALLIED CONVOY SYSTEM 1939-1945

SHIP NAME	CONVOY	LOSS DATE	PGE
CITY OF MANILA	SL 118	19/08/42	146
CITY OF OXFORD	HG 84	15/06/42	179
CITY OF PERTH	MKS 10	26/03/43	146
CITY OF SIMLA	OB 216	21/09/40	155
CITY OF VENICE	KMS 18B	04/07/43	171
CITY OF WATERFORD	OG 74	19/09/41	177
CLAN ALPINE	OS 44	13/03/43	170
CLAN CAMPBELL	MW 10	23/03/42	193
CLAN CHATTAN	MW 9	14/02/42	193
CLAN CHISHOLM	HG 3	17/10/39	179
CLAN FERGUSON	PEDESTAL	12/08/42	193
CLAN MACNAB	SL 68	18/03/41	145
CLAN MACTAGGART	MKS 1X	16/11/42	146
CLAN OGILVY	SL 68	21/03/41	145
CLARK MILLS	MKS 42	09/03/44	146
CLONLARA	OG 71	22/08/41	177
COCKAPONSET	HX 126	20/05/41	132
COCLE	ON 92	12/05/42	161
CONCH	HX 90	02/12/40	131
CONDYLIS	SC 94	10/08/42	137
CONVALLARIA	SC 7	18/10/40	136
CORACERO	HX 229	17/03/43	132
CORINALDO	SL 125	30/10/42	146
CORTES	HG 73	26/09/41	179
COUNSELLOR	HX 22	08/03/40	130
COURLAND	HG 53	09/02/41	179
CREEKIRK	SC 7	18/10/40	136
CRESSADO	HG 82	08/05/42	179
CRISTALES	ON 92	12/05/42	161
CULLEN (See R J CULLEN)			
CUMBERLAND	OB 202	23/08/40	155
CURRY (See J L M CURRY)			
CYRUS H MCCORMICK	HX 348	18/04/45	133
DAGHILD	SC 118	07/02/43	137
DAGMAR I	HG 53	09/02/41	179
DALBLAIR	OA 204	28/08/40	149
DALCAIRN	HX 72	21/09/40	131
DALCROY	SC 107	02/11/42	137
DALEBY	SC 107	04/11/42	137
DALLAS CITY	OA 178	04/07/40	149
DALVEEN	HX 73	28/09/40	131
DANIEL CHESTER FRENCH	UGS 33	06/03/44	181
DANIEL MORGAN	PQ 17	05/07/42	190
DANIEL WEBSTER	KMS 37	10/01/44	171
DARLINGTON COURT	HX 126	20/05/41	132
DARTFORD	ON 100	11/06/42	161
DARU	SL 85	15/09/42	146
DAVANGER	HX 77	11/10/40	131
DAYDAWN	OB 244	21/11/40	155
DEFOE	OS 41	24/09/42	170
DEKABRIST	OP FB	04/11/42	191
DELPHIN	SC 6	09/10/40	136
DENPARK	SL 109	12/05/42	146
DERRYNANE	SL 64S	12/02/41	145
DEUCALION	OA 178	04/07/40	149
DEUCALION	PEDESTAL	12/08/42	193
DEVIS	KMS 18B	05/07/43	171
DIONYSSIOS STATHATOS	HX 91	12/12/40	131
DIXCOVE	SL 87	24/09/41	146
DJAMBI	OS 44	13/03/43	170
DJURDJURA	SL 76	13/06/41	145
DOKKA	OB 228	17/10/40	155
DOLIUS	ONS 5	05/05/43	164
DONAX	ON 139	22/10/42	161

SHIP NAME	CONVOY	LOSS DATE	PGE
DONBASS	INDEP	07/11/42	191
DORSET	PEDESTAL	13/08/42	193
DUMFRIES	MKS 71	23/12/44	146
DUNAFF HEAD	OB 293	07/03/41	155
DUNBAR CASTLE	OA 69	09/01/40	149
DUNSTAN	OB 306	06/04/41	155
DVINOLES	HX 173	04/02/42	132
EARLSTON	PQ 17	05/07/42	190
EASTERN STAR	OB 318	07/05/41	155
EDWARD BATES	UGS 30	01/02/44	181
EDWARD BLYDEN	SL 87	22/09/41	146
EDWARD H CROCKETT	RA 60	29/09/44	191
EFFINGHAM	PQ 13	30/03/42	190
EGYPTIAN	SC 121	07/03/43	137
EIDANGER	ON 67	24/02/42	161
EIRINI KYRIAKIDOU	SL 76	13/06/41	145
EL ALMIRANTE	HX 235	22/04/43	132
EL ARGENTINO	OS 52KM	26/07/43	170
EL CAPITAN	PQ 17	10/07/42	190
EL COSTON	CU 15	26/02/44	184
EL OCCIDENTE	QP 10	13/04/42	190
EL OSO	HX 14	11/01/40	130
ELIN K	HX 229	16/03/43	132
ELISABETH DAL	HX 300	03/08/44	133
ELISABETH VAN BELGIE	ON 127	10/09/42	161
ELMBANK	HX 72	21/09/40	131
ELMCREST	OA 178	04/07/40	149
ELUSA	HX 126	21/05/41	132
EMBASSAGE	OS 4	27/08/41	170
EMILE FRANCQUI	ON 153	16/12/42	161
EMMY	ON 94	25/05/42	161
EMPIRE ABILITY	SL 78	27/06/41	145
EMPIRE ADVENTURE	OB 216	20/09/40	155
EMPIRE ANTELOPE	SC 107	02/11/42	137
EMPIRE BANNER	KMS 8	07/02/43	171
EMPIRE BEAUMONT	PQ 18	13/09/42	191
EMPIRE BOWMAN	SL 126	30/03/43	146
EMPIRE BREEZE	ON 122	25/08/42	161
EMPIRE BRIGADE	SC 7	19/10/40	136
EMPIRE BURTON	SC 44	20/09/41	136
EMPIRE BYRON	PQ 17	05/07/42	190
EMPIRE CELT	ON 67	24/02/42	161
EMPIRE CLOUGH	ON 100	10/06/42	161
EMPIRE COMMERCE	MKS 26	30/09/43	146
EMPIRE COWPER	QP 10	11/04/42	190
EMPIRE CROSSBILL	SC 42	11/09/41	136
EMPIRE DEFENDER	ASTROLOGER	15/11/41	193
EMPIRE DELL	ON 92	12/05/42	161
EMPIRE DORADO	SC 53	22/11/41	137
EMPIRE ENERGY	SC 52	04/11/41	136
EMPIRE EVE	KMS 14	18/05/43	171
EMPIRE FROST	SC 23	13/03/41	136
EMPIRE FUSILIER	ON 60	09/02/42	161
EMPIRE GEMSBUCK	SC 52	03/11/41	137
EMPIRE GILBERT	OP FB	02/11/42	191
EMPIRE GOLD	HX 348	18/04/45	132
EMPIRE HARTEBEESTE	SC 100	20/09/42	137
EMPIRE HAWKSBILL	OS 34	19/07/42	170
EMPIRE HERITAGE	HX 305	08/09/44	133
EMPIRE HERON	SC 48	15/10/41	136
EMPIRE HOMER	ON 57	15/01/42	161
EMPIRE HOPE	PEDESTAL	12/08/42	193
EMPIRE HOUSMAN	ON 217	31/12/43	162
EMPIRE HOWARD	PQ 14	16/04/42	190
EMPIRE HUDSON	SC 42	10/09/41	136

SHIP NAME	CONVOY	LOSS DATE	PGE
EMPIRE IBEX	HX 245	02/07/43	132
EMPIRE IMPALA	SC 121	07/03/43	137
EMPIRE KESTREL	UGS 13	16/08/43	181
EMPIRE KUDU	SC 46	26/09/41	136
EMPIRE LAWRENCE	PQ 16	27/05/42	190
EMPIRE LEOPARD	SC 107	02/11/42	137
EMPIRE LOTUS	SC 79	12/04/42	137
EMPIRE LYNX	SC 107	03/11/42	137
EMPIRE MALLARD	SC 46	26/09/41	136
EMPIRE MANOR	HX 276	28/01/44	133
EMPIRE MERSEY	SC 104	14/10/42	137
EMPIRE MINIVER	SC 7	18/10/40	136
EMPIRE MOAT	OG 74	20/09/41	177
EMPIRE MOONBEAM	ON 127	12/09/42	161
EMPIRE MORDRED	MKS 7	08/02/43	146
EMPIRE NORSEMAN	UC 1	23/02/43	186
EMPIRE OAK	OG 71	22/08/41	177
EMPIRE OCELOT	OB 218	28/09/40	155
EMPIRE OIL	ON 127	11/09/42	161
EMPIRE PELICAN	ASTROLOGER	14/11/41	193
EMPIRE PURCELL	PQ 16	27/05/42	190
EMPIRE RAINBOW	ON 113	26/07/42	161
EMPIRE RANGER	PQ 13	28/03/42	190
EMPIRE REDSHANK	ON 166	22/02/43	161
EMPIRE REINDEER	SC 94	10/08/42	137
EMPIRE RIDGE	HG 61	19/05/41	179
EMPIRE ROWAN	KMS 11	27/03/43	171
EMPIRE SAILOR	ON 145	21/11/42	161
EMPIRE SHACKLETON	ON 154	29/12/42	161
EMPIRE SKY	OP FB	06/11/42	191
EMPIRE SOLDIER	SC 100	16/09/42	137
EMPIRE SONG	TIGER	09/05/41	193
EMPIRE SPENSER	HX 217	08/12/42	132
EMPIRE STARLIGHT	IN PORT	03/04/42	190
EMPIRE STEVENSON	PQ 18	13/09/42	190
EMPIRE STREAM	HG 73	25/09/41	179
EMPIRE SUNRISE	SC 107	02/11/42	137
EMPIRE SURF	ON 55	14/01/42	161
EMPIRE TOURIST	RA 57	04/03/44	191
EMPIRE TRADER	ON 166	23/02/43	161
EMPIRE UNION	ON 154	27/12/42	161
EMPIRE VOLUNTEER	SC 3	15/09/40	136
EMPIRE WAGTAIL	ON 154	28/12/42	161
EMPIRE WEBSTER	KMS 8	07/02/43	171
EMPIRE WHALE	SL 126	29/03/43	146
ENSEIGNE MAURICE PREHAC	SL 110	27/05/42	146
ERATO	OG 69	27/07/41	176
ERIK BOYE	HX 47	15/06/40	130
ERVIKEN	SC 48	16/10/41	136
ESMOND	OB 318	09/05/41	155
ESSEX LANCE	ONS 20	16/10/43	164
ESTRELLANO	HG 53	09/02/41	179
ETRIB	HG 84	15/06/42	179
ETTRICK	MKF 1YG	15/11/42	174
EUGENIA CAMBANIS	SC 13	28/11/40	136
EUGENIE S EMBIRICOS	ON 57	21/01/42	161
EULIMA	ON 166	23/02/43	161
EVEROJA	SC 52	03/11/41	137
EVROS	SC 48	16/10/41	136
EXECUTIVE	RA 53	05/03/43	191
EXPOSITOR	ON 166	23/02/43	162
EXTERMINATOR	QP 13	05/07/42	190
FAGERSTEN	SC 104	13/10/42	137
FAIRFIELD CITY	PQ 17	05/07/42	190

204

INDEX OF SHIP LOSSES

SHIP NAME	CONVOY	LOSS DATE	PGE	SHIP NAME	CONVOY	LOSS DATE	PGE	SHIP NAME	CONVOY	LOSS DATE	PGE
FERM	HX 112	16/03/41	131	HAWKINGE	OG 69	27/07/41	176	JOHN RANDOLPH	QP 13	05/07/42	190
FINNANGER	ON 67	24/02/42	161	HEDRUN	OB 197	16/08/40	155	JOHN WITHERSPOON	PQ 17	06/07/42	190
FIRCREST	HX 65	25/08/40	131	HEFFRON	QP 13	05/07/42	190	JONAS LIE	ON 277	09/01/45	162
FJORDHEIM	ON 251	02/09/44	162	HEINA	SC 67	10/02/42	137	JONATHAN HOLT	OB 289	24/02/41	155
FLORISTAN	OS 17	19/01/42	170	HEKTORIA	ON 127	12/09/42	161	JONATHAN STURGES	ON 166	24/02/43	162
FLYNDERBORG	SC 52	03/11/41	137	HELLE	SC 26	04/04/41	136	JOSEPH SMITH	ON 218	11/01/44	162
FORT BATTLE RIVER	KMS 10G	06/03/43	171	HENRY BACON	RA 64	23/02/45	191	JURA	HG 53	09/02/41	179
FORT BELLINGHAM	JW 56A	26/01/44	191	HENRY MILLER	GUS 63	03/01/45	183	JUSTITIA	SC 11	22/11/40	136
FORT CEDAR LAKE	SC 122	17/03/43	138	HENRY R MALLORY	SC 118	07/02/43	137	JUTLAND	PQ 15	02/05/42	190
FORT FITZGERALD	UGS 18	04/10/43	181	HIDLEFJORD	HX 114	01/04/41	131	KAAPAREN	HX 194	14/06/42	132
FORT HOWE	MKS 26	30/09/43	146	HINDANGER	ON 127	11/09/42	161	KAIMOKU	SC 94	08/08/42	137
FORT JEMSEG	ON 202	23/09/43	162	HINDPOOL	SL 67	08/03/41	145	KALLIOPI	SC 118	07/02/43	137
FORT RAMPART	HX 233	17/04/43	132	HOBBEMA	SC 107	03/11/42	137	KARLANDER	OB 321	14/05/41	155
FRANCIS W PETTYGROVE	MKS 21	13/08/43	146	HOMESIDE	SL 62	28/01/41	145	KASONGO	OB 290	27/02/41	155
FREDERICK BARTHOLDI	HX 270	25/12/43	133	HONOMU	PQ 17	05/07/42	190	KATHA	OS 45	02/04/43	170
FREDERICK DOUGLASS	ON 202	20/09/43	162	HOOSIER	PQ 17	10/07/42	190	KATVALDIS	ON 122	25/08/42	161
FRESNO CITY	HX 84	05/11/40	131	HOPECASTLE	SL 125	29/10/42	146	KAVAK	HX 90	02/12/40	131
FRESNO CITY II	HX 232	12/04/43	132	HORACE BUSHNELL	JW 65	20/03/45	191	KELLWYN	OG 69	27/07/41	177
GARM	SC 42	11/09/41	136	HORACE GRAY	BK 3	14/02/45	191	KELSO	SC 94	08/08/42	137
GARTBRATTAN	OG 45	05/11/40	176	HOUSATONIC	OB 287	19/02/41	155	KENBANE HEAD	HX 84	05/11/40	131
GEORGE CLEEVE	GUS 31	22/02/44	183	HUMBER ARM	HX 53	08/07/40	130	KENTUCKY	PQ 18	18/09/42	191
GERALDINE MARY	HX 60	04/08/40	130	HURUNUI	OA 228	14/10/40	149	KENTUCKY	HARPOON	15/06/42	193
GERMANIC	HX 115	29/03/41	131	HYBERT	QP 13	05/07/42	190	KERAMIAI	OA 80G	30/01/40	149
GHARINDA	ONS 5	05/05/43	164	HYLTON	HX 115	29/03/41	131	KERVEGAN	SC 22	09/02/41	136
GLEN HEAD	OG 63	06/06/41	176	IJORA	QP 8	07/03/42	190	KIEV	QP 10	13/04/42	190
GLENEDEN	HG 15	25/01/40	179	ILA	SC 48	15/10/41	136	KING ALFRED	HX 60	04/08/40	130
GLENORCHY	PEDESTAL	13/08/42	193	IMPERIAL STAR	HALBERD	27/09/41	193	KING EDGAR	SC 167	02/03/45	138
GLITTRE	ON 166	23/02/43	162	INDEPENDENCE HALL	SC 73	07/03/42	137	KING EDWARD	ON 154	27/12/42	161
GOGOVALE	HX 60	04/08/40	130	INDIAN PRINCE	KMS 31	11/11/43	171	KING GRUFFYDD	SC 122	17/03/43	138
GOGRA	OS 45	02/04/43	170	INDIER	SC 26	03/04/41	136	KING IDWAL	OB 244	22/11/40	155
GOODLEIGH	HX 90	02/12/40	131	INDUNA	PQ 13	30/03/42	190	KING ROBERT	SC 19	29/01/41	136
GOOLISTAN	QP 15	23/11/42	191	INGA I	OG 69	27/07/41	177	KINGSBURY	SC 122	17/03/43	138
GRACIA	OB 287	19/02/41	155	INGRIA	ON 166	24/02/43	162	KINROSS	OB 336	24/06/41	155
GRADO	SC 129	11/05/43	138	INGRID	ON 57	19/01/42	161	KIRNWOOD	SC 57	10/12/41	137
GRAIGWEN	SC 6	10/10/40	136	INVERARDER	ON 67	24/02/42	161	KOLCHIS	SC 13	23/11/40	136
GRANGEPARK	KMS 3G	20/11/42	171	INVERILEN	HX 224	03/02/43	132	KOLGA	OA 178	04/07/40	149
GRANVILLE	SC 122	17/03/43	138	INVERSHANNON	HX 72	21/09/40	131	KOLLBJORG	HX 223	24/01/43	132
GRAY RANGER	QP 14	22/09/42	191	IRENEE DU PONT	HX 229	17/03/43	132	KORSHAMN	HX 112	17/03/41	131
GRAYBURN	HX 133	29/06/41	132	ITALIA	HX 47	14/06/40	130	KOSMOS II	HX 212	28/10/42	132
GREGALIA	OB 318	09/05/41	155	IXION	OB 318	07/05/41	155	KRASNY PARTIZAN	INDEP	29/01/43	191
GRETAVALE	SC 52	03/11/41	137	J B WHITE	HX 112	17/03/41	131	KUMASIAN	SL 81	05/08/41	146
GREYLOCK	RA 52	03/02/43	191	J H SENIOR	HX 252	19/08/43	132	KURDISTAN	SC 57	10/12/41	137
GUNBORG	SC 7	18/10/40	136	J L M CURRY	RA 53	07/03/43	191	KUZNETZ LESOV	QP 15	23/11/42	191
GURNEY E NEWLIN	HX 212	27/10/42	132	J PINCKNEY HENDERSON	HX 252	19/08/43	132	KYNO	HX 66	28/08/40	131
GYPSUM QUEEN	SC 42	10/09/41	136	JACKSONVILLE	CU 36	30/08/44	184	KYRIAKOULA	OB 290	26/02/41	155
H H ROGERS	ON 167	21/02/43	162	JAMAICA PLANTER	HX 326	27/12/44	133	LA ESTANCIA	HX 79	20/10/40	131
HAHIRA	SC 107	03/11/42	137	JAMES OGLETHORPE	HX 229	17/03/43	132	LACONIKOS	SL 128MK	07/05/43	146
HALIZONES	OS 52KM	27/07/43	170	JAMES RUSSELL LOWELL	GUS 18	15/10/43	183	LADY GLANELY	HX 90	02/12/40	131
HALLFRIED	SL 138MK	31/10/43	146	JEAN JADOT	KMS 7	20/01/43	171	LAFIAN	SL 87	24/09/41	146
HAMPTON LODGE	MKS 6	20/01/43	146	JEANNE M	OG 46	02/12/40	176	LAHORE	SL 67	08/03/41	145
HARBURY	ONS 5	05/05/43	164	JEDMOOR	SC 42	16/09/41	136	LANCASTER CASTLE	IN PORT	14/04/42	190
HARLINGEN	SL 81	05/08/41	146	JEREMIAH VAN RENSSELAER	HX 224	02/02/43	132	LANCASTRIAN PRINCE	ON 176	12/04/43	162
HARMALA	SC 118	07/02/43	137	JERSEY CITY	OB 191	31/07/40	155	LANGUEDOC	SC 7	17/10/40	136
HARMODIUS	SL 67	08/03/41	145	JESSMORE	OG 53	21/02/41	176	LAPLAND	OG 69	27/07/41	177
HARPAGUS	HX 126	20/05/41	132	JEYPORE	SC 107	03/11/42	137	LAPWING	HG 73	26/09/41	179
HARPALION	QP 10	11/04/42	190	JHELUM	SL 68	21/03/41	145	LARISTAN	ON 57	15/01/42	161
HARPALYCE	HX 65	25/08/40	131	JOEL R POINSETT	ON 225	04/03/44	162	LAVINGTON COURT	OS 34	19/07/42	170
HARPERLEY	ONS 5	05/05/43	164	JOHN BANVARD	UGS 57	31/10/44	181	LEISE MAERSK	SC 11	23/11/40	136
HARRY LUCKENBACH	HX 229	17/03/43	132	JOHN BELL	UGS 14	26/08/43	181	LEONIDAS Z CAMBANIS	SC 26	03/04/41	136
HARTINGTON	SC 107	02/11/42	137	JOHN HOLT	SL 87	24/09/41	146	LIMBOURG	HX 115	29/03/41	131
HARTLEBURY	PQ 17	07/07/42	190	JOHN P PEDERSEN	HX 126	20/05/41	132	LISIEUX	SC 13	27/11/40	136
HASTINGS	ON 166	23/02/43	162	JOHN PENN	PQ 18	13/09/42	190	LLANISHEN	OA 203	23/08/40	149
HATARANA	SL 118	18/08/42	146					LLANOVER	ON 92	12/05/42	161
HATIMURA	SC 107	03/11/42	137					LLANWERN	OB 290	26/02/41	155
								LOCHKATRINE	ON 115	03/08/42	161

◇ THE ALLIED CONVOY SYSTEM 1939-1945

SHIP NAME	CONVOY	LOSS DATE	PGE
LORNASTON	OS 115KM	08/03/45	170
LOT	UGS 10	22/06/43	181
LOWTHER CASTLE	PQ 16	27/05/42	190
LYNTON GRANGE	ON 154	29/12/42	161
MAASDAM	HX 133	26/06/41	132
MACBETH	PQ 18	13/09/42	191
MACEDONIER	HX 92	12/12/40	131
MAHANADA	OB 290	26/02/41	155
MAHRATTA	HG 1	06/10/39	179
MAIDAN	HX 84	05/11/40	131
MAIDEN CREEK	ON 152	31/12/42	161
MAKALLA	OA 203	23/08/40	149
MALABAR	HX 5	27/10/39	130
MALANTIC	SC 121	09/03/43	138
MALAYA II	HX 133	26/06/41	132
MANCHESTER BRIGADE	OB 218	26/09/40	155
MANCHESTER MERCHANT	ON 166	25/02/43	162
MANDALIKA	SL 68	18/03/41	145
MANGEN	OG 47	20/12/40	176
MANIPUR	HX 55	17/07/40	130
MANSEPOOL	OB 289	24/02/41	155
MARCELLA	OS 44	13/03/43	170
MARDINIAN	SC 2	09/09/40	136
MARGARETA	HG 73	27/09/41	179
MARINA	OB 213	18/09/40	155
MARITIMA	SC 107	02/11/42	137
MARNIX VAN ST ALDEGONDE	KMF 25A	06/11/43	174
MAROUKO PATERAS	SC 52	03/11/41	137
MARY LUCKENBACH	PQ 18	14/09/42	191
MARY SLESSOR	MKS 7	08/02/43	146
MASSMAR	QP 13	05/07/42	190
MATHERAN	HX 79	19/10/40	131
MATRA	HXF 7	13/11/39	133
MCKEESPORT	ONS 5	29/04/43	164
MEANDROS	OB 274	16/01/41	155
MELMORE HEAD	ON 154	28/12/42	161
MELROSE ABBEY II	ON 154	27/12/42	161
MERVYN	OB 28	01/11/39	155
MEYER LONDON	UGS 37	16/04/44	181
MICHIGAN	UGS 7	20/04/43	181
MIDDLETON	SC 21	18/02/41	136
MILCREST	ON 132	07/10/42	161
MILL HILL	HX 66	30/08/40	131
MILOS	SC 121	11/03/43	138
MOBEKA	OS 17	19/01/41	170
MOLLY PITCHER	UGS 6	17/03/43	181
MONT VISO	KMS 30	03/11/43	171
MONTENOL	OS 28	21/05/42	170
MORMACSUL	PQ 16	27/05/42	190
MOSTYN	HG 50	23/01/41	179
MOUNT KASSION	SC 94	08/08/42	137
MOUNT PARNES	ON 92	12/05/42	161
MOUNT PELION	SC 107	02/11/42	137
MOUNT TAURUS	ON 144	17/11/42	161
MUNERIC	SC 42	09/09/41	136
N T NIELSEN ALONSO	ON 166	22/02/43	162
NAGARA	SL 126	28/03/43	146
NAGPORE	SL 125	28/10/42	146
NAILSEA COURT	SC 121	10/03/43	138
NAILSEA RIVER	SL 45	15/09/40	145
NALON	SL 52F	06/11/40	145
NARDANA	SL 67	08/03/41	145
NARIVA	HX 229	17/03/43	132

SHIP NAME	CONVOY	LOSS DATE	PGE
NAVARINO	PQ 17	04/07/42	190
NAVASOTA	OB 46	05/12/39	155
NELLIE	SC 104	13/10/42	137
NEW BRUNSWICK	OS 28	21/05/42	170
NEW SEVILLA	OB 216	20/09/40	155
NEW WESTMINSTER CITY	IN PORT	03/04/42	190
NEWTON ASH	SC 118	07/02/43	137
NICETO DE LARRINAGA	SL 87	22/09/41	146
NIDARDAL	SC 58	16/12/41	137
NIGARISTAN	HX 150	24/09/41	132
NIKOLINA MATKOVIC	SC 104	13/10/42	137
NIRITOS	SC 7	18/10/40	136
NIVOSE	KMS 31	11/11/43	171
NORDEFLINGE	KMS 51	30/05/44	171
NORFJELL	BK 3	14/02/45	191
NORITA	OG 69	28/07/41	177
NORMAN MONARCH	HX 126	20/05/41	132
NORNE	HX 66	30/08/40	131
NORSE KING	ON 154	29/12/42	161
NORTIND	HX 223	26/01/43	132
NOVASLI	SC 167	02/03/45	138
OBERON	SL 78	27/06/41	145
OCEAN FREEDOM	IN PORT	13/03/43	191
OCEAN HUNTER	KMS 37	10/01/44	171
OCEAN VOICE	QP 14	22/09/42	191
OHIO	PEDESTAL	15/08/42	193
OILFIELD	HX 121	28/04/41	131
OLIVER ELLSWORTH	PQ 18	13/09/42	191
OLOPANA	PQ 17	08/07/42	190
ONOBA	OB 274	16/01/41	155
OPORTO	OS 44	13/03/43	170
ORANGEMOOR	HG 31	31/05/40	179
OREGON	SC 94	10/08/42	137
OREGON EXPRESS	ON 202	23/09/43	162
OREGONIAN	PQ 18	13/09/42	191
OROPOS	ON 152	19/12/42	161
OSWESTRY GRANGE	SL 64S	12/02/41	145
OTAIO	OS 4	28/08/41	170
OTTERPOOL	HG 34F	20/06/40	179
P.L.M.21	OS 97KM	03/12/44	170
P.L.M.22	SL 78	27/06/41	146
PACIFIC GROVE	HX 232	12/04/43	132
PACIFIC PIONEER	ON 113	29/07/42	161
PACIFIC RANGER	HX 77	12/10/40	131
PACIFIC STAR	SL 125	27/10/42	146
PALEMBANG	MKS 67	06/11/44	146
PAMPAS	MW 10	26/03/42	193
PAN ATLANTIC	PQ 17	06/07/42	190
PAN KRAFT	PQ 17	05/07/42	190
PAN-NEW YORK	HX 212	29/10/42	132
PAN-PENNSYLVANIA	CU 21	16/04/44	184
PAN ROYAL	UGS 5	09/02/43	181
PANAMA	ON 294	11/04/45	162
PARISMINA	ON 144	18/11/42	161
PARRACOMBE	TEMPLE	02/05/41	193
PARTHENON	SC 107	02/11/42	137
PAUL HAMILTON	UGS 38	20/04/44	181
PAULUS POTTER	PQ 17	05/07/42	190
PEGU	OB 40	24/11/39	155
PELAYO	HG 84	15/06/42	179
PENELOPE BARKER	JW 56A	25/01/44	191
PERSEUS	SL 64S	12/02/41	145
PETER KERR	PQ 17	05/07/42	190
PETREL	HG 73	26/09/41	179

SHIP NAME	CONVOY	LOSS DATE	PGE
PINCKNEY HENDERSON (See J PINCKNEY HENDERSON)			
PINK STAR	SC 44	20/09/41	136
PINTO	HX 305	08/09/44	133
PORT AUCKLAND	SC 122	18/03/43	138
PORT DENISON	OA 220	27/09/40	149
PORT GISBORNE	HX 77	11/10/40	131
PORT HARDY	HX 121	28/04/41	131
POSSIDON	SC 2	08/09/40	136
PRESIDENT FRANCQUI	ON 154	29/12/42	161
PRESIDENT DOUMER	SL 125	30/10/42	146
PRESIDENT SERGENT	ON 144	18/11/42	161
PRIMER ENRIQUE	HG 88	03/09/42	179
PRINS HARALD	KMS 3G	20/11/42	171
PRINS WILLEM III	KMS 11	26/03/43	171
PUERTO RICAN	RA 53	09/03/43	191
PYRRHUS	OG 18	17/02/40	176
R J CULLEN	ON 57	15/01/42	161
RACELAND	PQ 13	28/03/42	190
RADCHURCH	SC 94	09/08/42	137
RAMSAY	ON 100	10/06/42	161
REGENT LION	UGS 72	17/02/45	181
REIGH COUNT	SC 133	05/06/43	138
REMUERA	HX 65	26/08/40	131
RICHARD BLAND	RA 53	05/03/43	191
RICHARD HENDERSON	UGS 14	26/08/43	181
RICHARD OLNEY	KMS 26	22/09/43	171
RINOS	SC 107	02/11/42	137
RIVER AFTON	PQ 17	05/07/42	190
RIVER LUGAR	SL 78	26/06/41	146
ROBERT E HOPKINS	SC 118	07/02/43	137
ROBERT H COLLEY	HX 209	04/10/42	132
RODINA	QP 13	05/07/42	190
ROGERS (See H H ROGERS)			
ROHNA	KMF 26	26/11/43	174
ROSARIO	ON 167	21/02/43	162
ROSEWOOD	SC 121	09/03/43	138
ROSSINGTON COURT	HX 26	13/03/40	130
ROTHERMERE	HX 126	20/05/41	132
ROTORUA	HX 92	11/12/40	131
ROTULA	SC 22	01/03/41	136
ROWALLAN CASTLE	MW 9	14/02/42	193
ROYAL STAR	UGS 38	20/04/44	181
ROYSTON GRANGE	SL 8	25/11/39	145
RUCKINGE	HG 76	19/12/41	179
RUPERRA	HX 79	19/10/40	131
RUTH I	SC 156	06/04/44	138
RYDBOHOLM	OB 290	26/02/41	155
RYM	SC 48	16/10/41	136
SALLY MAERSK	SC 42	10/09/41	136
SALONICA	SC 11	23/11/40	136
SALTWICK	MKS 28	21/10/43	146
SAMA	ON 67	22/02/42	161
SAMBRE	OB 188	27/07/40	155
SAMSUVA	RA 60	29/09/44	191
SAMUEL DEXTER	ON 220	24/01/44	162
SAN CONRADO	HX 114	01/04/41	131
SAN FERNANDO	HX 49	22/06/40	130
SAN GABRIEL	OB 205	30/08/40	155
SANTA ELENA	KMF 25A	06/11/43	174
SANTA ELISA	PEDESTAL	13/08/42	193
SANTOS	HX 252	19/08/43	132
SARANAC	OA 172	25/06/40	149
SAUGOR	OS 4	27/08/41	170
SCANIA	SC 42	11/09/41	136
SCEBELI	ON 178	21/04/43	162

◇ 206

INDEX OF SHIP LOSSES

SHIP NAME	CONVOY	LOSS DATE	PGE
SCHIE	OB 336	24/06/41	155
SCORESBY	SC 7	17/10/40	136
SCOTTISH MAIDEN	HX 83	05/11/40	131
SCOTTISH MINSTREL	HX 55	17/07/40	130
SCOTTISH STANDARD	OB 287	21/02/41	155
SEAKAY	CU 17	19/03/44	184
SEATTLE SPIRIT	ON 102	18/06/42	161
SEDGEPOOL	SC 7	19/10/40	136
SEGUNDO	OS 4	27/08/41	170
SEGUNDO ENRIQUE	HG 88	03/09/42	179
SELVISTAN	ONS 5	05/05/43	164
SEMBILANGAN	OS 44	13/03/43	170
SENIOR (See J H SENIOR)			
SERBINO	SL 89	21/10/41	146
SHEAF MOUNT	ON 122	25/08/42	161
SHETLAND	MKS 15	23/06/43	146
SHILLONG	HX 231	04/04/43	132
SHIRAK	HX 79	19/10/40	131
SHREWSBURY	SL 64S	12/02/41	145
SIDI-BEL-ABBES	UGS 7	20/04/43	181
SILVER SWORD	QP 14	20/09/42	191
SILVERBELLE	SL 87	22/09/41	174
SILVERCEDAR	SC 48	15/10/41	136
SILVERWILLOW	SL 125	30/10/42	146
SIREMALM	HG 73	27/09/41	179
SITALA	HX 79	20/10/40	131
SKJELBRED	ON 202	23/09/43	162
SLEMDAL	HG 84	15/06/42	179
SNEFJELD	SC 7	19/10/40	136
SOCONY	HX 148	09/09/41	132
SOEKABOEMI	ON 154	27/12/42	161
SOEMBA	HX 100	07/01/41	131
SOESTERBERG	SC 7	19/10/40	136
SOLFERINO	OB 290	26/02/41	155
SOLOR	HX 332	27/01/45	133
SOLOY	HX 133	24/06/41	132
SOMERSET	SL 72	11/05/41	145
SOURABAYA	HX 212	27/10/42	132
SOUTH AMERICA	SC 156	06/04/44	138
SOUTH WALES	SC 46	26/09/41	136
SOUTHERN EMPRESS	SC 104	13/10/42	137
SOUTHERN PRINCESS	HX 229	17/03/43	132
SPAR	SC 94	05/08/42	137
ST CLAIR II	SL 87	24/09/41	146
ST DUNSTAN	OB 202	23/08/40	155
ST ESSYLT	KMS 18B	04/07/43	171
ST GLEN	SL 44	06/09/40	145
ST MALO	HX 77	12/10/40	131
ST MIHIEL	CU 65	09/04/45	184
ST SUNNIVA	ON 158	23/01/43	161
STALINGRAD	PQ 18	13/09/42	190
STANGRANT	HX 77	13/10/40	131
STANMORE	KMS 27	02/10/43	171
STAR OF LUXOR	SC 57	10/12/41	137
STARCROSS	SL 73	20/05/41	145
STARGARD	SC 42	10/09/41	136
STEEL VOYAGER	ONS 18	23/09/43	164
STEEL WORKER	MINED IN PORT	03/06/42	190
STENTOR	SL 125	27/10/42	146
STIGSTAD	ON 166	21/02/43	162
STIRLINGSHIRE	HX 90	02/12/40	131
STOCKPORT	ON 166	23/02/43	162
STONEPOOL	SC 42	11/09/41	136
STORK	OG 71	23/08/41	177
STRATFORD	OB 218	26/09/40	155

SHIP NAME	CONVOY	LOSS DATE	PGE
STRATHALLAN	KMF 5A	22/12/42	174
SUKHONA	PQ 18	13/09/42	190
SUSANA	SC 104	13/10/42	137
SVEND FOYN	HX 229A	19/03/43	132
SVEVE	ON 127	10/09/42	161
SWEDRU	SL 69	16/04/41	145
SWIFTPOOL	SL 81	05/08/41	146
SWINBURNE	OB 290	26/02/41	155
SYROS	PQ 16	26/05/42	190
T J WILLIAMS	SC 44	20/09/41	136
TABERG	OG 63	06/06/41	176
TADORNA	CRUPPER	10/11/42	193
TALABOT	MW 10	26/03/42	193
TANIMBAR	HARPOON	14/06/42	193
TAPANOELI	SL 68	17/03/41	145
TASMANIA	SL 125	31/10/42	146
TASSO	HX 90	02/12/40	131
TEJO	HG 53	09/02/41	179
TENNESSEE	SC 100	22/09/42	137
TERJE VIKEN	OB 293	07/03/41	155
TERKOELI	HX 229	17/03/43	132
THALIA(Gk)	SC 7	19/10/40	136
THEODORE DWIGHT WELD	ON 202	20/09/43	162
THERMOPYLAE	MW 8A	19/01/42	193
THIARA	OB 188	27/07/40	155
THISTLEGLEN	SC 42	10/09/41	136
THOMAS G MASARYK	UGS 37	16/04/44	181
THOMAS DONALDSON	JW 65	20/03/45	191
THOMAS HOOKER	ON 168	07/03/43	162
THOMAS SCOTT	RA 64	17/02/45	191
THOMAS STONE	KMF 1	07/11/42	174
THORNLEA	OB 206	02/09/40	155
THORNLIEBANK	OS 12	29/11/41	170
THURSO	HG 84	15/06/42	179
TIELBANK	SL 67	08/03/41	145
TITAN	OA 207	04/09/40	149
TIVIVES	MKS 28	21/10/43	146
TOLKEN	ON 92	13/05/42	161
TORINIA	HX 72	21/09/40	131
TOWA	HX 92	11/12/40	131
TOWARD	SC 118	07/02/43	137
TREGENNA	HX 71	17/09/40	131
TREHATA	SC 94	08/08/42	137
TREMODA	OS 4	27/08/41	170
TRENTBANK	KMS 3	24/11/42	171
TREVERBYN	SL 89	21/10/41	146
TREWELLARD	HX 84	05/11/40	131
TRITON	SL 118	17/08/42	146
TROLLA	ON 122	25/08/42	161
TSIOLKOVSKY	QP 11	01/05/42	190
TUCURINCA	HX 228	10/03/43	132
TUDOR	HG 34F	19/06/40	179
TUVA	ON 19A	02/10/41	161
UFA	INDEP	26/01/43	191
UGANDA	HX 79	19/10/40	131
ULEA	HG 75	28/10/41	179
ULYSSES	HX 232	12/04/43	132
UMARIA	SL 126	30/03/43	146
URLANA	SL 135MK	05/09/43	146
USKBRIDGE	OB 228	17/10/40	155
VACLITE	OA 80G	30/01/40	149
VARANGBERG	HG 73	26/09/41	179
VARNA	HG 53	09/02/41	179
VENETIA	HX 112	16/03/41	131

SHIP NAME	CONVOY	LOSS DATE	PGE
VESTFOLD	HX 222	17/01/43	132
VICTORIA	OB 244	21/11/40	155
VILLE DE ROUEN	ON 154	28/12/42	161
VILLE DE TAMATAVE	ON 160	24/01/43	161
VINEMOOR	OB 188	26/07/40	155
VIRGINIA DARE	UGS 33	06/03/44	181
VOLTURNO	MKS 15	23/06/43	146
W B WALKER	SC 19	29/01/41	136
W C TEAGLE	SC 48	16/10/41	136
W HENDRIK	HX 90	03/12/40	131
WACOSTA	PQ 18	13/09/42	191
WAIMARAMA	PEDESTAL	13/08/42	193
WAIRANGI	PEDESTAL	13/08/42	193
WALMER CASTLE	OG 74	21/09/41	177
WALTER Q GRESHAM	HX 229	18/03/43	132
WANDBY	HX 79	20/10/40	131
WANSTEAD	ONS 3	21/04/43	164
WARFIELD	OS 58/KM	15/08/43	170
WARKWORTH	ON 23	10/10/41	161
WARLABY	SL 64S	12/02/41	145
WAROONGA	HX 231	06/04/43	132
WARWICK CASTLE	MKF 1X6	14/11/42	174
WASHINGTON	PQ 17	05/07/42	190
WAZIRISTAN	PQ 7A	02/01/42	190
WENTWORTH	ONS 5	05/05/43	164
WEST MADAKET	ONS 5	05/05/43	164
WEST MAXIMUS	ONS 5	05/05/43	164
WESTBURY	SL 64S	12/02/41	145
WESTPOOL	SC 26	03/04/41	136
WHITE (See J B WHITE)			
WHITFORD POINT	HX 79	20/10/40	131
WIDESTONE	ON 144	17/11/42	161
WIGRY	ON 53	15/01/42	161
WILHELMINA	HX 90	02/12/40	131
WILLIAM C GORGAS	HX 228	11/03/43	132
WILLIAM CLARK	OP FB	04/11/42	191
WILLIAM EUSTIS	HX 229	17/03/43	132
WILLIAM HOOPER	PQ 17	04/07/42	190
WILLIAM S THAYER	RA 59	30/04/44	191
WILLIAMS (See T J WILLIAMS)			
WILLOWBANK	SL 34	12/06/40	145
WINDSOR CASTLE	KMF 11	22/03/43	174
WINDSORWOOD	OA 172	25/06/40	149
WINKLER	ON 166	23/02/43	162
WINNIPEG II	ON 139	22/10/42	161
WINTERSWIJK	SC 42	10/09/41	136
WROTHAM	OG 69	28/07/41	177
WYOMING	UGS 6	15/03/43	181
YAKA	ON 144	18/11/42	161
YORKMAR	SC 143	09/10/43	138
YORKSHIRE	HG 3	17/10/39	179
ZAAFARAN	PQ 17	05/07/42	190
ZAANLAND	HX 229	17/03/43	132
ZANNES GOUNARIS	SC 6	09/10/40	136
ZARIAN	ON 154	29/12/42	161
ZOUAVE	SC 122	17/03/43	138
ZUIDERKERK	SL 119	28/08/42	146

ABOUT THE AUTHOR

Arnold Hague, born 1930, entered the Royal Navy in 1949 as a National Service rating. Promoted Midshipman in the Supply & Secretariat Branch in August 1949, he completed his full time service, joined the Reserve Division in London and finally retired in 1979 as a Lieutenant-Commander. During that time he served in several appointments, including command of two Reserve Communications Centres and the Sea Cadet Corps in the West Midlands area.

He has written a number of previous books, THE TOWNS, DESTROYERS FOR GREAT BRITAIN, SLOOPS 1926-1946, CONVOY RESCUE SHIPS, and co-authored CONVOYS TO RUSSIA. He also served as a sub-editor to JANE'S FIGHTING SHIPS in the late 1960s, and has made numerous contributions to naval publications during the last forty years.

He has researched the naval war 1939-1945 since 1949, largely in collaboration with the late John K Burgess of Toronto and latterly Calgary, and the assistance of official resources in London. In particular he has specialised in naval movements and operations and, as shown in this publication, the convoy system and details of that period.

Married to a former Reserve Officer, they have a son and daughter and a grandson. In retirement he lives in Surrey, England where he continues his interest, research and writing.